Uprooted Americans : essays to honor Oscar Handlin / edited by
Richard L. Bushman ... ₍et al.₎. — 1st ed. — Boston : Little,
Brown, c1979.

xvii, 366 p. : ill. ; 24 cm.

"Selected Bibliography of the published works of Oscar Handlin ₍by₎ Robert
Mirak": p. 351-365.
CONTENTS: Solomon, B. M. A portrait of Oscar Handlin.—Demos, J.
Witchcraft and local culture in Hampton, New Hampshire.—Scott, A. F. Self-
portraits: three women.—Bushman, R. L. "This new man": dependence and
independence, 1776.—Berthoff, R. Independence and attachment, virtue and
interest.—McLoughlin, W. G. Cherokee anomie, 1794-1809.—Goodman, P.
The politics of industrialism: Massachusetts, 1830-1870.—Harris, N. Utopian

(Continued on next card)

79-11095
MARC

79

Uprooted Americans

Uprooted Americans

Essays to Honor Oscar Handlin

EDITED BY

Richard L. Bushman, Neil Harris,
David Rothman, Barbara Miller Solomon,
Stephan Thernstrom

Little, Brown and Company
BOSTON　　　　TORONTO

FIRST EDITION

The contributors and publisher are grateful to the following libraries, societies, publishers, and individuals for permission to reprint material as noted.

Princeton University Press for material from *The Letters of Benjamin Franklin and Jane Mecom,* ed. with an Introduction by Carl Van Doren (copyright 1950 by the American Philosophical Society).

The University of North Carolina Press for material from *The Letterbook of Eliza Lucas Pinckney, 1739–1762,* edited by Elise Pinckney. © 1972 The University of North Carolina Press. By permission of the publisher.

The Historical Society of Pennsylvania for material from the diary of Elizabeth Drinker.

Macmillan Publishing Co., Inc., and William Heinemann, Ltd., for material from *The Melting Pot* by Israel Zangwill (copyright 1909, 1914 by Macmillan Publishing Co., Inc., renewed 1937, 1942 by Edith A. Zangwill).

The Estate of Edith A. Zangwill for excerpts from the Edith Zangwill–Annie Yorke correspondence.

Lydia Hansen for excerpts from the correspondence of Marcus Lee Hansen.

Columbia University and Arthur M. Schlesinger, Jr., for material from *The Reminiscences of Arthur M. Schlesinger,* 1959, in the Oral History Collection of Columbia University.

The Henry E. Huntington Library for material from the F. J. Turner Papers, T.U. Box 35.

Library of Congress Cataloging in Publication Data
Main entry under title:

Uprooted Americans.

"Selected Bibliography of the published works of Oscar Handlin [by] Robert Mirak": p.
CONTENTS: Solomon, B. M. A portrait of Oscar Handlin. — Demos, J. Witchcraft and local culture in Hampton, New Hampshire. — Scott, A. F. Self-portraits: three women. [etc.]
1. United States — Civilization — Addresses, essays, lectures. 2. Minorities — United States — Addresses, essays, lectures. 3. Handlin, Oscar, 1915– Addresses, essays, lectures. I. Handlin, Oscar, 1915–
II. Bushman, Richard L.
E169.1.U76   973   79-11095

ISBN 0-316-11810-9

MV

Designed by D. Christine Benders

*Published simultaneously in Canada
by Little, Brown & Company (Canada) Limited*

PRINTED IN THE UNITED STATES OF AMERICA

Acknowledgments

The editors express appreciation to Bernard Bailyn and Donald Fleming, who aided in the early planning, and to Richard McDonough and Katie Kramer of Little, Brown and Company for tactfully leading a dozen authors through the last stages of manuscript preparation and publication.

The secretaries of the History Department at Harvard University and of the Committee on Higher Degrees in the History of American Civilization provided the names of Oscar Handlin's graduate students. Debby Beardsley, Mr. Handlin's secretary, assisted Robert Mirak with the compilation of the bibliography.

A number of Handlin students who are unrepresented in this volume gave the editors help in many forms.

Contents

Introduction

Richard L. Bushman

This volume samples the current work of twelve scholars who prepared their Ph.D. dissertations at Harvard University in history or the history of American civilization under the direction of Oscar Handlin. Between 1951 and 1978 Professor Handlin supervised the dissertations of seventy-two candidates. The students who eventually published book-length monographs were invited to submit essays. This book is a selection of their work.

As with all books of this kind, the resulting collection raises a question about the influence of the man in whose honor the essays were prepared. In this case, the character of the collection makes the question unusually difficult to answer. Scholars identified with a certain approach or a single period can be said to focus students' attention on a topic, or to structure the nature of their inquiries. The essays presented here range over the entire span of American history and treat subjects from politics to witchcraft, just as Professor Handlin himself has worked the broad field. The breadth of his interests, by excluding a simple answer, reduces to its purest form the question of how the mind of a teacher acts upon his students.

Speaking as one among many, I have the impression that the Handlin teaching style never made students feel they were being shaped. As Barbara Solomon says in her sketch of Oscar Handlin, he was as notable for his silences as for his direction. The most common admonitions were "get busy" or "see what you find." In criticisms of papers he dealt with language as much as with interpretive perspective. The mood of the Handlin seminar was laissez-faire. In my experience, students had no sense of forbidden or preferred paths. Add to this the multiplicity of influences playing on historians over the past thirty years, and only by a specious artifice could one pretend to see the teacher's hand guiding the pens of his students.

We come at the question of influence better by asking why so many ambitious and competent graduate students have chosen to work with Oscar Handlin over the past thirty years. What has he stood for in graduate training at Harvard? Subject matter may be part of it. Although his courses dealt with everything from immigrants, social structure, economics, and cities to religion, literature, law, politics, and education, Oscar Handlin's interest ran to the study of ordinary lives, paralleling the flow of historiographical currents in recent years. He carried the older social history of his teacher, Arthur Schlesinger, Sr., forward into our time. The virtues of Schlesinger's work have gone unappreciated, while *Boston's Immigrants,* with its tables, maps, and above all the close examination of a substantial population in one community, although first published in 1941, went through nine printings between 1968 and 1974. Stephan Thernstrom's *Progress and Poverty* and Sam Bass Warner, Jr.'s, *Streetcar Suburbs* built directly on Oscar Handlin's work on immigrants and the city. Whatever their particular interest, students felt that he gave them access to new perspectives, new themes, and particularly to the systematic study of plain people.

System was an important part of the appeal. Pots and pans, sewing machines and automobiles did not in themselves add up to social history. On the other hand, the system of analysis did not borrow from the social sciences, whether sociology, demography, or economics. One sensed an implicit aversion to formalized hypothesizing or overwrought social-scientific methodology. Apparently always informed when theory came up, Handlin invariably turned discussion away from abstract conceptions to historical realities. By his own account, novels and plays opened his thinking as much as sociology or psychology. The key was to ask a good question and to work logically and empirically toward an answer. I could detect no formal method beyond the forceful and intelligent use of fact and reason. The classic question students joked about was why the railroads went east and west, when north-south lines like the Illinois Central made more money. Why did farmers buy automobiles when horses cost less and produced manure? One big question did not inform the inquiry, but lots and lots of little ones, based on some puzzle in the historical situation itself.

In the Handlin seminar I took, we read on a theme, one student raised questions for discussion, and near the end, after having said virtually nothing for an hour or more, Professor Handlin summarized our talk and raised a question of his own. Usually it was very simple, and very hard to answer. The students slugged away at the puzzle until they or the time were exhausted and then listened to a brief logical answer based not on greater knowledge but on having tested the alternatives more rigorously. In retrospect it can be seen that the point was less to find the answer than to learn to make good questions — difficult, penetrating, and concrete enough to be answerable. A well-wrought question, we saw, led rapidly into a great deal of knowledge.

This mode of teaching carried over into the lectures. They conveyed surprisingly little conventional information. It was not necessary to take extensive notes. Their beauty lay in the unfolding patterns and the vivid images of how life worked. Many of those pictures have survived the twenty years since I left graduate school, and surface again and again in my lecturing and writing.

The system and power of Oscar Handlin's thought are not evident in all of his books. *The Wealth of the American People* (1975) and the two-volume text *The History of the United States* (1967) pull together original answers to myriad original questions, but because space did not permit a full explication of the questions, the force of the answers is sometimes blunted. The best exemplification of Oscar Handlin's system of thought is *Chance or Destiny: Turning Points in American History* (1955), a tour de force of historical analysis. Professor Handlin chose to tie together eight essays on war and diplomacy, which originally appeared in the *Atlantic Monthly*, with the philosophical question of the title, the role of accident in history. One of the virtues of the book is that the format gave him space to analyze the complexity of events. Why did Napoleon fail to send his fleet to the Caribbean and thus carry out his American plan, which included retention of Louisiana? Why didn't the British come to the aid of the Confederacy when their support might have changed the outcome of the war? That the essays showed large developments turning on happenstances — early ice in a harbor, or a chance encounter of Southern troops, scavenging for boots, with the advance guard of the Union army — is less important than the analytical processes by which Handlin followed intricate causal chains from point to point across oceans and continents through circumstances trivial and grand. *Chance or Destiny* reveals most clearly the nature of the analysis and the fullness of factual comprehension underlying the hundreds of summary observations in books like *The Wealth of the American People,* and suggests the rhetorical problems of presenting in brief span all that his system of thought opened up.

The famous essay "Origins of the Southern Labor System" (1950) was based on a characteristic Handlin question: why were black servants in the seventeenth century treated differently than whites? Perhaps more than any other single piece of writing, this essay showed the power of his questions to stir debate and stimulate research. After two and a half decades the controversy is not closed.

Graduate students may have recognized the analyst in Oscar Handlin before they perceived the artist. *The Uprooted* (1951) surprised me. It was so personal, so evocative, so humane. It seemed to be a daring book, not because it left aside the conventional apparatus, but because it revealed so much of the author. The book was personal, not because of the autobiographical echoes, but as a novel is personal in speaking of intimate matters. *The Uprooted* linked Handlin in my mind with his contemporary at Harvard Perry Miller, whose Widener study was next door to Handlin's on the seventh floor. Rather than mirrors of the past, they were candles, artists in their own right, who lit up reality, not merely reflected it. Both men invested much more human sensibility in history than students ordinarily expected.

That boldness gave implicit license to students to lay aside the note cards at times and tell the story. We were freed to recover the whole of life as far as intelligence and feeling could encompass it.

What was less apparent then and still remains to be explicated is the nature of Oscar Handlin's artistic vision. A particular, complex perspective distinguishes his work, somber, highly conscious of sorrow and frustration, and yet not tragic. In the divine sense the vision is comic. In *The Uprooted* the son is set free in a new land. The origins of slavery reveal racism to be a recent historical fabrication and therefore subject to dissolution by current historical forces. After centuries of toil, America has largely acquired the wealth it so long sought. The cosmic optimism, the refusal to see viciousness at the heart of life or to take pleasure in despair partly account for the discord between Oscar Handlin and the student ethos of the late sixties.

But the optimism is cosmic, not immediate. Life is filled with travail and losses accompany every gain. The son in *The Uprooted* loses touch with the world of the fathers. Americans created magnificent machinery for producing affluence and then found they did not know the purpose of wealth. Americans of all sorts forever discover "the glory and the grief of being free."[1] Irony lies at the very heart of history and life.

In a recent essay, "Living in a Valley" (1977), the Handlin vision finds a new metaphor. The meditation at the end explains in quite personal language how the promise of the peak draws the climber on and up, even though intervening dark chasms bar the way and demand ever-renewed exertion. Each achievement discloses new difficulties and the need for more effort. The essay points once more to what America and life require of those who would live — a willingness to go on taking risks, venturing forth, stoically accepting losses with gains, never yielding to weak indulgence in outrage or the dulling intoxication of cheap sensuality. "However painful be the effort, now or then, to stand alone or walk the unfamiliar path, only thus do humans discover the power to try the will, only thus discover themselves."[2]

The celebration of achievement and courage, the rays of hope glinting through history, rather than being banal optimism, are offered as a foundation for continued struggle against hardship, meaninglessness, and despair. Handlin ends his recent book on youth, *Facing Life* (1971), with a comment on the loss of direction in postwar America. "The children cannot follow when the parents do not lead. The parents cannot lead when the path has vanished and the destination is not known." But with an ironic twist, he turns his spatial image around to convert hopelessness into hope. "Is it emptiness or openness about us? The absence of familiar paths may be the opportunity for discovery; and the destination unknown may only demonstrate the limits of our vision."[3]

"Living in a Valley" begins by contrasting mountain people and valley people. Three anecdotes coming out of the Handlins' experiences in the Swiss mountains where they vacationed define a mode of living sharply different from that of the valley people almost in sight below. So far as I know Oscar Handlin has never systematically invoked the words "traditional" and "modern" as formal terms of historical analysis, but "Living in a Valley" draws attention to the fact that this has frequently been his theme. He speaks here of peoples driven out of old centers and finding refuge finally in the mountains where the rhythms and outlooks of traditional life persist. That movement is an analogy for the flow of history in many of his books. Not just the immigrant driven from European villages into the flat, open American city suffers the pains of alienation from an older order, but the Commonwealth of Massachusetts passing from corporatism to individualism, American youth entering the directionless postwar world, and the American economy overcoming poverty to discover the boredom and confusion of plenty. The immigrant is archetypical of all who have migrated into a new time and suffered from disorientation. "Alienation, formerly the penalty of migration, was now the lot of many people whose whole existence passed anonymously in impersonal communities, so massive that they assured no one recognition, so fluid that they held no one in place."[4]

I do not believe that Oscar Handlin has been widely thought of as a historian of modernization, and just as well. So often abused and distorted, that concept will pass with its predecessors, and those too closely associated with it will be thought of, justifiably or not, as obsolete. But it is noteworthy that in the 1950s, as his teaching and scholarship reached full maturation, Oscar Handlin remained aloof from the historiographical fashions of the decade: consensus history, status strains, social mobility figure lightly in his work. His themes emerged from a perspective that transcended the United States and the immediate issues of the decade. He clearly revealed his own view of modern history in *The Uprooted:* "A time came for many men when the slow glacial shift of economic and social forces suddenly broke loose in some major upheaval that cast loose the human beings from their age-old setting. In an extreme form this was the experience of the immigrants. It was also in some degree the experience of all modern men."[5] While other historical conceptions have faded with the years, the power of that idea to evoke speculation and energize research has been unfailing.

In their maturity scholars and teachers cease to call upon the models of their graduate teachers for hints and guides. A host of other influences, some welling up from deep within themselves, replace conversations with a dissertation director. And yet we must note that eight of the eleven essays in this volume follow communities, or politics, or culture across the divide between the traditional and the modern world, the boundary which Oscar Handlin has so assiduously explored. Rowland Berthoff and I confront the theme directly in our discussion of dependence and independence, as those ideas migrated from the eighteenth century via the Revolution to economic individualism in the early nineteenth century. John Demos starts with witchcraft in a seventeenth-century village, but instead of dropping it when eighteenth-century secularism suppresses "superstition" in the traditional order, he follows the fortunes of the village witch down to the latest variant in the legends of a twentieth-century town.

The pains of departure from the traditional life are poignantly portrayed in William McLoughlin's study of the Cherokee in the years preceding their great trek. McLoughlin points out that the Cherokee, often considered the best disciplined and organized of the tribes, passed through two decades of cultural confusion before finding the resources to adapt to the pressures of new circumstances. The Whig elite whom Paul Goodman watches deteriorate in the mid-nineteenth century had less resilience than the Cherokee. They lost power entirely to a new breed of democratic politicians. In the Handlin spirit, Goodman touches on the irony of the triumph of democratic forces. Was Massachusetts better served by Benjamin Butler than by John Quincy Adams?

The essays by Neil Harris and William Taylor observe American novelists and photographers coping with the spiritual issues of modernization at the end of the nineteenth and beginning of the twentieth centuries. Harris finds amateur novelists asking what man's place was in the world science discovered and technology made. Taylor's photographers questioned how humans were to picture the towering cities they built for themselves. New structures and new powers in the environment forced the observers to look at themselves in search of spiritual strength or a new vision of life equal to the awesome powers at work around them.

In his discussion of the idea of a melting-pot America, Arthur Mann sees in its most zealous exponent, the playwright Israel Zangwill, the contradictions common in people of two cultures. They yearn to blend imperceptibly with the new while clinging tenaciously to the old. Zangwill's was the anguish of many uprooted Americans.

It would be too much to attribute the convergence of themes in these eight essays to the influence of one teacher. Other historiographical forces have focused attention on the breakup of old orders and the construction of new. But it is certainly true that none of these essays is foreign to the spirit of Oscar Handlin's work. At least it can be said that he early identified one of the master concepts of history making in our time, and that he and his students have fruitfully explicated its meaning.

A book to honor Oscar Handlin, the longtime general editor of the Little, Brown Library of American Biography and author of *Al Smith and His America* (1958) would be incomplete without biographical studies. Anne Firor Scott draws portraits of three eighteenth-century women, Jane Mecom (Benjamin Franklin's sister), Elizabeth Sandwith Drinker of Philadelphia, and Eliza Lucas Pinckney of Charleston, founder and grand dame of the illustrious Pinckney line. Moses Rischin's essay on Marcus Lee Hansen, besides explicating important connections in the development of history writing in the twentieth century, tells us where immigrant history was when Oscar Handlin came on the scene.

Each essay in this volume reflects in some way the consequences of one man's teaching and scholarship conveyed to, transformed by, and carried forward in the mind of a student. Altogether they are meant as a tribute and appreciation. Ultimately, of course, the most complete measure of Oscar Handlin's achievement is the list of his published works prepared by Robert Mirak, joined with the list of graduate students who worked under his direction. Together they represent the ground of printed words, research, and talk on which Oscar Handlin stands, and the group of students who, pleased with the new land he showed them, sank roots in nourishing soil.

Notes

1. Oscar Handlin, *The Uprooted,* 2nd ed. (Boston: Little, Brown, 1973), p. 298.
2. *Ibid.,* p. 278.
3. Oscar and Mary F. Handlin, *Facing Life: Youth and the Family in American History* (Boston: Little, Brown, 1971), p. 289.
4. *The Uprooted,* p. 278.
5. *Ibid.,* p. 272.

A Portrait of
Oscar Handlin

Barbara Miller Solomon

Barbara Miller Solomon, senior lecturer at Harvard University on history and literature and on the history of American civilization, is the author of *Ancestors and Immigrants: A Changing New England Tradition* (1956), and *Pioneers in Service* (1956). She is the editor of Timothy Dwight's *Travels in New England and New York* (1969), and is currently completing a book on American women and the historical meanings of their higher education.

AS OF JUNE 1978, seventy-two men and women had written Ph.D. dissertations in American history and the history of American civilization under the direction of Oscar Handlin. A group of these students gathered in April 1975 to honor the professor and his wife, Mary. Many did not know each other, for the celebrants spanned several academic generations, but they found that they shared a unique experience: the special fellowship of Handlin students. Those not able to attend sent letters that communicated the same feeling of identification. For the occasion, contemporaries, professors, and colleagues of Oscar's contributed personal recollections to which he responded in kind.* A portrait of Oscar Handlin emerged from these varied perspectives.

Oscar was the firstborn, in 1915 in New York City, of three children of Joseph and Ida Handlin, immigrants from Tsarist Russia. The child was father to the man; the schoolfellow was the scholar and professor to be. A small boy, observed delivering groceries to his father's customers in Brooklyn, had in hand the book he had been reading before he jumped off the wagon. A quiet, shy lad, he did not lack confidence. Before he was eight,

*All quotations are from letters, greetings, and speeches prepared for the occasion.

3

young Oscar knew he would write history books better than those he read. He meant to be a scholar.

Not an easy pupil, he became the *enfant terrible* of the public school systems of three states. Sometimes he was expelled, sometimes promoted, but he was never lost. In 1930, Oscar at fifteen landed at Brooklyn College. The school was a recent extension of the New York City colleges, open to those who qualified by examination. Oscar was soon conspicuous. An instructor in the history department who taught him in his first year could not believe that a first-term freshman could write the paper he submitted. Suspecting a case of plagiarism, she called him in, only to acknowledge the mistake. This young man was exceptional. He could write, and he had something to say.

Oscar went his own thinking way in a college where intense questioning flourished during the Great Depression. While undergraduate Marxists of varying shades debated vociferously, he was, in the recollection of classmate Bernard Frizell, "gazing out even then through thick-lensed glasses," viewing the tumult with "a skeptical eye." No joiner, Oscar remained independent; already he resisted easy solutions to the complexities of history and of contemporary life.

With his first degree in hand, the nineteen-year-old arrived in Cambridge in September 1934, along with Frizell, who reports that a Harvard dean's statement that "nobody up here has heard of Brooklyn College" did not faze "thin rosy-cheeked" Oscar. He was ready for Harvard, and Harvard proved ready for him.

As at institutions Oscar had previously attended, faculty members of the History Department and other students sensed something different about the newcomer. Oscar's style as a graduate student became legendary. Was it true that he took no notes at lectures? Richard Leopold has verified the fact. Such curious behavior puzzled peers and professors alike. Moreover, the young man argued more than others did; he seemed to "seize upon every occasion to differ," William Langer recalled. But the question of whether or not Oscar was merely contentious was settled after his general examination. The brilliant performance added to the legend of the young man from Brooklyn. He had, as Frank Collier heard from the current professorial grapevine, "astounded his committee by the depth of his knowledge and skill in fielding their probing questions." The "youngster" was, in the perspicacious judgment of Ray Billington (who was slightly ahead of Oscar), "fated to rank among the great historians of our day."

Fellowships supported Oscar's progress, culminating in a Sheldon which took him to London and Dublin for research on his doctoral thesis. With its completion he received the Ph.D. in 1940, and its publication as *Boston's Immigrants* in 1941 brought the J. H. Dunning Prize of the American Historical Association.

Within a few years Oscar's reputation for scholarly productivity enhanced the Handlin legend. When as a graduate student I wanted to study the history of immigration, F. O. Matthiessen suggested that I work with Oscar Handlin, but cautioned that I not be intimidated by this "young man with a long bibliography."

Oscar Handlin had attacked the work of earning the doctorate with a fierce joy. The same quality in the professor dazzled his first students. In these neophytes, he generated the conviction that historical knowledge mattered, that finding and transmitting it was a neccessity.

The bibliography became longer and longer, and in its making there was a partner from the beginning. Mary Flug Handlin, his wife from 1937 to her death in 1976, was not a mere assistant but an independent thinker, demanding and indefatigable in research, his critic and editor, the full participant in what became their collaboration. Oscar and Mary demonstrated their faith in the scholar's enterprise. It was more than a vision for them; it was a business, a craft. They assumed that no product was made without drudgery, discomfort, and pain. If one complained that writing was hard, the professor said, "Good. It should not come too easily."

The pressure to respond to the high standards by which Oscar lived was unrelenting, but it was tempered by his sympathetic awareness of the problems each student confronted. Yehoshua Arieli, a stranger from Israel, somewhat older than other seminar members, gained encouragement, because, despite Professor Handlin's brevity in conversation, he gave "the feeling that he understood my situation." Moreover, although Oscar Handlin was the professor, Mary Handlin was the unofficial teacher — seemingly withdrawn in a corner of the Widener study — who often broke the professor's silence when it seemed to overwhelm the unprepared or floundering victim. Those who came into the Handlin orbit gained untold benefits from one or the other partner over the years.

Always his students knew that their work was taken seriously. They discovered that writing a thesis was the beginning of writing a book. Under Oscar Handlin's patient but persistent prodding students' expectations rose. With women whose marriages and babies interrupted doctoral progress, the professor was firm. "Glad to hear the baby arrived safely. Are you back at work?" Anne Firor Scott heard the question and knew what it meant. Dorothy Burton Skårdal, raising a family in Norway, was not sufficiently removed to escape the professor's expectations. When Oscar, Mary, and their three children arrived in her mountain village, Dorothy had the inevitable chapter and yet knew the inevitable comeback: "Start the next."

The pressure operated whether one was in Telemark, in Cambridge, or in Las Vegas. Only a younger student in the Handlin fold, however, could have had the experience of Henry Binford, who, after the ordeal of his doctoral examination with Oscar, turned on the television to forget. "As the screen glowed and came to life, whose image should appear but that of Oscar Handlin." The professor was omnipresent and inescapable.

The first generation of Handlin students had a relatively young man, almost a contemporary, as their mentor in the 1940s. Most students were only a few years younger than the professor, and a few were older. To that generation Oscar Handlin was less awesome or formidable, even though he was compelling and demanding of one's best efforts. With the publication of the Pulitzer Prize–winner *The Uprooted* in 1951, undergraduates and the general public more often sought Oscar Handlin. The small classes on "The Immigrant in American History" and "The Boston Community" in the Social Relations Department gave way to large lectures on the social history of the American people. Later graduate students became the disciples of a recognized scholar, one with responsibilities in the university and the larger world.

In 1954 Oscar Handlin became professor of history at Harvard. He had taught for one year at Brooklyn College in 1938–1939, and then returned to Harvard to rise from instructor in 1939–1940 to full professor fifteen years later. Thereafter he occupied a series of chairs. He was named Winthrop Professor of History in 1962, Charles Warren Professor of American History in 1965. On a year's sabbatical he served as Harmsworth Professor of American History at Oxford University. The climax of these appointments came in 1973, when Oscar Handlin was made Carl H. Pforzheimer University Professor at Harvard.

In addition to teaching, Oscar contributed to the advance of research by organizing and directing the Center for the Study of the History of Liberty in America, 1958–1967, and the Charles Warren Center for Studies in American History, 1965–1973. He also served successively as vice-chairman, 1962–1965, and chairman, 1965–1966, of the United States Board of Foreign Scholarships, popularly known as the prestigious Fulbrights. Moreover, throughout these years Oscar gave his expertise to many other academic and communal projects. These included the Committee on Research in Economic History; the Brandeis University Board of Overseers; the Ford Hall Forum; the New York Public Library; the American Jewish Committee; the American Council for Nationalities Service.

Oscar Handlin had become the busiest of academic men, engaged as consultant, confidant, and guide at all levels of the university community, yet no less concerned with the welfare of his graduate students. One colleague described him as "the most patiently submissive to intrusions and to calls for assistance." Although his students found it took longer to penetrate the reserve of the professor, eventually most succeeded and were richly rewarded. As earlier, for Oscar and Mary, relationships with students did not end with their acquisition of the Ph.D. Friendships with former students, spouses, and offspring remained important to the Handlins, whose curiosity and sympathy matched their forthright judgments about standards for the professional man or woman. In the inevitable crises, the Handlins were always available to help in decisions about jobs, fellowships, and drafts of later books. Fittingly, Sam Bass Warner toasted Oscar and Mary as "guides to young professionals."

Over time the familial relationships of the Handlins and their students expanded to include the students of the students. Dedications in their first books identify the influence of Oscar Handlin upon still younger members of the profession. Arthur Mann noted, "the Handlin students and grandstudents make an extended family of historians."

Oscar Handlin has shaped a tribe of Americanists for forty years. When his students gathered to honor him, they affirmed the communal sense they have enjoyed as historians trained by him. Oscar did not dominate their choices of historical inquiry. Consciously, the professor used the weapon of listening to teach. Thus he gave students freedom to find and develop their own strengths. The variety of books his students have written reflects the openness of the teacher. Their writings, like his, range from the colonial era to the present; the themes encompass not only immigration and ethnicity but also economics, politics, religion, and the arts. What has bound the works of the professor and his students is a common sympathy for the many forms of human experience of individuals and groups. Oscar Handlin's creativity has offered, not one, but numerous models to follow. He is scholar and poet, the artist of American history.

Witchcraft and Local Culture in Hampton, New Hampshire

John Demos

John Demos, professor of history at Brandeis University, is completing a book-length study of witchcraft, from which the current essay is excerpted. He is the author of *A Little Commonwealth: Family Life in Plymouth Colony* (1970).

A TRIAL FOR witchcraft was invariably a powerful *event*, a moment of intense drama in the lives of all those who supported the proceedings, or sought desperately to defend against them, or merely stood by and watched. But such trials were just the high points on a variable "curve" of personal and communal anxieties. The survival in quantity of court records, and the relative paucity of material on everyday circumstance, may lead us into errors of emphasis. We must periodically remind ourselves that witchcraft — or a concern therewith — was a *persistent* feature of life in early New England.

The history of Hampton (until 1679 a part of the province of Massachusetts Bay, but belonging thereafter to New Hampshire) seems especially well suited for making this point. For more than twenty years the people of Hampton worried and gossiped about the dubious character of their neighbor Goodwife Eunice Cole. On at least three occasions they brought her to court for conduct indicating "familiarity with the Devil." She became, in truth, a local celebrity, familiar not only to Hamptonites but also to residents of neighboring towns and to passing boatmen who traded along the New England coast. From a variety of local records it is possible to grasp the long-term continuity in the experience of this alleged witch, and in the town's dealings with her. One can even trace lines of personal contact along which her reputation passed through time and across generations, adding new recruits to the legion of her accusers and victims.

"Goody" Cole was the first and most notorious "witch" at Hampton, but she was not the last. As she grew older, attention shifted to other women. New arrests were made, testimony taken, bonds filed — although, in the end, matters were resolved short of actual convictions. After 1680 there were no further legal actions of this sort, but witchcraft remained a part of the popular consciousness. Well into the eighteenth century Hamptonites sensed the Devil at work around them.

Hampton was founded in 1639 by a small band of families moving north from Essex County, Massachusetts. Its early years were notable chiefly for chronic turmoil and contention. Virtually from the start there was difficulty over boundaries, with neighbors both to the east (Exeter) and the south (Salisbury). More painful still was the presence of much internal strife. In the early 1640s Hampton was embroiled in a bitter dispute over the pastor, Reverend Stephen Bachiller. Incredibly — for he was then an octogenarian — Bachiller stood accused of "soliciting the chastity of his neighbor's wife." In fact the problem ran also to keenly felt differences of religious belief and of geographical origin in old England. In 1646 there was new controversy, concerning the division of town lands. Repeatedly, the contesting parties appealed for outside support; and, repeatedly, the authorities at Boston sought to mediate. As Governor Winthrop noted in his journal: "Diverse meetings . . . [with] magistrates and elders" might temporarily dampen the conflict, but then "it brake out presently again, each side being apt to take fire upon any provocation." It was not until the decade of the 1650s that the community achieved a *modus vivendi* with which most, if not all, of the citizens were reasonably comfortable.[1]

The formal history of witchcraft in Hampton begins with the year 1656. That there was an *in*formal history, extending some time farther back, seems likely — but not provable from extant materials.[2] In any case, by the spring of 1656 Hamptonites were giving evidence on a wide scale, looking toward the prosecution of Goodwife Eunice Cole. An initial brace of depositions were taken by magistrates in Essex County that April, and were forwarded to Boston for use in a trial before the General Court the following September. The court solicited further testimony of its own, so that some two dozen witnesses eventually took part.[3] Nine manuscript depositions survive today, and provide at least a sampling of the charges against Goody Cole. Two of these imputed illness and death (a grown man, an infant girl) to her *maleficium;* three others alleged acts of destruction against domestic animals. The same materials noted a variety of suspicious and seemingly occult phenomena: strange scrapings against houses, fierce cats appearing suddenly and then disappearing, a private conversation that was somehow known to the accused.[4]

But who was Goody Cole? What can be learned of her character? And what was the pattern of her relations with others? Actually, the trial testimonies themselves yield some parts of the answer to such questions. She was, first of all, a woman given to threats and curses against those she perceived as antagonists. ("Goodwife Cole said that if this deponent's calves . . . did eat any of her grass, she wished it might poison or choke them.")[5] She was herself quite ready to proclaim the influence of witchery. ("Goodwife Cole said that she was sure there was a witch in the town, . . . and that thirteen years ago she knew one bewitched as Goodwife Marston's child was.")[6] She was not reluctant to confront established authority. ("At a meeting with the selectmen, Eunice Cole came in . . . and demanded help of the selectmen for wood or other things; and the selectmen told her she had an estate of her own, and needed no help of the town.")[7]

These scattered glimpses of Eunice Cole interacting with her accusers can be supplemented by evidence of other kinds. She had arrived in New England some two decades before, together with her husband, a carpenter named William. A bill from November 1637 noted the manner of their coming: "William Cole . . . to pay unto Matthew Craddock of London, merchant, the sum of ten pounds of current money . . . for his and his wife's passage, and so to be free of their service to Mr. Craddock."[8] (Twenty years later Craddock took the Coles to court over this debt, "to this day never satisfied.") There was no reference, here or elsewhere, to any younger Coles, and it seems safe to assume that the couple was childless.

It is evident, too, that the Coles were quite poor. Recently freed from service to an English merchant, they assumed a modest position in the little community of Mount Wollaston (later Braintree) just to the south of Boston.[9] Mount Wollaston was the initial base of the controversial "antinomian" preacher, Reverend John

Wheelwright; it was from there that he and his followers set out to found the town of Exeter. Because they moved beyond the reach of any provincial authority, the Exeter group drew up special articles of "combination" as a basis for self-government. All of the firstcomers set their hands to these articles, promising thereby to "submit ourselves . . . to Godly and Christian laws." Included on the list is the name of William Cole, undersigned with a crude personal mark.[10]

The Coles spent five uneventful years in Exeter. A land division among early householders, with the usual pattern of unequal shares, finds William near the middle of the list.[11] Twice he went to court in minor actions — once as plaintiff, once as defendant.[12] In 1643 he served as fence viewer, the only civil office he ever held in New England.[13]

It is not known why the Coles moved to Hampton in 1644, but this change marked a sharp downward turn in their fortunes.[14] In remarkably short order they incurred the enmity of their new neighbors. In 1645 Eunice was charged at Salisbury Court with having made "slanderous speeches" against other Hampton goodwives.[15] Two years later the Coles were sued for the recovery of several pigs which plaintiff alleged they had wrongfully withheld. The court decided against them, and when the constable went to execute the verdict a violent ruckus ensued. Witnesses reported that Eunice cried "murder, murder," while William ranted about "thieves in the town"; together they bit the constable's hands, knocked him down, and "pulled the swine from him."[16] From this sequence the authorities developed additional, and more serious, charges — whose resolution is not recorded. In 1651 Eunice was admonished at court for new "misdemeanors," and in 1654 she was "presented" to still another jury.[17] There were, moreover, additional trials for which records are now lost.

If the Coles, and especially Eunice, were increasingly marked as deviant from a legal standpoint, they also gravitated quickly toward the bottom of the local status hierarchy. Hampton tax lists from 1647 to 1653 show William Cole "rated" fifty-first among sixty householders in the former instance, and dead last out of seventy-two in the latter.[18] A floor plan for the meetinghouse, dated 1650, finds William seated near the rear (among men far younger than himself), and Eunice consigned to the back bench of a gallery that was yet to be constructed![19]

But what of the community in which the Coles found themselves so invidiously placed? Careful demographic reconstruction, focused on the year 1656, has yielded the following overall picture.[20] The total population was a little more than 350, the number of households approximately 65, the average size of household 5.6 persons. The age structure was heavily skewed toward youth (62 percent of the inhabitants were less than twenty years old); among people fully adult there were nearly equal numbers in brackets of thirty to thirty-nine, forty to forty-nine, and over fifty years. Among heads of household and their wives, fully half had lived in Hampton since the time of its founding; two-thirds had been there for at least ten years; and all but a handful for at least five. Of those whose place of origin in England can be traced, some 70 percent came from the eastern counties of Norfolk, Suffolk, and Essex. (It was to the influence of this majority that Stephen Bachiller ascribed his own downfall.) Before settling in Hampton, nearly all had stopped at least briefly in some other New England community — Watertown and Exeter, most especially; also Salem, Newbury, Ipswich, and Dedham.

The spatial arrangement of Hampton was relatively simple. Most of the population lived in a central, nucleated village, clustered on all sides of the "meetinghouse green." Several families, however, had home lots along the roadways that connected the village with the ocean shore (two miles east), or with a ships' "landing" just to the south on Taylor's River.[21] The social structure of Hampton embraced a familiar range of ranks and statuses. Year after year a cadre of perhaps a dozen families filled most of the major town offices, paid the highest taxes (because they controlled the most property), and occupied the coveted front-row seats in the meetinghouse.[22]

Here, then, was Hampton on the eve of its first witchcraft trial: a community no longer new, increasingly stable, self-contained, and self-sufficient — a fully formed social organism, by the standards of its own time and culture. The prosecution of Eunice Cole itself affirms this impression of integrated structure, for the people who testified against her represented a notably broad spectrum of local townsfolk; no single descriptive category will suffice to characterize them. For example, their spatial derivation within the town was almost random. Three sides of the village green produced witnesses for the trial; so, too, did the settlements along the outlying roads.[23] Nor was place of origin a significant determinant of trial participation; East Anglians predominated, but not disproportionately to their numbers in the town — and other regions of old England were represented as well.[24] A strong majority of the witnesses belonged to the families of "firstcomers," but several had arrived only within the previous decade.[25] The sexes were evenly represented (eleven apiece); and, with the exception of three young persons and one elderly widower, all the witnesses were married. Only the categories of age and social position yield anything like an uneven distribution. The age group thirty to thirty-nine was somewhat more heavily represented (relative to its overall size) than other ten-year brackets.[26] And the status group classified "high," as against "middle" and "low," was also distinctly preponderant. (The "low" group produced its fair share of witnesses, while the "middle" was somewhat *under*represented.)[27]

In sum, this analysis of the witnesses to Eunice Cole's "witchcraft" reveals a general movement against her, led by people of recognized standing in the community. Her prospects must, then, have seemed rather bleak, in the summer of 1656, as her case headed for trial before the Court of Assistants.

Unfortunately, the verdict in this case is nowhere recorded. All previous writers on Hampton have assumed a conviction — and a punishment by whipping and long imprisonment.[28] There is, however, reason to conclude otherwise. Witchcraft was a capital crime in Massachusetts Bay, and a judgment of guilt invariably brought the death sentence. Yet Goody Cole was certainly *not* executed. Indeed, she was back in Hampton by at least 1658, creating new difficulties for herself and her neighbors.[29]

The sequence of her life in these, and succeeding, years is extremely difficult to follow, for only some parts are documented. In 1660 she was prosecuted for "unseemly speeches . . . in saying to Huldah Hussey [a young neighbor], 'where is your mother Mingay, that whore? . . . She is abed with your father, that whore-master.' "[30] A short while later she was again in jail at Boston, petitioning the court "for her liberty." (With considerable pathos she pleaded her own "condition" as an "aged and weak woman," and the special needs of her husband — "he being 88 years of age, and troubled often with swellings and aches in his body . . . at which times I do take such pains with him as none but a wife would do.")[31] In October 1662 the court granted her request, upon certain conditions, and she evidently returned to Hampton before the end of the year.[32]

Her husband, however, had died that summer, and local authorities were already in the process of settling his estate. William Cole had written a will in May 1662, leaving Eunice only her "clothes which she left with me," and giving the rest of his property to a neighbor named Thomas Webster "upon condition of his keeping of me comfortably during the term of my natural life."[33] Eunice could hardly have been pleased with this plan, but the records do not show her own part in the probate arrangements. Subsequently the court elected to modify William Cole's will, dividing the estate evenly between Webster and the unfortunate widow. After various debts had been paid Eunice's share came to a mere eight pounds and this, in turn, was ordered withheld from her "to be improved" by the selectmen "for her necessity."[34] Almost certainly, these proceedings left a residue of bitter feelings, sufficient to energize still another charge of witchcraft — ten years later.[35]

Meanwhile Eunice Cole continued to bounce back and forth between Hampton and the Boston jail. The spring of 1665 found her approaching the General Court with a new petition for release from imprisonment — which was granted "upon her [giving] security to depart from, and abide out of, this jurisdiction."[36] It does not appear that she accepted these terms: how, after all, would an elderly, impoverished widow start over in an entirely new setting? Perhaps, then, she remained a prisoner for some years longer;[37] there is no further trace of her at Hampton until about 1670.

Whatever the legal troubles of Goody Cole in the decade of the 1660s witchcraft was *not* among them. Other crimes (such as "unseemly speeches") served to sustain her adversary relationship with the townspeople of Hampton. But there is no reason to think that her reputation for witchcraft had been dissipated; on the contrary, it flourished as vigorously as ever. One episode, recalled much later, will serve to illustrate. The setting was Hampton, on an evening near the end of the year 1662; a selectman named Abraham Perkins was approaching her house on an errand, when

I heard a discoursing . . . and, harkening, I heard the voice of Eunice Cole and a great hollow voice answer her, and the said Eunice seemed to be discontented with something, finding fault, and the said hollow voice spake to her again in a strange and unworldly [?] manner . . . as if one had spoken out of the earth or in some hollow vessel. . . . And I being much amazed to hear that voice, I went and called Abraham Drake and Alexander Denham, and we three went to her house and harkened, and heard the said Eunice Cole speak and the said strange voice answer her diverse times, and the said Eunice Cole went up and down in the house and clattered the door to and again, and spake as she went, and the said voice made her answer in a strange manner . . . and there was a shimmering of a red color in the chimney corner.[38]

This exchange, so patently terrifying to the men who watched and listened, would eventually sustain a formal indictment, charging that "Eunice Cole of Hampton, widow, . . . not having the fear of God before her eyes, and being instigated by the Devil, did on the 24th of November in the year 1662 . . . enter into covenant with the Devil . . ."[39] Significantly, however, the indictment was not returned until 1673. Doubtless, in the interim there was much local gossip about the "shimmering" presence which had visited Widow Cole on that fateful November evening; but for ten years it remained gossip — and nothing more.

This sequence raises obvious questions of *timing,* and invites further investigation of the history of Hampton during the intervening years. Why did the community wait so long before renewing its legal battle against witchcraft? As mentioned previously, Eunice Cole may have spent much of this period in prison at Boston; if so, the incentive for a new prosecution would have been somewhat diminished. That is not, however, the whole story; for during the decade of the 1660s Hamptonites were increasingly preoccupied with *external* risks and dangers. The problem which faced them was not new, but now — as never before — it threatened their property, their political rights, and the integrity of their community.

In order to understand this situation, it is necessary to trace the history of the so-called Mason patent for northern New England.[40] Deriving from grants by King Charles I to a minor courtier and colonial adventurer named Captain John Mason, the patent remained until mid-century largely undeveloped. Meanwhile, settlers arrived in the designated region, establishing new towns (including Hampton) under the administrative oversight of Massachusetts Bay. In 1650 John Mason's grandson and principal heir obtained in England a judgment favorable to the family claim — which, however, was immediately contested by the Bay Colony. Out of favor with the Cromwell regime, the Masons had no quick opportunity to break this impasse.

But their prospects brightened considerably following the restoration of the monarchy in 1660. The new king's attorney general reaffirmed that "Robert Mason . . . had a good and legal title to the Province of New Hampshire."[41] And the royal "commission" sent to New England in 1664–1665 sharpened the issue by making it for the first time immediate and *personal*. Among other things, the commissioners challenged the jurisdiction of Massachusetts over the New Hampshire towns; indeed, at Portsmouth they appointed new officials directly responsible to the king. The whole region experienced, as a result, an extreme public agitation.[42] The political status of the various towns seemed suddenly unclear, and their territorial rights insecure; moreover, detached from Massachusetts, they would be far more vulnerable to the designs of Robert Mason.

As one of the communities directly involved, Hampton shared in the general excitement. During the summer of 1665 the town held special meetings to consider various strategies of response. Eventually a committee was appointed to "remonstrate" with the commissioners, and to "make answer to any claims or objections" that might be made against the rights of the local citizenry.[43] Subsequent meetings declared the strong desire of Hamptonites to retain their connection with Massachusetts. In all this they cooperated closely with their neighbors at Exeter, Portsmouth, and Dover.[44] Toward the end of the year the commissioners returned to England, with the issue still unresolved. The people of New Hampshire obtained thereby a brief period of remission; but Mason continued to press his interests as best he could, and he would find new — and better — openings in the future.

In 1672 the long-festering currents of fear and spite converged to produce the second major witchcraft prosecution at Hampton. Two developments seem to have opened the way. First, the "crisis" of the previous decade had temporarily abated, permitting the reassertion of *internal* concerns; and second, Eunice Cole had definitely returned to town, in circumstances that were bound to create difficulty. The record suggests that she was now wholly a public charge. Apparently she was living in a small hut erected by the town; individual householders took turns in supplying her daily needs for food and fuel.[45]

As in her previous trial for witchcraft, the prosecution mounted a large body of testimony against Eunice Cole. Fourteen depositions, taken between October 1672 and April 1673, are still extant;[46] they record the impressions of sixteen different witnesses, about twelve distinct episodes. Once again the *range* of the witness group seems notable — whether measured in terms of age, sex, social position, or place of residence.

But most striking of all, in this 1673 case, is the blending of old and new material. Several major depositions return to events from a much earlier period: an angry encounter with the defendant "about 16 or 17 years ago";[47] a Sabbath service "many years since," when a "small creature . . . fell out of the bosom of Eunice Cole";[48] the mysterious death of a newborn child to whom Eunice had been denied access, "about ten years ago";[49] her alleged "covenant" with the Devil, made on a November evening in 1662.[50] The court accepted such evidence, "though it speaks of what was done many years since, because it was never brought in against her before."[51]

Of course, there was much new evidence as well. The town constable, whose task it was to deliver to Eunice Cole the maintenance donated by the townspeople, recounted a series of recent misadventures. Eunice, he noted, "would be often finding fault with him about her provision, and complaining that it was not so good as was brought in to him" — whereupon his own bread turned rotten, and for weeks together "we could never make any bread . . . at home but it would stink and prove loathesome." Inevitably, the deponents grew "suspicious that goody Cole had enchanted our oven."[52] On another occasion Eunice quarreled with a local night watchman, and "the next day [he] fell sick, and lay sick about a fortnight."[53] There were renewed allegations that imps "sucked" on Eunice during Sabbath services.[54] But most important among the newer charges, it was claimed that she had repeatedly used devious means on a young girl named Ann Smith, "all tending to entice her to live with her."[55]

Four different witnesses gave evidence on this latter point: Ann Smith herself (called "about the age of nine years"), Anna Huggins (age fourteen), Sarah Clifford (age thirty), and Bridget Clifford (age fifty-six).[56] One episode, in particular, exemplified the larger pattern:

Bridget Clifford . . . saith [that] the last summer . . . she sent Ann Smith into the cabbage yard, and some [time] after my daughter Sarah said that she heard her cry in the orchard. And . . . when she came crying out of the orchard, I asked her what she ailed, and she said she knew not, but when she came she spake these words: "she will knock me on the head; she will kill me." And . . . my daughter Sarah took her up and carried her into her house which was near mine. And when she had laid her in the cradle, the child related to us two that when she was in the cabbage yard there came an old woman to her in a blue coat and a blue cap and a blue apron and a white neckcloth, and took her up and carried her under the persimmon tree, and told her that she would live with her. Then, said she, "the old woman struck me on the head with a stone"; and then she turned into a little dog and ran up the tree, and flew away like an eagle.[57]

Among the many intriguing aspects of this testimony, the "enticement" theme commands special attention. Evidently this was not a new accusation against Goody Cole. The court noted that "it was her design formerly to insinuate herself into young ones," and recalled an earlier trial when another local girl had testified "how many ways, and in how many forms, she [i.e., Eunice] did appear to her."[58] There is pathos, as well as terror, in these charges. Herself childless through many years of marriage, Eunice Cole may have sought in her widowhood to become a "parent" after all. It would be easy enough to understand her yearning in this direction, given a culture which consistently affirmed child-rearing as a central part of life.

But there are further questions to raise here. Why, for example, was Ann Smith the particular object of the widow's interest? How did this one girl fall under the shadow of those dark fears and pressures which had attached to Goody Cole from a much earlier time? To explore such issues is to commit oneself to some painfully complicated demographic reconstruction; but the outcome will fully repay the effort.

Ann Smith's personal history begins with her birth, at Exeter, in the year 1663.[59] She was the second child of one Nicholas Smith; her brother, Nathaniel, was three years older.[60] Her mother died when she was still an infant, and both Ann and Nathaniel were subsequently "placed" in the family of William Godfrey of Hampton. Their natural father remarried within a few years, but evidently made no effort to reclaim the children for his own household. William and Margery Godfrey, thenceforth foster parents for the two young Smiths, were already well along in life.[61] Each had been previously married and widowed; each had children by the former spouse. In addition, they had raised a son and two daughters of their own. The latter ranged in age from about eighteen to twenty-four, when the Smiths came into the household.

William Godfrey died in 1671, and soon thereafter his widow made her third marriage — to a Hampton neighbor named John Marion.[62] Nathaniel Smith remained with his adoptive mother through these various changes.[63] Ann, however, was by 1672 transferred to still another family, headed by Goodman John Clifford.[64] The Clifford household was itself extremely complex, for John had been married twice previously, and his current wife, Bridget, at least once; moreover, there were children from all of their earlier unions.[65] As of 1672 the Clifford *ménage* comprised the following persons:

John Clifford	age 57
Bridget [————] (Huggins) Clifford	age 56
Hannah Clifford (dau. of John & first wife)	age 23
Bridget Huggins (dau. of Bridget & first husband)	age 21
Israel Clifford (son of John & first wife)	age 19
Joseph Richardson (son of John's second wife and her previous husband)	age 17
Benjamin Richardson (son of John's second wife and her previous husband)	age 15
Elizabeth Clifford (dau. of John & second wife)	age 13
Anna Huggins (dau. of Bridget & first husband)	age 13
Nathaniel Huggins (son of Bridget & first husband)	age 12
Esther Clifford (dau. of John & second wife)	age 10
Isaac Clifford (son of John & second wife)	age 8
Ann Smith (dau. of Nicholas Smith; adoptive dau. of William Godfrey)	age 9

Meanwhile, John Clifford, Jr. (son of John and his first wife), was living in the next house, with his bride of two years, Sarah (Godfrey) Clifford.[66]

This situation requires summary, from the particular vantage point of Ann Smith. The Cliffords' was the *third* household in which she had lived. She had experienced the loss by death, first of her natural mother, and later of her adoptive father; and, in each case, the surviving parent (natural father, adoptive mother) had acceded in her transfer to a new setting. Her current family was composed of thirteen persons, including eleven children with four different surnames.

To be sure, fosterage was not uncommon in early New England; more than a few families were rearranged by the death of one spouse and remarriage of the other. But the complexity of the Clifford household was extreme, and the changes experienced by young Ann Smith were unusually frequent and jarring. Under all these circumstances, Ann might well have felt her new position (*chez* Clifford) to be somewhat uncomfortable, even precarious. Where was her real home? To whom did she finally belong? Was it fanciful to suppose, as life continued to move her about, that she might one day fall into the clutches of a witch-mother?

These data help to explain why Eunice Cole, longing for a child "to live with her," might have fastened her interest on Ann Smith. They also suggest why Ann herself might have been made especially jittery by an overt approach. But there is still more to ask about the circumstances which brought these two together. How had Ann come to learn of the widow's "witchcraft," in the course of her childhood years? To what extent was she prepared, by those around her, for what would happen in the summer of 1672?

It is clear, in the first place, that the Clifford family supported her charges against Eunice Cole; three of them supplied personal testimony for the prosecution. But these three — Bridget Clifford, Sarah Clifford, and Anna Huggins — were themselves recent arrivals in the household; and, in each case, it was *prior* experience that shaped their participation in the 1673 trial. Bridget had served as a witness in the first witchcraft prosecution, seventeen years before.[67] She was then the wife of John Huggins — who, as town constable, had once been responsible for whipping Goody Cole.[68] Anna Huggins was Bridget's daughter by her first husband. And Sarah Clifford was originally Sarah Godfrey, daughter of William; her brother, John, was another of the witnesses at the earlier trial.[69]

The Godfrey connection was important in one final way. William Godfrey's wife, Margery, was the mother by a previous marriage of Thomas Webster — the same man whom William Cole designated as his principal legatee.[70] This suggests the following possibilities, hypothetical but hardly fanciful. Widow Cole would likely have resented Thomas Webster's claim to property that she regarded as rightfully her own. And Webster, knowing her reputation as a grasping sort, surely *expected* such resentment; more, he anticipated some form of retaliation. These anxieties were freely expressed in the home of his mother — where Ann Smith, young and impressionable, was living as a foster child. Time and again, she would hear of the spiteful widow in terms that left too little, or too much, to the imagination. (Had Goody Cole muttered a curse as she passed by the gate this morning? What was she doing beside Thomas Webster's barn on the day his cows took sick?) This much, we can reasonably suppose, Ann Smith carried with her in moving from one foster family to the next.

To summarize: the lives of Eunice Cole and Ann Smith were joined in a social web of many strands and complicated structure; Smiths, Godfreys, Websters, Cliffords, Hugginses — each of these families contributed something to the sequence that would eventually bring the orphaned girl and the elderly widow into fateful contact. It remains now to characterize the entire *group* of witnesses in the 1673 trial, so as to show their collective relation to the defendant through time and space. Of sixteen deponents, three had also participated in the trial of 1656. Five more were relatives of people who had witnessed on that earlier occasion. Four had moved into Hampton since 1656, and four were from neighboring towns. Among all of these together, at least seven (and perhaps as many as nine) were under the age of thirty-five. The total picture reveals, first, some widening of the defendant's reputation beyond the borders of Hampton proper,[71] and, second, a process of transmission from one generation to the next. Like Sabbath services and barn raisings, Goody Cole's "witchcraft" had become a local institution.

Convicted in the minds of her Hampton neighbors, Eunice would still have her day in court at Boston. In April 1673 the Essex County magistrates ordered her committed to jail "in order to her further trial."[72] Her case was called late that summer, and the grand jury approved her indictment.[73] But the final verdict turned in her favor — just barely: "In the case of Eunice Cole, now prisoner at the bar, [we find her] not legally guilty according to indictment, but [there is] just ground of vehement suspicion of her having had familiarity with the Devil."[74] So back she went, to whatever was left of her life in Hampton.

Several years later Hampton undertook its third, and last, prosecution for witchcraft. Interestingly, Eunice Cole was no longer the leading figure; other women had now been pushed to center stage. The case began with the death of a little child — Moses Godfrey, age fifteen months — in July 1680. A jury of inquest found "grounds of suspicion that the said child was murdered by witchcraft."[75] Naming no names, the jurymen nonetheless alluded to "a party suspected," and the following day the court took bond from one John Fuller to guarantee that "Rachel, his wife, shall appear . . . to answer what shall be charged against her in point of witchcraft."[76]

Lengthy depositions, taken by the same court, supplied the full story. Rachel Fuller had visited the Godfrey household a few weeks earlier, when the child already lay ill. Her appearance that morning was extremely strange — "her face daubed with molasses" — and her behavior was more peculiar still. She sought to hold the sick child's hand, but was prevented from doing so by Goody Godfrey. And then "the said Rachel Fuller turned . . . and smote the back of her hands together sundry times, and spat in the fire. Then she, having herbs in her hands, stood and rubbed them in her hand and strewed them about the hearth by the fire. Then she sat down again, and said, 'Woman, the child will be well,' and then went out of the door."[77] Goody Fuller appears to have claimed for herself the powers of a healer; but there was strong doubt, among her neighbors, whether she used such powers for good or for ill. In the case of the Godfrey child, death — not healing — followed her bizarre ministrations.

Other testimony portrayed her as a generally eccentric figure. Often she had played the role of an expert on witchcraft, describing "how those that were witches did go abroad at night." Once she had named "several persons that she reckoned as witches and wizards in the town."[78] (Her list included Eunice Cole.) On another occasion she had told a neighbor of "a great rout at goodman Roby's . . . when [witches] had pulled Doctor Reed out of the bed, and with an enchanted bridle did intend to lead a jaunt."[79] Moreover, when the Godfrey infant was ill, she advised the family to "lay sweet bays under the threshold; it would keep a witch from coming in." As things turned out, this procedure served to implicate Rachel herself.

One of the girls . . . laid bays under the threshold of the back door all the way, and half way of the breadth of the fore door. And soon after Rachel Fuller came to the house. And she had always formerly come in at the back door, which is next her house, but now she went about to the fore door, and though the door stood open, yet she crowded in on that side the bays lay not, and rubbed her back against the [door-]post so as that she rubbed off her hat. And then she sat down, and made ugly faces, and nestled about. . . . And when she was in the house, she looked under the door where the bays lay.[80]

Rachel Fuller diverged, in one respect, from the usual pattern in these cases; at twenty-five, she was among the *youngest* persons ever to stand trial for witchcraft in colonial New England. Married just three years before, she had two small sons of her own. Her father, John Brabrook, had been an early and prominent settler at Watertown;[81] Rachel, however, did not know him, for he died in the year of her birth.[82] Her mother was left to raise eight small children. As time passed, the family became increasingly dependent on public assistance.[83] (Even before John Brabrook's death there was a house fire, which devastated the family properties.)[84] Several Brabrook children were farmed out into foster households. Rachel lived for some period with an uncle — a *rich* uncle, at that — in Newbury.[85] Her marriage to John Fuller of Hampton came in 1677. Like Rachel, Fuller had been raised by an uncle, and tasted wealth and prestige without really sharing in it.[86] Perhaps these ambiguities, these elements of social and personal dislocation, contributed indirectly to the process from which Rachel emerged as "suspect." Many accused witches came from similarly checkered backgrounds. Surely, however, the immediate source of the feeling against her was her manifest eccentricity — and her strong interest in all things occult. Such a woman, however youthful, could not but alarm her neighbors.

A second person was charged as a witch that summer at Hampton. Isabella Towle by name, she was a woman in her late forties, married, and the mother of nine children.[87] Her husband, Philip, was first a "seaman," and later a "yeoman" of average position in the community. Beyond this the record does not speak. Particularly unfortunate is the lack of any material on the substantive charges against Goodwife Towle. All that survives is a court order, from September 1680, that "Rachel Fuller and Isabel Towle, being apprehended and committed upon suspicion of witchcraft . . . still continue in prison till bond be given for their good behavior of £100 apiece, during the Court's pleasure."[88] Both defendants were discharged in the following year.

But were there *other* defendants, in addition to these two? A single, stray reference supplies a familiar name: "At a quarter court held at Hampton, . . . 7 September 1680, . . . Eunice Cole, of Hampton [was] by authority committed to prison on suspicion of being a witch; and, upon examination of testimonies, the Court vehemently suspects her so to be, but [there is] not full proof. [Defendant] is sentenced and confined to imprisonment, and to be kept in durance until this court take further order, with a lock to be kept on her leg. In the meantime, the selectmen of Hampton [are] to take care to provide for her as formerly, that she may be retained."[89]

The timing of these events invites further comment. As noted previously, the "Mason patent" had claimed the attention of Hamptonites at intervals since at least mid-century; here, indeed, was the single greatest threat to their life as a community. In the 1650s, when the town produced its first witchcraft prosecution, the Masons could find no good openings to press their case. In the 1660s events turned sharply in their favor, and Hampton, like the other New Hampshire settlements, was preoccupied with questions of political defense; meanwhile there were no indictments for witchcraft.

The same inverse correlation can be posited for the 1670s. In the early part of this decade the threat from outside had temporarily abated, and the years 1672–1673 brought new efforts in court to rid the town of its most notorious "witch." But soon thereafter the Masons returned to the attack. In 1675 they gained more legal judgments in their favor.[90] And in 1676 Edward Randolph, the crown's leading troubleshooter for colonial affairs, arrived in Boston to press various claims against New England — including that of the Masons.[91] Randolph went to New Hampshire in person, and aroused a flurry of anxious reaction. At

Hampton, for example, the minister and other leading men drafted an urgent statement "to clear [the townspeople] from having any hand in damnifying Mr. Mason . . . and for the full vindication of their rights."[92] The upshot was renewed litigation in England — and, finally, a decision to constitute the New Hampshire towns as a separate, *royal* province. A commission from the king in 1679 established new machinery of government, providing considerable scope for the colonists themselves.[93] Once again, the Mason threat seemed to recede — and, once again (in 1680), Hamptonites made witchcraft their central point of concern.

But the Masons were not done yet. Disappointed in their hopes for political control of New Hampshire, they still held claims to ownership of the *land*. In 1681 Robert Mason visited the colony, and sought to persuade (or frighten) individual settlers into accepting leases for their property.[94] These efforts were largely unsuccessful, so Mason returned to England and mounted a new strategy. In 1682 his friend Edward Cranfield received appointment as governor of New Hampshire, under a commission that conferred extraordinarily wide powers.[95] The following years were tumultuous ones for New Hampshire; charges of "rebellion" and "tyranny" flew back and forth between the Cranfield administration and the local citizenry. At Hampton, in fact, plans were laid for armed protest — plans that were frustrated only by prompt intervention from the governor himself. The insurgent leader, one Edward Gove, was arrested, tried for "high treason," convicted, and condemned to death; eventually, however, his sentence was commuted to imprisonment in the Tower at London.[96] So it was that Hampton — and "Gove's Rebellion" — has a modest claim to be considered in the story of resistance to imperial oppression.

Meanwhile, the governor had issued a new proclamation, requiring the people of the colony to take leases on their houses and lands from Robert Mason. A spate of lawsuits followed — most of them decided, allegedly by packed juries, in favor of Mason.[97] Inevitably, there were appeals, which prolonged the controversy through the Andros regime of the late 1680s and beyond.

The political history of Hampton need not detain us further, for we have reached a terminus in the sequence of local witchcraft trials. But if the *trials* ended in 1680, the belief in witches — and the fears which attended such belief — continued long thereafter. Here we must leave the relatively firm ground of documentary evidence (contemporaneous to the events described), and enter the uncertain area of folk "tradition." Such material is not susceptible to detailed analysis; but it deserves to be sampled, if only briefly.

The lore of Hampton mentions at least two local "witches" from the eighteenth century. One was a woman named Brown — apparently elderly, widowed, and extremely poor. She lived by herself on an isolated road, and at least some Hamptonites were fearful of passing that way. The only printed reference to her "witchcraft" notes the mysterious disappearance of some pigs, whose owner had stopped one day to visit with her. While she lived, there must have been many similar stories — circulating by word of mouth among the townspeople, and becoming in time a staple part of everyday gossip.[98]

The second eighteenth-century "witch" at Hampton cuts a strikingly different figure. "General" Jonathan Moulton carried the name of an old and extremely prominent local family. He served with distinction in various Indian wars and in the Revolution itself.[99] He was frequently a town officer and a deputy to the colonial legislature; he was also elected as a delegate to the convention that drew up the state constitution. He was a businessman of great energy and wide interests. For many years his "store" was the hub of economic life in Hampton; moreover, he owned a number of local mills. After the Revolution he speculated heavily in lands all over New Hampshire.[100] From these activities he prospered greatly — some thought, too greatly. His reputation was that of a "sharp dealer." On one occasion, at least, his property was vandalized by a "violent, riotous, and tumultuous" mob, which accused him of turning an unfair profit from goods washed up on Hampton beach in a shipwreck.[101] But this man's reputation reached out in other directions as well. Shrewd and sharp as he was, his great wealth seemed to some Hamptonites inexplicable except by reference to supernatural influence. Rumor declared that Moulton was in league with the Devil.

One incident served to crystallize the full range of these attitudes. Late on a March night in 1769, Jonathan Moulton's house burned to the ground. It was, in truth, a mansion by the standards of the time, and the fire made sensational news, reported in detail as far away as Boston.[102] There was no injury to persons, but the loss in property was estimated at a full three thousand pounds. Evidently, there were many in Hampton who felt that Moulton had simply received his due. Indeed — according to later tradition —

the report was at once spread far and wide that the fire had been set by the Devil, because the General had cheated him in a bargain. . . . The "facts" have been stated thus: The Devil was to have the General's soul after a certain number of years, in consideration of which, at stated periods he was to fill the General's boot with gold and silver — the boot being hung up in the chimney for that purpose. Whether a bootful at a time was not sufficient to meet his demands for money is not stated; but on a time when [the Devil] came to fill the boot, he found it took a quantity so vast that he descended into the chimney to see what the matter was, and to his surprise he found that the General had cut off the foot of the boot! And the room below was so full of money that he could not proceed to the door, and was compelled to go back up the chimney again.[103]

This account diverged at many points from the pattern in comparable cases a century earlier. The suspect was a man of the highest social and economic position. His "witchcraft" was entirely a matter of acquisitiveness, not malice and destruction for its own sake. Moreover, there was no obvious victim here — save the Devil himself. Moulton may be viewed as an early capitalist, in a society whose main features were still *pre*capitalist. His great and distinctive talent was the use of money to create *more* money. This form of enterprise was equated with "cheating," not only because of its prodigious success, but also because it ignored traditional values.

Financial manipulation was, indeed, central to the story of Moulton's transactions with the Devil. A bootful of money can become a roomful — if clever "tricks" are employed. (It is striking, by way of contrast, that seventeenth-century witchcraft rarely seemed to involve money; instead, the property at risk typically comprised domestic animals, food, housing, furnishings, and the like.) But if greed was Moulton's sin, the *envy* of his detractors seems equally evident. There is even a hint of admiration here; how many men, after all, had managed to fool the Devil? Finally, there is humor; then, as now, such a tale would surely evoke amusement. But again, these attitudes marked a change in the lore of witchcraft. They belonged to the world of eighteenth-century folk culture, where the Devil and his legions wore a new, less menacing aspect than theretofore.

The burning of his house was only a temporary setback for Jonathan Moulton; quickly he built a new one, more grand than the first. His later years brought additional honors and greater prosperity — but no discernible mellowing of private attitudes toward his person and career. A local historian writes "that news of his death [in 1788] was carried to the haymakers on the marsh; and the cry 'General Moulton is dead!' was passed along from mouth to mouth for miles, in no regretful tones."[104] And there is one more story attached to his death. His body, having been prepared for burial, was suddenly missing from the coffin. The people of Hampton were not surprised. "The Devil," they whispered knowingly to one another, "has got his own at last."[105]

As time passed, new names and new events were added to the lore of Hampton witchcraft; but always, it seems, Eunice Cole retained a pride of place. Well down into the nineteenth century the legend of her deeds and misdeeds was embellished through constant retelling. About 1840 a Hamptonite wrote of Goody Cole as follows: "Whatever may have been the old woman's crimes and misfortunes, still many a mother has been indebted to her for hushing their crying children. The fear of her name would alarm the most courageous, or subdue the worst temper, from generation to generation."[106]

These elements of local tradition go well beyond the documentary record from the various trials of Eunice Cole. Their relation to the historical reality of seventeenth-century Hampton is quite uncertain; but they do reveal much about the place of witchcraft in the minds of *later* generations of Hamptonites. What, then, were the tales which subdued tempers and hushed the cries of children? A few examples will have to suffice.

A carpenter named Peter Johnson, born and raised at Hampton in the settlement years, was one of several young men who dared to "torment" Goody Cole, "playing upon her many a trick." On a particular occasion, while Johnson was framing a house, Goody Cole stood by and taunted him about his work. In a flash of anger the carpenter hurled his ax in her direction. The ax missed its target and stuck in the ground, "the handle upwards" — and Johnson could not pull it free. Eventually, he made apologies and asked Eunice "to give him his axe again"; whereupon she lifted it out "with the greatest ease." On an evening not long thereafter, several "young folks" peeked in at Goody Cole's window, "and saw her busily engaged in turning a bowl with something in it, apparently in the shape of a boat; at last she turned it over and exclaimed, 'there, the Devil has got the imps.' That night news came that Peter Johnson, carpenter, and James Philbrick, mariner, were drowned at the same hour in the river near the creek now [i.e., c. 1840] known as Cole's creek."[107]

Vengeance, of terrible proportions, was always a central theme in the legend of Goody Cole. One special instance was memorialized long afterward by a famous American poet. In the autumn of 1657 a boat had capsized in Hampton harbor with dreadful result, as noted in the town records: "The sad hand of God [came] upon eight persons, going in a vessel by sea from Hampton to Boston, who were all swallowed up in the ocean. . . ."[108] But the "sad hand of God" was not the only way to explain this disaster. A quite different version was preserved in folklore — and then in a poem, "The Wreck of Rivermouth," by John Greenleaf Whittier:

> Once in the old colonial days,
> Two hundred years ago and more,
> A boat sailed through the winding ways
> Of Hampton River to that low shore . . .
>
> "Fie on the witch!" cried a merry girl,
> As they rounded the point where goody Cole
> Sat by her door with her wheel atwirl,
> A bent and blear-eyed poor old soul.
> "Oho!" she muttered, "ye're brave today!
> But I hear the little waves laugh and say,
> 'The broth will be cold that waits at home;
> For it's one to go, but another to come!' "
>
> "She's cursed," said the skipper; "speak her fair.
> I'm scary always to see her shake
> Her wicked head, with its wild gray hair,
> And mouth like a hawk, and eyes like a snake,"
> But merrily still, with laugh and shout,
> From Hampton River the boat sailed out . . .

They saw not the shadow that walked beside,
They heard not the feet with silence shed,
But thicker and thicker a hot mist grew,
Shot by the lightnings through and through,
And muffled growls, like the growl of a beast,
Ran along the sky from west to east. . . .

Veering and tacking, they backward wore;
And just as a breath from the woods ashore
Blew out to whisper of danger past,
The wrath of the storm came down at last!
The skipper hauled at the heavy sail:
"God be our help," he only cried.
As the roaring gale, like the stroke of a flail,
Smote the boat on its starboard side.

Suddenly seaward swept the squall;
The low sun smote through cloudy rack;
The shoals stood clear in the light, and all
The trend of the coast lay hard and black.

But far and wide as eye could reach,
No life was seen upon wave or beach.
The boat that went out at morning never
Sailed back again into Hampton River.[109]

Goody Cole's own end is not mentioned in the town records; but once again "tradition" has preserved a chilling account. In her last illness she remained alone in her house, with all the windows and doors boarded up save one. Presently the neighbors, seeing no further sign of her, mustered their courage and forced their way in. They found her quite dead. As quickly as they could, they dug a hole in the ground beside the house. They threw the body down, covered it, and then "drove a stake through it, with a horseshoe attached, to prevent her from ever coming up again."[110]

The alleged site of this strange burial is still a point of interest among the people of Hampton. So, too, is the Cole house lot, with its ancient well. For the latter, special claims are made. It is said that shipmasters used to stop there to fill their casks, in the belief that the water would never become brackish.[111]

In 1938, on the three hundredth anniversary of the founding of Hampton, the town took official action to square accounts with Goody Cole: "*Resolved,* that we, the citizens . . . of Hampton, in

33

the town meeting assembled, do hereby declare that we believe that Eunice (Goody) Cole was unjustly accused of witchcraft and familiarity with the Devil in the 17th century, and we do hereby restore to the said Eunice (Goody) Cole her rightful place as a citizen of the town of Hampton."[112] The resolution was passed by unanimous vote.

In fact, the legend of Goody Cole has become a cherished part of the local culture. A bronze urn in the town hall holds some material purported to be her earthly remains. A stone memorial on the village green affirms her twentieth-century rehabilitation. There are exhibits on her life in the museum of the local historical society. There are even some *new* tales in which she plays a ghostly, though harmless, part: an aged figure, in tattered shawl, seen walking late at night along a deserted road, or stopping in the early dawn to peer at gravestones by the edge of the green.[113]

And now an author's postscript. Picture the living room of a comfortable house in Hampton. A stranger has come there, to examine a venerable manuscript, held in this family through many generations. Laboriously, his eyes move across the page, straining to unravel the cramped and irregular script of a bygone era. Two girls, aged nine or ten, arrive home from school: after a brief greeting they move off into an alcove and begin to play. Awash in the sounds of their game, the stranger looks up from his work and listens. "Goody Cole," cries one of the girls, "I'll be Goody Cole!" "Yes," responds the other, "and I'll be the one who gives you a whipping — you mean old witch!"[114]

It is a long way from her time to ours, but Goody Cole has made the whole trip.

Notes

1. J. K. Hosmer, ed., *Winthrop's Journal*, 2 vols. (New York, 1908), II, 179. For other references to Hampton controversies, see *ibid.*, I, 266, and II, 45–56. On all aspects of the early history of Hampton, the basic source is Joseph Dow, *History of the Town of Hampton, New Hampshire*, 2 vols. (Salem, Mass., 1893). See also: V. C. Sanborn, "The Grantees and Settlement of Hampton, N. H.," in *Essex Institute Historical Collections*, LIII (1917), 228–249; Charles H. Bell, *History of the Town of Exeter, New Hampshire* (Exeter, N.H., 1888); John F. Cronin, ed., *Records of the Court of Assistants of the Colony of Massachusetts Bay*, 3 vols. (Boston, 1926–1928), I, 236; Nathaniel B. Shurtleff, ed., *Records of the Governor and Company of the Massachusetts Bay in New England*, 5 vols. (Boston, 1853–1854), III, 66 ff., 253; *Winthrop Papers*, in *Collections of the Massachusetts Historical Society*, 4th ser., IV, 69, 446–449; J. Franklin Jameson, ed., *Johnson's Wonder-Working Providence, 1628–1651* (New York, 1910), pp. 188–189; Charles E. Banks, *Topographical Dictionary of 2885 English Emigrants to New England, 1620–1650* (Philadelphia: Brownell, 1937), *passim; The New England Historic Genealogical Register*, XII (1858), 272, XXXXVI (1892), 58–64, 157–161, 246–251, 345–350; Sybil Noyes, Charles Thorton Libby, and Walter Goodwin Davis, *Genealogical Dictionary of Maine and New Hampshire* (reprinted, Baltimore: Genealogical Publishing Co., 1972), 81–82 and *passim;* the Town Book of Hampton, I–II (ms. volumes, Town Offices, Hampton, N.H.).
2. For example, the following testimony from the trial of Eunice Cole in 1656: "Goody Marston and Goodwife Susannah Palmer . . . saith that goodwife Cole said that . . . thirteen years ago she knew one bewitched as goodwife Marston's child was and she was sure that party was bewitched for it told her so . . . and she had prayed [for] this thirteen years that God would discover that witch." Ms. deposition, Apr. 8, 1656, in Massachusetts Archives, vol. 135, fol. 2.
3. There is a manuscript list of persons who had "expended time in witnessing against Eunice Cole on trial for witchcraft" in Suffolk Court Files, fol. 26203, Clerk's Office, Supreme Court of Suffolk County, Boston, Mass. The list contains eighteen names. Six more persons can be identified, from other materials, as having joined in this prosecution.
4. See: Massachusetts Archives, vol. 135, fols. 2–3, ms. depositions by Goody Marston and Goodwife Susannah Palmer (Apr. 8, 1656), Thomas Philbrick (undated), Sobriety Moulton and Goodwife Sleeper (Apr. 10, 1656), Mary Coleman (undated), Richard Ormsby and Ensign Goddard (Apr. 12, 1656), Abraham Perkins and John Redman (Sept. 4, 1656), Abraham Drake (Sept. 4, 1656); Suffolk Court Files, Clerk's Office, Supreme Court of Suffolk County, Boston, Mass., fol. 256a, ms. deposition by Joanne Sleeper, Sept. 4, 1656; "Trials for Witchcraft in New England," documents collected by Samuel G. Drake, Houghton Library, Harvard University, Cambridge, Mass., ms. deposition by Thomas Coleman and Abraham Drake, Sept. 5, 1656.
5. Ms. deposition by Thomas Philbrick (undated), in Massachusetts Archives, vol. 135, fol. 2.
6. Ms. deposition by Goody Marston and Susannah Palmer (Apr. 8, 1656), *ibid.*

7. Ms. deposition by Thomas Coleman and Abraham Drake, Sept. 5, 1656, in "Trials for Witchcraft in New England," documents collected by Samuel G. Drake, Houghton Library, Harvard University, Cambridge, Mass. There was a suspicious aftermath to this incident. Denied the assistance she sought, Eunice Cole allegedly complained to the selectmen that "they could help goodman Robie, being a lusty man, and [yet] she could have none." The man she referred to, one Henry Robie, "lost a cow and a sheep very strangely . . . two or three days after this."

8. See Middlesex County Court Papers, Middlesex County Courthouse, Cambridge, Mass., paper no. 1219. There are also copies of a claim filed by Craddock's "agent" on June 26, 1657, for payment of this bill, and of the court's decision in the case.

9. A small grant of land to William Cole was noted in the Town Records of Boston, Feb. 20, 1637. See *Second Report the Record Commissioners of the City of Boston* (Boston, 1877), p. 15.

10. This document is reprinted in John Demos, ed., *Remarkable Providences: The American Culture, 1600–1760* (New York: Braziller, 1972), pp. 192–193. Three other manuscript documents bear the name of William Cole with an accompanying signature mark. (See his bill to Matthew Craddock, Nov. 16, 1637, in Middlesex County Court Papers, Middlesex County Courthouse, Cambridge, Mass., paper no. 1219; petition from Exeter, to General Court of Massachusetts Bay, 1643, in Massachusetts Archives, vol. 112, fol. 9; and the petition from Hampton on behalf of Lieut. Robert Pike, 1654, in Massachusetts Archives, vol. 10, fol. 299–300.) This evidence makes it seem probable — though not certain — that Cole was illiterate. His wife also used a signature mark. (See her petition to the governor and General Court of Massachusetts Bay, undated, in Massachusetts Archives, vol. 10, fol. 281.)

11. The list is printed in Bell, *History of Exeter,* p. 436.

12. Both actions were decided on Sept. 5, 1643. See Bell, *History of Exeter,* pp. 444, 445.

13. *Ibid.,* p. 445.

14. The Coles had received land in Hampton, as part of the general "division" of June 30, 1640. (See the Town Book of Hampton, I, 21, Hampton Town Offices, Hampton, N.H.) It is clear, however, that Exeter remained their place of residence for four years thereafter.

15. See *Records and Files of the Quarterly Courts of Essex County, Massachusetts* 8 vols. (Salem, Mass., 1911–1920), I, 88.

16. Presentments to court held at Ipswich, Sept. 28, 1647, in Essex County Court Papers, I, folio not numbered; see also Records of the County Court, Ipswich, Nov. 1645 to May 1663, fol. 12. (These ms. volumes are in the Clerk's Office, Essex County Courthouse, Salem, Mass.)

17. Norfolk County Court Papers, 1650–1680, fols. 30, 50 (ms. volume, Clerk's Office, Essex County Courthouse, Salem, Mass.).

18. See town rate, in the Town Book of Hampton, I, 34. (This list is not dated, but can be attributed from internal evidence to the latter months of 1647.) The original copy of the rate for 1653 has apparently been lost; however, a copy was included by Edmund Willoughby Toppan in his "Manuscript History of Hampton," 3 vols. (unpublished), II, 187. These volumes are currently owned by Mrs. Wilma White, Hampton, N.H.

19. See the Town Book of Hampton, I, 28–29. The plan is reprinted in Noyes et al., *Genealogical Dictionary,* p. 55.

20. This summary reflects a detailed effort to reconstruct the entire population of Hampton at the time of Eunice Cole's first formal trial for witchcraft. The reconstruction is based primarily on the superbly full and accurate information in Noyes et al., *Genealogical Dictionary,* and on the genealogies in Dow, *History of Hampton,* vol. II. Additional material has been taken from various genealogies of individual families, and from the Town Book and Vital Records (ms. volumes, Town Offices, Hampton, N.H.). The information as to place of origin in England has been drawn chiefly from Banks, *Topographical Dictionary.*

21. For a most useful map of Hampton in the early years, prepared by Lucy E. Dow and A. W. Locke, see Dow, *History of Hampton,* inside back cover. This has been checked against the original land records, in the Town Book of Hampton, II.

22. An effort has been made to construct a "status ladder" for the various Hampton families, by analyzing the extant tax lists, the meetinghouse plan of 1650, wills and

inventories, and patterns of local office holding. See the Town Book of Hampton, I, 34; E. W. Toppan, "Manuscript History," II, 187; *The Probate Records of Essex County, Massachusetts,* 3 vols. (Salem, Mass., 1916–1920); Noyes et al., *Genealogical Dictionary,* p. 55; Dow, *History of Hampton,* I, 563–578; the Town Book of Hampton, *passim.*

23. Witnesses came from two families living west of the green, four families on the north side, and six on the east. Four more resided in other parts of the town.

24. Among fifteen witnesses whose place of origin can be traced, nine came from eastern England (among a total of fifty-six adults associated with that region, in the overall population of Hampton). For other regions, the figures are as follows: *north,* two (out of four); *center and west,* one (out of seven); *south,* three (out of twelve).

25. Among twenty witnesses whose arrival in Hampton can be dated, thirteen came in the years 1638–1640, one in 1641–1645, four in 1646–1650, and two in 1651–1655.

26. Among twenty-two witnesses whose ages can be approximately determined, eight (out of a cohort of thirty-seven in the total population) were between the ages of thirty and thirty-nine. Four (of thirty-eight) were twenty to twenty-nine; four (of thirty-three) were forty to forty-nine; and four (of twenty-nine) were fifty or over. In addition, there were two witnesses younger than twenty years old.

27. A "scoring system," based on considerations of wealth, officeholding, and seating in the meetinghouse, has been used to divide the adult population into three status groups of roughly equal size. Eleven witnesses against Eunice Cole are thereby classified "high" (out of forty-six, in the population as a whole); four are "middle" (out of forty-one); and seven are "low" (out of forty-one).

28. See, for example, Dow, *History of Hampton,* I, 44–54; and James W. Tucker, "Eunice 'Goody' Cole: The Only Woman Ever to Be Convicted of Witchcraft in New Hampshire" (pamphlet, privately published).

29. An obscure, but important, reference in the town records seems to establish this point. Under a heading entitled "The accounts of the County of Norfolk for the Court held at Salisbury, the 12th [day] of the 2nd month 1659," there is the following entry: "To Rich. Ormsby, for expense about G. Cole, [16]58: 00.05.00." Ormsby, a local constable, could not have had any responsibilities for Eunice Cole unless she was, at the time designated, physically present in Hampton. See the Town Book of Hampton, II, 343. There is also the evident fact that she was soon thereafter (perhaps 1659?) charged with making "unseemly speeches" about her neighbors (see text, below.)

30. Norfolk County Court Papers, 1650–1680, fol. 16, 18 (ms. volume, in Clerk's Office, Essex County Courthouse, Salem, Mass.).

31. "The Humble Petition of Eunice Cole, Wife of William Cole of Hampton, Now Prisoner at Boston," in Massachusetts Archives, vol. 10, fol. 281. The petition is not dated. Other writers have assigned it to the year 1662, however, and this appears, from internal evidence, to be accurate.

32. See *Records of the Governor and Company of the Massachusetts Bay in New England,* vol. IV, pt. 2, 1661–1674, p. 70. The evidence on this point is somewhat confusing, for the court made it a "condition" of Eunice Cole's release that she "depart, within one month . . . out of this jurisdiction, and not to return again upon penalty of her former sentence being executed against her." She appears, nonetheless, to have returned to her home in Hampton (still within the "jurisdiction" of Massachusetts Bay), for there, on Nov. 24, 1662, she was observed in conversation with a strange presence alleged to be the Devil. See below, pp. 17–18. Note also that in Nov. 1662 the county court ordered payment to Henry Green of Hampton "for watching one day and one night with Eunice Cole." This procedure is not otherwise explained, but, again, it seems to establish Goody Cole's reappearance in the town. See *Records and Files of the Quarterly Courts of Essex County, Massachusetts,* III, 4.

33. A manuscript copy of William Cole's will is in Essex County Probates, no. 6001, Registry of Probates, Salem, Mass. There is also an inventory of Cole's estate, taken by Thomas Webster acting as "executor." The estate included a house lot and housing (valued at £20), an acre of meadowland, two cows, a heifer, a pig, a feather mattress and other bedding, a Bible, small quantities of yarn and hemp, and a variety of kitchen furnishings (mostly described as "old," and valued low). The total value of these properties was estimated at £53, 19s.

34. See court orders of Oct. 14, 1662, Apr. 14, 1663, and Oct. 13, 1663, in "County Court, Norfolk, 1648–1678," fols. 56 (reverse side), 60 (reverse side), 65 (ms. volume, Clerk's Office, Essex County Courthouse, Salem, Mass.).

35. See below, pp. 19–25.

36. Court order, May 3, 1665, in *Records of the Governor and Company of the Massachusetts Bay in New England*, vol. IV, pt. 2, p. 149.

37. According to one source, the prison keeper at Boston was receiving payment "for keeping goodwife Cole," as late as June 1668. See Samuel G. Drake, *Annals of Witchcraft in New England* (Boston, 1869), p. 101. The documents which support this assertion are not specified by Drake, however; they may indeed have been lost between his time and ours.

38. Ms. deposition by Abraham Perkins, Sr., Apr. 7, 1673, in Suffolk Court Files, vol. 13, fol. 1228. The deposition dates this episode to a time "when William Fifield was constable." Fifield was constable at Hampton only once, in 1662.

39. See Massachusetts Archives, vol. 135, fol. 16.

40. See Charles E. Clark, *The Eastern Frontier — The Settlement of Northern New England* (New York: Knopf, 1970), pp. 16–18, and *passim*.

41. Quoted in Dow, *History of Hampton*, I, 90.

42. *Ibid.*, pp. 91–92.

43. *Ibid.*, p. 91.

44. *Ibid.*, p. 93.

45. This arrangement is mentioned in the deposition by Robert Smith, Aug. 29, 1673, in Massachusetts Archives, vol. 135, fol. 11. See also Dow, *History of Hampton*, pp. 79–80.

46. See Massachusetts Archives, vol. 135, fols. 4–15, and Suffolk Court Files, vol. 13, fol. 1228.

47. Ms. deposition of Jonathan Thing, Sept. 5, 1673, in Suffolk Court Files, vol. 13, fol. 1228.

48. Ms. deposition of Mary Perkins, Apr. 1673, in Massachusetts Archives, vol. 135, fol. 7.

49. Ms. deposition of Hopestill Austin, Sept. 5, 1673, in Suffolk Court Files, vol. 13, fol. 1228.

50. Ms. deposition of Abraham Perkins, Apr. 7, 1673, *ibid.*

51. Ms. paper entitled "In the Case of Eunice Cole," undated, in Massachusetts Archives, vol. 135, fol. 13. This document contains decisions handed down by the court with reference to several questions of evidence in the 1673 trial.

52. Ms. deposition of Robert Smith, Aug. 29, 1673, in Massachusetts Archives, vol. 135, fol. 11.

53. Ms. deposition of John Mason, Apr. 7, 1673, in Suffolk Court Files, vol. 13, fol. 1228.

54. Ms. deposition of Elizabeth Shaw, Apr. 8, 1673, *ibid.*

55. Ms. paper "In the Case of Eunice Cole," in Massachusetts Archives, vol. 135, fol. 13.

56. These depositions are all in Massachusetts Archives, vol. 135, fols. 4, 5, 6, 8.

57. Ms. deposition of Bridget Clifford, Apr. 7, 1673, *ibid.*, fol. 8.

58. Ms. paper "In the Case of Eunice Cole," *ibid.*, fol. 13.

59. These genealogical reconstructions are based on materials in Noyes et al., *Genealogical Dictionary*, pp. 151, 269, 355–356, 646, 731; in Dow, *History of Hampton*, II; and in the Town Records of Hampton, *passim*.

60. Nicholas Smith, born about 1629 in England, came to Exeter before 1658. The name of his first wife is not known. They had children: Nathaniel (born Sept. 3, 1660), and Ann (born Feb. 8, 1663). Nicholas Smith married, second, Mary [Satchell] Dale, about 1666. He died June 22, 1673.

61. William Godfrey was born, probably in one of the eastern counties of England, between 1600 and 1608. He was a resident at Watertown, in Massachusetts Bay, by 1639, and moved to Hampton in 1649. He married, first, Sarah [——————], about 1630; they had one child, John, born about 1632. He married, second, Margery [——————] Webster, in 1638; they had three children, Issac (born 1639), Sarah (born 1642), and Deborah (born 1645). William Godfrey died Mar. 25, 1671. Margery Webster, born about 1609, was the widow of Thomas Webster (who died in Norfolk County, En-

gland, in 1634). By her first husband she had one child, Thomas, born in 1631. She married, third, John Marion, Sept. 14, 1671, and died May 2, 1687.

62. John Marion was born, probably about 1610, in Essex County, England, was briefly at Watertown in Massachusetts Bay (early 1640s), and came to Hampton in 1645. He married, first, Sarah Eddy, before 1640, who died Jan. 26, 1671. They had at least four children, born between 1641 and 1650. John Marion was living as late as 1684; his death is not recorded.

63. Note the following order, by the County Court at Salisbury, Apr. 10, 1677: "Nathaniel Smith, being given to Deacon William Godfrey and his wife Margery as their own, and they having kept him from [the time when he was] a child, [and] Deacon Godfrey being now dead, and his widow having married John Marion, the Court orders that Smith shall continue and abide with the said Marion and [his] wife until he comes to age of one-and-twenty years, and shall do them faithful service." (Quoted in Dow, *History of Hampton*, II, 978.) On July 31, 1680, Nathaniel Smith was found dead "in a canoe at the landing place, with his face bloody"; an inquest decided that "water was the cause of his death by drowning" (*ibid.*, II, 978).

64. See the grand jury "presentment" of Eunice Cole, Oct. 9, 1672, in Massachusetts Archives, vol. 135, fol. 7. This document mentions both Ann Smith and John Clifford, Sr., "who hath charge of her by her father." There is also a separate reference to Clifford and "a child [again, Ann Smith] which was committed to his wife's tuition." See the paper entitled "In the Case of Eunice Cole," Massachusetts Archives, vol. 135, fol. 13.

65. John Clifford was born, about 1615, in Nottingham County, England. He was an original proprietor of the town of Salisbury, in 1640, and was resident at Hampton by 1642. He married, first Sarah [————], about 1640; she died about 1655. They had children: John (born about 1640), Hannah (born 1649), Elizabeth (born 1651), Israel (born about 1653). John Clifford married, second, Elizabeth [Wiseman] Richardson, Sept. 28, 1658; she died Dec. 1, 1667. They had children: Elizabeth (born 1659), Mahitable (date of birth uncertain, died young), Ester (born 1662), Isaac (born 1664), Mary (born 1666, died 1669). John Clifford married, third, Bridget [————] Huggins, Feb. 6, 1672. He died in 1694. Bridget [————] Huggins was born about 1617 in England. She married, first, John Huggins, about 1638. John Huggins was born in England (perhaps in Norfolk County) about 1609. He was in Dedham by 1638, and came to Hampton in 1639. He and his wife had children: Susannah (born 1640), Ester (born about 1642), John (born about 1646), Elizabeth (born about 1648), Mary (born 1650, perhaps died young), Bridget (born 1651), Martha (born 1654), Anna (born 1659), and Nathaniel (born 1660). Bridget Huggins was living in 1680; her death is not recorded.

66. John Clifford, Jr., married Sarah Godfrey, Aug. 18, 1670. They had eight children, the first of whom (John) was born Feb. 7, 1672.

67. Bridget Huggins's testimony from the earlier case does not survive. Her name, however, is included on a list of witnesses against Eunice Cole, from the year 1656, in Suffolk Court Files, fol. 26203.

68. See ms. deposition of Ephraim Winsley, Apr. 29, 1673, in Suffolk Court Files, fol. 1228.

69. The name of John Godfrey is included on a list of witnesses against Eunice Cole in the 1656 trial, *ibid.*, fol. 26203.

70. See above, p. 17, and note 34.

71. One episode, recounted as part of the prosecution case, appears to have taken place in Boston. See ms. depositions by Hopestill Austin, Sept. 5, 1673, and Elizabeth Person, Sept. 5, 1673, in Suffolk Court Files, fol. 1228.

72. Order of the county court, held at Salisbury, Apr. 29, 1673, in Massachusetts Archives, vol. 135, fol. 7.

73. *Ibid.*, fol. 16.

74. *Ibid.*, fol. 15.

75. See Nathaniel Bouton, ed., *Documents and Records Relating to the Province of New Hampshire*, I (Concord, N.H., 1867), 415.

76. *Ibid.*
77. Deposition of Mary Godfrey, July 14, 1680, *ibid.*, p. 416. The same episode was described by John Godfrey (Mary's husband) in his own deposition of July 14, 1680 (*ibid.*, p. 418).
78. Deposition of Elizabeth Denham and Mary Godfrey, July 14, 1680, *ibid.*, pp. 416–417.
79. Deposition of Nathaniel Smith, July 14, 1680, *ibid.*, pp. 417–418. Curiously, this witness was the elder brother of Ann Smith, whose role in the prosecution of Eunice Cole (1673) has been fully discussed above. Nathaniel died, apparently from drowning, a scant two weeks after giving this testimony (see note 63).
80. Deposition of Mary Godfrey, July 14, 1680, *ibid.*, p. 417.
81. On Brabrook's affairs in Watertown, see *Watertown Records,* I (Watertown, Mass., 1894): pt 1, pp. 14, 26, 28, 29, 30, 34, 38, 39, 40, 43, 44, 45, 46, 47, 51, 53, 55, 59, 77, 78, 82, 92, 93, 100; also pt. 2, 122; and pt. 3, pp. 8, 10.
82. The date of John Brabrook's death is not recorded. His name appeared for the last time in the town records on Oct. 14, 1654; by Jan. 1655 his wife was being mentioned as "the widow Brabrook." *Ibid.*, pt. 1, pp. 38–40, 44.
83. In Jan. 1655 the selectmen of Watertown appointed three men to oversee the affairs of the Brabrook family. For several years thereafter the town made *ad hoc* grants of money to Widow Brabrook, and arranged for the "hiring" of her land, cows, and other property. By 1663 the town was forced to provide "for the keeping of widow Brabrook" for one full year at a time. In 1668 the selectmen ordered "Brabrook's house and land (being seized by execution) . . . sold to pay the town's debts." *Ibid.*, pp. 44, 77, 78, 82, 100.
84. Town order, Dec. 20, 1651: Brabrook was to be compensated £30, "toward his loss by fire." *Ibid.*, p. 26.
85. On June 28, 1668, Joseph, Sarah, and Rachel Brabrook petitioned the county court "that Henry Short of Newbury and Simon Thompson of Ipswich be appointed their guardians" (*Probate Records of Essex County,* II, 130). In Sept. 1669 Rachel Brabrook testified in a court case involving members of Henry Short's family. It appears, moreover, that she was the "ward" in the Short household who experienced some "lewdness" at the hands of a neighboring manservant (see *Records and Files of the Quarterly Courts of Essex County, Massachusetts,* IV, 179–180). Henry Short, brother of Rachel's mother, was an early and prominent settler of Newbury; he held many local offices, up to and including that of selectman. After his death, his estate was valued at more than £1800 (see *Probate Records of Essex County,* II, 345–349).
86. John Fuller was born in Ipswich in about 1643. (His father, also named John, had come from England in 1635, and had married Elizabeth Emerson, daughter of another Ipswich resident.) When still a boy, John Jr. was sent to live in the household of his uncle, William Fuller, at Hampton; his brother — a second William — went along. William Fuller, Sr., had no children of his own, and seems to have treated these nephews more or less as adopted sons. When John Fuller, Sr., died, he made only token bequests to his sons, John Jr. and William, because "their uncle hath undertaken to give them sufficient portions." William Sr. paid the highest rate among all Hampton householders in 1647; moreover, his name is found near the top of two subsequent rate lists. He held many local offices, and was twice elected deputy from Hampton to the Massachusetts General Court. But John Jr. — his allegedly "sufficient portion" notwithstanding — never approached the same level of wealth and prestige. On a town list of 1680, for example, his "rate" falls among the bottom third of the householders. See William H. Fuller, *Genealogy of Some Descendants of Captain Matthew Fuller* (n.p., 1914), pp. 175–176; "John Fuller of Ipswich, Mass., 1634," in *The New England Historic Genealogical Register,* II, 57–61. See also *Probate Records of Essex County,* II, 57–61.
87. This woman was born Isabella Austin, daughter of Francis and Isabella [Bland] Austin, in about the year 1633. Her father, an early resident of Hampton, died in 1642, and her mother was remarried soon thereafter to Thomas Leavitt. The Bland connection, on the mother's side, was a distinguised one; "Mr." John Bland was an early and prominent settler of Martha's Vineyard. Moreover, Thomas Leavitt was a

man of considerable stature within Hampton itself. Isabella Austin married Philip
Towle, Nov. 19, 1657. Towle's origins are not known, though local tradition makes
him out an Irishman. He arrived in Hampton just a short while before his marriage.
Philip and Isabella [Austin] Towle had children: Philip (born 1659), Caleb (born
1661, killed by Indians 1677), Joshua (born 1663), Mary (born 1665), Joseph and
Benjamin (twins, born 1669), Francis (born 1672), John (born 1674), Caleb (born
1678). Philip Towle died in 1696, aged about eighty; his widow died in 1719. See
Noyes et al., *Genealogical Dictionary,* pp. 68–69, 95–96, 425, 689, and the Town Book
of Hampton, *passim.*
88. Quoted in Dow, *History of Hampton,* I, 85.
89. From a quarterly court, held at Hampton, Sept. 7, 1680, quoted in D. Hamilton
Hurd, *History of Rockingham and Stratford Counties, New Hampshire* (Philadelphia,
1882), p. 322.
90. See Dow, *History of Hampton,* 94.
91. See Michael G. Hall, *Edward Randolph and the American Colonies* (Chapel Hill: University of North Carolina Press, 1960), pp. 36–37, and Dow, *History of Hampton,* I, 94.
92. Dow, *History of Hampton,* I, 94.
93. See Clark, *Eastern Frontier,* 56–58, and Dow, *History of Hampton,* I, 95–97. The new
framework of government included a president, a council, and an assembly. The
latter was to consist of deputies chosen by the various towns. The councillors were
appointed from London, but at first these appointments fell entirely to residents of
New Hampshire.
94. See Dow, *History of Hampton,* I, 100.
95. *Ibid.,* pp. 101–102.
96. Various materials pertaining to this affair are printed in Bouton, *Documents and
Records,* I, 458–462. See also Dow, *History of Hampton,* I, 103–105.
97. Dow, *History of Hampton,* I, 106.
98. Roland D. Sawyer, "History of Earlier Hampton: The Witchcraft Days," ms. in possession of the Meeting House Green Memorial and Historical Association, Inc.,
Hampton, N.H.
99. On various particulars of Jonathan Moulton's life, see Dow, *History of Hampton,* I, 209,
212, 215, 249, 251, 255, 262, 264, 268, 270, 271, 273, 278, 287, 399, 403, 404, 406,
536, 550, and II, 870. Moulton was born, the son of Jacob and Sarah [Smith] Moulton, in about 1726. He married, first, Abigail Smith, Feb. 22, 1749. They had children: Joseph (born 1749), Sarah (born 1752), Jonathan (born 1754), Mary (born
about 1756, died 1760), Abigail (born 1758), Benning (born 1761), Anne (born
1763), William (born 1766), Elizabeth (born 1768), Jacob (born 1770), Joseph (born
1772). Jonathan Moulton married, second, Sarah Emery, Sept. 11, 1776. They had
children: Sally (born 1779), Emery (born 1782), John (born 1783), Nathaniel (born
1787).
100. *Ibid.,* I, 278. The grand scale of his business operations may be illustrated by reference to a circular of 1785, in which Moulton advertised sale of some 80,000 acres of
land (comprising most, or all, of eight separate townships). Apparently, this circular
was directed especially to Ireland.
101. *Ibid.,* pp. 212–214.
102. Passages from the report of this fire in the *Boston Chronicle,* Mar. 20, 1769, are quoted
in *ibid.,* p. 215.
103. This story is quoted from Drake, *Annals of Witchcraft,* pp. 156–157.
104. Dow, *History of Hampton,* I, 278.
105. Drake, *Annals of Witchcraft,* p. 157.
106. Toppan, "Manuscript History," III, 45.
107. *Ibid.,* pp. 40 ff. See also Hurd, *History of Rockingham and Stratford,* p. 322.
108. Quoted in Dow, *History of Hampton,* 57.
109. John Greenleaf Whittier, *The Complete Poetical Works of John Greenleaf Whittier* (Cambridge, Mass., 1894), pp. 245–246. "The Wreck of Rivermouth" was written in 1864.
The verses quoted here are only a part of the entire poem. Whittier wrote a second
poem entitled "The Changeling," in which Eunice Cole also figures as a principal. See
ibid., p. 251.

110. Slightly different versions of this story may be found in Toppan, "Manuscript History," III, 45, and Hurd, *History of Rockingham and Stratford*, p. 332.
111. Local tradition; see ms. holdings of the Meeting House Green Memorial and Historical Association, Inc., Hampton, N.H.
112. Art. 16, Town Meeting, Mar. 8, 1938, quoted in James W. Tucker, "The Witch of Hampton" (pamphlet, privately printed; Meeting House Green Memorial and Historical Association, Inc., Hampton, N.H.).
113. Tucker, "Witch of Hampton."
114. Personal observation, Nov. 16, 1971; house of Mrs. Wilma White, Hampton, N.H.

Self-Portraits: Three Women

Anne Firor Scott

[Collections of letters] heap up in mounds of insignificant and often dismal dust the innumerable trivialities of daily life, as it grinds itself out, year after year, and then suddenly they blaze up; the day shines out, complete, alive, before our eyes. . . .

— Virginia Woolf, "The Pastons and Chaucer"

Anne Firor Scott, professor of history at Duke University, is author of *The Southern Lady* (1970) and of various other books and articles dealing with the social history of American women. She is presently at work upon the relationship between higher education and women's changing self-perceptions, the first fruit of which is the article "What, Then, Is the American: This New Woman?" (1978).

THE EIGHTEENTH CENTURY, to borrow Bernard Bailyn's phrase, was not incidentally but essentially different from the present, and many of the elements of that essential difference can be most clearly seen in the lives of women. Colonial history has so long been written in terms of high achievement, of political theory, of founding fathers, of economic development, of David-and-Goliath conflict, that it is easy to forget how small a part such things played in most individual lives. Seen from the standpoint of ordinary people, the essential theme of the eighteenth-century experience was not so much achievement as the fragility and chanciness of life. Death was an omnipresent reality. Three children in one family die on a single day from epidemic disease; fathers are lost at sea; adolescents mysteriously waste away; mothers die in childbirth; yet life goes on to a constant underlying murmur of "God's sacred will be done." In these circumstances, how is the meaning of life perceived? What social structures do people build to sustain the spirit? What, in this context, become the central values? What is the texture of daily life?

The life histories of three colonial women give some clues.

The three women are Jane Franklin Mecom of Boston, Elizabeth Sandwith Drinker of Philadelphia, and Eliza Lucas Pinckney of Charleston. Taken together their lives cover nearly a century, from 1712 when the first was born to 1807 when the youngest died. Their experience encompassed three cultures — Puritan, Quaker, and plantation — and covered a broad spectrum of colonial social classes. The life of each is illuminating, each in a different way. All three loved to write, and each created a self-portrait — two in letters, one in a journal she kept from the time she was twenty-four until a few days before her death. Various depredations have washed out important parts of their life histories; and many things went unrecorded. Yet the documents which have survived bring us into the midst of daily experience, and reveal, from time to time, their most deeply held cultural values.

I. Jane Franklin Mecom

Jane, youngest of Josiah Franklin's seventeen children, was born in 1712, six years after Benjamin. Because in later life she would become her brother's favorite correspondent, we know more about her than about any other woman of her social class in eighteenth-century Boston.

She was eleven when Benjamin made his famous getaway, breaking his apprenticeship and embarking upon the legendary career which would make him the archetypal self-made American. In old age both looked back with favor upon their early childhood: "It was indeed a Lowly Dweling we were brought up in but we were fed Plentifully, made comfortable with fire and cloathing, had sildom any contention among us, but all was Harmony: Especially betwen the Heads — and they were Universally Respected, & the most of the Famely in good Reputation, this is still happier liveing than multituds Injoy."[1]

Even allowing for the rosy glow the passage of time creates, the recollections of both brother and sister suggest that the parents were remarkable people, and that such education as children get at home, both had gotten. The things Jane Mecom singled out for recollection were central values all her life: a good reputation and the respect of the community. She always tried to "live respectable," and her fondest hope was that her children should do so.

At the age when her brother had run away to begin his climb to fame, Jane Franklin married a neighbor who was a saddler. Her brother sent a spinning wheel, an appropriate gift for a seven-

46

teenth child who could expect no dowry. The best efforts of both spouses would be required to keep up with a growing family, as — for a quarter of a century — every second year brought a new baby. Three died in infancy, but nine survived to be fed, clothed, and trained for self-support.

By the time we catch another glimpse of Jane Mecom she was already thirty, living in a house owned by her father, taking in lodgers and caring for her aging parents. Her twelve-year-old son was learning the saddler's trade, and she was searching for appropriate apprenticeships for the younger ones. Between caring for parents, children, lodgers, and her husband's shop it is no wonder that the only written word of hers which survives from this period is a postscript to a letter her mother wrote to Benjamin. His letters to her began a pattern which would last a lifetime, as he spoke of sending "a few Things that may be of some Use perhaps in your Family."[2]

His help was more than financial. Busy making his own way in Philadelphia, he took time to find an apprenticeship for his namesake, Benny Mecom, who gave some promise of talents similar to his own. There were problems "such as are commonly incident to boys of his years," although, Franklin added, "he has many good qualities, for which I love him."[3] Diligence was not one of those qualities, and Jane Mecom was deeply concerned lest Benny never learn to work. He never did, at least not steadily, and would continue to cause his mother anxiety as long as he lived.

We get our next clear glimpse of Jane Mecom when she was fifty-one and entertaining her brother in her own house. While he was there she enjoyed what would ever after be her measure of "suitable Conversation," and shone, however briefly, in the reflected glory of Dr. Franklin as Boston admirers paid court to him at her house. The fact that he chose to domicile himself with the Mecoms, rather than with the far more affluent and equally welcoming "cousen Williams," says something about the quality of her conversation, or, perhaps, about his sensitivity to her feelings.

That interval of pleasure was brief. Four of the twelve Mecom children were already dead; now Sarah, at twenty-seven a "Dear and Worthy child," died, leaving a husband and four children who promptly moved into Jane Mecom's house. Within six months two of the four grandchildren were dead. She was still grieving for them when Edward Mecom, her husband of thirty-eight years, also died. She wrote one of the two comments about him to be found in any of her letters: "It pleased God to call my Husband out of this Troblesom world where he had Injoyed Little and suffered much by Sin & Sorrow."[4] Two years later she lost her youngest and favorite, Polly, at eighteen: "Sorrows roll upon me like the waves of the sea. I am hardly allowed time to fetch my breath. I am broken with breach upon breach, and I have now, in the first flow of my grief, been almost ready to say 'What have I more?' But God forbid, that I should indulge that thought. . . . God is sovereign and I submit."[5]

In 1766 she was fifty-five. Of five surviving children the oldest was thirty-four and the youngest twenty-one, but none was in a position to support a widowed mother. Two sons had been bred to the saddler's trade; one had died and the other gone to sea. Peter, a soap-boiler like his grandfather, showed signs of the mental illness which would eventually incapacitate him, and the feckless Benjamin was not earning enough to support his own wife and children. Her son-in-law Flagg was an unskilled workman, hard put to take care of his two children. The one daughter who still lived with her was a melancholy and sickly young woman.

Jane Mecom's thoughts turned, therefore, to self-support. She continued to take in lodgers and her brother sent from England a small stock of trading goods which arrived just as Bostonians decided to boycott English goods in protest of the Stamp Act. Poverty, she concluded, "is Intailed on my famely."[6]

She was acutely aware of her dependence on her brother's help. She tried to repay him with reports on life in Boston. "The whol conversation of this Place turns upon Politices and Riligous contryverces," she wrote, adding that her own sentiments were for peace. With his reply he sent her a set of his philosophical papers, which she proudly read.[7]

Somehow in 1769 she contrived a trip to Philadelphia, where Franklin's wife and daughter found her "verey a greabel" — so much so that he was moved to suggest, from London, that she consider staying on permanently.[8] But Boston was home, and back she went into the midst of the rising conflict with Great Britain.

Her brother, though thoroughly engrossed in the same conflict in London, took time to write Jane Mecom asking for detailed instructions as to the making of "crown soap," a family secret which he feared might be lost if it were not preserved for the next generation. Here at last was something she could do in return for all his help; her instructions were given in minute detail.

At about this time her letters began to grow longer and more revealing. Perhaps her visit to Deborah Franklin had reduced her awe of her famous brother; perhaps confidence in her own capacities was growing. Whatever the reason, she began to speak more freely, range more widely, and fill out — for us — the scanty self-portrait belatedly begun.

An admirer of Thomas Hutchinson and a lover of peace, Jane Mecom was no early patriot. By 1774, however, "Proflegate soulders" making trouble and harassing citizens on the streets of Boston pushed her closer to the rebel position. The battle of Lexington finished what the soldiers had begun, as she locked her house, packed such goods as she could carry, and took refuge in Rhode Island.

In some ways the war changed her life for the better. Catherine Ray Greene, with whom she stayed at first, became her good friend. Her granddaughter, Jenny Flagg, married Elihu Greene, brother of General Nathanael Greene, a solid farmer, merchant, and entrepreneur. A man of his standing could well have demanded a dowry, but his willingness to marry Jenny for love marked a change in the hitherto unbroken stream of Mecom bad luck.

In the fall of 1774 Franklin came home after a decade in England, and not long after took his sister for a prolonged stay in Philadelphia. His wife, Deborah, had died, and Jane was able to be helpful to him until he went off to France. In two years General Howe's decision to occupy Philadelphia sent her back to Rhode Island to her granddaughter's house, where she was "much Exposed & . . . under constant Apprehensions" that the British would invade.[9]

Yet the British were not as troublesome to her as a personal crisis brought on by wartime inflation. The country woman who cared for her son Peter suddenly demanded more money for that service than Jane Mecom had or could see any way to get. Dependence on her brother was galling enough when he anticipated her needs; now she had to ask for help. Her spirits felt "so deprest" that she could scarcely write, but what else could she do?

The war had disrupted communication and her letter was a

long time reaching him. Meanwhile, relief came in a painful guise: Peter died. Accustomed as she was to accepting God's will, Jane Mecom reflected that Peter had been "no comfort to any won nor capable of injoying any Himself for many years."[10] His death was a blessing.

But at the same time she had heard nothing for five months from her daughter Jane Collas in Boston, and began to worry lest this last remaining child might be going the way of her brothers into insanity. Apologizing for burdening a busy and important man, she wrote her fears to Franklin: "It gives some Relief to unbousom wons self to a dear friend as you have been & are to me. . . ."[11]

Her daughter was, it turned out, physically rather than mentally ill, but sick or well she was never able to live up to her mother's standards of energy and enterprise. "You say you will endeavour to correct all your faults," Jane Mecom wrote in 1778 when Jane Collas was already in her thirties, and proceeded to outline in some detail what those faults were: a tendency to look on the dark side of "God's Providence," an inclination to despair and to extravagance, laziness and a lack of ingenuity in working to meet her material needs, an unseemly fondness for a great deal of company. She also tended to lie abed late, which her mother found "a trouble to me on many accounts." To top it off, she aspired to gentility without the means to support her aspiration — a tendency Jane Mecom scorned whenever she encountered it.[12]

Nine children had survived infancy and none had fulfilled their mother's hopes. Most had died in early adulthood. Benjamin simply disappeared during the Battle of Trenton and no trace of him was ever found. Peter's tragic end has already been noted. The fate of her children pushed Jane Mecom to a rare moment of questioning God's will: "I think there was hardly Ever so unfourtunate a Famely. I am not willing to think it is all owing to misconduct. I have had some children that seemed to be doing well till they were taken off by Death. . . ."[13] But there was nothing to be done. One must accept these things or go mad.

In the late seventies the long train of bereavement, displacement, and struggle abated for a while. Her granddaughter Jenny Greene, with whom she was living, was a most satisfactory young person whose conversation and attention to her comfort she much appreciated, and whose husband she respected. Though there was no neighbor for two miles, many visitors dropped in. She herself never left home unless someone sent a carriage (the Greenes owning none) since "I hant courage to ride a hors."[14] She made and sent to Franklin several batches of crown soap which he wanted for his friends in France, took care of Jenny Greene in her successive lyings-in, helped with the babies, supervised the household, and, from time to time, sold "some little matter" from the small store of goods she had brought from Boston in 1775. "My time seems to be filld up as the Famely I am in Increases fast," she wrote. She was sixty-eight and very energetic, though "as I grow older I wish for more Quiet and our Famely is more Incumbered as we have three children Born since I came & tho they give grat Pleasure . . . yet the Noise of them is sometimes troblesom. . . ."[15] She knew "but little how the world goes Except seeing a Newspaper some times which contains Enough to give Pain but little satisfaction while we are in Armes against each other. . . ."[16] In spite of the inflation and the losses the Greenes were suffering as many of their ships were captured, her life was pleasanter than it had been since childhood. "I contineu very Easey and happy hear," she wrote in 1781, "have no more to trroble me than what is Incident to human Nature & cant be avoided in any Place, I write now in my own litle chamber the window opening on won of the Pleasantest prospects in the country the Birds singing about me and nobod up in the house near me to Desturb me. . . ."[17]

Life had taught Jane Mecom to be wary when things were going well. Ten months after that happy note her granddaughter died, giving birth to the fourth child in four years, and at seventy Jane Mecom was suddenly again the female head of a household of young children who needed, she thought, "some person more lively and Patient to watch over them continualy"; but since there was no one else, she did it anyway.[18] Fortunately she found them a comfort as she grieved for her beloved grandchild, sacrifice to the age's custom of unbroken childbearing. She was too busy to pine, though the war had cut off her communication with Franklin for three years.

His first postwar letter included a "grat, very grat, Present," for which she thanked him extravagantly, adding that his generosity would enable her to live "at Ease in my old Age (after a life of Care Labour & Anxiety). . . ."[19]

By 1784 she was back in Boston, in a house long owned by her brother, where she was able to "live all ways Cleen and Look Decent."[20] It was a great comfort. She had leisure to read and write, a minister she respected with whom to discuss theology and other things, the care and companionship of her granddaughter Jenny Mecom, the regular attention of her nephew-in-law Jonathan Williams. Her grandchildren and great-grandchildren were often a source of pride and pleasure.

One grandchild, Josiah Flagg, turned up in Philadelphia and, as she saw it, presumed upon his relationship to persuade Franklin to take him on as a secretary. He beseeched his grandmother to conceal the fact that he, Josiah, had once been a shoemaker, thus bringing down upon himself the scorn she reserved for false pride. She lectured him severely, betraying trepidation lest her demanding relatives threaten her warm relationship with her brother. Fortunately Josiah turned out to be an excellent penman and behaved well in the Franklin family.

With her brother back in Philadelphia, correspondence quickened. He was still concerned that someone in the family be trained to carry on the tradition of the crown soap. Might she teach the younger Jonathan Williams, or even Josiah Flagg, how to make it? She would think about it. She had thought earlier of teaching her son-in-law Peter Collas, whose difficulties in earning a living had become almost ludicrous. Whenever he took berth on a ship it was promptly captured. But she had decided that the soap required a man of "Peculiar Genius," and that Collas was not.[21] Meanwhile she continued to make the soap herself, sending batch after batch to Franklin.

He felt the urge for some "cods cheeks and sounds," a favorite New England delicacy. She managed to acquire a keg to send him. She wished him well in the enterprise of the federal convention, and when the Constitution arrived in Boston she reported that while some quarrelsome spirits opposed it, those of "Superior Judgement" were going to support it.

She assured him that she followed his advice about taking exercise and walked even when a chaise was available, "but I am so weak I make but a Poor Figure in the Street."[22] She had her chamber painted and papered against the day she might be confined to it.

A ship captain friend took a favorable report of her to Philadelphia, for which she was grateful: "The Gratest Part of my time when I am sitting at home I am apt to Imagine as Samson did when He lost his Hare, that I can Arise & Shake my Self & Go forth as at other times but on Tryal Like him I am wofully disapointed & find my Feet cripling & my Breath short, but I am still chearful for that is my Natural Temper."[23]

In January 1788, replying to his request for a "very peticular" account of how she lived, she provided a detailed description:

I have a good clean House to Live in my Grandaughter constantly to atend me to do whatever I desier in my own way & in my own time, I go to bed Early lye warm & comfortable Rise Early to a good Fire have my Brakfast directly and Eate it with a good Apetite and then Read or Work or what Els I Pleas, we live frugaly Bake all our own Bread, brew small bear, lay in a little cyder, Pork, Buter, &c. & suply our selves with Plenty of other nesesary Provision Dayly at the Dore we make no Entertainments, but some Times an Intimate Acquaintance will come in and Pertake with us the Diner we have Provided for our selves & a Dish of Tea in the After Noon, & if a Friend sitts and chats a litle in the Evening we Eate our Hasty Puding (our comon super) after they are gone; It is trew I have some Trobles but my Dear Brother Does all in His Power to Aleviat them by Praventing Even a wish, that when I Look Round me on all my Acquaintance I do not see won I have reason to think Happier than I am and would not change my neighbour with my Self where will you Find one in a more comfortable State as I see Every won has ther Trobles and I sopose them to be such as fitts them best & shakeing off them might be only changing for the wors.[24]

Six more years of life remained to her. The new Constitution was inaugurated, George Washington took office, merchants and politicians concerned themselves with their own and the nation's prosperity, foreign conflicts flamed and threatened. Jane Mecom, for her part, worried about Benjamin Franklin's illness with "the stone," and prayed for his tranquillity in the face of pain. Their correspondence ranged around topics mostly personal and family, and upon reflections on life as they had lived it. "I do not Pretend to writ about Politics," she said, "tho I Love to hear them. . . ."[25]

Franklin's death in 1790 was a blow, but she was now seventy-eight herself, and prepared to be philosophical about this, as she saw it, temporary separation from her best friend. In his will he provided for her, and when she died four years later this woman who had lived so frugally was able to leave an estate of a thousand pounds to Jane Collas (in trust — she still worried about her daughter's extravagance!) and to her fifteen grandchildren and great-grandchildren.

When the historians came to treat the years covered by her life they dwelt on wars and politics, on the opening of land and trade and manufacture, on the economic development of a fertile wilderness, the rapid growth in population, the experiment in representative government.

That all these things shaped Jane Mecom's life experience there can be no doubt. Yet life as she perceived it was mostly made up of the small events of which great events are composed: of twenty-one years of pregnancy and childbirth which, multiplied by millions of women, created the rapid population growth; of the hard struggle to "git a living," and to make sure her children were prepared to earn theirs; of the constant procession of death which was the hallmark of her time; of the belated prosperity and happiness which came to her in old age. What added up to a wilderness conquered, a new nation created, was often experienced by individuals as a very hard life somehow survived. It is only in retrospect that all the separate experiences together create something we call "economic development," or "manifest destiny," or — simply — "history."

The events of Jane Mecom's life might have destroyed a weaker person, but some combination of natural resilience, good health, belief in the virtues of diligence, industry, and ingeniousness, and firm faith that God had good reasons for all the pain and sorrow which befell her, carried her through. Perhaps her final judgment on the whole experience was summed up in that sentence: "Every won has ther Trobles and I sopose them to be such as fitts them best & shakeing off them might be only changing for the wors."

In chapter three of Virginia Woolf's *Room of One's Own* there is a clever and moving fantasy: what if Shakespeare had had a sister as gifted as himself? The end of the fantasy is tragic, for Shakespeare's imaginary sister, born with a great gift, was so thwarted and hindered by the confines of "woman's place" that she killed herself. In Jane Mecom we have a real-life case, for of the sixteen siblings of Benjamin Franklin, she alone showed signs of talent and force of character similar to his. At the age of fifteen one ran off to Philadelphia and by a combination of wit, luck, and carefully cultivated ability to get ahead began his rise to the pinnacle among the Anglo-American intelligentsia. At the same age the other married a neighbor and in a month was pregnant. From that time forward her life was shaped almost entirely by the needs of other people. Like her brother she had a great capacity for growth, though the opportunity came to her late and was restricted by her constant burden of family responsibilities. The Revolution broadened her experience as it did his, yet she was almost never without children to care for, even in her seventies. Her letters showed a steady improvement in vigor of style, and even in spelling. Her lively intelligence kept Franklin writing her even when he was very busy. Perhaps she had herself half in mind when she wrote in 1786: "Dr. Price thinks Thousands of Boyles Clarks and Newtons have Probably been lost to the world, and lived and died in Ignorance and meanness, mearly for want of being Placed in favourable Situations, and Injoying Proper Advantages, very few we know is able to beat thro all Impedements and Arive to any Grat Degre of superiority in Understanding."[26]

The "impedements" in her own life had been many, some might have thought insuperable, yet clearly by the age of eighty she had arrived at the "superiority in Understanding" which makes her letters a powerful chronicle of an eighteenth-century life.

II. Elizabeth Sandwith Drinker

Jane Mecom's life emerges full of interest from the most fragmentary records. Elizabeth Drinker, by contrast, left the most detailed record of any eighteenth-century American woman, one which provides an intimate view of daily life among the tight little community of Philadelphia Quakers of which she was a part.

Born Elizabeth Sandwith, of Irish inheritance, she was orphaned in her teens, and lived with her sister in another Quaker family. In 1759 when she was twenty-four she began a laconic record of how she spent her time ("Went thrice to meeting; drank tea at Neighbor Callender's") which gradually grew into a regular journal wherein she recorded the details of her life and speculated a little upon them. The last entry was made a few days before her death in 1807.

55

As a child she had had the great good fortune to go to Anthony Benezet's school, and she knew English, Latin, and French. To a solid basic education she brought an inquiring mind — science and medicine were particularly fascinating to her — and a touch of intellectual (though not religious) skepticism.

At twenty-six after a long courtship she married Henry Drinker, a widower her own age, who after an apprenticeship to a merchant firm, and the requisite trading voyage, had been taken into the company.

For thirteen months the journal lay untouched but for one minor entry, and by the time she began to keep it regularly again "my dear little Sal" had already joined the family. For the ensuing nineteen years pregnancies, miscarriages, births, deaths of four infants and the weaning and raising of the other five formed the principal focus of her life. Henry, for his part, was on the way to becoming one of the busiest men in Philadelphia, constantly "from home" on business or on Quaker affairs, for his progress in business was paralleled by his gradual accumulation of responsibility in the world of the Friends.

As child after child was born and lived or died, the journal became in part a medical record. Capable of serving as midwife for her friends, Elizabeth Drinker could do little to ease her own very difficult childbirths, "lingering and tedious," as she called them. She liked to nurse her babies, but was often forced for reasons of health to put them out to nurse. Though the family could afford the best doctors in Philadelphia, she was an independent-minded practitioner herself who often went contrary to their advice. When one of her sons fell out of a tree and broke a collarbone, she was pleased to find herself able to help the doctor set it. When newly acquired indentured servants (often under the age of ten) arrived with the itch and with lice and without smallpox inoculation, she undertook to deal with all these problems. Her husband and children fell ill with astonishing frequency. Along the way she read weighty medical books and speculated, sometimes in conversation with her good friend Benjamin Rush, about the cause and cure of various diseases.

The conflict with Great Britain marked a turning point in Elizabeth Drinker's development. Quakers tried to remain aloof, both for religious reasons and because those who were merchants had much to lose. One consequence was that in 1777 Henry

Drinker and a number of others were arrested, and taken off to prison in Winchester, Virginia. At forty-two Elizabeth Drinker was suddenly head of a household composed of her sister Mary, five children, and five indentured servants, and the British army was about to occupy Philadelphia. While she dutifully trusted that "it will please the Almighty to order all for the best," it was clear that she would have to lend Him a hand, and she prayed for resolution and fortitude.[27]

There were daily challenges. Barrels of flour disappeared and rumors of widespread looting sped through the town: "Tis hardly safe to leave the door open," she noted; "I often feel afraid to go to bed." Henry's business affairs had to be attended to. One of her servants was first "very impertinent and saucy," and then ran away altogether with an audacious British soldier. Meeting the soldier on the street, Elizabeth Drinker confronted him, demanding that he pay for the servant's time. The British began commandeering blankets, and other things. Horses were stolen; wood was scarce; other servants disappeared, to the point that "we have but 9 persons in our Family this winter; we have not had less than 13 or 14 for many years past."[28]

As if they had overheard her, the British authorities arranged to enlarge the family again by quartering a certain Major Crammond, his two horses, two cows, and a Hessian stableboy in the Drinker household. The major kept the family awake with late dinner parties.

In the midst of the effort to keep the household fed, warmed, and healthy, she joined with other wives of incarcerated Friends to visit George Washington on behalf of their absent spouses. By some means which the journal does not make clear, release was arranged and she could thankfully turn back the headship of the household to H.D., as she always called him.

His return was quickly followed by the British evacuation. People who had been too friendly with the enemy were now turned out of their houses, their goods were confiscated, and a few, including some Quakers, were hanged. The Drinkers were understandably nervous, but only one member of the family, Henry Drinker's brother, ran directly afoul the American government. Still, the Americans were worse than the British in expropriating what they wanted (calling it taxation), and good furniture, pewter, blankets, and provisions were hauled off under their eyes. Servants continued to disappear, and they found themselves with only one. When news of Cornwallis's defeat arrived, Quakers who refused to illuminate their houses in celebration were subjected to a mob. Seventy panes of glass were broken in the Drinkers' house.

By the time the treaty of peace was signed, she, like the new nation of which she was somewhat reluctantly a part, had reached a new stage of life. "I have often thought," she wrote in later years, ". . . that women who live to get over the time of Childbareing if other things are favourable to them, experience more comfort and satisfaction than at any other period of their lives."[29] When that was written in 1797 she was certainly commenting upon her own life, which by our standards would not seem to have been precisely one of comfort, whatever it might have enjoyed of satisfaction. Though her last child had been born when she was forty-six, illness continued to be a major theme of the Drinker experience through the rest of her life.

Eleven pregnancies had left her own health uncertain at best; her son William had tuberculosis; H.D. was a constant victim of intestinal disorders and even more of the heroic treatment he received for them; one child had yellow fever and the whole family lived through three yellow fever epidemics; everyone sooner or later had malaria; in the household someone, husband, children, grandchildren, and servants, was always ill. Yet this seemed to interfere very little with the daily routine. Sick people entertained visitors along with the rest of the family, and people down with chills and fever one day were riding their horses off to the country the next. To the twentieth-century mind the whole situation is quite baffling.

Though she regularly worried about the ill health of her daughters, all three married and began at once to have children of their own. One daughter, the youngest, caused a family crisis by running away and marrying "out of meeting" a perfectly respectable young Friend whose only disability, apparently, was that he did not wear the plain dress. Henry Drinker took a hard line: no one was to visit the miscreant daughter. Elizabeth Drinker, after a few months, defied him, noting without contrition: "I feel best pleased I went."[30] Henry finally relented, and Molly and her husband became part of the growing clan of sons and daughters and in-laws.

Elizabeth Drinker attended each of her daughters in childbirth, assisting the midwife and the doctor. After a hard time with Sally's fourth, she recorded that she had slept only two of the preceding fifty hours and noted that she was "much fatigued, bones ache, flesh sore, Head giddy, etc. but have at the same time much to be thankful for."[31] Mother and child had both survived.

Two years later Molly and Sally were in labor at the same time. Sally's delivery was a very hard one; Molly's baby was stillborn. "The loss gives me great concern, not only being deprived of a sweet little grandson, but ye suffering of my poor Child, who lost, what may be called the reward of her labour . . . [and who] may pass through, if she lives, the same excruciating trouble a year the sooner for this loss."[32] In 1799 Sally was in labor with her sixth child, and very depressed. Elizabeth Drinker tried to cheer her, reminding her that she was now thirty-nine and that this "might possiably be the last trial of this sort, if she could suckle her baby for 2 years to come, as she had several times done hereto-fore. . . ."[33] It is odd that Elizabeth Drinker should have offered this particular argument, since she herself had twice become pregnant while nursing a baby, but it was standard advice from mothers to daughters in the eighteenth century. Neither she nor her daughters made any bones about their dislike of pregnancy and childbirth, though it seems in no way to have diminished their affection for the children themselves. Indeed, rather the contrary, since the burgeoning family was the center of Elizabeth Drinker's life. Children, in-laws, grandchildren moved in and out of the house daily, and formed the subject for much of what she wrote. All her children lived nearby, and visited each other as well as their parents constantly, sharing carriages, lending servants, sharing summer houses, exchanging children. In 1799 Eliza Downing, a granddaughter, came to spend the winter with Elizabeth and Henry Drinker. "I trust it will be for the child's good," her grandmother wrote, "[I] having no other little ones to attend to."[34] She was much concerned to teach the young people "wisdom and prudence."

The Drinkers included servants in their conception of fam-ily — bound boys and girls or indentured adults. Often they came as children of seven or eight. Once there were three black boys under ten at the same time. Elizabeth Drinker gave them careful attention, mending their clothes and trying to teach them. "I have much to do for the little black boys; these small folk ought to be of service when they grow bigger, for they are very troublesome when young. . . ."[35] Pretty bound girls were likely to flirt, or, worse, to get pregnant. One who had lived with them since she was ten gave birth to a mulatto baby, at the Drinker's expense. There followed much soul-searching as to what the child's future should be, but it died before they could decide. Elizabeth Drinker, who had raised the mother, thought she was as good a servant as she ever had, but for this "vile propensity" for getting pregnant. She was hard put to understand how all her training in moral values had gone for naught.

There was no doubt in her mind that the "poorer sort" were different from herself, yet some of her former servants were close friends who came back often to visit. When one favorite servant came down with yellow fever the family reluctantly decided to send her to the yellow fever hospital where, of course, she died. The matter weighed on Elizabeth Drinker's conscience.

She recognized that much of the comfort and satisfaction of her later life was because of Mary Sandwith, who never married, and who chose to care for household things, leaving her sister free to "amuse myself in reading and doing such work as I like best."[36]

The natural world interested her greatly: insects, butterflies, turtles were brought for her inspection by children and grand-children who knew of her curiosity about such things. Eclipses fascinated her. She speculated as to the causes of all sorts of natural events, and she loved to read about science.

Her reading, indeed, was prodigious. She felt constrained to note in her journal that it was not her sole occupation; but it was certainly an increasingly important part of her life as she grew older. She kept lists of books read, and they encompass most of what eighteenth-century Philadelphia had to offer. She read Mary Wollstonecraft's *Vindication of the Rights of Women* and noted that "in very many of her sentiments, she, as some of our friends say, *speaks my mind*. . . ."[37] Then she read William Godwin's memoir of Mary Wollstonecraft, and modified her opinion: "I think her a prodigious fine writer, and should be charmed by some of her pieces if I had never heard of her character."[38]

She read Tom Paine and abhorred what she took to be his dangerous principles. She took *Gargantua and Pantagruel* from the library and, after one quick look, hastily sent it back. She was equally shocked by Rousseau's *Confessions.* She read Swift, and seven volumes of Sterne, tracts by Madame Roland, dozens of religious books, Plutarch's *Lives, The Letters of Lady Russell,* medical books, *The Whole Duty of Woman* ("a pretty little book which I have read several times within forty years"),[39] a book on logic, Mugo Park's *Travels in the Interior of Africa,* Edmund Burke, Maria Edgeworth, Wordsworth's *Lyrical Ballads,* Francis Bacon's *New Atlantis,* Paley's *Principles of Moral Philosophy,* and on and on.

While she read and wrote, children and grandchildren (by 1804 there were seventeen) moved steadily in and out; often twenty people came to dinner. Friends from other towns arrived for the Yearly Meeting and lodged with the Drinkers. Henry continued to be the busiest man in Philadelphia, and she remarked that if good works would take a person to heaven he would certainly get there. William, so careful of his health, was her companion for walks and talks. She was not in the best of health herself, but was "seldom Idle." She took snuff, and taught one of her grandchildren Latin. Nancy's husband had an urge to move to "ye back woods," and she dreaded the thought. Every year she took stock on the first of January, and was surprised to find herself still alive. More and more she enjoyed solitude, a thing which had been disagreeable to her when she was young.

Her son Henry went off to India on one of the Drinker ships and wrote home about seeing a widow burned on her husband's funeral pyre. An old black woman came to call who had been her slave fifty years before, when she and her sister were orphaned, and whom they had sold. Not long after they had been conscience stricken and tried to buy the child back, but the new owner refused. In the end he had freed black Judey in his will, and now here she sat in the kitchen telling her life story. Elizabeth Drinker observed and reflected on the life around her.

As she grew older her interest in politics quickened. When John Adams came to town as President her feelings were at war with her Quaker principles. "He went by our door attended by the Light-horse and a few others. Tho' I am not for parade of any sort, in ye general way, yet on this occasion, everything considered, I should have been pleased to see a little more of it."[40] In 1800 she took note of the disputed election and of Jefferson's popularity in Philadelphia. She read Fenno's paper and quoted it.

When the new century arrived she tried to make her own determination of the vexed question: did it begin on the first day of 1800 or the first day of 1801? She decided the latter.

Friend after friend died. The last pages of the journal recorded an endless succession of deaths and funerals, accompanied by the small sense of triumph that oneself was still alive. Sally's death at forty-six bore heavily on her spirit. I have had nine children, she mused, and now my first, third, fifth, seventh, and ninth are all dead.

She fell and bruised herself and the doctors wanted to bleed her, "which I would not comply with."[41] Old age had brought the courage to resist their violent treatments, of which she had long been rightly skeptical. On the eighteenth of November in 1807 she noted in her journal that the weather was clear and cold, and the moon out. One grandson dropped in; she sent William to make the rounds of all the family dwellings. He came back to report that, but for one toothache, all were in good health. With her world thus in as good order as it could be, Elizabeth Drinker died.

The newspaper spoke of her remarkable personal beauty, her superior education, her journal, and her goodness. Perhaps it was, as she was fond of saying of obituaries of her friends, a "just character." She had lived seventy-two years, born in a prosperous colony when no more than three-quarters of a million people lived in all British North America; she died a citizen of a nation of nearly seven million. Her own town had grown remarkably in those years, had been the scene of the Declaration of Independence, the Constitutional Convention, and the early years of the new government. James and Drinker, her husband's firm, had exemplified in microcosm much of the mercantile history of the colony and the new nation. Her son who sailed off to India and her son-in-law with a yen for the backwoods were both part of much larger movements.

Yet for Elizabeth Drinker, observant, thoughtful, well-read person that she was, life almost began and ended with family, work, and religion. From the day Sally was born until the day she herself died, she was deeply concerned with the welfare, first of children, then of grandchildren. They were part of her daily experience, even when they were grown and settled in their own houses. She was never without a child in her house and never ceased trying to teach them the ways of righteousness as she saw them. She abhorred idleness, and made sure that her journal noted this fact lest some future reader think she spent all her time reading books! And, like Jane Mecom, she believed the Almighty knew what He was about.

One of her descendants, who used her journal to write a medical history of the eighteenth century, confidently asserted that she was an invalid from the age of forty-nine.[42] It is a strange definition of invalid. Her household and medical responsibilities could each have counted for a full-time job, and while she used her uncertain health as the excuse to provide a certain amount of solitude, she never shirked work. In contrast to certain nineteenth-century women who used ill health as a way of avoiding the challenges of life, Elizabeth Drinker and her children seemed to take it as simply a part of life, a nuisance, perhaps, but not disabling.

Her descendants continued to flourish in Philadelphia, and it is pleasant fantasy to imagine the shock (but secret pleasure too) with which Elizabeth Drinker might read part of their story in Catherine Drinker Bowen's *Family Affair.*

III. Eliza Lucas Pinckney

Born almost midway between Jane Mecom and Elizabeth Drinker, in the West Indies, daughter of an army officer whose family had owned land in South Carolina (or just "Carolina," as the family invariably referred to it) and Antigua for three generations, Eliza Lucas came from more favored circumstances than either of the others. The contrast between Jane Mecom's rough-hewn prose and phonetic spelling, and her equally rough-hewn handwriting, and the elegant language, copperplate penmanship, and ritual formality of Eliza Lucas's early letters is remarkable. While Jane Mecom's friends and relatives included people in almost the whole range of the social scale, and Elizabeth Drinker belonged to the solid middle class, with Eliza Lucas we move at once to the top of the scale and stay there.

There had been money to send her "home" to England for a careful education, and when she was seventeen, her father had settled her, along with her mother and her younger sister, on one of his plantations in Carolina while he carried on his duties as governor of Antigua.

In contrast to the other two, we can see Eliza Lucas clearly in her youth, and an astonishing young person she was. As vigorous and enterprising as the young Franklin or the young Jefferson, she began at once to administer the work of three plantations. For five years she taught the three R's to her sister and the slave children, experimented with new plants, dealt daily with overseers and factors, wrote long letters on business matters to her father and to his business associates, taught herself law and used her knowledge to help her neighbors who could not afford a proper lawyer, and read so much in Locke, Boyle, Plutarch, Vergil, and Malebranche that an old lady in the neighborhood prophesied that she would damage her brain.

A touch of humor and of self-deprecation was all that saved her from being unbearably didactic when she wrote to her younger brothers or younger friends. With older people — especially her much admired father — she was witty and straightforward.

Given her talents and wide-ranging interests, it was no wonder that she found the run of young men dull. "As to the other sex," she wrote, "I don't trouble my head about them. I take all they say to be words . . . or to show their own bright parts in the art of speechmaking. . . ."[43]

Her father proposed two possible candidates for her hand. She thanked him but declined both suggestions, saying of one "that the riches of Peru and Chili if he had them put together could not purchase a sufficient esteem for him to make him my husband." She hoped her father would agree that she should remain single for a few years.[44]

So she continued happily as his agent, writing dozens of letters, dealing with the factor and with the agent in England, supervising planting, instructing overseers, paying debts and contracting new ones. "By rising early," said this female Poor Richard, "I get through a great deal of business."[45] It was an understatement.

The social life of Charleston appealed to her less than the work of the plantation. "I own," she wrote, "that I love the vigitable world extremely."[46] Loving it meant study, experiment, and constant attention. The most visible consequence of her love affair with vegetables was the development of indigo as a major export crop for South Carolina. At her father's suggestion she began to plant indigo seeds, and when, after several failures, a crop was achieved, she worked with servants he had sent from Antigua to refine the process by which it was prepared as a dye.

A true exemplar of the Enlightenment, she believed religion and right reason could coexist, and said that "the soports of the Xtian religion" enabled her to view life's hazards with equanimity. She endeavored to resign herself to events as they came, since "there is an all Wise Being that orders Events, who knows what is best for us," and she believed in subduing the passions to reason.[47]

Migraine headaches hardly slowed her down. It occurred to her to plant oak trees against the day when South Carolina might run out of hardwood. In a careful letter she compared the agriculture of England and South Carolina, somewhat to the advantage of the latter, and observed that "the poorer sort [here] are the most indolent people in the world or they could never be so wretched in so plentiful a country as this." Indolence was, in her view, pretty close to a deadly sin.[48]

This precocious young woman who found men her own age a little boring was intrigued by the intelligent conversation of a man in his forties, Carolina's first native-born lawyer, Charles Pinckney. She had met Pinckney and his wife soon after her arrival, liked them both, and carried on a lively correspondence across the ten miles that separated the plantation from Charleston. He lent her books, encouraged her to report to him on her reading, and enjoyed the discipleship of so eager a pupil. Once, in 1741, she absentmindedly signed a letter to him "Eliza Pinckney."[49]

Three years later in December 1744 Mrs. Pinckney died. On May 2, 1745, Eliza wrote her father thanking him for permission to marry Charles Pinckney and "for the fortune you are pleased to promise me." She also thanked him for the pains and money laid out for her education, which "I esteem a more valuable fortune than any you have now given me." She assured him that Mr. Pinckney was fully satisfied with her dowry.[50]

To a cousin who had warned that she was so particular she was bound to "dye an old maid," she wrote: "But you are mistaken. I am married and the gentleman I have made choice of comes up to my plan in every tittle . . . I do him barely justice when I say his good Sence and Judgement, his extraordinary good nature and eveness of temper joynd to a most agreeable conversation and many valuable qualifications gives me the most agreeable prospect in the world. . . ."[51]

She bore with equanimity the talk of the town about their

somewhat precipitate marriage, but was righteously indignant when gossip told it that the late Mrs. Pinckney had been neglected in her last illness. Writing to that lady's sister she said firmly that she would never have married a man who had been guilty of such a thing.[52] As she had earlier striven to please her father, so now she made every effort to please her husband. "When I write you," she told him, "I . . . desire . . . to equal even a Cicero or Demosthenes that I might gain your applause."[53]

Her father seems to have worried lest the strong-minded independence in which he had reared her might not sit well with a husband, and she reassured him that "acting out of my proper province and invading his, would be inexcusable."[54] She and Pinckney apparently agreed that her proper province was a spacious one, since she continued to supervise her father's plantations, assumed some responsibility for Pinckney's as well, and carried forward the experiments with indigo which were in midstream at the time of her marriage.

Her self-improving urge was as strong as ever. She wrote a long list of resolutions, and planned to reread them daily. With God's help she hoped not to be "anxious or doubtful, not to be fearful of any accident or misfortune that may happen to me or mine, not to regard the frowns of the world." She planned to govern her passions, improve her virtues, avoid all the deadly sins, be a frugal manager while extending hospitality and charity generously, make a good wife, daughter, and mother, and a good mistress of servants. At the end of this long list of injunctions to herself for ideal behavior she made a typical note: "Before I leave my Chamber recolect in General the business to be done that day." Good advice for any administrator.[55] Once she noted that "nobody eats the bread of idleness while I am here."[56] It might well have been her lifetime motto.

Her married life was as busy as her single life had been. In ten months Charles Cotesworth Pinckney was born. Perhaps the childlessness of Pinckney's first marriage explains the extraordinary eagerness of both parents to cherish "as promising a child as ever parents were blessed with." Eliza could see "all his papa's virtues already dawning" in the infant. A friend in England was asked to find a set of educational toys described by John Locke, while his father set about designing toys to teach the infant his letters. "You perceive we begin bytimes," Eliza added, "for he is not yet four months old."[57]

A second son was born and died. Then came Thomas and Harriott. Though Eliza Pinckney had slave nurses to suckle her infants, she was intensely preoccupied with the training, education, and shaping of her children.

In 1752 political maneuvering deprived Charles Pinckney of his seat as chief justice of the colony and he left for England to serve as South Carolina's agent there. The family took a house in Surrey and lived much like their neighbors. Eliza Pinckney was appalled at the amount of time the English gentry wasted, especially in playing cards. On the other hand, she loved the theater and never missed a new performance if she could help it. She called on the widowed Princess of Wales, and found her informality, her interest in South Carolina and in "little domestick questions" very engaging. The boys were sent to school, and Harriott was taught at home. It was a good life, and she was in no hurry to return to South Carolina.

Increasingly concerned by developments in the Seven Years' War, fearful that France might take over a large part of North America, the Pinckneys decided to liquidate their Carolina estate and move to England. To this end they sailed the war-infested sea in 1758, taking Harriott and leaving their sons in school. Three weeks after they landed Charles Pinckney was dead. Eliza Pinckney at thirty-five was once again in charge of a large and complex plantation enterprise. It was just as well, she thought, to have so great a responsibility; otherwise the loss of this most perfect of husbands would have undone her.

I find it requires great care, attention and activity to attend properly to a Carolina estate, tho but a moderate one, to do ones duty and make it turn to account, . . . I find I have as much business as I can go through of one sort or other. Perhaps 'tis better for me. . . . Had there not been a necessity for it, I might have sunk to the grave by this time in that Lethargy of stupidity which seized me after my mind had been violently agitated by the greatest shock it ever felt. But a variety of imployment gives my thoughts a relief from melloncholy subjects, . . . and gives me air and exercise. . . .[58]

In letter after letter she recited Pinckney's virtues; the same ones she had praised when she married him. His religious dedication, "free from sourness and supersitition," his integrity, charm, and good temper, "his fine address" — she thought she would never find his like again.[59]

Fortunately she still loved books, agriculture, and her children. It was for the children she told herself (and them) that she worked so hard, overseeing the planting, buying and selling, writing ceaselessly to England (in several copies since no ship was secure), nursing slaves through smallpox, supervising the education of Harriott. She expected reciprocal effort from her sons. She wrote Charles Cotesworth: ". . . though you are very young, you must know the welfair of a whole family depends in a great measure on the progress you make in moral Virtue, Religion, and learning. . . . To be patient, humble, and resigned is to be happy. It is also to have a noble soul, a mind out of the reach of Envy, malice and every Calamity. And the earlier, my dear boy, you learn this lesson, the longer will you be wise and happy."[60]

She was convinced that happiness for all her children depended in great measure on a "right Education," and she encouraged Harriott; she was "fond of learning and I indulge her in it. It shall not be my fault if she roams abroad for amusement, as I believe 'tis want of knowing how to imploy themselves agreeably that makes many women too fond of going abroad."[61]

She thought highly of female talent. Once a letter from a friend in England came with the seal broken. Perhaps someone had read the letter? No matter; "it may teach them the art of writing prettily . . . and show how capable women are of both friendship and business. . . .[62]

She fell ill, lay four months in her chamber, but was too busy to die. A friend in England wanted seeds of all the trees in Carolina, and she was happy to oblige. The planting at Belmont, her plantation, was following an old-fashioned pattern; she decided to modernize, working harder, she said, than any slave. She revived silk-making experiments begun when Pinckney was alive, and endeavored to teach the skill to other women. Harriott's education continued to be one of her chief joys: "For pleasure it certainly is to cultivate the tender mind, to teach the young Idea how to shoot, &c. especially to a mind so tractable and a temper so sweet as hers. . . ."[63]

Though she still talked of going back to England, of taking her sons to Geneva for their final polishing, any observer could have foretold that it would never happen. She was busy, and therefore happy, and the boys were doing well. Both, despite their long absence, were ardent in the American cause, and Thomas had astonished his schoolmates by his articulate opposition to the Stamp Act.

In 1768 Harriott at nineteen married a thirty-five-year-old planter, Daniel Horry, and set about replicating her mother's career. "I am glad your little Wife looks well to the ways of her household," Eliza wrote her new son-in-law; "the management of a Dairy is an amusement she has always been fond of, and 'tis a very useful one."[64] Harriott was soon running much more than the dairy.

While Harriott was busy in the country, her mother set about planting a garden at the Horrys' town house. In her own well-organized household five slaves had each their appointed tasks; none was idle and none, she said, overworked. She herself was constantly industrious.

In such good order, then, were the family affairs in 1769 when Charles Cotesworth Pinckney at last came home from his sixteen-year sojourn in England, already an American patriot. He was at once admitted to the bar, and in a month had been elected to the South Carolina Assembly. A year or so later Thomas arrived to join him. The children for whom she had seen herself as working so hard were all launched.

Perhaps, though it would have been out of character, other circumstances would have permitted Eliza Pinckney to slow down at forty-five. But public affairs were in turmoil, and in 1775 both her sons were commissioned in the first regiment of South Carolina troops. Their business and financial affairs remained in the hands of their mother and sister, who were quite prepared to carry on while the men went to war.

It was 1778 before the full force of hostilities reached the Pinckneys. They had chosen Ashepoo, the family plantation belonging to Thomas Pinckney, as the safest place for all their valuables. It was a bad guess. Augustine Prevost's forces burned it to the ground on their way to Charleston, leaving Thomas — as he thought — wiped out and his mother's interest severely damaged. Charles Cotesworth wrote from his military post that of course whatever he had left when the war ended would be divided with them. Eliza wrote to Thomas: "Don't grieve for me my child as I assure you I do not for myself. While I have such children dare I think my lot hard? God forbid! I pray the Almighty disposer of events to preserve them and my grandchildren to me, and for all

69

the rest I hope I shall be able to say not only contentedly, but cheerfully, God's Sacred Will be done!"[65]

The loss of Ashepoo was only the beginning. British troops impressed horses, took provisions, commandeered houses. Eliza Pinckney had to take refuge in the country, leaving her town property to who could know what depredations. In the midst of all this stress Thomas was wounded, Charles Cotesworth, already suffering from malaria, was imprisoned, and two grandchildren were born. In 1780 the British captured Charleston and by that time plenty had given way to pinched poverty. She owed sixty pounds to a creditor in England and could find no way at all to pay it. For a while it seemed that the fruit of thirty years' hard work was all lost.

Even before the war ended, however, it was clear that Eliza Pinckney's labors had accomplished much more than the building of a prosperous planting interest. She had created an enormously effective family. Planting and business, important as they were, had always taken second place to the upbringing and education of her children. Now, as adults, the three saw themselves, with her, as almost a single entity. The men, at war, often wrote their mother once, sometimes twice, a day. Harriott, who had been Tom's close friend and confidante before he was married, and whom he had always treated as an intellectual equal, continued after his marriage as his business agent and political adviser. For both brothers she managed plantations (as well as her own, after Daniel Horry died), handled money, looked after their wives and children. They, in turn, took time from their pressing military duties to oversee the education of her son.

After the war, the pattern continued. Both Pinckney men moved into public service. Charles Cotesworth was a member of the Constitutional Convention; Thomas was elected governor of South Carolina by an overwhelming majority and was in office when the state ratified the Constitution. Both were part of the developing Federalist party. Each was to be a foreign envoy, and to give his name to important treaties. These careers were made possible by the labors of their mother and sister.

In 1792 Eliza Pinckney developed cancer, and almost the entire family proposed to accompany her to Philadelphia, where a physician with considerable reputation in that field was to be found. She refused to go if they all came along: she could not risk the whole family on one ship. So, while Charles Cotesworth and his children reluctantly remained in Charleston, Harriott took her to Philadelphia. It was too late. She died and was buried there, George Washington at his own request serving as one of her pallbearers.

Building notable families was one of the things American colonials had to do for themselves when they came away from England. Franklin and Drinker were to become well-known family names because of the work and the public service of their men. Pinckney, too, became famous as a consequence of the public service of Thomas, Charles Cotesworth, and their cousin, also Charles. But the family was created, sustained, and developed a strong sense of itself as a consequence of the work, the vision, the exhortation, the constant attention of Eliza Pinckney. Her children carried on the vision to the end of their very long lives, and it is a measure of their success that a modern historian, dealing with eighteenth and early nineteenth century Charleston, chose to call his book *Charleston in the Age of the Pinckneys.*[66]

IV. Reflections on the Microcosm

"As families are such at last the Church and Commonwealth must be," James Fitch remarked in Boston in 1683. More than a century later Chief Justice John Marshall was moved to comment that he had "always believed that the national character as well as happiness depended more on the female part of society than is generally imagined."[67]

It is with similar assumptions that I have tried to learn from the records left by these three women what it was like to be an eighteenth-century person. They take us to the heart of daily life: to scenes of childbearing and nerve-racking struggle to keep babies alive, to scenes of mysterious illness and sudden death, of wartime stringencies and dislocations, to the struggle to "git a living" or — at another level — to get rich. Through their eyes we see the chanciness of life, and begin to understand the central role of kinship in providing such security as was possible in a world so filled with uncertainty.

Different as these women were, each put family at the center of life. Eliza Pinckney and her three children viewed the world, not as individuals, but *as a family*. A threat to one was a threat to all; fame and fortune were also shared. They took care of each other's interests, of each other's children, as a matter of course. Tom's rice crop failed and Charles Cotesworth's wife put five hundred pounds at his disposal, "cheerfully," his brother noted. The family wanted Tom to stay in London. Earlier, when the British burned most of the family's movable assets, Charles Cotesworth announced at once that all he had left was to be divided among the rest of them. When the brothers went abroad, Harriott had their power of attorney; she made sure their plantations were cared for, their debts paid. Together they took responsibility for the younger generation. Young Daniel Horry was a spendthrift and showed signs of becoming a monarchist. His grandmother and his uncles tried to set him right, and his debts were settled as a family responsibility. Meanwhile the young women in the family were trained by their aunt and grandmother so that they, too, could run plantations. By the time Eliza Pinckney died the family had a full-fledged "tradition" for many of its activities, and doubtless no one remembered that it had all been created in two generations.

The Drinkers were equally knit together by kinship. The sons-in-law were brought into the family business, and encouraged to help each other. When one had business reverses, the whole family helped out. The cousins were grouped around the grandparents, and encouraged to see the family as their most basic commitment.

Jane Mecom's life was shaped by her relationship to Benjamin Franklin, but beyond the two of them lay a wide network of Franklin kin, in-laws, cousins in various degrees. Late in life Benjamin asked his sister to send him a detailed and complete list of all their kinfolk in Boston which he could use for reference. He was constantly being asked for help of one kind or another, and he wanted to be sure that he gave the proper priority to blood relations. In-laws were addressed as "sister" and "brother," and were entitled to at least formal statements of affection. They clearly recognized some members of the clan as more "valuable" than others, but blood created a responsibility even for ne'er-do-wells. While historical demographers argue about nuclear and extended families, we must pay close attention to the actual experience of families, and beware of false dichotomies.

Deism may have flourished in certain circles in the eighteenth century, but women's lives were too close to tragedy for such cool beliefs to be very satisfying. A deep need to believe that all the deaths, particularly of children, had meaning encouraged them to believe in a personal God, and in life beyond the grave.

No one who reads these pages will doubt that women's lives were different from those of men. In a day when contraception was all but unknown there is no mystery about a sexual division of labor which allotted men tasks in the public sphere and women those which could be carried out at home. Each of these women was pregnant within a month of marriage, and two continued to bear children into their late forties. Eliza Pinckney's family was unusually small for the time, but she was widowed at thirty-five. Shortly before his death Charles Pinckney had discussed with the Princess of Wales his plans for his next son.

Nor was it only their own children who kept women close to home. All three of these women were as much involved in raising the second generation as they had been with the first, and Jane Mecom, for a time, was responsible for four great-grandchildren. Grandmothering was an important part of their lifework.

All three believed in work as a moral value. They reserved their strongest criticisms for indolence in any form, and none of them saw old age as justification for idleness. For Jane Mecom and Elizabeth Drinker, "work" was largely domestic, though both dealt also in some mercantile ventures. Jane Mecom ran her own little shop for a while, and Elizabeth Drinker kept accounts for her husband's firm. Eliza Pinckney's work encompassed the larger world of plantation trade. Through most of her life she was busy with shipments, payments, factors, and the like, while she also planned and supervised the actual production of rice, indigo, silk, and the hundred other products of the relatively self-sufficient plantation. Though nominally working, first for her father, then for her husband, and finally for her children, she seems not to have felt any inhibition about acting in her own name, making her own decisions. The fact that legal ownership belonged to father or husband was of no great operational significance.

Woman's life in the eighteenth century was fundamentally influenced by marriage. In a day when conventional wisdom had it that for both men and women it was wise to marry close to home, all three did so. But the luck of the draw varied widely. There is little record of Edward Mecom's life, but circumstantial evidence suggests that Jane Mecom might have done better on her own. Elizabeth Drinker admired Henry, and his success in business provided her with a life of material comfort. Gradually as she grew older he was replaced at the center of her emotional ties by her son William, and her other children and grandchildren preoccupied her mind.

Eliza Pinckney was convinced that Charles Pinckney was incomparable, and despite various offers she never married again. During her marriage she had played the role of the properly subservient wife; her father had written to her husband the directions he had once sent to her; and her time had been much engaged in childbearing and child care. Widowed, she assumed the role of head of the family, and continued to make vital decisions even when her sons were grown and had families of their own. With their help she created the "Pinckney Family."

These were only three of millions of women who lived and worked and died in colonial America. In this age of statistical sophistication, it is a bold historian who builds any case upon three examples, yet in these lives we see exemplified cultural values which were those of many of their contemporaries. In their experience we see much of the common life of eighteenth-century woman, no matter what her social class. In another sense, of course, all three were uncommon women, whose achievements tell us something about the possibilities as well as the probabilities for women in their day and generation.

Notes

1. Jane Mecom to Benjamin Franklin, Aug. 16, 1787, in Carl Van Doren, ed., *The Letters of Benjamin Franklin*, VII (New Haven: Yale University Press, 1965), 515n. Sparks 296. Note her use of the plural: "Heads."
2. *Ibid.*, p. 52.
3. *Ibid.*, p. 43.
4. *Ibid.*, p. 84.
5. The original of this letter is lost. It is here reprinted from Jared Sparks, ed., *The Papers of Benjamin Franklin*, VII (New Haven: Yale University Press, 1965), 515n. Sparks corrected spelling and punctuation.
6. Van Doren, *Letters*, p. 114.
7. *Ibid.*, pp. 106–107.
8. *Ibid.*, p. 111.
9. *Ibid.*, p. 183.
10. *Ibid.*, p. 189.
11. *Ibid.*
12. *Ibid.*, p. 174.
13. *Ibid.*, p. 171.
14. *Ibid.*, p. 197.
15. *Ibid.*, p. 208.
16. *Ibid.*, p. 210.
17. *Ibid.*
18. *Ibid.*, p. 214.
19. *Ibid.*, p. 221.
20. *Ibid.*, p. 245.
21. *Ibid.*, p. 206.
22. *Ibid.*, p. 230.
23. *Ibid.*, p. 263.
24. *Ibid.*, p. 306.
25. *Ibid.*, p. 322.
26. *Ibid.*, p. 275.
27. H. D. Biddle, *Extracts from the Journal of Elizabeth Drinker* (Philadelphia: Lippincott, 1889), p. 49.
28. Typescript of manuscript journal, Historical Society of Pennsylvania, Dec. 7, 11, 14, 1777. Cited hereafter as Ms. Journal.
29. *Ibid.*, Feb. 26, 1797.
30. Biddle, *Extracts*, pp. 292–293.
31. Ms. Journal, Apr. 5–8, 1795.
32. *Ibid.*, June 14, 1796.
33. *Ibid.*, Oct. 23, 1799.
34. *Ibid.*, Dec. 20, 1798.
35. *Ibid.*, Dec. 26, 1794.

36. *Ibid.*, Jan. 1, 1802.
37. *Ibid.*, Apr. 22, 1796.
38. *Ibid.*, 1799 (n.d.).
39. *Ibid.*, 1799 (n.d.).
40. Biddle, *Extracts,* p. 313.
41. Ms. Journal, Jan. 1, 1807.
42. Cecil K. Drinker, *Not So Long Ago* (New York: Oxford University Press, 1936), p. 10.
43. Elise Pinckney, ed., *The Letterbook of Eliza Lucas Pinckney* (Chapel Hill: University of North Carolina Press, 1972), p. 27.
44. *Ibid.*, p. 6.
45. *Ibid.*, p. 7.
46. *Ibid.*, pp. 34–35.
47. *Ibid.*, p. 49.
48. *Ibid.*, pp. 29, 19.
49. *Ibid.*, pp. 39–40.
50. Harriott Horry Ravenal, *Eliza Lucas Pinckney* (New York: Scribner's, 1896), pp. 69–70.
51. *Ibid.*, p. 94.
52. Eliza Lucas Pinckney to Miss Bartlett, Manuscript Division, William R. Perkins Library, Duke University.
53. Ravenal, *Pinckney,* p. 90.
54. *Ibid.*, p. 100.
55. *Ibid.*, pp. 115–118.
56. *Ibid.*, p. 245.
57. Eliza Lucas Pinckney to Miss Bartlett, Manuscript Division, William R. Perkins Library, Duke University.
58. Pinckney, *Letterbook,* p. 144.
59. *Ibid.*, pp. 100–102.
60. *Ibid.*, p. 168.
61. *Ibid.*, p. 142.
62. *Ibid.*, p. 152.
63. *Ibid.*, p. 181.
64. *Ibid.*, p. 243.
65. *Ibid.*, p. 276.
66. George C. Rogers, *Charleston in the Age of the Pinckneys* (Norman: University of Oklahoma Press, 1969). The Pinckney Family Papers in the Library of Congress provide ample evidence that the three children of Eliza Lucas Pinckney continued to operate as a family through the rest of their long lives. From Charles C. Pinckney's receipt book we learn that in 1796 Harriott was acting as "attorney for General Pinckney" and paying his bills. It is clear that through the whole time Tom was abroad she took care of both his plantation and his financial affairs. In August 1815 Charles wrote Harriott asking her to look into and inform him about a certain machine he had heard of for the manufacture of cotton goods. As late as 1822 the two of them were cooperating in the search for black-seed cotton to plant. These are only samples of their continued habit of working as a unit. The large number of "My dear Harriott" letters from both brothers would make an interesting book.
67. Fitch is quoted in Edmund Morgan, *The Puritan Family* (New York: Harper, 1966) p. 143. The Marshall quotation is found in Frances Mason, ed. *My Dearest Polly: Letters of Chief Justice John Marshall to His Wife,* Richmond: Garrett and Massie, 1961, p. 140.

"This New Man": Dependence and Independence, 1776

Richard L. Bushman

Richard L. Bushman, author of *From Puritan to Yankee: Character and the Social Order in Connecticut, 1690–1765* (1967), is professor of history and chairman of the History Department at the University of Delaware. He is working on a study of political culture in provincial Massachusetts.

IN A FAMOUS LETTER to Hezekiah Niles in 1818, John Adams rhetorically asked a question of abiding interest: "But what do we mean by the American Revolution?" Then in dialogue with himself: "Do we mean the American War? The Revolution was effected before the War commenced. The Revolution was in the Minds and Hearts of the People." Not stopping there, Adams went on to say what sentiments of mind and heart had changed. One was the "habitual affection of England as their Mother-Country" that turned to "Indignation and Horror" when they found her "a cruel Beldam, willing like Lady Macbeth, to dash their Brains out." The other had to do with monarchy. "While the King, and all in Authority under him, were believed to govern, in Justice and Mercy according to the Laws and Constitution," Americans had "thought themselves bound to pray for the King and Queen and all the Royal Family." When the king turned against the people and purposed to destroy "all the Securities of their Lives, Liberties and Properties," Americans thought it their duty to "pray for the Continental Congress and all the thirteen State Congresses."[1] The second change meant most to Adams and to his contemporaries. They summed up the Revolution in the contrast of monarchy and republic, the end of government by the king and the king's officers, and the institution of a government of popularly elected officials.

Much earlier, on the eve of independence, Adams had elaborated on the cultural meaning of the Revolution. "It is the form of Government which gives the decisive Colour to the Manners of the People, more than any other Thing," he had written to Mercy Warren. A republic "will produce Strength, Hardiness, Activity, Courage, Fortitude and Enterprise"; monarchy produces "Taste and politeness," "Elegance in Dress," "Musick and Dancing," "Horse Racing and Cockfighting," "Balls and Assemblies."[2] Far from being narrowly political, monarchy and republic were societal types. They shaped culture and personality — or so Adams seemed to be saying. If true, the overthrow of monarchy disturbed deep cultural foundations, and the revolution in government implied a formidable transformation of society.

What did monarchy mean in the American colonies in the eighteenth century? Did it penetrate below the surface of provincial culture? Was its removal anything more than cosmetic surgery? Monarchy was so commonplace, so pervasive, that like the air its social importance is easily missed, especially in the North American provinces, where the splendor of royal rituals and the political presence of the king were but dimly reflected in the proceedings of royal governors. And yet the moral structure of monarchy was not irrelevant in America. The ancient covenants between king and people sounded in the language and the protocols of government at the farthest reaches of the empire and echoed outward through society.

In the last stages of the revolutionary controversy, when American publicists reviewed the fundaments of political allegiance, they laid bare the foundations of monarchical society. Why did people yield to the monarch? Submission, it was said repeatedly, was based on the ancient formula that protection compels allegiance. Thus James Wilson: "Allegiance is the faith and obedience which every subject owes to his prince. This obedience is founded on the protection derived from government: for protection and allegiance are the reciprocal bonds which connect the prince and his subjects."[3] The primary forms of that protection were security against foreign enemies and the distribution of justice, forms symbolized by two mythic images, one of the king personally leading the troops into battle, and the other of him present in each court of justice in the person of the magistrate.

The larger principle working in both settings was the safety of the people and more particularly the preservation of their rights.

Protection went beyond obvious enemies, foreign and domestic, to include enemies of the people among the king's own officers, corrupt judges, or conniving governors. The appeal to the king for redress upon the parliamentary invasion of colonial rights in 1765 was a customary response. In the same spirit the rejoicing upon repeal of the Stamp Act of 1766 took the form of thanks to the benevolent monarch for manifesting once more his royal concern for his people's rights.

The emotional structure of the king-people relationship was officially conveyed by the language of family. The quasi-legal obligation of the people to obey their protector or for the king to protect the obedient was ordinarily subordinated to the images of tender father and affectionate children. The king's care went beyond the contractual obligations to repel foreign enemies and administer justice. The people's whole welfare was his province — their bread, their children, their health. The people yielded voluntarily, out of gratitude to their common father, not merely from interest or duty. That was how the relationship was depicted in governors' speeches and in petitions and addresses from the assemblies. The language of the familial protectorate was the rhetorical matrix in which all political debate proceeded.

The abbreviation for the entire relationship was dependence. The word implied a hierarchical relationship of a superior caring for inferiors, and inferiors gratefully acknowledging the superior's authority and yielding to his will. Magnificence was an essential part. The king's ermine and crown, his palaces and retinue, his place at the peak of royal processions were visible attestations of power, but power which achieved poignant beauty because wielded on behalf of the people. In contests over the governors' salaries, assemblies freely acknowledged that governors required an income adequate to sustain their "dignity." Their office as representatives of the king's power called for a commensurate measure of magnificence, not for the governor's sake, but for the people whom he protected. Dependence caught up all of this: an elevated protector, set off by visible symbols of his station, exercising power for the benefit of lesser men who willingly submitted to his governance.

No one could match the king for might or magnificence, nor at this point in English history replace him in the courts or on the battlefield. He stood apart from all others in status and function. As a general mode of relating, however, protection and allegiance were anything but unique in monarchical society. Dependence was typical. It extended from king to lords to gentlemen of every kind, thence to tenants, laborers, servants, retainers. Protection was the obligation of the nobles — noblesse oblige. Every officer of the king acted in his stead as protector. By the same token, dependencies sprang into being wherever a great man offered protection or favor, whether office, land, or payment for a work of art. Whoever benefited from the largesse of a patron became a dependent. Colonial governors typically depended on the favor of an influential person in England for the grant of office in the first place and for protection thereafter. The obsequious correspondence accompanying the negotiations, disgusting to modern ears, was merely the language of dependence, struck from the same block as the assemblies' petitions to the crown.

Harold Perkin has suggested that in preindustrial England "the relationship of patronage was the module of which the social structure was built. It was all pervasive from the Court and Cabinet to the parish poor."[4] English society can be conceived as vast networks of dependencies formed by the exercise of various forms of protection — favors, gifts, offices, and above all land. The dependence of tenant on landlord was meant to be much more than the relationship of owner and renter. Normative values placed on the landlord the obligation to protect his tenants, and they, it was assumed, would invariably yield to the lord's will, just as officeholders and children yielded to their benefactors. Such dependencies were the elemental social units of power, and the management of power, including political power, can be understood as the manipulation of various networks of dependence formed from innumerable links of patrons and pendant clients.

However many exceptions and lacunae there were in actuality, the dependency networks were sufficiently real to eighteenth-century Englishmen to form the basis of Trenchard's and Gordon's social analysis. In letter eighty-five, Cato asked if republicanism would work in England. Somewhat regretfully he answered no, and gave as reason the fact that English social structure forbade it. Dependence was too prevalent, and dependencies took their life from monarchy. The nobility and gentry through "Birth and Fortune" gained admission to the legislature; "and their near Approach to the Throne gives them Pretences to honourable and profitable Employments," which when dispensed to their followers "creates a Dependence from the inferior Part of Mankind." Besides the disposal of offices, "the Nature of many of their Estates, and particularly of the Mannors, adds to that Dependence." These landlords with their train of tenant-dependents must ever favor monarchy since "Monarchy supports and keeps up this Distinction and subsists by it. It is senseless to imagine, that Men who have great Possessions, will ever put themselves upon the level with those who have none, or with such as depend upon them for Subsistence or Protection, whom they will always think they have a Right to govern or influence, and will be ever able to govern, whilst they keep their Possessions, and a monarchical Form of Government, and therefore will always endeavour to keep it."[5] Monarch and lords reciprocated support: the monarch provided the offices which gentlemen distributed to enhance their power, and they in turn sustained the king, their protector and provider. For Cato, dependence was the characteristic structural mode of monarchical society and the source of its strength. To this analysis, it can be added that as the chief protector of the people, the monarch was the exemplar of all that was good in dependence, the moral anchor for lesser patrons.

The fundamental assumptions about the reciprocal obligations of rulers and people were as widely held in America as in England. Royal governors demanded compliance from assemblies by perpetually reminding the representatives of His Majesty's protection and favor. The governors' own moral authority grew from their agency in providing the tender care the king intended for his people. At the other end of the scale, petitioners to the assemblies addressed the government as humble suppliants appealing to superiors for help. At virtually every level of government, all the elements were there: the assumption of a hierarchical relationship, expectations of protection, and the promise to obey. As a principle of politics the protection-allegiance formula was beyond debate. The more interesting question has to do with colonial society. Was colonial America, like Cato's England, constructed of many lesser protectorates extending into dependence structures which rose from servants and tenants, to local magnates, the governor, and the king?

There was certainly a ruling group in every colony to whom the people voluntarily deferred. Because of wealth, family, experience, and personal qualities, a small number of men came to hold a vastly disproportionate number of public offices. In the South and along the Hudson the preeminence of a few families has always been recognized. Recent work has shown the same pattern in New England, in the most democratic quarter of colonial America. In Windham, Connecticut, quite typically, between 1755 and 1786, 7 percent of the town families overwhelmingly dominated the top town offices. When offices are weighted by importance and points assigned, a single family will garner a third to a half of the points over a twenty-year period and two or three families more than two-thirds of the total. We now have evidence to support John Adams's observation that the office of representative in Massachusetts towns has "generally descended from generation to generation in three or four families at most." Deference was not merely a matter of familiarity either. When a Jeremiah Gridley or a Timothy Ruggles moved into town, the inhabitants immediately put him into office. There was everywhere a rough-hewn gentry who were generally recognized as most able to act on behalf of the people in public affairs.[6]

A colonial aristocracy to whom the populace habitually deferred, however, was not by itself enough. The crux of the matter was dependence. John Adams, reflecting on the Massachusetts social structure in 1787, observed that "among the wisest people that lives there is a degree of admiration, abstracted from all dependence, obligation, expectation, or even acquaintance which accompanies splendid wealth, ensures some respect, and bestows some influence."[7] Adams was making an important distinction between deference and dependence. Deference, "abstracted," as he said, "from all dependence," was a simple respect for social superiority, family, wealth. Dependence included in addition a grant or favor from superior to inferior, typically of office or land, binding one to the other and setting up a mutually acknowledged obligation. The recipient of protection was materially indebted to his patron. Falling out of favor entailed a palpable loss. More important, a dependent was morally bound by far stronger bonds than mere respect for rank or grandeur. Gratitude imposed a duty to yield his will to his patron's.

Were many colonists dependent in 1776? Did they look to their superiors for land or office, for employment or favors, thus entangling themselves in powerful moral and social obligations? The royal governors did all in their power to surround themselves with clients and where possible to extend their influence in the assemblies through the distribution of appointments, contracts, and whatever else they commanded. In Maryland and New Hampshire a substantial patronage existed which made the replication of the English system more than a dream. Elsewhere population growth and the consequent increase in local officers — justices of the peace and militia officers — without a concomitant increase in delegates to the assemblies may have given mid-eighteenth-century governors greater patronage leverage in the assemblies than their predecessors had. But for reasons that are well known, the governors' efforts were comparatively feeble. The British ministry sucked up colonial offices to enhance their own power, filling the best posts with their own dependents, not the governors'. Frequent elections kept local magnates as dependent on their constituents for office as on the governor. Any inclination to toady doomed a politician at the polls. Most important for the analysis of the total society, there was precious little political patronage which the circle of favorites around the governor could themselves dispense. The governor could perhaps tie a small group to him — his council, the major military officers, the justices of the superior courts. But what could this group in turn offer to men in their communities? An occasional court clerkship, a provisions contract, lesser offices in the militia? The paucity of patronage is perhaps best reflected in differential English and American tax rates. Years ago, Lawrence Henry Gipson estimated that the per capita tax rate in England was many times that of the most burdened colony. Add to taxes, customs revenues and the funds drained from Ireland into the English treasury, and the total available for expenditure in England vastly exceeded American expenditures. There simply was not enough government money available in the colonies for much to seep down to counties or towns. Local magnates, though in a measure dependent on the governor for office, received little from him to create dependents in their own spheres of influence. The network of places radiated from governor to a handful of associates and not much farther.[8]

Various studies have asserted that social differentiation was becoming more marked in the eighteenth century. The distance between poorest and richest was increasing, and the number of men with large estates was expanding. New classes of great planters, landlords, and merchants were coming into existence.[9] How did this fact affect colonial society? Were the rich surrounding themselves with dependents, using their wealth to dispense favors and create obligations? Contemporary historians have concentrated on stratification, the crystallization of social groups into distinct classes defined by wealth and economic interest. The issue for eighteenth-century social analysts, who were fully as interested in the concentration of wealth, was not the separation of classes, which implies independence, but amalgamation, the binding of lesser men to the rich. It was the formation of dependencies rather than of classes, the suppressing of conflict rather than its generation, which struck eighteenth-century radicals as significant and ominous. As heirs of Harrington they fully expected men of property to exercise influence in this mode. Did that happen in the colonies as wealth concentrated in the eighteenth century?

Powerful, wealthy men, the justices of the peace or militia majors in their towns or counties, doubtless had innumerable small favors within their command: licenses for ordinaries, for ferries or mills, loans to small operators, assistance with legal technicalities, minor employments for tradesmen or the sons of a neighbor. John Adams observed that "all the rich men will have many of the poor in the various trades, manufactures, and other occupations in life dependent upon them for their daily bread; many of small fortunes will be in their debt and in many ways under obligations to them." Besides these were the social favors and chastisements, the proverbial "smiles and frowns" of the great: an invitation to dinner, a letter or conversation, a visit to a sick child, attendance at a funeral. Again Adams: "Others, in better circumstances, neither dependent nor in debt, men of letters, men of the learned professions, and others, from acquaintance, conversation, and civilities, will be connected with them and attached to them."[10] Considering all of these, are we right in thinking colonials were enmeshed in networks of dependencies like subjects of the king in England?

The shortest answer is that eighteenth-century observers addressing the question did not think so. However much Crèvecoeur's Enlightenment exaggerations are discounted, he put his finger on an important point. America was "not composed, as in Europe, of great lords who possess everything, and of a herd of people who have nothing." The ordinary American, so it was believed, was a freeholder. One English under secretary, William Knox, with a half-dozen years' experience in Georgia, attributed the colonists' strong republican tendencies to this fact. At the beginning of settlement, land was "granted out in small tracts to each Individual in perpetuity, with the reservation of a small Quit Rent payable to the Crown, and thus every Male Inhabitant became a Freeholder." The form of tenure colored all subsequent social relationships. "This mode excluded all ideas of subordination and dependence. The relation between Landlord and Tenant could have no existence where every Man held by the same tenure and all derived immediately from the Crown." Recognition of increasing colonial wealth in the eighteenth century did not cause Knox to qualify his analysis. American "Republicanism" was a tendency "which increased with their Wealth, and in a little time, if their prosperity had continued, must have swallowed up the Monarchic powers."[11]

There is a small mystery in the certainty of men like Knox and their virtual unanimity on the question of dependence. They seemed to have overlooked the great proprietors in Virginia, New Jersey, Pennsylvania, and New York whose vast empty estates began to fill up in the eighteenth century, and the lesser landlords in Maryland, where as many as half of the farmers were tenants. Perhaps comparison with England was enough to shrink the significance of American lordships. By 1790 one-fifth of all English farmland was held by four-hundred great landlords; three-quarters of all the cultivated land was owned by landlords of some kind and worked by tenants. Only rarely was any portion of the colonial landscape so dominated. Knox himself made another point about landlord influence. "The superior industry or better fortune of some enabled them to extend their possessions by purchase," he noted; "others became wealthy thro' successful trade, but their riches brought them little Influence." Why? Because if they "parcelled out their Lands it was upon the same tenure as they held it, only requiring a stated rent," without any familial affection or associated obligations. The relationship was of owner and renter — contractual, financial, impersonal — not lord of the soil and dependent, a modern rather than feudal connection. The payment of rent was the sum of it.[12]

To Knox's reasons we can add the fact of remoteness. Penn and Calvert in England could never win the affection and gratitude of their American tenants. Many properties of Lord Fairfax, the notable exception to nonresident proprietors among the titled landlords, were at a great remove across the mountains, occupied by people who scarcely knew him. These tenants of Fairfax's may have held him in awe as young Devereaux Jarratt growing up in Virginia did the periwig, but in both instances the awe was partly attributable to the infrequency of the gentry's appearances. The personal bonds of patron and client could hardly mature among strangers. Rowland Berthoff and John Murrin have said of the filling in of the large proprietorships, "In terms of genuine feudalism the revival was thus grossly imperfect, more a matter of economic profit for the proprietor than of mutual obligations between lord and man or landlord and man that might have harmonized the relationship."[13]

Knox, the returned colonial bureaucrat, felt compelled to stress the absence of subordination and dependence to his superiors at home. It must have been difficult for Englishmen with experience restricted to the realm to grasp the limited influence property and rank afforded American gentlemen. William Gordon reported in his history of the Revolution that the home government characteristically made this error. "The British ministry have been greatly mistaken, in supposing it is the same in America as in their own country. Do they gain over a gentleman of note and eminence in the colonies they make no considerable acquisition. He takes few or none with him and is rather despised, than admired to by former friends. He has not as in Britain, dependants who must act in conformity to his nod. In New England especially, individuals are so independent of each other, that though there may be an inequality in rank and fortune, everyone can act freely according to his own judgment."[14] The difficult point to grasp was that in America economic inequality did not entail dependence. Political managers had to adopt another calculus in the absence of ties which could be assumed in England's monarchical society.

Colonial rulers could expect a large measure of deference but not that deeper control afforded by material dependence extending into the extremities of society.

What form did a revolution against monarchy take in this anomalous society, deferential yet not dependent? Did social repercussions follow from the constitutional abandonment of monarchy? Obviously the Revolution endangered all forms of dependence. Both ideology and events undermined aristocracy. Not that radical Whiggery was entirely unambivalent on the point. English Whigs did not deny the merit of innocent dependence. In Whig writing, the antithesis of the bad governor, the lawless tyrant, was the good patron, the faithful protector. The only true relation in government, Cato said, was that of "Father and Children, Patron and Client, Protection and Allegiance, Benefaction and Gratitude, mutual Affection and mutual Assistance." How could he say otherwise when country gentlemen, the radical Whigs' natural audience, were themselves landlords and protectors, patrons with many clients, and besides, men staunchly loyal to the protector king?

Aside from infrequent comments about benevolent patrons, however, Trenchard and Gordon dwelt almost exclusively on the corruptions of dependence, the abuse of loyalty, and the contrivance of false allegiances. Radical Whig scenarios featured the courtier who flattered his way into power, great lords collecting dependents to swell their followings and serve their pride, bankers buying dependents with fraudulent stocks, the king's ministers corrupting the legislature with places, pensions, bribes, and a long train of "Debauchees, riotous Livers, lewd Women, Gamesters, and Sharpers" who subsisted on the leavings of their patrons.[15] Radicals in Britain and America alike exalted the untainted independent man, free of entanglements with patrons, quick to resist encroachments because his will was untrammeled, and his spirit brave, incorruptible, energetic. Dickinson's Pennsylvania farmer was the archetypical independent gentlemen with his small farm, a few good servants, a little money at interest, and a disposition to espouse the sacred cause of liberty to the utmost of his power. The radical press in America had its *Independent Advertiser* and *Independent Reflector* well before the Revolution; by 1784 there were five newspapers in the United States with "independent" in their titles.

The word proclaimed the integrity of the paper and its trustworthiness as a defender of popular rights. The independent was in no man's employ.[16]

The Declaration of Independence ended whatever ambivalence existed in the American Whig views of personal dependence. Dependence was tolerable in a monarchy; in a republic it was contradictory. The sovereign citizen could not be dependent on the will of another. Republican principles required that all men be equal — not equal in ability or wealth, nor even in opportunity to gain wealth. They were to be equal in dominion. No man had the right by nature to rule another. All were to enjoy equal liberty.

In its essence the concept of equality was political, having to do with authority to govern, but it was not narrowly political. Dominion took many forms and the exercise of the state's coercive powers was but one. Influence was another, including the influence exercised by patrons over their dependents. Joseph Priestley, the English republican, stated the principle concisely: "Those who are extremely dependent should not be allowed to have votes in the nomination of the Chief Magistrates; because this might, in some instances, be only throwing more votes into the hands of those persons on whom they depend." The tenant or laborer could not be entrusted with suffrage. By the same token, as Harrington had argued a century earlier, the concentration of wealth with the associated control over land, offices, and innumerable lesser favors militated against a commonwealth. Those lacking property sank into subordination to those who controlled it, losing the capacity for independent judgment and the will to defend liberty. People think for themselves where there is an equal distribution of property, Samuel Adams had argued. On the other hand, "an enormous Proportion of Property vested in a few Individuals is dangerous to the Rights, and destructive of the Common Happiness, of Mankind." The redistribution of property was not advocated from "a drastic desire to distribute wealth more evenly," as Caroline Robbins has observed, but for strictly political reasons, because "too great an accumulation of wealth in a few hands might disturb the balance of the state." The Federalist Noah Webster in a tract advocating ratification of the Constitution declared point-blank that "an equality of property, with a necessity of alienation, constantly operating to destroy combinations of powerful families, is the very soul of a republic."[17]

The impulse to economic reform, present in the mix of revolutionary ideology, did not pass without effect. It was to protect the "soul of the republic" that Jefferson introduced legislation to abolish primogeniture and entail, a modest version of Harrington's agrarian law. The explicit purpose was to facilitate the alienation of land and to undermine "combinations of powerful families." The Hudson River manors in New York were stripped of their remaining baronial privileges, and entail and primogeniture abolished there too. Here and there other proposals to equalize property were voiced, but the sum of the reforms was actually very small. The ideological conviction that "a republic could succeed only if property was equally distributed" put little pressure on the vested interests. Carter Braxton's prediction that Americans would not submit to the agrarian laws of ancient republics proved accurate. Differences in wealth, even the growing concentration of wealth, failed to precipitate economic reforms. The reason is not hard to find. The crucial issue for the revolutionaries was not political and economic equality. Leveling was never on the agenda of reforms. The key was dependence. American ideologies, like their English counterparts, did not respond so much to sheer inequality as to subordination resulting from economic dependence, and they perceived American farmers as already independent. However inaccurate in detail, the colonists' view of themselves as typically independent freeholders, a view confirmed by European observers, undercut in advance postrevolutionary reforms. Ezra Stiles blandly repeated Harringtonian propositions that "dominion is founded in property," and that therefore "a free tenure of lands, and equable distribution of property enters into the foundation of a happy state." The affirmation was painless and self-congratulatory because in New England, Stiles reminded his hearers, "we have realized the capital ideas of Harrington's Oceana." So long as Americans were independent, inequalities were harmless.[18]

Because so few social changes resulted from the Revolution, we probably underrate the social significance of republicanism. Above all we must recognize that the Revolution discredited the entire ethic on which traditional society was based, the values surrounding protection, patronage, and dependence. The new egalitarian frame of mind was revealed in a host of small things rather than a single major upheaval: the entry of the word *aris-*

tocrat into political discourse, for example, as a new term of opprobrium; or frequent comments about imposing on the people with "Shew and Parade" at every display of magnificence reminiscent of aristocracy. The Republican *Pittsfield Sun* compared Governor Christopher Gore's visit to Berkshire County in 1809 to the arrival of a royal procession. "Whether it was touched off exactly in the style of an English prince or noble, dashing down among his tenants, before an election, his Excellency from his long residence in England, is better qualified, than we are, to decide."[19] George Washington on his ceremonial visit to Boston wisely wore his old wartime uniform and rather than entering the city by carriage simply rode a horse. Details like these signified the fall of the ancient social morality.

Republicanism's aversion to dependence cast a longer shadow on the coming social order than on society in 1776. Manufacturers with their armies of dependent workers and banks with their beholden debtors and stockholders flatly contradicted republican principles. As Jefferson observed in his comment about manufactures, work as an employee of someone else was actually dangerous: "Dependence begets subservience and venality, suffocates the germ of virtue, and prepares fit tools for the designs of ambition." The opposition to Hamilton's program in the 1790s was at least in part ideologically inspired.[20]

Ideology was, of course, too frail a reed to lay athwart the course of the financial and industrial juggernaut. Despite all republican objections, the percentage of workers employed by others increased from an estimated 12 percent in 1800 to 40 percent in 1860. Republicanism could not halt or even deflect the great economic forces gathering momentum in Jefferson's administration. But it could shape a characteristic attitude toward factory work, the belief that work in another's employ should be temporary. A factory job was to be transitional, merely preparation for independence as farmer or detached artisan. Abraham Lincoln spoke of hiring out as a stage in the life cycle: "The prudent, penniless beginner in the world, labors for wages awhile, saves a surplus with which to buy tools or land, for himself; then labors on his own account another while, and at length hires another new beginner to help him." A fundamental aim of the National Trades Union was to facilitate workers' escape from their "humiliating, servile dependence, incompatible with the inherent natural equality of men."[21]

In the long run republicanism did work changes in American society. It did not prescribe drastic alterations in the distribution of property. Property was already sufficiently well distributed to shield the citizenry from undue influence and assure equality in the political sphere. The changes took place in the realm of values and attitude. The Revolution infused the American mentality with an aversion to dependence, dependence of all kinds, economic and political. Ideally a citizen stood alone, independent politically, because independent in his work. The enduring vision of a nation of freestanding capitalists thus did not originate in economic conditions alone. Its lineage went back to the republican idea of the good citizen. The freehold farmer and autonomous craftsman were originally valued for their civic qualities, for political judgment unconstrained by obligations to employer or master. At its source, American individualism was a political conception, sustained by economic plentitude, but charged and focused in 1776 by republicanism and the colonial revolt against monarchy and traditional dependence.

Notes

1. John Adams to Hezekiah Niles, Feb. 13, 1818. Charles Francis Adams, ed., *The Works of John Adams* (Boston, 1850–1856), X, 282.
2. John Adams to Mercy Warren, Jan. 8, 1776. *Warren-Adams Letters, Being Chiefly a Correspondence among John Adams, Samuel Adams, and James Warren* (Boston, 1917), I, 201–202.
3. Robert Green McCloskey, ed., *The Works of James Wilson* (Cambridge: Harvard University Press, 1967), II, 743.
4. Harold Perkin, *The Origins of Modern English Society, 1780–1880* (London: Routledge & Kegan Paul; Toronto: University of Toronto Press, 1969), p. 50.
5. John Trenchard and Thomas Gordon, *Cato's Letters; or, Essays on Liberty, Civil and Religious, and Other Important Subjects* (reprinted, New York: Russell and Russell, 1969), III, 160–161.
6. William F. Willingham, "Deference Democracy and Town Government in Windham, Connecticut, 1755 to 1786," *William and Mary Quarterly*, 3rd ser., XXX (Oct. 1973), 407; Bruce C. Daniels, "Family Dynasties in Connecticut's Largest Towns, 1700–1760," *Canadian Journal of History*, VIII (Sept. 1973), 99–110; Adams, *Works*, VI, 393; Clifford K. Shipton, *Sibley's Harvard Graduates* (Boston: Massachusetts Historical Society, 1945, 1956), VII, 525, and IX, 202 (cf. obituary of Samuel Prince in *New England Weekly Journal*, July 15, 1728); Patricia U. Bonomi, *A Factious People: Politics and Society in Colonial New York* (New York and London: Columbia University Press, 1971), pp. 36, 38. Edward M. Cook, Jr., has found a greater proclivity to elect representatives of wealthy, well-established families to high office in large cities than in small towns. See *The Fathers of the Towns: Leadership and Community Structure in Eighteenth-Century New England* (Baltimore: Johns Hopkins University Press, 1976).
7. Adams, *Works*, VI, 392.
8. Bernard Bailyn, *The Origins of American Politics* (New York: Knopf, 1968), pp. 72–91, 107–124; David Curtis Skaggs, *Roots of Maryland Democracy, 1753–1776* (Westport, Conn.: Greenwood Press, 1973), pp. 14–18; John Murrin, "Review Essay," *History and Theory*, XI (1972), 261; L. H. Gipson, "Connecticut Taxation and Parliamentary Aid Preceding the Revolutionary War," *American Historical Review*, XXXVI (July 1931), 721–793, and "The American Revolution As an Aftermath of the Great War for Empire, 1754–1763," *Political Science Quarterly*, LXV (1950), 97.
9. Thomas Jefferson Wertenbaker, *Planters of Colonial Virginia* (Princeton: Princeton University Press, 1922); James E. Henretta, "Economic Development and Social Structure in Colonial Boston," *William and Mary Quarterly*, 3rd ser., XXII (1965), 75–92; Gary B. Nash, "Urban Wealth and Poverty in Pre-Revolutionary America," *Journal of Interdisciplinary History* V (1976), 545–584; Linda A. Bissell, "From One Generation to Another: Windsor, Connecticut," *William and Mary Quarterly*, 3rd ser. XXXI, (1974), 79–110. For further citations in this vein, see the historiographical essay by Bernard Bailyn, *Lines of Force in Recent Writings on the American Revolution* (XIV International Congress of Historical Societies, San Francisco, August 22–29, 1975),

pp. 13–16, and the essays in Alfred F. Young, ed., *The American Revolution: Explorations in the History of American Radicalism* (Dekalb: Northern Illinois University Press, 1976). For a critique of the studies of social stratification in Boston, see G. B. Warden, "The Distribution of Property in Boston, 1692–1775," *Perspectives in American History*, X (1976), 81–128.

10. Adams, *Works*, VI, 392.
11. J. Hector St. John Crèvecoeur, *Letters from an American Farmer* (Garden City, N.Y.: Doubleday, n.d.), p. 46; Jack P. Greene, "William Knox's Explanation for the American Revolution," *William and Mary Quarterly*, 3rd ser., XXX (Apr. 1973), 299.
12. Rowland Berthoff and John M. Murrin, "Feudalism, Communalism, and the Yeoman Freeholder: The American Revolution Considered As a Social Accident," in Stephen G. Kurtz and James H. Hutson, eds., *Essays on the American Revolution* (New York: W. W. Norton, 1973), pp. 256–288, esp. p. 271; Gregory A. Stiverson, "Landless Husbandmen: Proprietory Tenants in Maryland in the Late Colonial Period," in Aubrey C. Land et al., *Law, Society, and Politics in Early Maryland* (Baltimore: Johns Hopkins University Press, 1977), pp. 197–211; Skaggs, *Roots of Maryland Democracy*, pp. 39–43; G. E. Mingay, *English Landed Society in the Eighteenth Century* (London: Routledge & Kegan Paul, 1963), pp. 19–24; Greene, "William Knox's Explanation," pp. 299–300; Stephen Innes, "Land Tenancy and Social Order in Springfield, Massachusetts, from 1652 to 1702," *William and Mary Quarterly*, 3rd ser., XXXV (Jan. 1978), 33–56.
13. Berthoff and Murrin, "Feudalism," p. 271.
14. William Gordon, *The History of the Rise, Progress, and Establishment of the Independence of the United States of America* . . . (Freeport, N.Y.: Books for Libraries Press, 1969), I, 143.
15. David L. Jacobson, ed., *The English Libertarian Heritage, from the Writings of John Trenchard and Thomas Gordon* in the Independent Whig *and Cato's Letters* (Indianapolis: Bobbs-Merrill, 1965), p. 118; Trenchard and Gordon, *Cato's Letters*, III, 162.
16. John Dickinson, *Letters from a Farmer in Pennsylvania*, in Forrest McDonald, ed., *Empire and Nation* (Englewood Cliffs, N.J.: Prentice-Hall, 1962), p. 3; the "Independent" newspapers are listed in Charles Evans, ed., *American Bibliography* (Chicago, 1903–1934), VI, 294, 295.
17. Joseph Priestley, *An Essay on the First Principles of Government*, 2nd ed., (London, 1771), p. 13, quoted in Chilton Williamson, *American Suffrage: From Property to Democracy, 1760–1860* (Princeton: Princeton University Press, 1960), pp. 71–72; William V. Wells, *The Life and Public Service of Samuel Adams* (Boston, 1865), II, 251; *An Essay of a Declaration of Rights* (Philadelphia, 1776), art. 16, quoted in Gordon S. Wood, *The Creation of the American Republic, 1776–1787* (Chapel Hill: University of North Carolina Press, 1969), p. 89; Caroline Robbins, *The Eighteenth Century Commonwealthman* (New York: Atheneum, 1968), p. 15; Noah Webster, *An Examination into the Leading Principles of the Federal Constitution* . . . (Philadelphia, 1887), in Paul Leicester Ford, ed., *Pamphlets on the Constitution of the United States* (Brooklyn, 1888), p. 59.
18. For some of the antiprivilege reforms see references in Wood, *Creation of the American Republic*, p. 72n; Jeremy Belnap to E. Hazard, "Belnap Papers" in Massachusetts Historical Society, *Collections*, 5th ser., II (1877), 313; [Carter Braxton], *An Address to the Convention of . . . Virginia; on the Subject of Government* . . . (Williamsburg, 1776), quoted in Wood, *Creation of the American Republic*, pp. 96–97; Ezra Stiles, *The United States Elevated to Glory and Honor* . . . (New Haven, 1783), in John Wingate Thornton, ed., *The Pulpit of the American Revolution* (Boston, 1876), p. 404 (cf. p. 341).
19. *Pittsfield Sun*, Aug. 5, 1809.
20. Thomas Jefferson, *Notes on the State of Virginia*, edited by William Peden (Chapel Hill: University of North Carolina Press, 1954), p. 165; Drew R. McCoy, "Republicanism and American Foreign Policy: James Madison and the Political Economy of Commercial Discrimination, 1789 to 1794," *William and Mary Quarterly*, 3rd ser., XXXI (Oct. 1974), 633–646.
21. Stanley Lebergott, "The Pattern of Employment Since 1800," in Seymour E. Harris, ed., *American Economic History* (New York: McGraw-Hill, 1961), p. 292; *The Political Thought of Abraham Lincoln* (Indianapolis: Bobbs-Merrill, 1967), p. 134; *The Man*, Aug. 30, 1834, in Edwin C. Rozwenc, ed., *Ideology and Power in the Age of Jackson* (Garden

City, N.Y.: Doubleday, 1964), pp. 124, 126. Herbert G. Gutman develops the use of antifeudal rhetoric, with an accompanying stress on independence, in *Work, Culture, and Society in Industrializing America: Essays in American Working-Class and Social History* (New York: Random House, 1977), pp. 49–53.

Independence and Attachment, Virtue and Interest: From Republican Citizen to Free Enterpriser, 1787–1837

*Rowland Berthoff**

*I wish to thank Richard L. Bushman, David T. Konig, J. G. A. Pocock, and Warner Berthoff for helpful criticism of earlier drafts of this essay.

Rowland Berthoff, the author of *British Immigrants in Industrial America, 1790–1950* (1953), and of *An Unsettled People: Social Order and Disorder in American History* (1971), is currently at work on a study of republican liberty and social equality in America. He is William Eliot Smith Professor of History at Washington University (St. Louis).

"CORRUPTION" — the sad corruption of republican virtue — has been the lament of Americans from Shays's Rebellion down to Watergate. Even the Revolution that won the independence of the republic, so it seemed in 1788 to the chronicler of the Shays affair, had not been free of it. All the brave pledges of life, fortune, sacred honor, and homespun frugality had failed to suppress a corrupt attachment to self-interest. "Precarious wealth" gained from war profiteering had led to "voluptuousness" among the newly rich, which in turn undermined the virtues of "diligence and economy" — "the best support of all governments, and particularly of the republican" — among people of every class. Most deplorable of all, as the recent uprising of farmers in western Massachusetts showed, "the discipline and manners of the army had vitiated the taste, and relaxed the industry of the yeomen" — had corrupted, that is, the fundamental virtues of the self-reliant, public-spirited, independent citizen.[1]

Corruption of the virtuous citizen through unduly selfish attachment to the victorious republic was a danger that thoughtful patriots had been led to expect. The political theory that they had taken over from the English "Country" opposition to the novel executive government of Sir Robert Walpole (1721–1742) and his successors, and ultimately from James Harrington's *Oceana* (1656) and Niccolò Machiavelli's *Discourses on Livy* (c. 1519), warned that degeneration was the ironic fate of the most successful of republics. Material prosperity and expanding empire, by attaching the private interest of the citizen to government in various corrupt ways, would eventually subvert his personal independence and with it the very bedrock of civic virtue on which the republic had grown and conquered. In the end tyranny, perhaps after a period of either anarchy or oligarchy, would rise on the ruins of liberty.[2]

This classical theory of politics, which looked back for both inspiration and warning to the Roman republic (sometimes also to a mythical Saxon or "Gothic" age of English liberty and communal equality), held up an ideal that was fundamentally static rather than progressive. The citizens of the true republic were self-reliant but disinterested property owners, attached above all to the common good, armed against the threat of tyranny, deferential to the special virtues of those of both higher and lower rank, but none among them rich or powerful enough to reduce others to dependence. (Dependents there of course would be — servants, women, children, the poor and propertyless — but they accordingly were not citizens.) In this republican equilibrium no sort of change could be seen as commendably progressive and modern. Even though prosperity and power were the necessary consequences of republican virtue, the course of empire inevitably hastened the dismal onset of self-interest, personal dependence, civic corruption, and eventual collapse of the republic itself. At best the downward cycle might be checked or even brought back into balance for a time, but only to begin again.

Although Americans began to lose any coherent memory of this systematic theory almost as soon as it was simplified into the striking phrases of the Declaration of Independence, their history ever since has characteristically been seen, by historians as well as others, in terms of classical cycles of civic virtue, corruption, and then again reform seeking to recover the pristine ideals of the Founding Fathers. In spite of the constitutional checks and balances which the latter devised, the moment of crisis — the "Machiavellian moment" of incipient degeneration — has kept recurring. For a Jeffersonian like Albert Gallatin in 1807 the approach of another war, with its "necessary increase of Executive power and influence, the speculation of contractors and jobbers, and the introduction of permanent military and naval establishments," raised the question "whether the awakening of nobler feelings and habits than avarice and luxury might not be necessary to prevent our degeneration, like the Hollanders, into a nation of mere calculators."[3] It was the self-interested calculation of bankers and stockholders against which that imperious republican Andrew Jackson rallied, in 1832, the "independent spirit," the "moral character," and the "habits of economy and simplicity which are so congenial to the character of republicans."[4] Again, the new Republican party of the 1850s, true to its name, sought to restore the same virtuous standard of "free labor" of free men settled upon free soil.[5] Although by that time economic growth and spreading prosperity were the hallmarks of American development, progress still was assumed to mean not change so much as, it has recently been noted, a "return to original truth."[6]

The republican ideal survived the Civil War and indeed received its apotheosis in Lincoln's invocation of liberty at Gettysburg, but applying it to the modern world proved increasingly awkward in the years that followed. This was more than a matter of the venal politicians of the Tweed and Grant era or of the high-minded but overly abstract civil-service reformers of the time. The essentially republican doctrine of free labor or free contract — of uncoerced agreement between autonomous individuals — was generally understood to forbid any practical enforcement of the state and federal laws that were intended, in the late 1860s, to guarantee that same freedom, whether for white industrial workingmen in the North or for the black freedmen of the South.[7] Such deadlocks eventually led the latter-day liberals of the twentieth century to impose limits on certain kinds of liberty in the hope of yet restoring to the modern citizen the essential independence of the classical ideal. Modern conservatives are understandably distressed over a liberalism that finds it necessary to destroy liberty in order to save it. But the dilemma would have been familiar enough to the eighteenth-century Country theorists who feared that the more freely were republican virtues practiced, the more surely would they lead to gross inequality in wealth and power, dominion of some citizens over others, a truly imperial government, and finally corruption of the essential civic virtue itself. Americans have forever been waking to find that literal independence for everyone is in truth only an American dream.

It could hardly be otherwise. Classical republicanism was already anachronistic when the circumstances of the American Revolution transformed it into a national ideology. What historians have recently discovered about the colonial eighteenth century, now that they are looking for something more in it than democratic "seeds" of the Revolution, suggests that the republican ideal expressed a reaction against the tendencies actually dominant in colonial society and not their political fulfillment. The "truly revolutionary thing" about the Revolution, Gordon S. Wood concludes, was not the struggle to preserve colonial self-government from imperial dominion (genuine though that was) but rather the hope of establishing an ideal American republic on the archaic Country or Commonwealth principle of "the sacrifice of individual interests to the greater good of the whole." As the patriots saw it, they were engaged in a classic cycle of self-reformation against corruption from within as well as self-defense against subjection to England, a "desperate attempt," Wood calls it, because by the 1760s the economic and social basis capable of sustaining such an ideal in America "had long been disintegrating, if it ever existed."[8]

As varied as the original purposes of the English colonizers of North America had been — economic and spiritual, national and personal, communal and selfish — during the eighteenth century the society of each of the colonies tended to become more like that of contemporary England. The mother country provided, however, no static or stable model. England was in the throes of modernization: agricultural improvement and reorganization of agrarian society; new commercial and financial institutions, including the Bank of England and a national debt; the beginning of the transportation and industrial revolutions; establishment of a regular or standing army; and — on grounds of national interest in an age of imperial wars — executive domination of Parliament, through patronage and "influence" in the hands of a prime minister, instead of the constitutional balance of King, Lords, and Commons established by the Whig Revolution of 1689. It was specifically this modern English political-military-financial complex that the opposition Country coalition of Old Whigs, Tories, and backward-looking radicals denounced as hopelessly corrupt more than a generation before the American Revolution.[9]

The North American colonies were rushing down the same modern road as fast as their more limited opportunities permitted. The population, doubling in every generation through natural increase and immigration, crowded the older seaboard towns and counties and was rapidly filling up the backcountry.[10] Although, by comparison with English tenants and other clients of the great, American proprietors of farms and shops might seem to fulfill the Country ideal of self-sufficient independence, they too were already subject to the remote contingencies of trans-oceanic or at least provincewide trade. And most willing devotees of the capricious Goddess of Commerce they were. In every channel open to them — land speculation; production of tobacco, rice, or wheat for export; coastal and transatlantic shipping; land banks and paper money; even a rudimentary trust for keeping candlemakers' costs down and profits up — colonial Americans sought to develop their corner of the British commercial empire.[11] Neither the homeland nor the colonies had abandoned the principle of public regulation of the economy, but in practice this "mercantilism" was mainly promotional and more an accumulation of *ad hoc* decisions than a coherent system of political economy. What was left of the old social and theological restraints on economic enterprise would have been inadequate even if they had not been weakened by the materialism of the age — and perhaps also, though inadvertently, by the otherworldly individualism of the Great Evangelical Awakening of the 1740s.[12] By the 1760s Americans needed a new system of ideas to harness the dynamism of the emerging modern world almost as much as their English and Scottish cousins did.

What these overseas contemporaries of the yet unpublished Jeremy Bentham and Adam Smith hit upon would surely have been different if the imperial crisis of 1765–1775 had not intruded.[13] If American national independence had been delayed, like that of Canada, Australia, or New Zealand, until there was more of a homegrown social basis for it, the new republic might not have felt impelled to reject outright the political ideas and practices currently prevailing in England — nor to do so in terms borrowed from a very old-fashioned faction of English dissidents. Before 1765 it had been at least as credible to imagine America as someday the center of the British Empire as to prophesy her independence from it; the colonists had not particularly sought to prove their identity as a separate people — certainly not an old-fashioned people, even though European savants liked to think of them as arcadian primitives. Still regarding England as "home" after three or four generations in America, the colonists had thrown themselves into the work of modernization, or Anglicization, as it has been called, without undue nostalgia for a half-mythical golden age.[14]

Had they been able to continue along the same path uninterrupted by the actual Revolution, Americans might eventually have understood their modern condition in terms adequate for dealing with it. The process of modernization, under way in the western world since the end of the Middle Ages, has progressively set the individual free from the traditional primary bonds of church, family, community, and fixed status. Sooner or later, however, it has imposed on him the remote, impersonal, and unpredictable imperatives of a world economy and mass society. The result has been uncertainty and anxiety perhaps oftener than true self-reliance. It has nevertheless been the perennial American dream to attain not only personal independence but through it, somehow, social stability and harmony as well. Other means to the good society, though in practice not entirely excluded, have been most fully accepted when disguised as "democratic" expansion of individual rights.

American reluctance to consider a more realistic range of ways of dealing with modernity owes a great deal to the kind of revolution in which the United States was born. A people familiar with Walpole's politico-financial centralization only through Country denunciations — no comparably systematic "Court" defense had yet been articulated — inevitably handed down to their descendants an ingrained distrust of any similar modern arrogation of power.[15] In 1840, for instance, the common republicanism of all Americans, by compelling the new Whig party to outdemocrat the Democrats, obscured the fact that Whig policy would have been better served by a thoroughly forward-looking, dynamic theory of a progressive republic with a plurality of diverse but regulated, balanced, and interdependent interests — what Alexander Hamilton had earlier hinted at as "a nation of cultivators, artificers, and merchants," of labor and capital, of private enterprise and neomercantilist public policy.[16] A thoroughly modern "American system" of that sort would presumably have been no less concerned to defend civil liberties than the Old Whig liberalism of the Revolution had been, but it would not have been so obsessed by an unattainable standard of civic virtue nor by exaggerated fears of corruption and hopes of reform.

At the time of the Revolution, however, the old-fashioned English ideology that the ineffectual but eloquent Country writers had been expounding for fifty years past, in their "quarrel with modernity," seemed to the rebellious Americans to explain the source of their current troubles precisely.[17] British encroachment on colonial self-government must obviously spring from the notorious Walpolean system of rule by corrupt influence, patronage, and standing armies. Americans easily fell into the pose of the Roman citizen or Saxon freeman, not merely defending private property from arbitrary taxation but rescuing their own civic virtue from the latter-day stew of self-interest into which they had been falling. A struggle thus conceived of as half rebellion, half self-reformation encouraged them to forswear the sordid temptations of material ambition, to overlook their actual dependence on commerce, and to believe that if left alone they would willingly subordinate private interest to the common good. It was gratifying, indeed vital for the cause, to contend that they were only so many self-reliant yet selflessly patriotic citizens, each one "equally free and independent" (in the classic phrase of the Virginia Declaration of Rights of June 1776), no man having "any degree or spark of . . . a right of dominion, government, and jurisdiction over [an]other" (as the Northampton, Massachusetts, town meeting added in 1780).[18] This handily covered over all the actual differences that the accelerated course of development in the eighteenth century had driven among them, distinctions of ethnic origin and religion, political advantage and power, wealth and status — and the self-seeking ways in which the latter had been gained — in all the regional variations from New England and the Middle Colonies to the plantation and backcountry South.

A neoclassical republic, its citizens imbued, as John Adams wrote in 1775, with "a spirit of true virtue and honest independence": such was the ideal of American nationality that the Revolution enshrined, however much they owed their hard-won victory to alliances with European monarchs, British military miscalculation, and their own mixture of patriotism, profiteering, persecution, doggedness, and luck.[19] "Such as we are we have been from the beginning," Joseph Story could still rejoice fifty years after: "simple, hardy, intelligent, accustomed to self-government, and self-respect, . . . never enfeebled by . . . vice or luxuries."[20] It was easy for nineteenth-century Americans to see themselves in the image of the "brave patriotic yeomanry, who, with giant strength, met the invaders of our land, and won our independence."[21]

The farther the classical ideal receded from the dynamic reality of the nineteenth-century American economy, the more Americans liked to think of themselves in its terms. Businessmen who were investing in the vast new mines, factories, banks, and railroads, or who managed them for others, could claim to be defending — especially against regulation by the society that their enterprises were transforming — both the "personal independence" of their employees and the "principle of personal ownership" and control of property just as the embattled farmers of 1775 had done. The multimillionaire John D. Rockefeller did not hesitate, as late as 1907, to attribute his business success to the old yeoman virtues of "economy, thrift, honesty, and perseverance."[22] The farmers of the time, who likewise engaged in commercial production on the largest scale possible to them, bought and sold land itself as a profitable commodity without for a moment giving up their special claim to the yeoman tradition.[23] Even tenant farmers and agricultural and industrial wage laborers, who had figured in classical republican theory as mere dependents, subservient to the will of others, were expected — and usually expected it of themselves — to become independent; until then they should at least behave like autonomous individuals rather than try to get ahead collectively through trade unions or other class-bound combinations. The fact that workingmen, farmers, and businessmen were all caught up in a continental and international economy, shaken by the same blasts of prosperity and depression, caused a good deal of doubt and worry, but as late as the Great Depression of the 1930s few of them were quite free of the nagging feeling that business failure, farm foreclosure, or the loss of a job must be due to some personal deficiency in the virtues expected of citizens of the republic.

In retrospect it may seem astonishing that the classical self-image was not abandoned by the 1830s, fifty years after the Revolution, to say nothing of the 1930s. Instead, it was during that half century between the Revolution and the age of Jacksonian democracy that the old categories of republicanism were stretched to explain away — indeed, to justify — the practical economic and social contradictions in which supposedly hardheaded, pragmatic Americans, then and since, have perpetually found themselves. Unfortunately a set of self-concepts that was already half obsolete, half fanciful when first adopted could so persist only through casual blurring of original distinctions and misapplication of originally compatible ideas to increasingly divergent phenomena.

There had been no theoretical incongruity in 1776 when the Virginia Declaration of Rights associated the equal freedom and independence of the citizen with his "attachment to the community," since personal independence included the "means of acquiring and possessing property"; sufficient property was the sign, in turn, of that "permanent common interest" which merited its owner's participation in public affairs.[24] The freeholder's self-interest thus accorded with "the great object" of government, which, as John Adams was still asserting in 1820 as he had in 1776, was "to render property secure," as "the foundation upon which civilization rests."[25] The man who lacked property to support himself, Adams added, citing Harrington, would be particularly dangerous as a voter because he was "too dependent upon other men to have a will of [his] own. . . . Such is the frailty of the human heart, that very few men who have no property, have any judgment of their own. They talk and vote as they are directed by some man of property, who has attached their minds to his interest."[26] For the same reason, so the Essex County convention of 1778 advised the Massachusetts General Court, correct republican policy denied the vote to other classes of persons who lacked "sufficient discretion" — namely, minors, for their "want of years and experience," and women, because of "the natural tenderness and delicacy of their minds, their retired mode of life, and various domestic duties" — and also to those "so situated as to have no wills of their own," notably slaves.[27] "Dependence," as Thomas Jefferson put it in an oft-quoted letter of 1787, "begets subservience and venality, suffocates the germ of virtue, and prepares fit tools for the designs of ambition."[28] The citizen who could afford independent judgment, on the other hand, could be relied upon to consult the general welfare and to respect his fellow citizens' right to life and liberty as well as to property. Personal independence meant civil attachment, not detachment of private interests. A stake in society involved not merely security for one's property but also a willing sense of personal responsibility to the commonwealth.

Land — *real* estate — was accordingly the preferable stake.

Property of other kinds, as the Northampton town meeting observed in 1780, "is very easily transferred from place to place," so that more than three times as much of it as of land was required, they reckoned, to "attach a man to the State."[29] Fortunately, at least in New England, John Adams noted with republican satisfaction in 1776, there had been from the beginning "a division of land into small quantities, so that the multitude [might] be possessed of landed estates." Maintenance of the old "equal liberty and public virtue" still required making "the acquisition of land easy to every member of society."[30] By the 1820s it was Adams's fellow conservatives, in the last states to adopt universal white male suffrage, who particularly extolled the "independence and discretion" of freeholders in public affairs.[31] Such natural virtue as the propertyless might have, the Whiggish planter Benjamin Watkins Leigh warned the Virginia constitutional convention of 1829, would be corrupted by dependence. The more honest a tenant was, indeed, the more dependent would simple gratitude for his landlord's favors make him: "the landlord holds such a tenant by the very strings of his heart."[32]

However the modern world might change, landownership remained, at the least, the great incentive to civic virtue. Adams in his old age came to doubt that the majority of New Englanders any longer owned enough land for them to be trusted not to "vote us out of our houses."[33] Some younger men were likewise content to retain the freehold qualification for voting, not only because "it was connected with many virtues, which conduced to the good order of society," but in the optimistic expectation (which continued to flourish long after the 1820s) that "in this country, where the means of subsistence were so abundant, and the demand for labor so great, every man of sound body could acquire the necessary qualification. If he failed to do this, it must be, ordinarily, because he was indolent or vicious."[34] Was it not, indeed, because of the property requirement and the practical hope of meeting it that "apprentices, and the sons of poor farmers were induced to lead a life of industry and economy"?[35]

No one disputed the desirability of a population of independent freeholders. In every congressional debate on western land bills from the 1790s to the 1830s there was general agreement that the West "should be compactly settled by honest, respectable yeomanry," as a Virginia congressman said in 1796.[36] "The poorer class of [our] citizens," a North Carolina colleague added, would thereby "be put into a situation in which they might exercise their own will, which they would not be at liberty to do if they were obliged to become tenants to others. To live in that dependent way had a tendency to vitiate and debase their minds, instead of making them free, enlightened, and independent."[37] "Real proprietors," even of small plots, "good Republicans instead of servile tenants," would be attached in the proper way to the government that had provided the opportunity.[38]

Thirty years later Thomas Hart Benton of Missouri, the perennial senatorial champion of the western settler — and the staunchest supporter of hard money and other rusty ideas among Jackson's partisans — took much the same line: "Tenantry is unfavorable to freedom. It lays the foundation for separate orders in society, annihilates the love of country, and weakens the spirit of independence. . . . The freeholder, on the contrary, is the natural supporter of a free government."[39] If landowning made possible the independent exercise of civic virtue, did not the virtuous citizen deserve land of his own? The "integrity, fair dealing, courage, generosity, and hospitality" of the western pioneers should be supported, Benton argued, by setting the price of public land as low as possible.[40] No matter how poor, such men were "the best of citizens . . . brave, hospitable, patriotic, and industrious, living upon their own labor, and that labor the primeval occupation of man and the first command of God."[41] Benton invoked the Gracchi and the Licinian law in good Country style; the Roman republic having given land to the ordinary man, "it was this interest in the soil of their country, which made the love of that country so strong a passion in the breast of the Roman citizen."[42]

Corrupt attachment to government was, on the other hand, as objectionable as ever. Thus the Jeffersonian and Jacksonian argument against a national debt and the Bank of the United States closely resembled the Country case, a century before, against governmental collusion with moneyed monopoly in England. It took considerable ingenuity, however, to detect comparably Walpolean kinds of corruption of the virtue of the ordinary citizen and voter. In 1820, pressing his bill to offer low prices and small tracts to land purchasers instead of the four-year payment plan on which many of them had defaulted in the current hard times, Representative George Robertson of Kentucky argued that "the relation of creditor and debtor ought not to exist between the Government and the people. It begets obligations, and interests, and feelings, incompatible with the genius of free institutions." In England the national debt might now be accounted a public blessing and the bulwark of the constitution, Robertson conceded, since it was in the interest of security holders, "the opulent and the influential," to maintain a stable government. But even there, if government were somehow to become not debtor but creditor — the relationship in which the federal government stood to land purchasers — then "who would preserve the Government from revolution?" If the United States persisted in keeping thousands of Westerners "in a state of dependency and tenancy," Robertson warned, the likely result would be armed resistance, anarchy, and sectional disunion.[43] Benton similarly belabored the federal government as a corrupt monopolist and "petty landlord" for its policy of leasing mineral rights on public land rather than selling outright. Much as in the unreformed politics of England, he darkly intimated, elections around the lead mines and saline springs of Missouri were "more or less influenced by the presence of men holding their leases at the will of the Federal Government."[44]

Even as old-fashioned a republican as Benton was beginning, however, to see in quite different kinds of enterprise the social benefits classically associated with landed property. What he had heard of English mining experience demonstrated to his satisfaction that the independence that was good for the farmer was good also for the entrepreneur and for the greater prosperity of the republic. Instead of being held under the vassalage of the federal leasing system, mining should be turned over "to the pursuit of individual industry, to the activity of individual enterprise, to the care of individual interest. . . . *Without a freehold in the soil,* . . . the riches of the mineral kingdom can never be discovered or brought into action."[45]

Such blurring of the republican distinction between land and modern industrial property was more characteristic, however, of the Whig opposition that coalesced in the 1830s. As they made the new sort of enterprise respectable, on the one hand, they raised doubts, on the other, whether land necessarily instilled civic virtue in its owner. Of course Whiggish opponents of Benton's periodic bills, in the 1820s and 1830s, for downward "graduation" of the minimum price for unsold, "refuse" land professed to share his classical desire to establish independent freeholders in the West. They feared, however, that overly rapid settlement would open the door to speculators and turn the farmers who went west into "large masses of laboring tenants, . . . the menials of some wealthy landlord, who fattens on the spoils of the industry and hard earnings of this valuable class of our citizens."[46] As for Benton's "refuse land" — evidently not the "Garden of the World" usually extolled by Democrats — was it good enough, after all, for "propagating the principles of equality, independence, and republicanism"?[47]

One obstacle in the path of admitting nonlanded property to the republican canon was the classical idea that the immovability of real estate — at least of the right sort — was what ensured its owner's firm attachment to the community. Owners of other kinds of property, no matter how rich, could always escape the threat of despotism by fleeing the country with their money and goods, Joseph Story observed in 1820: "But the hardy yeoman, the owner of a few acres of the soil, and supported by it, cannot leave his home without becoming a wanderer on the face of the earth. In the preservation of property and virtue, he has, therefore, the deepest and most permanent interest."[48] On that Southerners and New Englanders could agree. "That stout and generous yeomanry, the freeholders of this land," as Leigh put it, "are the only persons who have any stake that may not be withdrawn at pleasure, in the twinkling of an eye," to another county or state, as owners of personal property — "money, Bank stock, stock in the public funds" — all too easily could do. In the Virginia of 1829, he noted, such movables often included slaves, who "are more valuable in the South Western States than here."[49]

It was well enough for such conservatives to applaud the colonists for having made it easy for the virtuous to become settled freeholders, but Leigh's further argument that "any honest industrious citizen" could buy the required freehold for fifty dollars, and in some places for as little as five, amounted to conceding that real estate was no longer a fixed stake.[50] "Does not this interest in the soil pass from hand to hand?" a colleague asked; "is it not actually changing every day and hour?"[51] The fact that in the nineteenth-century land market a farm was apt to be a speculative investment for mere profit rather than the base for steady attachment to the community could hardly be denied.

By the 1830s eastern opponents of the western land rush made bold to doubt that freeholders any longer had a common interest to attach themselves to. The severing of old ties by migration appeared to be throwing individuals, property owners along with the rest, into "a violent, disorderly, and immoral mass" to which only time could "gradually give union and coherence."[52] Some congressmen were impatient with Bentonian "eloquence on the high virtues of squatters" and with their claim to "the peculiar favor of the Government." This "idle, profligate set of men, . . . their heads full of all sorts of schemes for living without profitable labor," were said to "perform no civil duties, and discharge none of the obligations of society, . . . [to] violate the laws, trespass upon the public property, and treat the authority of the Government with habitual contempt," all the while vilifying the honest land purchaser as an "avaricious speculator."[53]

Perhaps, on reflection, a lack of classical virtue was no new thing in the West. Looking back, in 1833, to the Kentucky of his youth, Henry Clay professed to be virtually unable to "recollect a single individual, or the descendents of any individual, who had remained on the lands which they had originally settled." Instead the first settlers had all along been the real speculators, driving up the price of land to those who came later.[54] "The value of the property of the yeomen of the country," who were still "decidedly the most important class in the community," might actually be damaged by a cheap-land policy, the more so because their spirit of independence, in all other instances most desirable, made them peculiarly "unable or unwilling" to combine for their own protection.[55] An overliberal policy might destroy the classical base for liberty.

The shifting sands that some, realistically enough, now detected beneath modern landownership had been thought by Country theorists to be the characteristic defect of commercial and financial property. Since modern merchants and bankers dealt in ephemeral goods and suppositious credit, the value of which depended on the government's ability to fund the public debt, they would be willing tools of politicians scheming to pay for their military ventures by taxing the solid estates of independent landed gentlemen and freeholders. The fluctuations of the market, as Jefferson noted in 1787, made merchants and even master artisans politically unreliable. Although they owned shops and countinghouses, they were too dependent "on the casualties and caprice of customers" to be as safe from "corruption of morals" as self-sufficient farmers could afford to be.[56]

There is more than one conceivable way in which spokesmen for the next generation of American merchants and bankers might have replied. One, which they did not take, would have been to concede the mutability of modern property of all kinds — goods, services, and public and private credit as well as land — which would at least have accorded with nineteenth-century reality, east and west, north and south, and could have been suitably expressed in the Romantic terms of boundless nature and human free will that were beginning to filter across from Europe. Instead they were content to claim the old-fashioned, fixed virtues of civic attachment and personal independence for merchants and, in effect, for property owners of other kinds to which they had become accustomed before the Revolution. Even land speculation, which it was still customary to denounce "as if it were a crime," a midwestern Whig senator ventured to say during the land boom of the mid-1830s, was simply another field for "the investment of accumulated capital" by the "industrious, enterprising, and intelligent"; senators who conjured up specters of landed aristocracy and dependent tenantry in the West seemed to think, he remarked, that wealth gained from business was less praiseworthy than poverty — which in reality was "too often the result of indolence and intemperance."[57] A few years later even a last-ditch opponent of universal suffrage could casually lump together "the independent yeomanry and men of business" as equally incorruptible exponents of the "democratic principles" of the republic.[58]

But while Jefferson's classical doubts about the civic virtue of merchants were being forgotten, his parallel wish never "to see our citizens occupied at a work-bench" in modern factories was not.[59] In a city like New York, the new mercantile conservatives now agreed, it was not they who were subject to the "caprice" of circumstance but rather "the motley assemblage of paupers, emigrants, journeymen manufacturers, . . . the poor and the profligate," who too easily became pawns of a new, demagogic set of political masters seeking to plunder and "control the affluent."[60] The only kind of property that still seemed a threat to republican virtue was the new industrial property, mainly because of the civic unreliability of its turbulent, dependent employees.

Once again, the pure Country theory was expressed only by Federalists and a few Old Republicans of the backward-looking sort. Since Jefferson's partisans were in power when the onset of the War of 1812 created a need for American manufactures, most of them now worried less about the theoretical capriciousness of dependent factory hands than about what the labor of such citizens could contribute to preserving the independence of the republic itself.[61] It was a Federalist antiwar congressman who still objected in 1810 that "you would never look to men and boys in workshops for that virtue and spirit in defence that you would justly expect from the yeomanry of the country."[62] So too Daniel Webster, as yet the champion of the old New England merchants rather than the new industrialists, announced himself "not in haste to see Sheffields and Birminghams in America," since, as he warned during the war, "habits favorable to good morals and free Governments" were unlikely to be formed in such places. Updating a republican idea as old as Aristotle, Webster observed that the factory hand was "necessarily at the mercy of the capitalist for the support of himself and family," because the modern technique of subdivision of labor left him "utterly incapable of making and carrying to the market on his own account the smallest entire article."[63] Such laborers, Webster was still asserting in 1820, "have no stake in society; they hang loose upon it, and are often neither happy in their own condition, nor without danger to the State."[64]

The new danger of anarchy from below, in eastern factory towns as on the western frontier, could be made to seem the same as the earlier threat from above of an oligarchy of wealth and power. Opponents of industrialization as well as of equal suffrage or cheap land reiterated the classical dictum that tenants and wage laborers alike were subject to the "whim and caprice," and for that matter the economic success or failure, of their landlords or employers.[65] "The whole body of every manufacturing establishment," Josiah Quincy advised the Massachusetts convention of 1820, "are dead votes, counted by the head, by their employer."[66] In New York State, Chancellor James Kent warned that "one master capitalist, with his one hundred apprentices, and journeymen, and agents, and dependents, will bear down at the polls, an equal number of farmers of small estates in his vicinity, who cannot safely unite for their common defence. Large manufacturing and mechanical establishments, can act in an instant with the unity and efficacy of disciplined troops."[67] In these classical terms democratization of the suffrage was arguably "one of the most aristocratic acts that has ever been recorded in this state. It will be turning over the votes of a great portion of manufacturers — day-labourers, poor mechanics, &c. into the hands of the rich man who feeds and employs them. It is not necessary that either force or corruption should be used; but the influence which the employer possesses, arising from the dependence of him who seeks to be employed, is sufficient to prostrate our republican institutions, and to raise up a deplorable aristocracy in our state."[68] Suffrage reformers would concede only that the old argument still applied to the free but "degraded" Negroes, "a peculiar people, unacquainted with civil liberty, and incapable of appreciating its benefits," whose "vote would be at the call of the richest purchaser."[69] The inveterate democrat Matthew Lyon, businessman and congressman first from Vermont and in 1810 from Kentucky, even proposed that the southern slaves would make ideal factory hands, since "no country can boast of a more abject, degraded set of people . . . nor a class more fitted to do all the drudgery of manufactures than our blacks."[70]

Democrats and industrial promoters joined, however, in defending from such old-fashioned republican suspicions of oligarchy the civic virtue of the new factory owners and their white male employees alike. In the New York constitutional convention of 1821 Martin Van Buren called for political equality for useful citizens of every sort, "mechanics — professional men — and small land holders, . . . the bone, muscle, and marrow of the population," who, even though some of them owned considerable personal property, had been excluded (by a $250 real-estate requirement) from voting for state senators. Why in particular, Van Buren asked, should anyone suppose that a factory owner, a man of property himself — including, for that matter, some real estate — would wish to march his so-called dependents to the polls for the sake of attacking the interests of other men of property?[71] Supposing it were true that "the rich control the votes of the poor," a fellow reformer added, "the result cannot be unfavourable to the security of property."[72] Property was property.

"Free-born" American laborers, for their part, might reasonably be conceded to be the equals of other citizens in republican virtue since, as the protectionist Mathew Carey observed in 1820, they too had a kind of patrimony, or property interest, in "the labour of their hands."[73] Jeffersonians too could grant the possibility, as early as the 1790s, that factory operatives had their share of natural virtue; although not "the class of citizens who provided at once their own food and their own raiment," they might nevertheless be relied upon to uphold "public liberty" and "public safety."[74] As for reports of "debaucheries and intemperance" in Birmingham or Sheffield, the Philadelphia scientist, statistician, and Democratic congressman Adam Seybert attributed them, in 1810, to "the want of prudence and . . . virtue" to be found among some men anywhere, "whether they are manufacturers or not."[75] Certainly men "who support their families reputably with their daily earnings" had as much "regard for country" as anyone, a Boston advocate of their right to vote asserted in 1820. The act of voting itself inculcated the very same civic virtue that had been held to qualify a man to vote. "The principle of character and independence which a man feels in exercising the privilege of a freeman" would be an even stronger safeguard for property than the ambition to own a freehold and would prevent the growth of a rebellious class of "Lazaroni" when Americans eventually became a great manufacturing people.[76] Not wage labor or poverty but lack of education made a man "liable to be imposed upon, misled, betrayed, and ruined," the *Lowell Journal* maintained in 1827. A proper republican schooling would be enough to sustain "good morals and virtuous sentiments, . . . general intelligence and political stability," in the "patriotick citizen."[77]

In the 1790s, before the industrial age was well begun in America, it could be credibly argued that the citizen would not be corrupted by factory labor because he would not be the one who did it, except perhaps as a sideline. Alexander Hamilton supposed that factories would positively enhance the self-sufficiency of farmers and other "industrious individuals and families" by "afford[ing] occasional and extra employment" in their off-seasons.[78] Actually it was more likely that the supplemental income that many farm families were already getting at home from spare-time weaving or shoemaking would be undercut by the new machinery, and those who gave up and went into the mills ceased to be farmers at all. The commonest prediction, however, was that the factory labor force would consist mainly, not of men, but of women and children, who had never been expected to be independent and "who otherwise would have little or nothing to do." Besides being rescued from debilitating idleness, they could acquire at least some of the virtues that made men independent: "In order that a community may be flourishing a vein of industry must run through the whole; all should be engaged in business useful to themselves and to the public. It is not enough that one half of the community be employed. Not only men, but women and children ought to be industrious."[79] Already, in 1791, it was cheerfully reported from Providence that child cardmakers "are prevented from contracting bad Habits, and are introduced thereby to a Habit of Industry, — by which we may hope to see them become useful Members of Society."[80] Thirty years later the need for such lessons still seemed evident to Henry Clay, as he surveyed "the crowds of little boys and girls who infest this Capitol, and assail us every day, at its very doors, . . . begging for a cent"; was not "constant occupation . . . the best security for innocence and virtue"?[81] The cotton mills of the 1820s delighted Clay with the "clock-work regularity" that they instilled in their working women and children.[82]

As it turned out, of course, men also worked in factories, but arguably at no loss to "virtue and happiness" if, as it appeared at the Waltham Mills in 1827, "their fixed position and regular profits" helped make morality at these "well-conducted manufacturing establishments" superior to that of most commercial and even farming centers, not to mention the colleges. The proof advanced for this moral superiority was, however, rather novel: "Among the several hundred persons of both sexes, mostly young, who have been employed there for ten or fifteen years, a single instance only of irregular intercourse had been discovered. Intemperance and vices punishable by law were unheard of."[83] The one instance was a mill girl accused of breaking the rule against being "found in the company of a male at an unseasonable hour." Although she pleaded her innocence, the accusation was enough to oblige the superintendent to fire her.[84] The classical civic virtues were being recast into a proto-Victorian code of personal behavior.

And not only for dependent women and children: the manly virtues of the republican citizen were practically narrowed down to the hard work, saving, and reinvestment that were supposed to be the best means for individual success and for the economic progress of the country. Idleness was the great danger to the republic, so Tench Coxe, the Hamiltonian promoter turned Jeffersonian, asserted in 1804. It was "the only evil that can be brought upon a State by the citizens: for it brings in its train, poverty, ignorance and discontent, the parents of sedition, tumult and civil war."[85] Andrew Jackson enunciated the positive side of the doctrine in praising, in his Bank veto message of 1832, "those habits of economy and simplicity which are so congenial to the character of republicans."[86] The same "industry and economy, . . . added to good sense, perseverance and the moral virtues," accounted for the enormous success of a millionaire merchant and banker like Stephen Girard, so it was commonly said after his death in 1831.[87] Nor were ordinary men dissatisfied that the lifelong practice of those virtues profited them far less. The farm laborer or tenant who just managed to become a small landowner, or the factory hand who, by dint of the constant toil of his wife and children as well as his own, penuriously scraped together enough to buy a house or a rundown farm, felt he too had won the personal independence celebrated by the Revolutionary tradition.[88] In the eyes of European immigrants that modest prospect, and not streets paved with gold, remained the perennial lure of America.[89]

The "attachment to liberty" that old-fashioned republicans prized could be demonstrated, the nineteenth century was coming to believe, in many ways.[90] A man could put his civic virtue to work in any honest occupation or enterprise in order to acquire property and advance the general welfare of the community. Thus the petition of the "Non-Freeholders of the City of Richmond," in 1829, denied that they were "destitute of interest, or unworthy of a voice," in the common good. Although they were "engaged in avocations of a different nature" from farming, these were "often as useful, pre-supposing no less integrity, requiring as much intelligence, and as fixed a residence." It would be "by no means easy or convenient," they went on, to withdraw from their own businesses or "from the support of their families" the price of the freehold still required for voting in Virginia; in any event, mere "attachment to property, often a sordid sentiment, is not to be confounded with the sacred flame of patriotism." With or without a freehold, the "free and independent" citizen, they concluded in the traditional words of the Virginia

Declaration of Rights, had his "common interest with, and attachment to, the community."[91]

No doubt it was highly unrealistic, in an age when property had become "pre-eminently a dynamic, not a static institution," to imagine that a mere shopkeeper, householder, marginal farmer, or wage laborer — or even an industrial entrepreneur — enjoyed the same self-sufficiency, the independence from economic pressures, and the ideal civic virtue that Country ideologues and Revolutionary patriots had attributed to the classic freeholder.[92] But the residue of the tradition defied the very reality it was used to defend. As late as the 1870s, and even after, when it had become patently foolish to suppose that industrial magnates were simply the most successful practitioners of antique republican virtue, a little flurry of "liberal" reform — and a spell of high wages and farm prices — usually sufficed to renew the faith that both private success and national prosperity flowed from simple hard work and self-denial.

Few by that time were aware of how completely those personal virtues had been detached from their old republican context. The Revolutionary generation had not simplemindedly supposed that material success was the gauge of civic virtue. "How many young men Neither Profligates nor idle persons," the town meeting of Mansfield, Massachusetts, asked back in 1780, "how many sensable, honest, and naturly Industerouss men, by Numberless Misfortins Never Acquire and possess propperty . . . ?"[93] Those who did, conservatives were still saying in the 1820s, were distinguished for their sense of "moderation" and "order," a "freedom from excessive ambition," as well as for "habits of industry" and other more active virtues.[94] But among the forward-looking of the nineteenth century, sheer personal ambition could quite credibly parade in old-fashioned patriotic guise.

Although the Revolutionary ideal of personal independence was now even more anachronistic than in 1776, to believe in it afforded the gratification of seeming to live by an older and far more honorific standard of individual rights than the laissez-faire theories of the Manchester economists. Of course Americans learned, by the 1830s, to cite these novel English doctrines when convenient. They had no need, however, of any invisible hand of "free trade" in order to transmute self-interest, as a mere private vice, into public benefits. To devote their own hands to work and accumulation, with a measure of after-the-fact philanthropy, seemed to them to be no vice at all but the very essence of civic virtue. The common speech of the time associated "vice and idleness," "idleness and vice," "vice and profligacy" as inherently unrepublican behavior.[95] The farther into the past the Revolution receded, the stronger grew the impression that free enterprise was the heart of the republican ethic that dated from the Declaration of Independence.[96]

Free enterprise — a category stretched, between the 1830s and 1850s, to include the publicly chartered business corporation — thus fell heir to the mantle of the classical republican citizen.[97] Just as the independent freeholder's landed estate had been supposed to attach his interests to the commonwealth, so the new entrepreneurial fortunes were seen as investment in the general welfare. From time to time, regrettably, the triumphant progress of the modern republic was interrupted by cycles of business depression and of such corruption as the peculations of the henchmen of President Grant or Mayor Tweed in the 1870s. Virtuous reformers could be expected to stamp out corruption, however, as surely as good times always followed bad.

But the much longer cycle that America ran in the course of the nineteenth century was far more destructive — a downward cycle of the nearly forgotten sort once prophesied for the republic of virtue by Country theorists and feared by the Founding Fathers. The anarchy and oligarchy that it produced were more insidious than any in ancient Rome or the England of Walpole, because the engine of change was the republican ideal itself. Long before the United States reached its centennial celebrations the "equally free and independent" citizen of 1776 had indeed been corrupted into what in 1876 was just beginning to be recognized as the modern embodiment of both those classical specters: the entrepreneur set free, by the American dream of virtuous independence, to dominate a society grown so narrowly acquisitive that it could only admire his success. Given the anachronism of the original ideal, the prophecy of fundamental corruption had been self-fulfilling. Should individualistic anarchy and corporate oligarchy someday proceed to the final stage of tyranny, Americans would have reason to believe their modern tyrant when he proclaimed his election simply the realization of the dream that had made America great.

Notes

1. George Richards Minot, *The History of the Insurrections in Massachusetts, in the Year MDCCLXXXVI, and the Rebellion Consequent Thereon* (Worcester, 1788), p. 12.
2. J. G. A. Pocock, *The Machiavellian Moment: Florentine Political Thought and the Atlantic Republican Tradition* (Princeton: Princeton University Press, 1975); Bernard Bailyn, *The Ideological Origins of the American Revolution* (Cambridge, Mass.: Harvard University Press, 1967).
3. Henry Adams, *The Life of Albert Gallatin* (Philadelphia, 1879), p. 362.
4. Marvin Meyers, *The Jacksonian Persuasion: Politics and Belief* (Stanford: Stanford University Press, 1957), p. 15.
5. Eric Foner, *Free Soil, Free Labor, Free Men: The Ideology of the Republican Party before the Civil War* (New York: Oxford University Press, 1970), pp. 11–33.
6. Major L. Wilson, "The Free Soil Concept of Progress and the Irrepressible Conflict," *American Quarterly*, XXII (1970), 770.
7. David Montgomery, *Beyond Equality: Labor and the Radical Republicans, 1862–1872* (New York: Knopf, 1967), pp. 73, 302–334, 379–380.
8. Gordon S. Wood, *The Creation of the American Republic, 1776–1787* (Chapel Hill: University of North Carolina Press, 1969), pp. 53–54, 59. Cf. Robert E. Shalhope, "Toward a Republican Synthesis," *William and Mary Quarterly*, 3rd ser., XXIX (1972), 49–80.
9. Isaac Kramnick, *Bolingbroke and His Circle: The Politics of Nostalgia in the Age of Walpole* (Cambridge, Mass.: Harvard University Press, 1968).
10. Philip J. Greven, Jr., *Four Generations: Population, Land, and Family in Colonial Andover, Massachusetts* (Ithaca: Cornell University Press, 1970); Kenneth A. Lockridge, *A New England Town, the First Hundred Years: Dedham, Massachusetts, 1636–1736* (New York: Norton, 1970).
11. Rowland Berthoff, *An Unsettled People: Social Order and Disorder in American History* (New York: Harper and Row, 1971), chs. 2–4; James B. Hedges, *The Browns of Providence Plantations: Colonial Years* (Cambridge, Mass.: Harvard University Press, 1952), pp. 94–112.
12. Richard L. Bushman, *From Puritan to Yankee: Character and the Social Order in Connecticut, 1690–1765* (Cambridge, Mass.: Harvard University Press, 1967); J. E. Crowley, *This Sheba, Self: The Conceptualization of Economic Life in Eighteenth-Century America* (Baltimore: Johns Hopkins University Press, 1974).
13. Unpublished, that is, as modern political economists: both Smith's *Wealth of Nations* and Bentham's *Fragment on Government* appeared in 1776, too late, despite the coincidence, to affect the resolution of American republicanism.
14. John M. Murrin, "Anglicization and Identity: The Colonial Experience, the Revolution, and the Dilemma of American Nationalism," paper read at meeting of Organization of American Historians, 1974.
15. Pocock, *Machiavellian Moment*, pp. 487–488.
16. Harold C. Syrett, ed., *The Papers of Alexander Hamilton* (New York: Columbia University Press, 1961–), X, 256. Cf. Robert L. Meriwether, ed., *The Papers of John C. Calhoun*

(Columbia: University of South Carolina Press, 1959–), I, 354–355; Daniel Webster, *Writings and Speeches* (Boston, 1903), XIII, 14. It seems significant that even James Madison's more limited pluralism, in the tenth *Federalist* paper, was not much recognized or appreciated until the twentieth century. See Douglass Adair, "The Tenth *Federalist* Revisited," *William and Mary Quarterly*, 3rd ser., VIII (1951), 48–67.

17. Pocock, *Machiavellian Moment*, p. 546.
18. Samuel Eliot Morison, ed., *Sources and Documents Illustrating the American Revolution, 1764–1788, and the Formation of the Constitution* (New York: Oxford University Press, 1929), p. 149; Oscar Handlin and Mary F. Handlin, eds., *The Popular Sources of Political Authority: Documents on the Massachusetts Constitution of 1780* (Cambridge, Mass.: Harvard University Press, 1966), pp. 580–581. The simpler "all men are created equal" of the Declaration of Independence and its separate mention of "life, liberty, and the pursuit of happiness" seem to have obscured the classical republican point that equality consisted in the liberty or independence of the citizen, not in any leveling of wealth or social status.
19. John R. Howe, Jr., *The Changing Political Thought of John Adams* (Princeton: Princeton University Press, 1966), p. 39.
20. *Bunker-Hill Aurora* (Boston), Dec. 6, 1828. I am indebted for this and the following reference to Judith Barry Wish, whose doctoral dissertation, "From Yeoman Farmer to Industrious Producer: The Relationship between Classical Republicanism and the Development of Manufacturing in America from the Revolution to 1850" (Washington University, 1976), expands on several of these same themes.
21. *New-England Farmer* (Boston), Jan. 20, 1826.
22. Rowland Berthoff, "The 'Freedom to Control' in American Business History," in David H. Pinckney and Theodore Ropp, eds., *A Festschrift for Frederick B. Artz* (Durham: Duke University Press, 1964), pp. 158, 179; Irvin G. Wyllie, *The Self-Made Man in America: The Myth of Rags to Riches* (New Brunswick: Rutgers University Press, 1954), p. 166.
23. Richard Hofstadter, *The Age of Reform: From Bryan to F.D.R.* (New York: Knopf, 1955), pp. 23–26, 62.
24. Morison, *Sources and Documents*, p. 149.
25. *Journal of Debates and Proceedings in the Convention of Delegates, Chosen to Revise the Constitution of Massachusetts, 1820–1821* (Boston, 1853), p. 278.
26. Charles Francis Adams, ed., *The Works of John Adams* (Boston, 1850–1856), IX, 376.
27. The existence of slavery was thus not simply an embarrassing anomaly in the new republic of liberty and equality; exclusion of slaves and other servile classes from equal citizenship was basic to republican theory. "Are slaves members of a free government? We feel the absurdity. . . ." "The Essex Result," in Handlin and Handlin, *Popular Sources*, pp. 340–341.
28. Thomas Jefferson, *Notes on the State of Virginia*, edited by William Peden (Chapel Hill: University of North Carolina Press, 1954), p. 165.
29. That is, either "two hundred pounds value in all estate" or "a freehold . . . of the annual income of three pounds," as qualification for voting for state senators. The proposed state constitution had not, however, made this distinction. Handlin and Handlin, *Popular Sources*, p. 575.
30. Adams, *Works*, IX, 376–377. Cf. *Journal of Convention of Massachusetts*, pp. 309–310 (Daniel Webster).
31. L. H. Clarke, *Report of the Debates and Proceedings of the Convention of the State of New-York* (New York, 1821), pp. 138 (John Duer), 144 (Ambrose Spencer).
32. *Proceedings and Debates of the Virginia State Convention of 1829–1830* (Richmond, 1830), p. 396.
33. *Journal of Convention of Massachusetts*, p. 278.
34. *Ibid.*, p. 247 (Warren Dutton). Cf. Clarke, *Report of Convention of New-York*, p. 13 (John Duer).
35. *Journal of Convention of Massachusetts*, p. 248 (Samuel Hoar, Jr.).
36. Rep. Robert Rutherford, *Annals of the Congress of the United States*, 4 Cong., 1 sess., p. 414, Mar. 3, 1796. See Mary E. Young, "Congress Looks West: Liberal Ideology and

Public Land Policy in the Nineteenth Century," in David M. Ellis, ed., *The Frontier in American Development: Essays in Honor of Paul Wallace Gates* (Ithaca: Cornell University Press, 1969), pp. 105–106, 110–112.

37. Rep. James Holland (Anti-Fed., N.C.), *Annals of Congress*, 4 Cong., 1 sess., p. 858, Apr. 5, 1796.
38. Rep. Jeremiah Crabb (Dem.-Rep., Md.), *ibid.*, p. 861, Apr. 5, 1796.
39. *Register of Debates in Congress*, 19 Cong., 1 sess., p. 727, May 16, 1826.
40. *Ibid.*, 20 Cong., 1 sess., IV, 625, Apr. 9, 1828.
41. *Congressional Globe*, 25 Cong., 2 sess., App., p. 143, Jan. 17, 1838.
42. *Register of Debates in Congress*, 20 Cong., 1 sess., IV, 624, Apr. 9, 1828.
43. *Annals of Congress*, 16 Cong., 1 sess., pp. 1872–1873, Apr. 18, 1820.
44. *Ibid.*, 17 Cong., 2 sess., p. 240, Feb. 14, 1823.
45. *Ibid.*, p. 241, Feb. 14, 1823 (emphasis added).
46. Sen. George Poindexter (Dem., Miss.), *Register of Debates in Congress*, 22 Cong., 2 sess., IX, 141, Jan. 19, 1833.
47. Sen. David Barton (Mo.), *ibid.*, 19 Cong., 2 sess., p. 42, Jan. 9, 1827; Sen. Samuel Foot (Conn.), *ibid.*, 21 Cong., 1 sess., VI, 442, May 20, 1830.
48. *Journal of Convention of Massachusetts*, p. 286.
49. *Virginia State Convention*, pp. 399–400.
50. *Ibid.*, p. 402.
51. *Ibid.*, p. 437 (P. P. Barbour).
52. Sen. Thomas Ewing (Whig, Ohio), *Register of Debates in Congress*, 22 Cong., 2 sess., IX, 169, Jan. 21, 1833.
53. Sen. John P. King (Dem., Ga.), *ibid.*, 24 Cong., 2 sess., vol. XIII, pt. 1, p. 657, Jan. 31, 1837.
54. *Ibid.*, 22 Cong., 2 sess., IX, 78, Jan. 7, 1833.
55. Sen. Committee on Manufactures, "Report on the Public Lands," *ibid.*, 1 sess., vol. VIII, pt. 3, App., p. 114, Apr. 6, 1832.
56. Jefferson, *Notes on Virginia*, p. 165.
57. Sen. Thomas Ewing (Whig, Ohio), *Register of Debates in Congress*, 24 Cong., 2 sess., vol. XIII, pt. 1, pp. 536–539, Jan. 24, 1837. Cf. Sen. Robert J. Walker (Dem., Miss.), *ibid.*, 420, Jan. 14, 1837.
58. Samuel Jones, *A Treatise on the Right of Suffrage* (Boston, 1842), p. 27.
59. Jefferson, *Notes on Virginia*, p. 165.
60. Clarke, *Report of Convention of New-York*, pp. 115–116 (James Kent).
61. See Wish, "From Yeoman Farmer to Industrious Producer," ch. 3.
62. Rep. Philip Barton Key (Fed., Md.), *Annals of Congress*, 11 Cong., 2 sess., p. 1906, Apr. 18, 1810.
63. *Ibid.*, 13 Cong., 2 sess., p. 1972, Apr. 6, 1814. See J. G. A. Pocock, *Politics, Language and Time: Essays on Political Thought and History* (New York: Atheneum, 1971), p. 93.
64. Webster, *Writings and Speeches*, XIII, 18.
65. Sen. Felix Grundy (Dem., Tenn.), *Register of Debates in Congress*, 22 Cong., 2 sess., IX, 117, Jan. 17, 1833.
66. *Journal of Convention of Massachusetts*, p. 251.
67. Merrill O. Peterson, *Democracy, Liberty, and Property* (Indianapolis: Bobbs-Merrill, 1966), p. 196.
68. Clarke, *Report of Convention of New-York*, p. 104 (Ambrose Spencer).
69. *Ibid.*, pp. 98 (John Z. Ross), 101 (Samuel Young).
70. *Annals of Congress*, 11 Cong., 2 sess., p. 1901, Apr. 18, 1810.
71. Clarke, *Report of Convention of New-York*, pp. 130, 134.
72. *Ibid.*, p. 125 (David Buel).
73. *Three Letters on the Present Calamitous State of Affairs* (Philadelphia, 1820), p. 34.
74. *National Gazette* (Philadelphia), Mar. 5, 1792, quoted in Wish, "From Yeoman Farmer to Industrious Producer," p. 51.
75. *Annals of Congress*, 11 Cong., 2 sess., p. 1895, Apr. 18, 1810.
76. *Journal of Convention of Massachusetts*, pp. 252–253 (James T. Austin).
77. *Lowell Journal*, May 4, 1827. I am indebted for this reference to Judith Barry Wish.

78. Syrett, *Papers of Alexander Hamilton*, X, 253.
79. *American Museum* (Philadelphia), VII (Jan. 1790), 25, quoted in Wish, "From Yeoman Farmer to Industrious Producer," p. 53.
80. Arthur Harrison Cole, ed., *Industrial and Commercial Correspondence of Alexander Hamilton Anticipating His Report on Manufactures* (New York: McGraw-Hill, 1928), p. 85.
81. James F. Hopkins, ed., *The Papers of Henry Clay* (Lexington: University of Kentucky Press, 1959–), II, 830.
82. *Ibid.* V, 467. Hamilton had foreseen, quite realistically, that foreign immigrants could also be hired for factory work "on reasonable terms in countries where labor is cheap." Presumably they too would learn the virtue of industry without compromising the independence of American-born citizens. See Cole, *Industrial and Commercial Correspondence*, p. 162.
83. [Alexander Hill Everett], *America, or a General Survey of the Political Situation of the Several Powers of the Western Continent, with Conjectures on Their Future Prospects* (Philadelphia, 1827), pp. 160–161.
84. *American Traveller* (Boston), Aug. 8, 1826, quoted in Wish, "From Yeoman Farmer to Industrious Producer," p. 168.
85. *An Essay on the Manufacturing Interest of the United States* (Philadelphia, 1804), p. 5.
86. Meyers, *Jacksonian Persuasion*, p. 15.
87. Sigmund Diamond, *The Reputation of the American Businessman* (Cambridge, Mass.: Harvard University Press, 1955), p. 7.
88. Merle Curti, *The Making of an American Community: A Case Study of Democracy in a Frontier County* (Stanford: Stanford University Press, 1959), chs. 7–8; Stephan Thernstrom, *Poverty and Progress: Social Mobility in a Nineteenth Century City* (Cambridge, Mass.: Harvard University Press, 1964), chs. 3–6.
89. Charlotte Erickson, *Invisible Immigrants: The Adaptation of English and Scottish Immigrants in Nineteenth-Century America* (Coral Gables: University of Miami Press, 1972), pp. 27–28.
90. Clarke, *Report of Convention of New-York*, p. 139 (John Duer).
91. *Virginia State Convention*, pp. 26, 27, 29.
92. James Willard Hurst, *Law and the Conditions of Freedom in the Nineteenth-Century United States* (Madison: University of Wisconsin Press, 1956), 10.
93. Handlin and Handlin, *Popular Sources*, p. 520.
94. James Kent, quoted in Peterson, *Democracy, Liberty, and Property*, p. 193; *New-England Farmer* (Boston), Jan. 20, 1826. I am indebted for the latter reference to Judith Barry Wish.
95. E.g., Clarke, *Report of Convention of New-York*, p. 138 (John Duer); Hopkins, *Papers of Henry Clay*, III, 718; Thomas Hart Benton (Dem., Mo.), *Register of Debates in Congress*, 21 Cong., I sess., VI, 407, Mar. 3, 1830.
96. It seems clear that the operative principles of nineteenth-century America did not stem from either laissez-faire economics, a specifically Protestant social ethic, Romantic ideas of nature and human will, or even a pragmatic aversion to all theories (as historians have variously argued). Classical republicanism — of which the "agrarian myth" was only the most obvious facet — provided the definitive ideas, as a lasting legacy of the American Revolution. See Pocock, *Machiavellian Moment*, pp. 526–546.
97. Oscar Handlin and Mary Flug Handlin, *Commonwealth: A Study of the Role of Government in the American Economy: Massachusetts, 1774–1861* (New York: New York University Press, 1947), *passim;* Louis Hartz, *Economic Policy and Democratic Thought: Pennsylvania, 1776–1860* (Cambridge, Mass.: Harvard University Press, 1948), *passim.*

Cherokee Anomie, 1794–1809: New Roles for Red Men, Red Women, and Black Slaves

William G. McLoughlin

"Anomie — a dissociation between culturally prescribed aspirations and socially structured avenues
for realizing these aspirations."

— Robert K. Merton

William G. McLoughlin is professor of history at Brown University. He is the author of *New England Dissent, 1630–1833* (1971). His most recent book is *Revivals, Awakenings and Reform* (1978). He is currently writing a history of the missionary movement among the Cherokee Indians, 1790–1870.

THE RISE OF the Cherokee Republic in the eastern part of the United States between 1794 and 1828 has generally been written as a success story with an unhappy ending: the Cherokees lifted themselves by their own bootstraps after their defeat in the American Revolution to become "the most civilized tribe" in America only to be forcibly ejected from their homeland in 1838. Standard histories of the Cherokees explain their rapid "acculturation" in terms of the benevolence of the federal government's civilization program, the dedicated zeal of evangelical missionaries, the able leadership of chiefs like Charles Renatus Hicks and John Ross, the brilliant invention by Sequoyah of a written Cherokee language, and the high percentage of Cherokees of mixed Indian-white ancestry who led the march to success.[1] A closer look at the record, however, indicates that their rise was not so simple an upward-curving arc. In fact, the true measure of Cherokee accomplishment can be appreciated only if we understand how totally disoriented their culture became between 1794 and 1809. They had to sink even lower than military defeat. Before their revitalization process began, they had first to drink the dregs of anomie.

They had taken a more fatal step than they realized by remaining loyal to the British in 1776. Joining hands with southern Tories in the summer of 1776, they initiated a concerted series of

127

destructive raids upon the white settlements from the Ohio River to the Carolinas. But the king and the Tories were unable to give them sufficient supplies or military assistance to sustain the attack. White frontiersmen quickly mobilized a massive counterattack which, by August 1777, so devastated the Cherokee villages and overwhelmed their warriors that the chiefs sued for peace. To gain that peace the tribe was forced to yield more than half of its 100,000 square miles of territory, forcing thousands of Cherokees to resettle within the shrunken nation. In addition, this defeat divided the tribe against itself.

Many younger chiefs, angry at the price the victors exacted, withdrew to the westernmost edge of their territory, taking their families with them. Aligning themselves with the Creeks on whose borders they settled, these dissidents founded a series of new towns along the lower Tennessee River Valley from Chickamauga to Muscle Shoals. Known as "the Lower Towns" or "Chickamaugans," this Cherokee faction continued to raid the white settlements in a guerrilla war which flared sporadically from 1780 to 1794. Refusing to be bound by treaties made with the new American government by the Upper Town chiefs in 1785, 1791, and 1792, the Lower Towns continued fighting long after the British had made peace. Time after time the white frontiersmen sent invading armies to burn the Lower Towns, destroy their crops, slaughter their livestock, burn their granaries. But the Chickamaugans always melted into the forest before them, returning later to rebuild the towns, reconstruct their homes and farms, continue their raiding parties. Enraged frontier settlers refused to distinguish between the friendly Upper Towns and the guerrillas in the Lower Towns. Invading peaceful Cherokee villages, they forced many of them to join the guerrillas. Eventually virtually every Cherokee village, of which there were close to sixty, was ravaged, often more than once. The population of the tribe was cut from an estimated 22,000 in 1770 to perhaps 14,000 in 1794. In 1809 there were only 12,395. Almost one thousand Cherokees left the East in these years to find peace in Spanish Territory across the Mississippi.

This devastating war back and forth across their land was only the military culmination of the gradual destruction of the Cherokee way of life. The Cherokees had first seen the white European in 1540 and since 1640 had been in continual contact with the English colonists. This contact slowly destroyed the old patterns of life and rapidly disrupted the equilibrium which existed among the various tribes in the Southeast. The original Cherokee economic system was only marginally subsistent, based upon a combination of hunting, fishing, food gathering, and agriculture.[2] Except for overpopulation (usually kept in environmental balance by famine, war, disease, and infanticide), they had managed like most Indians to live off the land without depleting its resources and without excessive effort. The soil was rich, the climate generally mild, the fish and game plentiful. The territorial imperatives necessitated by a similar economic system among the neighboring tribes kept up a constant warfare, but at the beginning of the eighteenth century a generally harmonious relationship among the Indians existed throughout the South. In that era tribal war served primarily socioeconomic purposes; it was a highly traditionalized system for maintaining vague hunting boundaries and a cultural process by which young braves established their status. But the European method of massive warfare, the political competition of empires to control the New World, and the economic restructuring brought by the fur trade radically altered Indian life. Moreover, the rapid influx of British settlers after 1640 and their expanding settlements forced the Indians into bitter wars in which the Europeans frequently manipulated the Cherokees to assist in the extermination of smaller eastern tribes.

The European concepts of permanent alliances, trade treaties, total war, and enforced land cessions compelled the Cherokees to create "kings" or "emperors" who were, at least in European logic, held responsible for the behavior of the whole tribe. This began a long process of limiting the local self-government of individual towns, the power of local chiefs, and the general concept of noncoercive consensus government which had formerly constituted what little governance there was. In addition, the trade alliances made the Cherokees partners in exploiting the game which had formerly been hunted only for food or clothing. It also made them increasingly dependent upon the manufactured goods of the Europeans — guns, traps, powder, lead, knives, axes, kettles, cloth, and blankets. Their own native skills in pottery and weaving deteriorated and, for some, spirituous liquor became a major necessity. As exploited employees of European trading companies, the Indians destroyed their own supply of game and found themselves thrown into the vagaries of European marketing fluctuations over which they had no control. Gradually new life-styles were introduced among them by English and Scottish traders who settled in their villages, married Cherokee wives, introduced European agricultural methods (including the use of black slaves), and taught them the uses of horses, cattle, pigs, and chickens. But prior to 1776 the acculturation process was essentially voluntary. The Cherokees took from the Europeans what seemed useful to them, while the major aspects of daily life and culture remained the same. Despite periodic epidemics from European diseases, the Cherokees managed to grow and thrive as a people. It was the warfare between 1776 and 1794 which destroyed them.

By 1800 their hunting grounds in Kentucky and Tennessee were wholly occupied by white Americans, and their role in the fur-trade economy was gone. Even by extended hunting expeditions across the Mississippi, it was impossible to obtain enough furs and hides to pay for the manufactured goods which had now become necessities. The only way to avoid starvation was to accept the white man's way of cultivation and animal husbandry. But the problems of such a social reorientation were almost overwhelming. Daily contact with white settlers who now surrounded them on three sides (leaving only their southwestern borders contiguous to other Indians) made the transition even more difficult. Charles Royce, writing of the Cherokees in these years, said that "they were, as a nation, being slowly but surely compressed within the contracting coils of the giant anaconda of civilization; yet they held to the vain hope that a spirit of justice and mercy would finally prevail in their favor. Their traditions furnished them no guide by which to judge of the results certain to follow. . . ."[3] The surrounding settlers, bristling with greed, contempt, and animosity, darted in and out of the tribal area, carrying on illicit trade, cheating, robbing, frequently assaulting the now defenseless Cherokees.[4] Ostensibly the treaties had left the political infrastructure of the tribe intact. Their chiefs and councils were still free to govern internal affairs. But with white men continually in their midst and encroaching upon their borders, with the critical control over crimes between whites and Indians fixed by treaty in the hands of white troops and courts, it was almost impossible for the local town chiefs to retain order under the old unwritten patterns of noncoercive authority and clan revenge. The efforts of tribal chiefs with broader authority to sustain order were thwarted by continuing animosity between the Upper Towns and the Lower.[5] They were harried from without and divided within.

Furthermore, the frequent cessions of land forced upon the Cherokees after 1777 (in the treaties of 1798, 1804, 1805, 1806, and 1807) cut the heart out of the original Cherokee homeland along the western borders of South Carolina, the eastern valleys of the Great Smokies, the upper valleys of the Tennessee and its tributaries in northeastern Tennessee.[6] In these years their oldest settlements fell into white hands and thousands of Cherokees made homeless by these cessions had to reestablish themselves in what remained of their land to the west and south. By 1800 more than forty of their towns had disappeared in the advancing white tide. More than two-thirds of their families were uprooted and forced to move — some two or three times. Resettling into already overcrowded and disorganized towns, they placed a severe strain upon limited resources, depleting precious supplies of grain and livestock. Before they could start new fields and harvest a crop these displaced families often reduced whole communities to virtual starvation.[7] To this great demographic disruption must be added the psychological and spiritual shock of leaving behind so many of their graves and sacred places; in an animistic or zootheistic religious culture, every spring, waterfall, mountain, cave, or lake had special supernatural significance. When villages were forced to abandon these sacred sites to white desecration, they lost basic spiritual landmarks as well as the territory itself. In addition, much of Cherokee medicine, as well as many religious potions, was based upon the gathering and concocting of certain kinds of herbs and flowers not always or so easily available in their new homes.

Cutting even deeper than economic hardships into cultural vitality was the breakdown of traditional patterns of enculturation — child-rearing and social maturation. It struck the southern Indians with particular pain to learn that they were no longer to be allowed to raise their sons and nephews to be warriors. In 1802 a Creek chief, speaking to the resident federal agent, informed him that he hoped the government would not see fit to prevent the customary small-scale warfare between the Cherokees,

Creeks, Choctaws, and Chickasaws. How else, he asked, were their young men to learn the skills to attain manhood and respect? "Brother, if we red men fall out, dispute and quarrel, you must look upon it as two children quarreling and you, our white friends and brothers, must remain neutral. There is among us four Nations old customs, one of which is war. If the young, having grown to manhood, wish to practice the ways of the old people, let them try themselves at war, and when they have tried, let the chiefs interpose and stop it. We want you to let us alone."[8] There was in Cherokee culture an achievement orientation which encouraged young and old warriors to measure their status by exploits of daring in war and hunting — through the number of their scalps or captives, the quantity of their furs and hides. These exploits were then celebrated in songs and dances for the edification and glory of all. More than self-achievement, they were measures of a man's importance to his family, clan, and tribe, and signs of his harmony with the spirits which controlled life. But what for the Cherokee was basic training, education, and testing was to the American government, after 1794, merely a source of troublesome "savagery." According to the treaties the Indians were to give up hunting and war for farming and book learning. The Cherokee treaty of 1791 stipulated that in order for "the Cherokee nation [to] be led to a greater degree of civilization and to become herdsmen and cultivators, instead of remaining in a state of hunters, the United States will, from time to time, furnish, gratuitously, the said nation with useful implements of husbandry."[9] Henceforth Cherokee boys were to prove their mettle by the sweat of their brows. Plowing a straight furrow, not shooting a straight arrow, was to be the test of a man. But this was not a skill their fathers, uncles, and chiefs could teach them.

What role, then, were the old to play and what respect could they sustain? Not only had they nothing worth teaching the young, but they were held responsible for the failure of the old system. Power, skill, prestige, and hence legitimate social authority now rested with "the white fathers," who found the warfare of the old chiefs merely a childish game. With the breakdown of the authority of the tribal elders, the disintegration of self-regulating custom, and the imposition of external force (the soldiers patrolling the borders, the government factor regulating trade, the federal agent enforcing their treaty obligations, the state constables and courts arresting and trying criminals) the internal political structure of the nation fell apart. It had no function to perform. Before the Cherokees could reestablish legitimate authority over their people, the chiefs and councils had to learn new roles, deal with new political and economic realities, accept the responsibility for inculcating new social values and sustaining new behavior patterns.

Even religious rituals and festive ceremonies had to be restructured. The old songs, rites, and dances associated with war (like the Eagle Dance) fell into disuse. The decline of hunting made the Bear and the Buffalo dances obsolete. The communal ceremonies of the new year and the relighting of the clan fires lost their meaning. The spiritual leaders of the community — priests or shamans — lost their authority as well. Cleansing and purification rites made sense only if one knew what values were being reaffirmed and what one owed allegiance to — what was pure and what impure. Of all the Cherokee ceremonies only the Green Corn Dance and the Ball Plays retained any vitality in these years. But even these became increasingly secularized. The Green Corn Dance, originally a harvest ritual, became a plaything of the federal agents, who worked with the chiefs to have it scheduled at times and places convenient to the government, either when annuities were to be distributed or when a treaty was about to be made. The government contributed provisions and whiskey for these occasions on the grounds that they put the Indians in a good mood for bargaining.

The Ball Plays, instead of communal festivals with religious overtones, became spectacles for white visitors and scenes of wild orgies of gambling, drunkenness, and brawling. Instead of replacing hunting and war as they might have done to enable young men to exhibit skill, strength, endurance, and daring, they became a kind of professionalized gambling, a quick way to make money (or to lose it) — a symptom of despair, not of vitality. In better days, and in the more conservative parts of the nation, the Ball Plays were hallowed by sacred prayers, dances, and rituals; players abstained from sexual intercourse prior to playing in order to retain their strength; to be chosen as a player was to be a person of high integrity and honor. But during the Cherokee nadir, all this was forgotten. In 1792 Governor William Blount reported two Ball Plays on two successive days in the Lower

Towns where Chief Eskaqua (or Bloody Fellow) "was on the losing side and having staked much bore it not quite well" the first day. "His getting drunk on Monday night was supposed to be a maneuver to get some of the best players of the adverse party in the same situation, which he effected. He did not play himself and none of his players drank to excess" so the next day Eskaqua's team recouped his losses because of the hangovers of the opposing team.[10] Bloody Fellow had previously been a mighty war leader; now he seemed to care only to enrich himself.

The distribution of the federal annuity itself became a great national holiday though it had no religious significance to the Cherokees. Its only purpose was the selfish one of getting all the liquor and booty one could for oneself. These occasions attracted hordes of disreputable white men — traders, gamblers, whiskey dealers — eager to extort some of these treaty funds from the Cherokees. The secretary of war instructed the agent to discourage the whole business in 1802, but not until the council regained its authority and asserted tribal control over the annuities in the form of a national treasury in 1817 did it come to an end.

Recognizing the importance of national holidays in establishing national pride, the Cherokee agent appointed by the government in 1801, Colonel Return J. Meigs, tried to encourage new ones more in keeping with the new status of the Indians as wards of the republic. A native of Connecticut and a loyal Jeffersonian, Meigs sought like a true *philosophe* to construct a new civil religion for his charges. Why not have "festival days [on] 4th July and New Year's Day, dividing the year equally," he wrote. "On those occasions political and moral sentiments will be diffused while the mind is alive and awakened by agreeable impressions made on such occasions not easily effaced."[11] No doubt he expected orations on the rising glory of America and the role of the Indian in that destiny, but nothing appears to have come of his suggestion. The Cherokees were not exactly moving in that direction.

For reasons not necessarily associated with Christianization, the Cherokees and other southern tribes appear to have adopted the festival of the Twelve Days of Christmas. The first New England missionaries noted this with surprise in 1818: "Christmas is a great day among the whites and half breeds in this country. It has been kept in such a manner that the Cherokees have given it the name which signifies shooting-day. Almost all the slaves have their time from Christmas to the end of the year and generally spend it in frolicking and drinking."[12] Few Cherokees were Christians at this time, however, and as the description implies, it was more a secular than a holy day. Trying to capitalize on it, some of the missionaries held a religious service on Christmas, but only the blacks attended. The obvious inference is that the more prosperous Cherokees adopted it from their slaves and not out of any respect for the founder of Christianity. Christmas had long been a slave holiday in the white South. It was probably brought into the tribe by white traders and Tory refugees, if not by the slaves themselves.

The first missionaries to ask to establish a mission station and school among the Cherokees were Moravians from North Carolina. Their first request to do this in 1799 was rejected, but approval came in 1801 when the Cherokees were convinced that it would be useful for their children to learn to read and write English. The Moravians did not accept their first pupils in Spring Place, Georgia, until 1804, and taught only a handful of children prior to 1810. A more successful missionary school was started near the federal agency in eastern Tennessee in 1804 by the Presbyterians, but it collapsed in 1810 for want of denominational support. By and large the missionaries provided little help to the Cherokees in these trying times, but by the same token, neither can they be blamed as a major source of their cultural disorientations.[13]

In 1800 the possibility that the Cherokees would ever recover their old tribal integrity and self-respect as a people must have seemed nonexistent. Nor did the alternative way of total assimilation offered by the American government appear feasible. Quite apart from the fact that few Cherokees possessed at that time the skill, the tools, or the capital to become successful farmers, almost everything about this new system ran counter to their traditions and beliefs. "Exclusive property" (the idea of private ownership of the land) ran counter to the staunch belief in tribal ownership of the land; private profit ran counter to communal sharing and the hospitality ethic; aggressive personal ambition ran counter to the high value placed upon self-effacement and affability. To leave the village, stake out a clearing in the woods, and start farming for oneself and family alone meant to repudiate neighborliness. Perhaps most important of all, it meant the establishment of a nuclear family system, patrilineal inheritance, the end of the clan relationships, and a reversal of roles for both men and women. Anomie at bottom meant for the Cherokees not only a loss of sovereignty and land but with the breakdown of cultural order it meant a loss of identity. What exactly did it mean after 1794 to be a Cherokee?

The changing role of Indian women in the years 1794 to 1810 was directly related, not only to the changing role of Indian men, but to the changing status of black men in the Cherokee Nation and in the white South. Where there were only whites and blacks in a community, the role of each was clearly defined. But among the Cherokees, there were red, white, and black men (not to mention mixed-bloods). Since the red was told that his future lay in adapting himself to white beliefs and behavior, the status of the black became even more problematic. In the eighteenth century the first blacks to enter the Indian nations, usually as runaways, were treated with lenience and familiarity. They provided useful skills and manpower and served as interpreters. There is evidence of black intermarriage and adoption and a number of freed slaves had an independent status. In the Revolutionary fervor for natural rights the Indian was considered by philosophers like Jefferson to be virtually equal to the white even if there were doubts about the black man. But as this fervor faded, as the white South moved toward the cotton kingdom, and as the Indian was forced to defend his own status as a "man of color" in the face of white frontier prejudice, the multiracial aspect of Cherokee society posed bitter problems for black and red.

Similarly, the new role of yeoman farmer or planter compelled a new relationship between Indian men and women. The Indian male, though he had in former days labored occasionally in the field with the women, never had his dignity as a warrior or hunter questioned for this any more than did the poor white who sometimes labored beside his slave. The respective status lines in both cases were established beyond doubt. But as the Cherokee woman went into the farmhouse to spin, sew, and cook, after 1794 she lost some of her former dignity and decision-making power in the tribal councils. At the same time, the Cherokee man, shorn of his primary status as a hunter-warrior and told to work steadily with ax and hoe, had to worry about how he could henceforth distinguish himself from black field hands.

Working in the fields was as hot and burdensome to the Cherokee as to the white Southerner. He did not share Jefferson's view of the nobility of that occupation. At first the Cherokee man considered it ignoble to be only and always working in the fields. Many years later, after the Cherokees had completed their transformation and could look back with less embarrassment on this problem, the editor of the *Cherokee Phoenix* wrote of the Cherokees at the turn of the century, "From the soil they derived a scanty supply of corn, barely enough to furnish them with gah-no-ha-nah [a corn dish] and this was obtained by the labor of women and grey headed men, for custom would have it that it was disgraceful for a young man to be seen with a hoe in his hand except on particular occasions."[14] Like his white southern counterpart the Cherokee hoped someday to own slaves to do his work. His model of American farming and capitalism was inevitably that of the southern cotton plantation, not the northern diversified subsistence farm which the federal government and eastern philanthropists held up to him. Hence to sustain his new role as a Cherokee man and his wife's as a Cherokee woman he would have to reduce the blacks to a servile laboring caste and transform his women into genteel mistresses of the hearth and home.

Eighteenth-century observations regarding the status of women among the Cherokees varied widely. James Adair argued in 1762 that their status was virtually equal to that of Cherokee men. Jefferson in 1783 believed they were little more than slaves: "The women are submitted to unjust drudgery. This, I believe, is the case with every barbarous people. With such, force is law. The stronger sex imposes on the weaker. It is civilization alone which teaches us to subdue the selfish passions and to respect those rights in others which we value in ourselves. Were we in equal barbarism, our females would be equal drudges."[15] A Tennessee historian of the Cherokees, drawing upon a wide variety of early sources, came closer to Adair's conclusion:

The Cherokees [in 1760] were just emerging, as were all Iroquoian people, from the matriarchal stage. "They have been a considerable while under petticoat government," Adair comments. Extraordinary respect was paid to womankind. When a Cherokee married, he took residence with the clan of his wife. His children were the property of the mother, and were classed as members of her clan. The wigwam and its contents belonged to the woman. She had a voice in the daily council and the deciding vote for chieftainships.

The women of each clan selected a leader. These leaders constituted the Womens' Councils, which did not hesitate to override the authority of the chiefs when it was thought that the welfare of the tribe demanded it. The head of the Womens' Council was the Beloved Woman of the tribe, whose voice was considered that of the Great Spirit speaking through her. . . . The white pioneer mother, with her large family, was far more of a drudge than her red sister.[16]

While the evidence is scanty and contradictory on details, there seems general agreement that prior to 1794 Cherokee women did have a participatory role of some kind in tribal decisions, a major interest in household property and care of the children, and that they did most of the work cultivating the fields. Thereafter, their role in tribal affairs became almost negligible. Part of the difficulty in "civilizing" the Indian was that it bothered nineteenth-century white Americans intensely to see women working in the fields. The government considered it a primary object of its civilization program to get the Indian women out of the field and into the kitchen. It was considered a marked step forward when Indian women began to take up spinning and weaving while the men grudgingly and of necessity took to the plow. In August 1802, the federal agent to the Cherokees reported the following items of husbandry and domestic manufacture which he had so far distributed among the Cherokees as part of the government's economic aid program: 58 ploughs, 13 mattocks, 44 hoes, 215 spinning wheels, 4 looms, 204 pairs of cotton cards, 53 sheep, 28 reels. He reported with mixed feelings that "the raising and man-ufacturing of Cotton is all done by the Indian Women; they find their condition so much bettered by this improvement that they apply for wheels, cards, etc. with great earnestness" and were disappointed that the government could not give them more. "The Indian men," however, "attend to the raising of Cattle and Swine — this costs them no labour, a thing they will avoid as long as possible."[17]

In 1805 Colonel Meigs reported that what seemed like progress to most white Americans was not so viewed by most Cherokee males. "Raising cotton, spinning and weaving is carried on the domestic way in almost every part of the nation, but this is totally done by the females who are not held in any degree of reputable estimation by the real Indian and therefore neither them [women] nor their occupation have any charms to tame the savage."[18] To the Cherokee man, whether the woman made clothes by preparing skins and furs or by spinning cotton, it was all the same. The great difficulty now was that she, not he, was providing the clothing for the family while he could contribute almost nothing. Only by growing a good crop could he sustain his prestige as a provider. The thwarting of the natural desire to maintain his old role as hunter-provider was frustrating in the extreme.

By 1802 Cherokee hunters who did not make the long trek across the Mississippi to hunt were bringing to the trading posts only the skins of small animals — "raccoons, foxes, and wild cats" — for which they received twenty-five cents each.[19] American Indian agents, observing the reluctance of the Indian men to undertake the onerous task of farming, concluded that they were inveterately lazy and shiftless: "Labour is painfull and the idea to most of them dishonorable; the love of ease is their predominant passion," wrote the Cherokee agent, Return J. Meigs, in 1808.[20] It never occurred to him that the Cherokee did not oppose all labor, but only that degrading to his status and lacking in that source of self-respect which came from the exercise of traditional skills.

Since working all day behind a plow, hoeing a cornfield, or feeding hogs was considered honorable and rewarding by a Connecticut Yankee, Return J. Meigs could not see why it had so little appeal to the Cherokees. What he saw as feckless Cherokee "roaming" in worn-out hunting grounds week after week was not a desire to avoid work but in part an urge to cling to an older way of life and in part a need to hide an ignorance of husbandry. It also was necessitated by lack of capital and tools to become a farmer. Despite its good intentions the government seldom provided more than a few hundred dollars' worth of agricultural tools per year; a Congress interested in keeping taxes low found it easy to cut the budget for nonvoting Indians. Consequently the Cherokees did not have in these years enough plows, hoes, or mattocks, and the few the government did supply were not evenly distributed.[21] Nor could the Indians keep the implements they did get in repair without a blacksmith, and these were always in short supply. Cherokees in mountainous regions or among the sandhills had little chance of making a living from farming. Even white frontiersmen who had grown up on farms in the East, who had some experience and capital and were able to pay for the services of blacksmiths, wheelwrights, or coopers, often had a difficult time starting out in the wilderness. Yet the Protestant ethic of hard work, self-discipline, and delayed gratification was assumed to be the divinely ordained system of values for all men. God had ordered Adam to support himself by the sweat of his brow and to cultivate the fields, and the sooner the Indian adopted this way of life the happier and more prosperous he would presumably be. The economic whip was there, but not the religious, social, or cultural incentive.

Those Cherokees, however, who were the sons and grandsons of white traders, Tory refugees, army deserters, and those white men who had married into the nation and cast in their lot with it made the most of the government's economic aid and got the lion's share of it. They also used their superior experience to take up the best farming land in the Cherokee Nation. And, most important of all, they had the capital to invest in slaves. By 1809 there were 583 black slaves in the Cherokee Nation, but they were owned by comparatively few of the two-thousand families. Not only did some have ten, fifteen, or twenty of them, but geographically the great bulk of them were in northern Georgia and Alabama where the rich black soil was fit for cotton plantations. Among that third of the Cherokees who lived in "the Valley Towns" of the Unicoi and Great Smokey mountains where there was the least intermixture of white ancestry and intermarriage, there were only five black slaves.[22] The Valley Towns long remained a center of traditionalist friction within the nation.

Eventually there were those who argued that the progress the Cherokees made toward civilization was primarily "oweing to the prevalence of slavery" among them.[23] Others argued that their progress resulted from the high proportion of white blood in their veins: "When every effort to introduce among them the idea of separate property as well in things real as personal shall fail, let intermarriages between them and the whites be encouraged by the Government. This cannot fail to preserve the race, with the modifications necessary to the enjoyment of civil liberty and social happiness."[24] The problem of relating red, white, and black among the southern Indians led them logically to wonder whether the white man was sincere, or honest with himself, in suggesting, as Jefferson and others did, the hope that the Indian could ultimately attain full and equal citizenship within white America.

Seeking to discover their new role within the American system now that they had agreed to give up the right of arms to sustain their sovereignty, the Cherokees received three conflicting answers. In official documents of the federal government, they were "wards" or "younger brothers" with a potential for full citizenship when they became fully "civilized" and "Christianized." To many American scientists they were "a dying race" more to be pitied than censured, but nevertheless incapable of meeting the challenge required to become part of that Anglo-Saxon people who stood at the forefront of human progress. And to the neighboring frontiersmen, they were irredeemable "savages," defeated enemies who had lost all right to their land and whose existence, on mere sufferance, was an irritating impediment to the westward march of white civilization. The only reason most frontier people tolerated them was that they wished the federal government to bear the expense of removing them. The federal government took pains to treat the tribes as quasi-independent states partly because they wanted them as a buffer zone or potential allies should France, Spain, or England press their claims to the Mississippi Valley and partly because it could not decide whether to "civilize" them where they were or remove them westward. (Prior to the Louisiana Purchase in 1803, there was no place to which to remove them, but one of Jefferson's reasons for acquiring the Louisiana Territory was to facilitate such a relocation.)

The ambivalence of the white American's attitude toward the native American is clearly revealed in an early missionary letter. The missionary who wrote it was a New England Federalist and philanthropist. Arriving in Tennessee he was shocked to find that "the sentiment very generally prevails among the white people near the southern tribes (and perhaps with some farther to the north) that the Indian is by nature radically different from all other men and that this difference presents an insurmountable barrier to his civilization."[25] The missionary, however, believed that "Indians are men and their children, education alone excepted, [are] like the children of other men." This same ambivalence prevailed among the Cherokees in different form. Colonel Meigs reported in 1805 that most Cherokees were not ready to accept white men as their equals: "Many of the Cherokees think that they are not derived from the same stock as the whites, that they are favorites of the great spirit and that he never intended they should live the laborious lives of the whites; these ideas, if allowed to have a practical effect, would finally operate [to] their destruction."[26]

Despite this theory of racial polygenesis — the belief that God had in effect created the races biologically different — there were Cherokees ready to take up the white man's ways and work toward the goal of ultimate citizenship. These civilizationists were generally Cherokees of mixed white and Cherokee ancestry, the so-called mixed-bloods, but not always. The chief whom James Mooney considered the leader of the "progressive" faction among the Cherokees after 1794, was a full blood called Doublehead. Colonel Meigs commented upon this theme in 1805: ". . . where the blood [of the Cherokees] is mixed with the whites, in every grade of it, there is an apparent disposition leaning toward civilization and this disposition is in proportion to its distance from the original stock. But it is evident at the same time that this does not arise from any augmentation of their intellectual power, for it is a fact that in this nation several of the Chiefs who are from unadulterated Indian [stock] have strong minds and more acute discernment than any of the Half Breeds."[27] Meigs fully sympathized with the federal government's plan to civilize and ultimately "incorporate" the Indians into the nation as citizens, but he recognized that it would take time. It might appear, he wrote to his subagent, Major William S. Lovely, in 1802, that "the civilization of a whole people of Savages seems sometimes a hopeless piece of business, but patience and perseverance will overcome great difficulties." It was the job of the federal agents to push this effort with vigor. The method, however, was ruthless in its disregard for their traditional way of life. "If it was within my power," said Meigs, "I would do away [with] every [Cherokee] custom inconsistent with civilized life." He noted with regret that "the Cherokees are extremely jealous of their Customs, Customs which have descended down to them from their Ancestors from time immemorial, many of which it is to be wished were done away [with]. . . ."[28] Meigs viewed his task as that of a latter-day, enlightened Pygmalion, hewing away with all the vigor at his command at the marble block of savagism within which the civilized man was held captive by the encrusted prejudices and superstitions of his forefathers. Government agents, he said, were to hammer away at the stone of culture until every vestige of the old ways was chipped away: "They, like that Statuary [sculptor] believe that the Statue is in the Block and that by the repeated strokes of the means, the desired effect will be produced."[29]

However, an irresistible urge to attribute white supremacy to hereditary or biological superiority provided Meigs with a convenient explanation for the apparent reluctance of many of the full bloods — "the real Indians" — to adapt to the white man's ways: "The number of the real Indians and those of Mixed Blood are nearly equal.[30] The last are almost without exception in favor of improvements and have very much thrown off the savage manner and habits: But those of the real Indians still hug the manners and habits of their ancesters [sic] and are unwilling to give [up] the pleasures of the shade and idleness. . . ."[31]

Almost all the attention focused by historians on families of intermarried whites and Cherokees has been given to that small but usually respectable element of resident traders and government officials (and later a few missionaries) who established themselves for life, married with serious intentions (and increasingly in Christian ceremonies), and accepted a certain responsibility to act for the best interests of the nation which had adopted them and bestowed full tribal rights upon them. It is the names of these families that have come down through the years as mixed-blood chiefs and influentials: Adair, McDonald, Ross, Lowery, McIntosh, Chisholm, Rogers, Riley, Baldridge, Vann, Foreman, Walker, McCoy, Pettit, Brown, Martin, Hicks. In later years, when the Cherokees became very conscious of their ancestry, it was fashionable to trace it back to the first respectable white trader or agent to intermarry, and for many of these families we can ascertain precise dates and places of entry into the nation. The children of such marriages tended to intermarry among the same group, creating what some considered a mixed-blood elite. Despite animosities between this group and the full bloods, their contributions to Cherokee life were considerable. They provided skills in trade, farming, domestic manufactures, technology, record keeping, and diplomacy which they put at the disposal of the Cherokees. They helped not only by their activities but by their example. More indirectly, but not less important, they inculcated a historical perspective and memory, they stressed the importance of long-range planning, the need to see Cherokee affairs in the broader perspective of the wider world around them. These contributions, however, were sometimes offset by their disdain for those Cherokees who did not zealously push toward acculturation and progress. They made few concessions to tribal custom, and insisted upon raising their children by white standards. These families caused serious internal problems after the 1790s by their disruption of clan kinship patterns and their desire to alter customs regarding private property and inheritance. Furthermore, because of their obvious advantages in dealing with whites, they began to assume important positions of leadership. Their children — normally called "half-breeds" by whites — grew up in the most difficult position of all, between two worlds. Their white fathers wanted them to live, act, and think like white men; their peers and Indian relatives wanted them to assert their Indian loyalty. The most popular, and yet typical, story illustrating this dilemma is the one told by Chief John Ross of his own childhood. His father, Daniel Ross, a Scottish trader from Baltimore, entered the Cherokee Nation in the 1780s on a trading trip, married the daughter of "Tory" John McDonald, who was then living at Chickamauga, and settled down to raise his family among the Cherokees. In 1797 young John Ross, then about seven years old, attended the festival of the Green Corn Dance. His mother, who was three-quarters white,

on this occasion had dressed him in his first suit of nankeen, brand new, made after the white man's style, and he sauntered out to meet his playmates with all the self-consciousness of one wearing, for the first time, his new spring suit. . . . Shouts of derision and taunts of "Unaka" [white boy] greeted him on all sides; even his most intimate friends held aloof. . . . While being dressed by his [Cherokee] grandmother the next morning, he burst into tears and after much coaxing told her of his humiliation the day before. She comforted him as grandmothers are wont to do . . . the nankeen suit came off, the hunting shirt, leggins, and moccasins went on, and the small boy ran shouting to his play, happy and "at home" again, as he termed it. . . .[32]

Ross's father, however, took care to hire white tutors to teach his son English and arithmetic so that he could learn his father's business, and Ross grew up to be a wealthy trader. His first marriage was to a Cherokee full blood; his second, after he had become principal chief, was to a well-to-do white Quaker lady who lived in Baltimore. Ross never overcame his "twoness." From the profits of trade he bought a large number of slaves to till his plantation fields and lived according to the style of a southern gentleman while defending to the last ditch the right of the Cherokees to remain on their homeland in the East. He was so unsure of his command of Cherokee language that as a chief he always spoke and wrote in English.

In regard to racial equality as well as in regard to adopting the white man's ways the Cherokee was left with an impossible dilemma: either he adopted a theory of polygenesis and racial separatism (that God had created the different races and they must not be mixed) — thereby throwing his weight on the side of reactionary bigots along the frontier — or he accepted the "enlightened" view of liberal philanthropists and accepted amalgamation, assimilation, and disappearance. Either route led to his extinction. I have found only one explicit statement by a Cherokee of what may have been a more general view, a faith that heredity and complexion were not the real issues. This occurred during a conversation which Meigs had early in the century with the Lower Town chief named Eskaqua, or Bloody Fellow. Meigs had tried to persuade him that it might be best if he led his people to the West since he appeared reluctant to adopt total acculturation. "Bloody Fellow replied that he had no inclination to leave the country of his birth. Even should the habits & customs of the Cherokees give place to the habits & customs of the whites, or even should they themselves become white by intermarriage, not a drop of Indian blood would be lost; it would be spread more widely, but not lost. He was for preserving them together as a people regardless of complexion."[33] It was this fundamental racial pride and confidence attached, let it be noted, to the critical notion of roots in their homeland, which sustained the Cherokees in their struggle for survival as a distinct people in the years ahead.

Although the Cherokees probably learned the importance which whites attached to racial differences primarily from daily experience with them, they also experienced their legal implications in various courtroom situations. Sometimes they found that there were advantages to be gained, as in the case of the Cherokee who was placed on trial for murdering, in a fit of drunken anger, a black slave owned by a white man. A white jury in Tennessee found him guilty of manslaughter, a crime punishable by branding. But when the judge examined the statute he discovered that it applied only to the killing of white men. Nevertheless, the attorney for the state demanded that the Indian be branded. The judge refused and the Cherokee was released. He had, however, learned an important lesson about the nice legal distinctions involved in interracial criminal justice. Meigs wrote that the Cherokees were pleased at the fairness of the trial and its outcome. But it was a fairness they seldom found in trials involving Indians charged with crimes against white men.[34]

While southern state courts may have shown partiality toward Indians who murdered black slaves, they were not prepared to deal in the same way with Indians accused of crimes against whites. Meigs discussed this matter with the secretary of war in 1812 when Governor Tatnall of Georgia demanded the arrest of two Cherokees accused of murdering two white Georgians. He said the Cherokees were "affraid of a trial" by a white jury. They had reminded Meigs that in a recent trial involving a white man accused of murdering a Cherokee, the case was dismissed for want of evidence because only Cherokees had witnessed the murder. The Cherokees, Meigs told Tatnall, had also informed him that there were at least eight recent cases where state courts refused to bring charges against white murderers. "This I have no doubt is true," Meigs told the governor. The reason the white murderers had not been tried was that there was "no proof but that of Indians" available as evidence. In such cases, he said, "the murderers could not be convicted and never will." He went on to remind the governor that "the state of the Indians is a deplorable one in this respect. We arraign them as moral agents, charge them with crimes that cannot be committed without including an idea that they are more like ourselves, at the same time we exclude them from all the advantages of beings capable of moral or religious conceptions; their testimony on oath is not admissible."[35]

Meigs had fought consistently against this double standard of American justice. Like a true Jeffersonian, he deplored the effort to read the Christian religion into the common law. Indians were denied the right to give legal testimony on the ground that they were heathens. Heathens did not believe in a God who administered rewards and punishments after death. Presumably, therefore, they would have no compunction about lying. Meigs was always eager to demonstrate that the Indians did indeed believe in a God and an afterlife. "I have been informed," he wrote to a lawyer in Tennessee who was trying to help an Indian named Stone (or Stone Carrier) on trial for horse stealing, "that the Moors have been admitted to give Evidence at Gibralter in Capital cases. The religion of the Cherokees is as good as that of Mahomet." Though not Christians, "the Indians believe in the being of a God and in the immortality of the soul; it is an instinctive idea with them."[36] He and Silas Dinsmoor, agent to the Choctaws, searched through Blackstone's *Commentaries* until they found support for their position. Dinsmoor wrote to Meigs about it in 1803: "In 3d Blackstone, Lib. 3, cap. 23, p. 369, it is said, 'All witnesses of whatever religion or country that have the use of their reason are to be examined except such as are infamous or such as are interested in the event of the cause. All others are competent witnesses though the jury from other circumstances will judge of their credibility.' This being the law, the Indians are and of right ought to be admissible as witnesses."[37]

Dinsmoor argued that it was not "absolutely necessary that an Indian should take an oath to make his testimony valid" because, as in the case of Quakers, "an affirmation might be sufficient." But even admitting that an oath was necessary and that an Indian had no idea of the being of a God nor of future existence, "Should these considerations bar an Indian from being admitted to oath and testimony? Which would be the most dubious testimony, the honest Indian who has never heard of or known a God or the Atheist or Deist who has convinced *himself* that there is none, or if there be, that he suffers the actions of men to pass unheeded and unnoted? Yet no one pretends to bar a whiteman on account of his religious opinions."[38] But despite Dinsmoor's arguments, he could not make the courts of the Mississippi Territory admit Indian witnesses any more than Meigs could in Tennessee or Georgia.[39] Even where Indians' cases were taken to court, Meigs frankly acknowledged, "it is a fact that they cannot have justice done to them in the courts of law." The judges, he said, were "just and liberal in their Sentiments and look on the human race with equal eye as far as related to distributive justice," but "a jury impaneled in the frontier Counties dare not bring in a Verdict to take the life of a Citizen for killing an Indian." The result was that Indians were regularly "accused, tried, and condemned and executed on the testimony of any white citizen of common character and understanding when at the same time a white man can kill an

Indian in the presence of 100 Indians and the testimony of these hundred Indians to the fact amounts to nothing and the man will be acquitted."[40] The impact of this upon the dignity and self-respect of the Indian was devastating. Richard Brown, one of the leading Cherokee chiefs, wrote to Meigs in 1811 about the feelings aroused in the Indians by their not being allowed to testify against white horse thieves: "We have found a horse belonging to an Indian near Dittoes landing or near Huntsville [in Mississippi Territory, now part of Alabama]. We cannot recover him without aid. The oath of the Indians is not known by your laws. Decide in some way to give us our right. Are we considered as negroes who cannot support our claims?"[41]

The Indians were always described as a proud people. They considered themselves the equals not only of white men but of the upper class of white men in the South. In 1760 Henry Timberlake noted that the Cherokees "are extremely proud, despising the lower class of Europeans; and in some athletick diversions I once was present at, they refused to match or hold conference with any but officers."[42] But after 1794 frontier whites became contemptuous of the rights of Indians, knowing that no white jury would ever convict them for anything they did to an Indian. In 1813 Meigs described four separate cases of Indian murders in which "prosecutions were instituted and all failed of producing punishment." It seriously undermined Meigs's faith in the republic: "Let us not advocate a system of Ethics that only subjects the weak and simple honest man to become the prey of the Bold villain who laughs at the restraints which bind the multitude."[43] The only means by which Meigs and the secretary of war could make a pretense of justice was to offer the family of a murdered Indian a cash compensation. In 1802 Secretary of War Henry Dearborn wrote to Silas Dinsmoor, the Choctaw agent, "You will endeavor to settle the disputes and if necessary engage to satisfy the Chickasaws for the loss of their friend by a pecuniary compensation not exceeding two or three hundred dollars to the family or friends of the deceased."[44] In this case the Chickasaw appears to have been murdered by a Delaware Indian, but the same "satisfaction" was offered for murders attributed to whites. In 1803 Dearborn authorized Meigs to provide "such pecuniary satisfaction as in your Judgement may be acceptable and proper" to the families of murdered Cherokees. He suggested a figure of "from one hundred to two hundred dollars for each man or woman actually murdered by white citizens since our last Treaty." Of course, the Cherokees were to be told that "the compensation is not intended to operate as an acquittal of the murderers."[45] But in effect such payments ended the agent's and the government's concern with the case.

The use of murder compensation payments continued until 1820 when John C. Calhoun, as secretary of war, decided to put a stop to it. "I have received your letter of the 14th November last," he wrote to Meigs, "submitting the claim of the Headmen of the Cherokees for the Indians killed by Americans." Grudgingly he acknowledged the precedents for the practice and said "you will accordingly pay the sum of $100 to the widow of the deceased." But he added, "You will inform the chiefs that the practice will not be continued in future as it is repugnant to those principles by which we govern ourselves in such cases."[46] Calhoun either had forgotten or did not realize that the practice had arisen in the first place because the principles by which the "Americans" governed themselves did not seem to be available to Indians. Nor did he take notice that the cost of an Indian's life had declined in twenty years from three hundred to one hundred dollars.

The failure of American jurisprudence in regard to white murderers was equally glaring in the much more frequent cases of fraud and theft perpetrated by white men upon the Indians: their horses, their furs, their traps, their guns — virtually anything they owned of any value was fair game for marauding whites. The federal agent, faced with trying to evaluate and adjudicate these claims, was compelled to establish his own investigatory and judicial system: "The nature of these kinds of claims cannot be equitably determined by strictly adhering to the law of evidence. The Indians cannot give legal testimony and by means of this disability the whites have an advantage; but by attending carefully to all the circumstances and to the character of the parties, justice can be done to the claimant for altho' the claims may be just, the parties, especially the Indians, cannot support their rights and some characters of each party cannot be credited; but by care here we can, with few exceptions, make equitable decisions."[47] In short, Meigs heard the evidence and made the decisions himself; they were forwarded to the Department of War, and they more or less had to accept his word for it in compensating the Indian or the white involved. Consequently much depended upon the honesty and ability of the agent; and not a little on how much money the War Department felt it could afford for this sort of thing. Meigs was an honest and conscientious agent; many agents were neither. Trying to explain to a friend why, after all the Americans had tried to do for them, the Cherokees still had certain "prejudices" against the white man, Meigs said, "It does not arise from pride, as ours does; it arises in the Indian from his humble conception of himself and of his race from the discovery he makes that we look down on him as an inferior being [which] has a tendency to make him despise himself as the offspring of an inferior race of beings."[48] Lack of respect by others led to loss of respect for himself. This self-rejecting rage, frustration, and despair often led Indians to drink themselves into oblivion, but at other times they found more objective vents for their anger. There were other ways to avenge themselves on their persecutors. Although some took vengeance into their own hands, as traditional tribal custom formerly prescribed, this was usually self-defeating. A more subtle and satisfying way to get even with the white man was to steal his horses. For several reasons horse stealing became a way of life for many Cherokees in these years of anomie.

According to all early accounts of the Cherokee people, they were notable for their honesty. Not only had they no locks on their own houses, barns, and stables, but a visitor might leave his horse, gun, or goods with any of them for months at a time and find them safe when he called for them. In a culture committed to sharing even the last piece of food with strangers as well as neighbors, neither avarice nor acquisitiveness was a virtue. Not placing a high value on personal property and seldom needing much, the Cherokees had no written laws governing theft, only social disdain for the thief. Robbery was not a crime included in clan revenge no matter what the object stolen. Not even the extensive use of western manufactures (guns, axes, kettles, and blankets) after 1700 seems to have produced any problem in this regard. So long as the cultural values were intact and healthy the Cherokees maintained their standards of honesty. But as the cultural system broke down, so did its values. By the last decade of the eighteenth century the problem of horse stealing and its allied vices rose to monumental proportions.

In times of war, horse stealing had always been an understandable and acceptable source of plunder. In times of peace it became a source of revenge, of excitement, of courageous achievement for those denied other means of self-esteem and success. Horse stealing had become a major problem during the guerrilla warfare of 1780–1794, and the treaty ending that war prescribed that "in future, to prevent the practice of stealing horses, attended with the most pernicious consequences to the lives and peace of both parties," the Cherokees were to "agree that for every horse which shall be stolen from the white inhabitants by any Cherokee Indians and not returned within three months, that the sum of fifty dollars shall be deducted" from the annuity which the government paid to the tribe annually for the land the Cherokees had sold to the government.[49] In addition, the congressional acts regulating trade and intercourse with the Indians passed in 1796, 1799, and 1802 all contained clauses designed to prevent this illicit traffic.

Horse stealing, of course, was not merely a symptom of the breakdown of Indian culture; it was so endemic upon the American frontier that it obviously represents also the breakdown of European culture on its outer fringes. Horse stealing provided one of the few areas of frontier life in which Indians and whites worked harmoniously together (sometimes in trying to catch the thieves who stole from both groups with equal disregard, sometimes in belonging to the "pony clubs" constituted to do the stealing). Slave stealing, while closely allied, was more dangerous as well as more profitable.[50] Cattle rustling was less profitable in the eastern woodlands because cattle were slow moving, noisy, and difficult to conceal. When out to steal, thieves might take whatever came first and most easily to hand, but only in regard to horse stealing was the traffic so common as to become a profession. The members of the pony clubs were thieves by vocation.

Horse stealing was directly related to the depletion of game in their old hunting grounds and the loss of status faced by Indian men who could not use their old skills to provide for their families. Return J. Meigs explained this (from the white man's viewpoint) in a letter to Benjamin Hawkins, the Creek agent, in 1805. He was justifying the government's effort to persuade the Indians to cede "the mountainous land lying between East and West Tennessee. . . . That land is of no use to them; there is not a single family [living] on it, and the hunting is very poor. Yet those of an idle disposition spend much time in rambling there and often return with a stolen horse which they have afterwards to pay for [from the annuity]. In fact, it is only a nursery of savage habits and opperates against civilization which is much impeded by their holding such immense tracts of wilderness."[51] The "savage habit" of stealing horses from an enemy was an old one, but too many otherwise honest Indians felt justified in resorting to it when their best efforts to support their families by hunting failed — largely because the whites had killed or chased away the game. How could a man return empty-handed from an extended hunting trip without feeling disgraced? While horse stealing had its roots in tribal warfare, in which booty taken from an enemy was always a sign of prowess and bravery, it also stemmed from the fact that Cherokees owned their land in common. Since no man could buy or sell land as a means of enriching himself this prime source of frontier enterprise was closed to them. (The fact that Indians had to measure private wealth in terms of personal property — horses or slaves — and not, as whites did, in terms of real estate, was of course part of the argument used by those who demanded that the Cherokees adopt the practice of owning their land "in severalty.") Hence movable or personal property became more important to them than to a white man as a means of investment or growing wealth once they were told to become capitalists. Moreover, horse stealing utilized many of the old-fashioned skills of the warrior and hunter: it was exciting; it tested a man's daring; it required quick wits and courage for, make no mistake about it, human life was at stake in these encounters. The respectable among the older generation frowned upon this practice and did not find it a valid substitute for war and hunting, but the elders had lost their right to command. Many young Indians preferred the risk of sudden death to the plodding routine of grubbing and hoeing in the fields day after day. And the profits from horse stealing were not only quicker but much larger than any Cherokee farmer could earn. Some less respectable chiefs managed to profit by it, if not to justify it.

But horse stealing, like slave stealing, was more than simply a way to vent one's anger on the white man or prove oneself a hell of a daring fellow. It also fulfilled an economic need on the frontier. The slave dealer provided cheap labor for a system desperately in need of it. The horse dealer provided a substitute for specie in an economy desperately short of cash. The dishonest vendors in stolen goods were simply providing more cheaply in the black market what there was a high demand for from the public. In this sense it was not strictly a white-Indian problem but a source of economic livelihood for those willing to take chances — the poor, the desperate, the angry, the alienated.[52]

Meigs readily recognized this aspect of the profession: "A considerable part of the land purchased in this country is paid for in horses; they serve as a kind of currency for this purpose all over this western country and hence arises the facility with which they are stolen by Indians and others."[53] Governor William Blount of Tennessee (the superintendent of Indian affairs for the southern district of the United States — south of the Ohio) noted this same bartering aspect when he asked James Carey, the official Cherokee interpreter, in 1793, "In what manner do the Indians dispose of stolen horses?" Carey answered, "Generally they sell them to the traders for a trifle, who run them out of the nation in a different direction to that from whence they came and barter them off for negroes or articles of merchandise."[54]

A detailed study of horse stealing on the frontier would reveal a great deal about its economic development and difficulties. For example, it seems evident that in the 1790s the Cherokees stole horses in the West and bartered them for goods in the East where the market was better, while in the early nineteenth century the need for specie on the frontier made it more profitable to steal horses in the East and trade them in the West. "This business is carried on by white people and Indians in combination," wrote Blount in 1792, "and as soon as a horse is stolen he is conveyed through the Indian nation to North or South Carolina or Georgia and in a short time to the principal towns on the seaboard for sale so as to effectually prevent recovery."[55] But fifteen years later Meigs reported, "The number of horses carried thro' and into this [Cherokee] country is almost incredible — from Georgia, both the Carolinas and Kentucky."[56]

The Indian nations were ideally situated for the business. Being centrally located between East and West, among various settlements scattered throughout the frontier, and being largely wilderness and without roads, the various Indian territories became common channels for shuttling stolen horses. "Considerable numbers of horses are stolen by citizens and by Indians," wrote Meigs, "that never will or can be detected on account of the Wilderness country, so that detection is easily avoided."[57] Not only was it difficult for victims to interrogate friendly Indians who might have been willing to help them trace the thieves, but the Indians themselves possessed no system of internal police to keep track of their own people and recapture their own horses. Since the traffic was interstate and through federal territory, the policing of it was the job of the federal government.

But with only one agent or two in the thousands of square miles of wilderness which constituted each Indian nation, it was impossible for the federal government to provide adequate policing. Even the licensing system under the trade and intercourse acts produced no convictions. "Horse stealing is a subject of complaint (almost continual) to me," wrote Governor Blount in 1792, "without my being able to give any redress. The only thing I can do is to give passports to the sufferers to go into the nation in search of their horses and letters to the chiefs which, as yet, has never been attended with recovery."[58] The chiefs, even if they knew who the thieves were, were hardly likely to turn them over to frontier justice. Consequently, horse stealing became one of the most constant causes of friction between Indians and whites on the frontier — each tending to lay the blame primarily on the other. "Horse stealing," Blount continued in this letter, "is the grand source of hostility between the white and red people in this district, and I fear will actually produce it if not desisted from. It is a subject on which the whites are very sore and with difficulty restrain themselves from taking what they call satisfaction, that is from killing some of the Indians."

While the Indians usually acted as the employees of white traders who paid them a trifle for the dangerous work and then shuttled the horses off to profitable sales in distant communities, more than once Indians bought stolen horses from each other — sometimes knowingly, sometimes not. On one occasion a white man forcibly took from a Cherokee a mare he said had been stolen from him by the Creeks. The Cherokee complained that the white man should pay him what he had paid the Creek for it. The white man refused, and the case was taken to Blount by a Cherokee chief. Blount told the chief that the white settler who "took possession of her brought her to me and proved her before a justice of the peace, by the oath of several disinterested evidences, to be his property; and by the law of the white people, he is entitled to keep her without paying anything. The [Cherokee] man when he bought her from a Creek must have known she had been raised by the white people [white people's horses were said to be rounder in the belly] and was stolen. Does not all your nation agree in informing me that the Creeks are daily stealing horses from the white people? Then why do they purchase horses from them?"[59]

There was of course no honor among thieves. They stole from each other and sold to each other and when questioned by white authorities blamed each other. Since there was no effective way to enforce the laws, both sides took the law into their own hands. Vigilantism prevailed and real or suspected horse thieves were frequently whipped, beaten, or shot by angry owners not too concerned about trying to differentiate one Indian from another. It was generally the Indians who suffered the most from vigilantes since they dared not assault any white man openly; yet their oath being unacceptable before a justice of the peace, it was impossible for them to "prove" legal ownership without written evidence or white witnesses. Even when Meigs accepted Indian evidence in his extrajudicial proceedings regarding depredations claims, they had no assurance of success. Meigs might trust their word, but the government auditors frequently demanded more concrete evidence before they would authorize payment.

I forward a number of claims of Citizens and Indians for damages stated by them to have been sustained, principally for Horse stealing, in which the citizens as well as the Cherokees have a share. It is very difficult to ascertain facts in these cases. The difficulty arises from the inaccuracy or want of testimony; the want of testimony arises from the impossibility of obtaining it in the places where the stealing is perpetrated being nearly all done in a wide wilderness principally in the Indian Country. This lays the white people under great distress to make legal proof of their losses. And the Indians suffer from the same cause, and in addition to that their testimony is not allowed to be valid in a legal sense.[60]

The shortcomings of horse stealing as a way of life were obvious, and it was never respectable. Still, what was respectable anymore? What options for a viable life-style with a hopeful future were there? Having lost faith in their own prowess, the Cherokees saw little they could depend upon in the white man's program. It might be said that the Cherokees had nowhere to go but up at the turn of the century. But in fact the miracle is that they did not, as did so many other Indian nations, disintegrate entirely. To their own surprise, as well as that of many of their closest observers, they discovered resources within themselves and their culture they had not realized were there.

The crisis which finally enabled them to regain a sense of their own dignity and self-respect was the effort made in the years 1806 to 1809 to persuade them to move west of the Mississippi. Their internal frictions reached a peak in 1807 when Doublehead, the "progressive" leader of the Lower Towns, was assassinated. The fact that he had been caught accepting bribes from the federal government, hidden in secret clauses of the treaties of 1805 and 1806, was only partly to blame. The deeper issue was his lack of consideration for the feelings of a large proportion of the tribe, particularly the conservative elements in the Valley Towns, who wished to find a middle ground between total assimilation and the old ways. In the press of the emergency which arose when Meigs, disillusioned by the murder of his favorite chief, tried to stampede the tribe into total removal to the West, a new group of leaders emerged.

Their first task was to reunite the various regions of the tribe in a concerted effort to hold on to what remained of their ancestral land. Their second task was to create a new instrument of political control — an elected executive body empowered to act on the nation's behalf when the council of chiefs was not in session. Although about one thousand Cherokees departed for Arkansas in 1810 in the wake of the crisis, the remaining twelve-thousand Cherokees acquired a new sense of solidarity and purpose. Henceforth the Cherokees knew that to be a Cherokee meant to live in the land of their forefathers and to put the unity and prosperity of the "nation" before the aggrandizement of individual sections or chiefs. With the new confidence gained from their successful resistance to disunion and removal, the Cherokees were ready to begin the more difficult task of restructuring their social order. This political revitalization culminated between 1817 and 1828 in a new form of government and a firm conviction that they must retain their own distinct ethnic identity. By their own effort, the Cherokees evolved a policy which avoided both of the white man's unpalatable alternatives. They would not assimilate and neither would they be moved. They would remain an independent, quasi-sovereign nation. Upon those fundamental principles the Cherokee people were reborn, like the phoenix, from the ashes of defeat and confusion.[61]

Notes

1. The standard histories of the Cherokee Nation are Henry T. Malone, *Cherokees of the Old South: A People in Transition* (Athens, Ga.: University of Georgia Press, 1956); Charles C. Royce, "The Cherokee Nation of Indians: A Narrative of Their Official Relations with the Colonial and Federal Governments," U.S. Bureau of American Ethnology, *Fifth Annual Report* (Washington, D.C., 1887); James Mooney, "Myths of the Cherokee," U.S. Bureau of American Ethnology, *Nineteenth Annual Report*, pt. I (Washington, D.C., 1900); Grace S. Woodward, *The Cherokees* (Norman, Okla.: University of Oklahoma Press, 1963); Marion L. Starkey, *The Cherokee Nation* (New York: Knopf, 1946); Gary E. Moulton, *John Ross: Cherokee Chief* (Athens, Ga.: University of Georgia Press, 1978); Rennard Strickland, *Fire and Spirits: Cherokee Law from Clan to Court* (Norman, Okla.: University of Oklahoma Press, 1975); Rudi Haliburton, Jr., *Red over Black: Black Slavery among the Cherokee Indians* (Westport, Conn.: Greenwood Press, 1977); Theda Perdue, *Slavery and the Evolution of Cherokee Society, 1540–1866* (Knoxville: University of Tennessee Press, 1978).
2. See Leonard Bloom, "The Acculturation of the Eastern Cherokees," *North Carolina Historical Review* XIX, no. 4 (Oct. 1942), 323–358; Fred Gearing, *Priests and Warriors: Social Structures of Cherokee Politics in the Eighteenth Century*, American Anthropological Association, Memoir No. 93 (Menasha, Wisc., 1962); William H. Gilbert, Jr., "The Eastern Cherokees," Bureau of American Ethnology, *Bulletin 133*, Anthropological Paper No. 23 (1943), pp. 169–413; John Philip Reid, *A Law of Blood: The Primitive Law of the Cherokee Nation* (New York: New York University Press, 1970).
3. Royce, "Cherokee Nation" p. 218.
4. For the inability, and often the unwillingness, of the federal government to uphold its treaty guarantees against white intruders in these years see ch. 7 in Francis P. Prucha, *American Indian Policy in the Formative Years* (Cambridge, Mass.: Harvard University Press, 1962) pp. 139–187.
5. For the political factionalism within the Cherokee Nation in these years see John P. Brown, *Old Frontiers: The Story of the Cherokee Indians from Earliest Times to the Date of Their Removal to the West, 1838* (Kingsport, Tenn.: Southern Publishers, 1938), pp. 148–453, and Mooney, "Myths of the Cherokee," pp. 82–87. For clan revenge, or "the blood law," see Reid, *Law of Blood*. According to this custom the closest male relative of a murdered man was personally responsible for avenging his death by taking the life of the murderer or a close relative of the murderer.
6. Royce, "The Cherokee Nation," provides detailed descriptions and maps of these cessions.
7. In 1804 and 1807 the tribe faced general starvation which only timely gifts of food from the federal agent alleviated. But in both cases he exacted a price in land cessions for this generosity.
8. Walter Lowrie, ed., *American State Papers: Indian Affairs* (Washington, 1832), I, 631. Hereafter cited as ASP (IA). As late as 1821 young Cherokees still were torn by the urge to establish themselves as warriors. One such youth left a missionary school that year: "He said he wished to leave this country and go [west] to war against the Osage."

Papers of the American Board of Commissioners for Foreign Missions, Houghton Library, Harvard University, 18.3.1, II, "Brainerd Journal," Nov. 15, 1821. Hereafter cited as ABCFM Papers.

9. Richard Peters, *The Case of the Cherokee Nation Against the State of Georgia* (Philadelphia, 1831), p. 253.

10. ASP (IA), I, 267.

11. Microfilm Records of the Cherokee Indian Agency in Tennessee, 1801–1835 (M-208), Roll 6, Records of the Bureau of Indian Affairs (RG 75), National Archives, [Dec.?] 1814. These records consist mostly of letters from the federal agent in the Cherokee Nation to the secretary of war. The microfilm has no frame numbers nor are the records paginated. The documents are given in chronological order. This undated document is placed between documents dated Nov. 1814 and Jan. 1815. Hereafter documents from this archive will be cited as M-208 with date.

12. ABCFM Papers, "Brainerd Journal," Dec. 25, 1818.

13. For the Moravian missionaries see Edmund Schwarze, *History of the Moravian Missions among the Southern Indian Tribes of the United States* (Bethlehem, Penna., 1923); for the first Presbyterian schools see Dorothy C. Bass, "Gideon Blackburn's Mission to the Cherokees," *Journal of Presbyterian History*, LII (Fall 1973), 203–226.

14. *Cherokee Phoenix*, Jan. 21, 1829. I have used the microfilm at the American Antiquarian Society, Worcester, Mass.

15. Thomas Jefferson, *Notes on Virginia*, in Adrienne Koch and William Peden, eds., *The Life and Selected Writings of Thomas Jefferson* (New York: Modern Library, 1944), p. 211.

16. Brown, *Old Frontiers*, pp. 18–19. See also Reid, *Law of Blood*, pp. 37–47, 67–70, 114–116, 119–121, 128–129, 187–188.

17. M-208, Return J. Meigs's "Journal of Occurrences," Aug. 1802.

18. *Ibid.*, Feb. 13, 1805.

19. ASP (IA), I, 676.

20. M-208, Jan. 3, 1808.

21. For the uneven distribution of government technical assistance and the complaints of the Upper and Lower Towns, see Mooney, "Myths of the Cherokee," pp. 82–83.

22. According to a census taken by Meigs in 1808–1809, the Valley Towns contained 3,648 out of 12,395 Cherokees, 5 out of 583 black slaves, 72 out of 341 whites in the nation as a whole. M-208, Oct. 17, 1808. By 1828 the Cherokees had developed a black code within their nation in order to protect their own status. See W. G. McLoughlin, "Red Indians, Black Slavery and White Racism: America's Slaveholding Indians," *American Quarterly*, XXVI (Oct. 1974), 367–385.

23. Secretary of War Lewis Cass quoted in the *Cherokee Phoenix*, Jan. 14, 1832.

24. Secretary of War William H. Crawford, ASP (IA), II, 28.

25. ABCFM Papers, "Brainerd Journal," Jan. 24, 1818.

26. M-208, Feb. 13, 1805.

27. *Ibid.*, Feb. 18, 1805.

28. *Ibid.*, undated, but filed between Dec. 25, 1801, and Jan. 1, 1802; *ibid.*, June 6, 1806.

29. *Ibid.*

30. This estimate is far too high and probably indicates that Meigs associated primarily with a special group of Cherokees and seldom ventured into the more remote regions of the nation. See *Cherokee Phoenix*, Jan. 1, 1831, for an estimate that "less than one-fourth" of the Cherokees were of mixed ancestry. An analysis of the federal census of the Cherokees in 1835 reveals that the figure was less than 23 percent.

31. M-208, July 27, 1805.

32. Rachel Eaton, *John Ross and the Cherokee Indians* (Muscogee, Okla., 1921) p. 3.

33. John Howard Payne Papers, Newberry Library (Chicago), II, 23.

34. M-208, Mar. 10, 1807, and May 1, 1807. Meigs noted of this crime, "It was an act perpetrated in a barbarous manner not in defence of life but in a rage of passion excited by the pride of the Indian to be opposed by a Negro, which even Indians effect to look down on with contempt." *Ibid.*, Feb. 22, 1810, Apr. 20, 1810. Meigs's phrase "even Indians" speaks volumes on this issue.

35. *Ibid.*, Mar. 19, 1812.

36. *Ibid.*, June 10, 1802.

37. *Ibid.,* July 26, 1803.
38. *Ibid.*
39. *Ibid.,* Apr. 7, 1801.
40. *Ibid.,* Apr. 6, 1812.
41. *Ibid.,* July 21, 1811.
42. Henry Timberlake, *Memoirs,* edited by Samuel C. Williams (Marietta, Ga.: Continental Book Company, 1948), p. 79.
43. M-208, Feb. 11, 1813.
44. Microfilm, Letters Sent by the Secretary of War Relating to Indian Affairs, 1800–1824 (M-15), Records of the Bureau of Indian Affairs (RG 75), National Archives, May 18, 1802. Hereafter cited as M-15.
45. M-15, May 30, 1803; Jan. 7, 1804.
46. *Ibid.,* July 6, 1820.
47. M-208, Feb. 22, 1810.
48. *Ibid.,* Aug. 3, 1817.
49. Treaty of June 26, 1794, cited in Richard Peters, *The Case of the Cherokee Indians* (Philadelphia, 1831), p. 254.
50. For an example of illicit slave trading among the Cherokees see ABCFM Papers, "Brainerd Journal," Oct. 10, 1819. A white man was purchasing Osage and other captive Indian children within the Cherokee Nation claiming they were "mulattos"; he sold them as black slaves to whites outside the nation. "This man," said the missionaries, "had endeavored to persuade another to join him in this business, stating that there were a number of [Indian] captives in the Cherokee Nation which he thought he could obtain at a low price."
51. M-208, Feb. 13, 1805.
52. My analysis here owes something to the chapter entitled "Crime As a Way of Life" in Daniel Bell, *The End of Ideology* (New York: Free Press, 1961).
53. M-208, Dec. 19, 1807.
54. ASP (IA), I, 438.
55. *Ibid.,* 265 (May 5, 1792).
56. M-208, Dec. 19, 1807.
57. *Ibid.*
58. Cited in Prucha, *American Indian Policy,* p. 204.
59. ASP (1A), I, 281 (Sept. 13, 1792).
60. M-208, Dec. 19, 1807.
61. For a discussion of the first removal crisis of 1806–1809 and the revitalization which emerged from it, see W. G. McLoughlin, "Thomas Jefferson and the Beginning of Cherokee Nationalism, 1806–1809," *William and Mary Quarterly,* 3rd ser., XXXII (Oct. 1975) 547–580.

The Politics of
Industrialism:
Massachusetts,
1830–1870

Paul Goodman

Paul Goodman, professor of history at the University of California, Davis, is the author of *Democratic-Republicans of Massachusetts: Politics in a Young Republic* (1964). He is currently working on a study of New England politics from 1830 to 1860.

"I CANNOT BUT REGRET that our state is put forward so prominently," lamented Robert C. Winthrop, Boston Brahmin and former Whig leader of the Bay State as civil war engulfed the nation in 1861. "Sumner at the Head of Foreign Affairs, Wilson at the Head of Military Affairs, Butler commanding one wing, Banks commanding another wing, Adams Minister to London. . . ."[1] The changing of the guard could hardly have been more complete or more painful to men like Winthrop: Charles Sumner, once a pariah cast out of the elegant parlors of Boston for the effrontery to challenge the claim of the Hub's elite to set moral standards; Henry Wilson, the coarse, ambitious Natick cobbler, once satisfied to do duty as a corporal in the Whig army, corralling working folks on election day; Ben Butler, the shady, foul-mouthed demagogue and Brahmin-baiter, self-proclaimed tribune of the people who sinuously piled up wealth and power for personal indulgence; Nathaniel Banks, formerly a bobbin boy in a Waltham factory, isolated as a member of the perennial Democratic minority who eventually scrambled from the workshop to become Speaker of the House of Representatives and governor; and finally Charles F. Adams, latest in a gifted line flawed by cranky independence and arrogant certainty that the well-being of the republic was never safe in the hands of State Street and Beacon Hill.

163

The ascendancy of men like Sumner, Wilson, Butler, Banks, Adams, and others who led the Massachusetts Republicans came only after a long battle that dethroned "Old Boston," as Henry Adams dubbed the metropolis's Whig elite. Their displacement, Adams thought, was a "necessary preliminary to growth."[2] Those whose entrepreneurial talents, vision, and financial resources had placed Massachusetts in the vanguard of industrial development in the United States and had given them, through the Whig party, a powerful voice in the affairs of state and nation, found themselves impotent after 1850, helpless to resist the new men, new measures, and new sentiments which thrust them aside.

To victors and victims alike the emergence of the Republican party, coming after the Free-Soil and Know-Nothing frenzies, appeared nothing less than a popular uprising, although a legal one, which toppled those accustomed to rule, an elite whose authority had once seemed unshakable. The Winthrops entered the political wilderness, explained Henry L. Dawes, a Republican politician from western Massachusetts, because such people had made the mistake of believing "as a class that the sun rises in Chelsea, comes up over State Street, hovers about the State House, and sinks in the waters of Back Bay."[3] The Republicans, of course, knew better. Their ascendancy rested on the support of "the great middling-interest class," explained Sam Bowles, editor of the *Springfield Republican*. "The highest class, aristocratically associated and affiliated," he explained, were "timid, afraid of change," paralyzed because they "held in their hands, the sensitive cords of commerce," while the poor were "fed by the rich man's money and led by the rich man's finger."[4] The Republican mass, by contrast, were those who "work with their own hands, who live and act independently, who hold the stakes of home and family, of farm and workshop, of education and freedom." Such were the folk of Worcester County, in the center of the state, who inhabited "a spot on the face of the earth where labor got the largest proportion of the joint product of labor and capital." The hardworking mechanics and farmers of Worcester prospered but they nursed "no pride of family or wealth."[5] Through the Republican party, people like them from Nantucket to the Berkshires sought in a troubled time a mastery over their state and the future. "The families which once controlled the city and state, which dictated opinion and put antislavery men in coventry, have vanished," exulted Edward Pierce, Charles Sumner's close friend.[6] Wealthy Boston businessman and dissenter from Brahmin orthodoxy John Murray Forbes agreed: "Mr. Lincoln must not depend upon the rich and aristocratic classes, nor upon the city," he warned in 1860, but rather "he must appeal to the hardhanded people of the country."[7]

The long political ascendancy and then sudden eclipse of the most prominent entrepreneurial elite in mid-nineteenth-century America is a tale embedded in the rise and fall of the Whig party and in the emergence of a new party system in the 1850s.[8] For a generation Boston's elite had assumed and received credit for the state's remarkable material development. Practical men of affairs, "Old Boston" had no taste for "anything like a principle," Henry Adams remarked, certainly not the antislavery principles preached by "the longhaired men and dythyrambic women" Beacon Hill had thought safely relegated to outer darkness. Bay State Whiggery's inability to contain the spread of the antislavery infection in the late 1840s eventually sealed the political doom of both the Whig party and the most powerful element within the Whig formation. Not the history of cotton textile manufactures but "the history of antislavery is the history of our country," intoned Henry Adams in 1876. Part, albeit a small part, of the "price and penalty paid" to end human bondage in the United States, Adams concluded, was the "breaking up in Boston of a social condition which had not the cement of impersonal truth."[9]

II

A quarter century earlier, Adams's father contemplated an instability that he thought threatened social order. "Our country has grown out of our means to control it," Charles Francis Adams confided to his diary in 1832. "Interests are so various and so opposite that it is not easy to say what the result will be."[10] Whatever may have been the case elsewhere, political instability, owing to corrosive competition among rival interests, was not the condition of the Adamses' native state. A powerful Whig party achieved hegemony in the 1830s by accommodating the competing interests of an increasingly heterogeneous society. The Whig synthesis fused the promise of unlimited material progress broadly diffused with the preservation of moral and social order. State aid for railroads went hand in hand with the modernization and expansion of public education and temperance. Massachusetts, proclaimed Rufus Choate, oracle of Bay State Whiggery, was "the most homogeneous community that ever existed," a society "without ranks, orders, classes; without antagonisms of interests, institutions, pursuits, or moral sentiments."[11] Boston, a city of some eighty-thousand souls in the 1830s, with another forty-thousand inhabiting its suburbs, had "no visible poverty, little gross ignorance, and little crime," boasted Brahmin George Ticknor, high priest of culture in the Athens of America. Even "the condition of the lowest classes of the people is so truly comfortable," Ticknor purred.[12] Classic Whig ideology, with its invocation of such notions as the harmony of interest and the universality of opportunity and prosperity, is hardly a reliable description of social realities; yet it exercised a powerful grip over significant portions of the citizenry, the more remarkable because in its heyday — the 1830s and 1840s — conflict between workers and employers, developing communities and backward ones, native born and foreign born, evangelicals and anti-evangelicals, old wealth and new wealth were increasingly straining the credibility of a theory of social harmony, just as a widening gap between rich and poor undermined confidence that equal opportunity was in fact a reality.

The proof of Whig persuasiveness in the Bay State came at the polls. Only twice in twenty years (1830–1850) did the party fail to capture the governorship and not once in these decades did the Bay State swerve from its Whig loyalty in presidential elections. The Democratic party was not in a hopelessly minority position — by the late 1830s it had gained sufficient strength to come within striking distance of victory and occasionally actually won. Yet the party's failure to turn Massachusetts into a competitive two-party state is surprising. The Massachusetts social order after 1830 was increasingly heterogeneous. Industrialization and a transportation revolution planted factories and workshops, large and small, throughout the once quiet countryside; towns swelled into large cities, and Boston grew into a metropolis with 18 percent of the state's inhabitants by 1850. The economic transformation stimulated the emergence of a working-class subculture rooted in the interests and consciousness that set wage earners apart, while professionals and white-collar workers formed another urban stratum (see Tables I, II). Strangers from Ireland added ethnic and religious diversity to a once all-Yankee populace; by 1855 the sons and daughters of Erin formed almost half the population of Boston. In these ways and many more, material progress brought heightened diversity, not the least of which was a tendency for great wealth to beget still greater wealth and for the distance between the most fortunate and the rest to widen and harden.[13] "The deformity of the present society," lamented the saint of Bay State Unitarianism, the Reverend William Ellery Channing, "is the separation of ranks, the immense disparity, the inhuman distance of different orders."[14]

Stratified by occupation, wealth, residence, and ethnicity, people after 1830 were more than ever set apart by denominational attachments. A once homogeneous Congregationalist commonwealth, Massachusetts in 1833 ended the ties between church and state which stretched back for two centuries. The downfall of the establishment was the unavoidable consequence of the cancerous spread of secularism and the fragmentation of religious faith among half a dozen competing denominations. By 1840 the numbers of Baptist, Methodist, and Universalist churches almost matched the numbers of Congregationalist-Unitarian congregations (see Table III). Complicating religious diversity was the spread of evangelical impulses in most of the major denominations, often dividing them in the process and provoking conflict with anti-evangelicals — both secular and religious — who resisted the pietist crusade to Christianize a social order by coercing temperance, abolishing slavery, banning Sunday mail, making the common schools inculcators of evangelical morality.[15] Yet despite the evangelical successes, nationally only about one in seven belonged to a church by 1850, after decades of revivalism.[16] In Massachusetts as elsewhere the nothingarians were legion. Some unaffiliated citizens were probably fellow travelers who leaned toward a particular denomination or at least shared its perspective on public questions; many were indifferent; and others were strongly hostile to efforts by the Christian "party" in politics to dictate personal behavior.[17]

The social diversity had alarmed Boston's Congressman Daniel Webster, who confessed in 1823 that politics back home disgusted him because, though "there is a federal interest, a Democratic

I. Leading Industrial Occupations in Massachusetts As a Percent of Total Industrial Occupations, 1837–1855

	1837 %	1855 %
Textile Manufacturing	24.5	19.9
Boot and Shoe	33.3	31.7
Leather	1.5	1.7
Apparel	4.1	7.0
Paper	1.0	1.1
Metals	1.8	5.7
Fabricated Metals	3.6	6.9
Lumber, Fabricated Wood	3.6	6.9
Foods	1.0	1.4
Shipbuilding	2.4	1.0
Fishing	17.2	8.9
	94.0	92.2
% Total Population Engaged in "Industry"	16.7	21.7

Note: Missing from the census of "industry" in 1837 and 1855 are the building trades and other skilled mechanics as well as unskilled laborers not employed in the industries included in the census. See Table II.
Sources: Secretary of State, *Statistical Tables: Exhibiting . . . Branches of Industry in Massachusetts . . . 1837* (Boston, 1838), pp. 201–209; Secretary of State, *Abstract of the Census of . . . Massachusetts . . . 1855* (Boston, 1857), pp. 162–173.

II. Occupational Distribution of Massachusetts Labor Force, 1855

	%		%
Farmers	16.9	Mechanics	36.7*
Factory Operatives	2.6	(Building Trades)	(8.1)
Laborers	18.1	Merchants	8.7
Mariners, Boatmen	4.9	Professionals	2.5
Manufacturers	1.6	Miscellaneous	7.9

*Includes boot and shoe workers

Occupational Distribution of Professionals, 1855

Doctors	21.3
Artists, Engravers	3.8
Clergy	21.1
Teachers	14.3
Lawyers	13.4

Occupational Distribution of Mechanics, Major Occupations, 1855

Blacksmiths	4.2	Tanners	2.5
Cabinetmakers	2.2	Stoneworkers	1.8
Carpenters	13.6	Carriagemakers,	
Machinists	6.2	Wheelwrights	1.8
Masons, Plasterers	3.4	Coopers	1.3
Painters	4.5	Clockmakers	1.3
Shipwrights	2.4	Foundrymen, Molders	1.4
Shoemakers	28.8	Building Trades	22.1
Tailors	2.7		

Source: Secretary of State, *Abstract of the Census of Massachusetts ... 1855* (Boston, 1857), pp. 162–173.

III. Religious Denominations in Massachusetts by Numbers of Churches, 1815–1860

	1815		1838		1860	
	N	%	N	%	N	%
Congregationalist	341	64.2	549	47.4	501	31.7
Presbyterian	6	2.4	—	—	10	.6
Episcopalian	10	1.9	39	3.4	73	4.5
Baptist	128	24.1	242	20.9	270	16.5
Methodist	26	4.9	188	17.4	295	18.1
Friends	12	2.3	16	1.4	36	2.2
Universalist	7	1.3	101	8.7	118	7.2
Roman Catholic	1	.2	9	.8	88	5.4
Unitarian	—	—	*	*	158	9.7
Other Christian	—	—	10	.9	85	5.2
Total	531		1,154		1,634	

*Unitarian churches included among Congregationalist
Sources: 1815: Timothy Dwight, *Travels in New England and New York,* ed. B. M. Solomon (4 vols.; Cambridge, 1969), IV, 322–324; 1838: *Massachusetts Register, 1838* (Boston, n.d.), pp. 127–143; 1860: *United States Census,* 1860, pp. 408–409.

interest, a Bankrupt interest, an Orthodox interest, and a middling interest," he saw "no national interest. . . ."[18] Yet the Whig party which Webster helped to build and lead established its supremacy in the Bay State precisely because it massed a broad spectrum of interests and perspectives under one political banner that a decisive majority of voters thought harmonized both particular interests and the general welfare.

The structure of the Whig vote in the 1830s and 1840s reveals the dimensions of the party's broad base. Whiggery's strongest following was in the large cities, the fishing towns, and in towns with only Congregationalist churches, that is, towns without "dissenting" congregations. The party ran less well in, though it usually carried, the nonindustrial towns, the boot and shoe towns, and those in which Baptists, Methodists, Universalists, and Quakers were numerous. The Whigs usually lost towns which had no Congregationalist churches, that is, "pure dissenting" towns where the only organized denominations tended to be Baptist and/or Methodist. The Democrats' best showing was in the agricultural towns least touched by industrial and commercial development, and in towns where dissenters were prominent, especially Baptists (see Table IV). The importance of denominationalism is suggested more sharply in Table V, which indicates that Democrats usually ran well ahead in religiously diverse towns in which the numbers of Baptist, Methodist, and Universalist churches exceeded the number of Congregationalist churches. Congregationalists, however, were by no means monolithically Whig, as in the case of Bristol County, which was the home of the Bay State's leading Democrat, Marcus Morton, himself an Orthodox Congregationalist most of his life. In eastern Massachusetts, where the Unitarian-Trinitarian split among Congregationalists was more extensive and bitter than anywhere else, the Orthodox of Bristol County may have leaned toward the Democrats because of the strong Unitarian tone Whiggery assumed in eastern Massachusetts, especially its leadership. There were striking differences in the voting patterns of those exclusively Congregationalist towns in which Unitarian splits occurred, and those which avoided fissure, as Table VI illustrates. "Pure" Trinitarian towns, for example, came close to giving the Anti-Masons a majority in 1834, whereas the third party ran much more poorly in towns which spawned Unitarian churches. Similarly

IV. Massachusetts Party Vote by Types of Towns, 1833–1845
(Whig and Democratic %=% two party vote; third party %=% three-party vote)

	1833 Governor			1839 Governor		1840 President		1845 Governor		
	Whig %	Demo. %	Anti-Mason %	W %	D %	W %	D %	W %	D %	Liberty %
Statewide	61.9	38.1	31.4	49.8	50.2	58.4	41.6	54.1	45.9	7.9
N=( )	(19)			(19)		(19)		(19)		
Cities	59.8	40.2	21.3	53.2	46.8	59.9	41.1	59.4	41.6	7.3
	(67)			(69)		(69)		(69)		
Nonindustrial Towns	54.7	45.3	31.2	44.6	55.4	52.1	48.9	50.3	49.5	7.2
	(22)			(22)		(21)		(22)		
Boot and Shoe Towns	55.3	44.7	46.6	50.3	49.7	59.1	41.9	56.2	43.8	10.8
	(15)			(15)		(15)		(18)		
Fishing Towns	61.4	38.6	30.8	54.4	45.6	60.4	39.6	60.2	39.8	9.1
	(11)			(11)		(11)		(11)		
Towns with No Congregational Churches	42.1	57.9	53.0	34.3	65.7	49.9	50.1	39.0	61.0	4.1
	(34)			(35)		(36)		(35)		
Towns with Only Congregational Churches	68.3	31.7	40.8	50.8	49.2	62.5	37.5	58.4	41.2	13.9
	(31)			(31)		(31)		(31)		
Baptist Towns	53.1	46.9	32.8	47.9	52.1	54.2	45.8	53.6	46.4	7.0
	(19)			(19)		(19)		(19)		
Methodist Towns	57.2	42.8	27.6	41.4	50.6	55.4	44.6	54.5	45.5	6.9
	(39)			(40)		(40)		(40)		
Universalist Towns	57.2	42.8	26.2	58.4	41.6	54.6	45.4	57.3	48.7	9.6
	(11)			(11)		(11)		(11)		
Quaker Towns	55.0	45.0	29.3	48.6	51.4	57.8	42.2	53.5	46.3	5.3
Boston	69.0	31.0	22.9	56.9	43.1	63.6	36.4	65.2	34.8	3.7

Note: Cities=towns with populations of 5,000+ in 1840; Nonindustrial Towns = towns in which 80%+ of the labor force in 1840 was engaged in agriculture; Boot and Shoe Towns = towns in which 25%+ of the population in 1840 was engaged in boot and shoe manufactures; Fishing Towns = towns in which 10%+ of population in 1840 was engaged in fishing; Baptist Towns = towns with two or more Baptist churches, excluding Boston in 1838; Methodist Towns = towns with two or more Methodist churches, excluding Boston in 1838; Quaker Towns = towns with one or more Quaker congregations, excluding Boston in 1838; Universalist Towns = towns in which a third or more of the churches were Universalist in 1838.

Sources: *United States Census,* 1840, for numbers engaged in agriculture, inhabiting cities of 5,000, and total population, pp. 36–47; Massachusetts Secretary of State, *Statistical Tables . . . 1837* (Boston, 1838) for numbers engaged in fishing and boot and shoe manufacturing; *Massachusetts Register and United States Calendar for 1838* (Boston, n.d.), pp. 127–143, for religious denominations by town. Election returns from Return of Votes for Presidential Elector, Return of Votes for Governor and Lieutenant Governor. Massachusetts Archives, Mss., Microfilm.

V. Religion and Politics: Party Voting in Dissenting and Nondissenting Towns, 1834–1845

		1833 Governor			1839 Governor		1845 Governor	
		W	D	Anti-Mason	W	D	W	D
Berkshire	Dissenting	42.4	57.6	10.3	36.0	64.0	41.9	58.1
	Nondissent.	55.9	44.1	10.9	46.5	53.5	53.1	46.9
Bristol	Dissenting	53.8	46.2	55.4	47.2	52.8	52.2	47.8
	Nondissent.	50.4	49.6	48.6	38.9	61.6	45.4	54.6
Hampden	Dissenting	44.5	55.5	8.2	40.1	59.9	44.0	56.0
	Nondissent.	64.7	35.3	14.9	46.0	54.0	51.0	49.0
Worcester	Dissenting	53.8	46.2	38.5	48.8	51.2	51.0	49.0
	Nondissent.	73.2	26.8	23.0	52.5	47.5	47.7	42.3

Note: Dissenting towns = towns where the number of Baptist, Methodist, and Universalist churches exceeded the number of Congregationalist churches.
Source: Massachusetts Register, 1838, pp. 127–143 for religious data; for election data, Returns of Votes for Governor and Lieutenant Governor, Massachusetts Archives, Mss., Microfilm.

VI. Towns with Only Congregational Churches, 1834–1845: Trinitarians vs. Unitarians

	1833 Governor			1839 Governor		1840 President		1845 Governor			1848 President		
	W	D	A-M	W	D	W	D	W	D	L	W	D	FS
Towns with Unitarian Churches, 1850	69.0	31.0	31.6	43.6	56.4	57.0	43.0	52.1	47.9	9.1	57.9	42.1	37.6
Towns without Unitarian Churches, 1850	67.6	32.4	47.3	56.3	43.7	67.5	32.5	64.1	35.9	17.4	71.0	29.0	23.9
All Towns with Only Congregational Churches	68.3	31.7	40.8	50.8	49.2	62.5	37.5	58.8	41.2	13.9	64.0	36.0	32.0

Note and Sources: Towns with only Congregationalist churches are in *Massachusetts Register, 1838*, pp. 127–143; those which had Unitarian churches by 1850 were located in *United States Census*, 1850, *Massachusetts Social Statistics*, Ms., National Archives. Prior to the 1840s, the *Massachusetts Register* did not differentiate between Trinitarian and liberal or proto-Unitarian Congregationalist churches. Separation of church and state in 1833 formalized splits that existed in heterogeneous Congregational churches. Many of the Unitarian churches of 1850 derived from such splits as is suggested by the striking differences in voting patterns in 1833 and later between those Congregationalist towns which developed Unitarian churches and those which did not. For election data see Table IV. Whig and Democratic percentages are the two-party vote; third party percentages are of the three-party vote.

Trinitarian towns stayed with the Whigs in the 1839 gubernatorial election when the party lost the state, in large measure because it had conceded to peitist demands for temperance legislation. In contrast, the divided towns switched to the Democrats.

Though the gross economic and denominational characteristics of a community — whether it was a small, rural town or an industrial and commercial hub, denominationally mixed or homogeneous — significantly shaped the structure of voting, other complex patterns of social relationships peculiar to a community influenced partisan attachments too. Boot and shoe towns, for example, tended to vote reliably Whig, but the Democrats polled well in Lynn, the nation's largest and oldest boot and shoe center. Lynn's economy was dependent on shoe manufacture, which meant that other commercial and maritime interests were negligible. By the 1830s Lynn had developed a labor force which, because of its size and industrial experience, was beginning to form a working-class consciousness that eventually spawned a militant labor movement and a workingmen's newspaper in the 1840s and 1850s. In addition, a variety of religious denominations, notably the Methodists, won great popularity in Lynn, and contributed to the evolution of a workingmen's subculture. Finally, few Irish or other immigrants settled in Lynn to complicate the development of solidarity along occupational lines. In such circumstances Whig influence was weaker than in other smaller and newer boot and shoe towns where the industrial experience of the labor force was more limited.[19]

In contrast, workingmen in Boston, differentiated by an immensely complex variety in kind and level of skill, and inhabiting a metropolis with large numbers of professionals, petty shopkeepers, and businessmen, were much more susceptible to the influence of entrepreneurial elements, who were overwhelmingly Whig. Charlestown across the river, however, was a Democratic town, and Whigs understood why. Repeatedly they sought to prevent the polls from remaining open late to allow workers who lived outside the city time to return home after a day's labor to cast their ballots remote from Boston's influence.[20]

Where Whig channels of influence were weak, Whig strength at the polls reflected that weakness. The small town of Mount Washington, in the northwestern extremity of Berkshire County, is an extreme example of a Democratic bastion in the 1830s and

1840s, a farming town which raised sheep and produced charcoal but was literally without institutions or an influential middle class. Though incorporated sixty-five years earlier, Mount Washington in 1835 had "no minister, no doctor, no lawyer, no post-office, and no tavern."[21] But it did have lots of Democrats, as did the five other Berkshire towns without a post office, church, or justice of the peace and quorum in 1838.

In contrast to such one-party towns was sharply divided Waltham. The coming of industry into this farming community doubled the population between 1810 and 1820, with the newcomers concentrated in the southern section of the town. The farmers and traditional leaders who resided in the northern and western sections saw their influence in jeopardy, as the two factions joined battle over the location of a new meetinghouse. "It was a contest for location between the farm aristocracy and the mill aristocracy," a Walthamite explained.[22]

Behind these voting patterns lay a web of historical and contemporary circumstances that made Massachusetts a solidly Whig state for two decades and gave the entrepreneurial elite in Boston, together with allied groups in commercial and industrial centers throughout the state, the dominant voice in the dominant party. The party traced its origins back to the 1820s when Bay State voters massed behind their native son John Quincy Adams in his campaigns for the presidency. Unity in presidential politics reflected the collapse of the first party system by 1824. Programmatic differences which a generation earlier had divided Republicans and Federalists had blurred if not disappeared, and Federalist elites accepted and integrated Republican leadership. A small Jackson party emerged in the late 1820s, consisting of a few unreconstructed Jeffersonians plus a coterie of officeseekers, but even though the party expanded its narrow base in the next decade, it could never catch up with Whiggery.

As the party of economic development wedded to the tariff, internal improvements, and a national bank, Massachusetts Whiggery demonstrated extraordinary appeal because of the pervasiveness of industrial and urban development. Elsewhere, a highly uneven diffusion of economic development created sharp contrasts between advanced and backward areas, with correspondingly different interests and attitudes toward developmental policy. Such differences formed a seedbed which nourished well-matched competitive party systems in the 1830s, with the Whigs appealing more to the developing areas, the Democrats to the less well endowed, underdeveloped elements. In Massachusetts, too, the Democrats' strongest appeal was to the rural towns least touched by change. But such towns were atypical. To an unusual degree, Bay State communities were affected, some more than others, by industrial development. By the 1850s railroads had reached every town of five-thousand or more with one exception, and of ninety-eight towns with between two-thousand and five-thousand souls, all but a dozen inland communities lacked rail connections. With one mile of rail for every seven square miles of territory, the Bay State was far in advance of New York, whose ratio was 1:28.[23]

Under Whig management, moreover, industrial advance came cheaply. The costs of government fell lightly on the shoulders of taxpayers. During much of the 1830s and 1840s, Massachusetts dispensed with even its modest state tax, relying on the bank tax for 82 percent of its revenues in 1837 and that together with two other business taxes for 86 percent in 1847.[24] Like other states, Massachusetts invested in internal improvements, but the Western Railroad proved to be a financial success. Massachusetts was spared the massive burden of public indebtedness, taxes, and the dangers of default other states encountered. The opportunities for the Democrats to profit as the party of retrenchment and economy were meager, the more so because of the comparative weakness, isolation, and rarity of have-not communities with an affinity for the Jacksonians. Nor could the antimonopoly theme get Democrats very far. Like the spread of the rail network, the diffusion of banking through liberal charter grants — from 66 in 1829 to 129 by 1837 — not only stimulated growth but mollified the desire of have-not towns for banking facilities and eased country-town jealousy of cities well endowed with banks.[25] When the crash came in 1837, Massachusetts Whigs could blame the Democrats for economic mismanagement and could contrast the relative soundness of Bay State banking and currency with the chaos elsewhere.

The extensive diffusion of economic development at low cost to the taxpayer minimized, though it did not erase, divisions between farming and industrial, rural and urban interests. So too did the shrewd sensitivity of urban Whigs to small-town apprehensions that progress was passing them by. A system of town representation established by the revolutionary constitution of 1780 remained intact in the 1830s, overrepresenting the small towns and underapportioning the growing communities. Bostonians pressed for reapportionment, but a constitutional amendment adopted in 1840 temporarily soothed small-town anxieties by leaving them still substantially overrepresented. To city Whigs this seemed a reasonable price to maintain party harmony, especially since on key issues — such as state aid to railroads — country Whigs eventually deferred to their city brethren's desires.[26]

The Whigs similarly demonstrated sensitivity to working people, a group whose political volatility is seen in the shifting voting patterns of the boot and shoe towns and the efforts by the Democrats to cultivate labor support. Skilled artisans had begun to organize unions and to strike for higher wages and shorter hours in the 1830s.[27] Employers fiercely resisted, but the Massachusetts Supreme Judicial Court — a bastion of Whig orthodoxy — refused to bring union activity under the ban of criminal conspiracy doctrine. *Commonwealth v. Hunt* (1840) demonstrated to workers that a Whig judiciary had not thrown its weight into the scales on behalf of employers. Organized workers were not immune from legal constraints, as strikes occurred ever more frequently over the next two decades, but the decision minimized the growth of a working-class consciousness rooted in the conviction that government was an enemy. That consciousness had failed to develop earlier in America, because in contrast to Europe, workers did not have to battle for the rights of citizenship. In Massachusetts those rights by 1840 included free association for purposes of collective bargaining.[28]

The expansion and improvement of common schools was still another sign that Massachusetts, under Whig guidance, recognized that the promise of equal opportunity in an industrial society necessitated that all children receive a fair start in the competitive race. Moreover, through the schools, the state could inculcate the ethic of self-improvement, an ethic that had extraordinary attraction among working folk. Public schools, like publicly assisted internal improvements, were the means by which a Whiggish government served as an agent of social progress. Horace Mann, first as a Whig legislative leader and then as secretary of the State Board of Education, championed them both.[29]

Just as Whigs carefully maneuvered among the state's economic and occupational interests, so too did the party's leaders cautiously navigate among the powerful and sometimes warring religious denominations. When disestablishment finally occurred in 1833, it was no partisan triumph. Orthodox Congregationalists, Baptists, and particularly the Universalists who led the final battle, were politically divided. Though anticlerical elements were proportionately more weighty among the Democrats, prominent members of that party opposed change.[30] Urban Whig elites, especially those with Unitarian leanings, were apprehensive about the consequences of disestablishment for the future of Unitarian parishes and the loss of ecclesiastical sources of social control, but most bowed before the inevitable. Massachusetts thereby was spared a bruising battle that would have split both parties. In other ways, too, cosmopolitan, Unitarian Whig elites accommodated, not without difficulty, their Trinitarian brethren. In Boston, citadel of rational Christianity, evangelicals forced the Unitarian merchants and lawyers to make room for pietists in the party councils in the 1820s.[31] Though religious liberals first tried to prevent the legislature from granting a charter to Orthodox-backed Amherst College in the 1820s, the Trinitarians ultimately prevailed. Similarly, Orthodox Congregationalists who charged that under Horace Mann's management the State Board of Education had become an instrument of Unitarian influence in the schools quieted down when given greater representation on the board.[32]

Yet the Orthodox-Unitarian accommodation was inherently unstable. The success of revivalism emboldened evangelical Congregationalists and enabled them to ally with other pietistically inclined elements to form a Christian "party" in politics. When Whig Governor Edward Everett caved in to evangelical demands for temperance legislation in 1838, the Whig party temporarily came to grief. Everett, though himself once a Unitarian minister and Harvard professor, had abandoned both the classroom and the pulpit for politics. A pliable, ambitious politician with a keen scent for political winds that would advance his career, Everett had cultivated the Orthodox in the early 1830s when their support of the Anti-Mason party threatened the Whig majority. Everett had small enthusiasm for the Fifteen Gallon Law which banned the retailing of liquor in quantities of less than fifteen gallons, but he had to go along or lose Orthodox votes. The result was an outcry from Unitarian Whigs, led by Harrison G. Otis, and anti-evangelical Democrats. Trapped, Everett went down to defeat in 1839. The Whigs suffered heavy losses in every type of town (see Table IV) except the Universalist towns, where the Whigs ran well ahead of their customary showing. The Democrats made dramatic gains in the "pure dissenting" towns without Congregationalist churches. Temperance was clearly a party splitter for the Whigs. After the Democrats repealed the measure in the 1840s, temperance subsided as a statewide issue until the 1850s.

The Whigs quickly learned the lesson of Everett's defeat and John Davis's failure in 1842. The next year the party tapped George N. Briggs to lead their ticket. For seven terms this self-made man from the Berkshires, who started as a hatter's apprentice, became a lawyer, and in 1830 entered Congress for six terms, proved just the man. Briggs was a prominent Baptist, a choice that avoided the necessity of selecting, as in the past, either an Orthodox Congregationalist or a Unitarian. A long-tenured trustee of Orthodox Williams College and president of the American Baptist Missionary Union, the American Temperance Union, and the American Tract Society, his ascendancy gave the pietists a symbolic victory, yet Briggs could be counted on to hew to the party line.[33]

The locus of that leadership appeared diffused. An Appleton, a Lawrence, and a Winthrop served in Congress, and great Boston businessmen, such as P. C. Brooks, could be found on the city's delegation in the General Court, but the party was no closed corporation. Talented but unconnected young men received recognition and enjoyed patronage. Horace Mann began as a young lawyer representing Dedham in the legislature, then proved his value to Boston capitalists as a skillful advocate of their views on Beacon Hill. At the urging of his Boston friends, he became a Suffolk County senator and tapped Boston money both in his professional role as educational reformer and for his own personal needs. Henry Wilson likewise rose rapidly in the Whig ranks because of the Natick shoemaker's gifts as a popular orator and party organizer who spoke the vernacular and mixed easily with the rank and file. Similarly, on Boston and Springfield city councils in the 1830s and 1840s sat not only men of wealth and social eminence but substantial contingents of skilled workers and small shopkeepers.[34] The Whig escalator thus deprived the Democrats of leadership material.[35] That party chronically suffered from a paucity of political talent, a condition resulting in part from its minority status, but also from a distinct odor of social unrespectability.

Massachusetts Whiggery was open to the ambitious, and flexibly accommodated a variety of groups and interests under its umbrella, but there was a center of gravity among the state's preeminent entrepreneurial elements, especially the merchants, manufacturers, and capitalists in Boston. Without the approval of the Boston "coterie," complained Congressman Edward Everett in 1828, advancement was difficult, and despite his recognition, he lamented exclusion from the "confidential councils" of the party.[36] That exclusion drove him to dallying with Anti-Masonry. Even Daniel Webster discovered that his career was hostage to the opinions of Boston's elite. For them, the unity of the Whig party nationally, not the advancement of Webster's presidential ambitions, was indispensable if Whig mercantile policy were to become public law.[37] In control of Boston's forty-man delegation in the General Court, employers of the state's most successful lawyers, advertisers in the leading newspapers, stockholders and directors of the commonwealth's richest and most powerful business enterprises, trustees of its leading philanthropies and its university, Boston's elite, in alliance with parallel elements in other urban communities such as Worcester, Springfield, Lowell, and Salem, was the most powerful constellation in the Whig galaxy. The state's leading entrepreneurs were not omnipotent, but on most matters of vital concern to their interests, they usually prevailed. Their most ambitious undertaking, for example, the Western Railroad, depended upon state aid. Economy-minded farmers and communities quarreling over the route stalled the project in the legislature, but the persistence of the road's promoters eventually paid off.[38] Similarly, though country Whigs managed to proliferate the number of banks, the state's Suffolk System, in which the large Boston banks had a leading voice, regulated and restrained the smaller interior institutions.

If anyone doubted its dominant voice in Bay State Whiggery, events in the late 1840s made Boston's power indelibly clear. First the annexation of Texas, then war with Mexico, and finally resolution of the sectional deadlock after the war divided the Whigs over slavery. Accustomed to getting their way in matters of great moment, Boston's Whig elite confidently assumed that the Free-Soil infection within their ranks, which jeopardized sectional peace and national party unity, could be put down, and it was. But the triumph was short-lived. The infection, repelled within the party, spread unpredictably to other parts of the body politic, and ultimately led to the Whigs' undoing.[39]

"The politics of Massachusetts are in a state of utter confusion," reported an alarmed Daniel Webster to President Fillmore, one month after the heroic labors that had saved the union through grand compromise in 1850. "Many Whigs are *afraid* to act a manly part," he complained, "lest they should lose the government," and instead were acting "a most mean part in their courtship of abolitionism."[40] That courtship, however, came too late. In the fall elections, a coalition of Free-Soil Whigs and office-hungry Democrats broke the Whig party's grip on the State House and laid the foundations for a new party system that dominated the commonwealth for more than seven decades. By the mid-1850s one could discern that the price of maintaining control of the Whig party had been to risk political oblivion. Try as leading Whigs might to preserve mastery by invoking the sanctified rhetoric of class harmony, insisting on the common interests of country and city, of workers and employers, of slave owners and free labor, and by declaring that the commonwealth's continued prosperity hinged on sectional harmony, and that people should keep their minds on the tariff and not the territories, it was no use. The old ideas fell on deaf ears; the old leaders fell out of step with those they presumed to lead. The finale was a democratic political revolution in the 1850s that thrust new men and new forces to the fore, sweeping aside whomever stood in the way.

III

The political revolution of the 1850s profoundly altered the lines of political cleavage which had structured the second party system.[41] The Democrats, always the minority party but not without prospects of occasional successes, shrank to a hopeless minority. The new Republican party, which captured more than 70 percent of the votes in the 1856 and 1860 presidential elections,

VII. Massachusetts Party Vote by Types of Towns, 1855–1860

(Whig, Republican, and Democratic % = % two-party vote; American % = % three-party vote; Constitutional Union and Breckenridge Democratic % = % four-party vote)

	1855 Governor			1856 President			1858 Governor			1860 President			
	Whig	Demo.	Amer.	Rep.	Demo.	Amer.	Rep.	Demo.	Amer.	Rep.	Demo.	Const. Union	Brecken-ridge Demo.
Statewide	66.9	33.1	66.5	73.6	26.4	11.8	65.7	34.3	28.7	72.2	27.8	13.2	3.5
N = ( )	(15)			(15)			(15)			(15)			
Cities	71.2	28.8	62.6	67.2	32.8	16.8	58.5	41.5	32.4	72.3	27.7	17.7	4.9
Nonindustrial Towns	(50) 64.1	35.9	58.9	(50) 74.4	25.6	10.3	(49) 65.9	34.1	23.8	(50) 77.0	23.0	10.4	6.0
Boot and Shoe Towns	(17) 66.1	33.9	76.3	(17) 73.3	26.7	9.6	(17) 67.3	32.7	29.1	(17) 70.9	29.1	11.0	1.5
Fishing Towns	(15) 72.0	28.0	65.6	(15) 83.0	17.0	12.5	(15) 76.8	23.2	34.3	(15) 89.9	10.1	12.5	5.6
Declining Towns	(28) 66.8	33.2	62.1	(28) 77.6	22.4	6.2	(28) 69.2	30.8	15.9	(28) 83.7	16.3	5.6	4.7
High-Growth Towns	(29)			(28)			(29)			(29)			

Towns with Only Congregational Churches	(12) 74.9	25.1	64.5	(12) 86.2	13.8	4.7	(12) 80.4	19.6	11.8	(12) 91.6	8.4	2.4	3.2
Towns without Congregational Churches	(32) 58.3	41.7	67.9	(34) 74.0	26.0	7.0	(33) 67.0	33.0	24.8	(35) 71.5	28.5	10.2	2.9
Baptist Towns	(33) 59.7	40.3	68.4	(32) 72.3	27.7	7.0	(33) 65.0	35.0	24.8	(33) 76.1	28.9	8.1	4.5
Methodist Towns	(44) 59.1	40.9	64.4	(44) 76.3	23.7	5.8	(43) 64.9	35.1	22.0	(44) 80.0	20.0	5.2	4.6
Unitarian Towns	(42) 73.1	26.9	62.9	(42) 77.7	22.3	13.9	(41) 68.3	31.7	35.4	(42) 79.8	20.2	16.2	3.7
Universalist Towns	(12) 53.0	47.0	67.4	(12) 70.4	29.6	12.9	(12) 63.5	36.5	22.7	(12) 75.5	24.5	12.6	3.1
Roman Catholic Towns	(33) 69.3	30.7	62.0	(32) 65.6	34.4	16.9	(33) 56.9	43.1	32.9	(33) 70.0	30.0	18.0	3.2
Boston	77.1	22.9	50.0	58.4	41.6	24.8	50.6	49.4	37.8	67.9	32.1	25.3	4.3

Notes: Cities = those with populations of 10,000+; Nonindustrial Towns = towns in which 5% or less of the 1855 population was engaged in manufactures or other nonagricultural employment in 1855 occupational census; Boot and Shoe Towns = towns in which 25%+ of the 1850 population was engaged in boot and shoe manufacture in 1855; Fishing Towns = towns in which 10%+ of the 1850 population was engaged in fishing in 1855; Declining Towns = towns whose populations declined 5% or more between 1850 and 1855, excluding declines because of boundary changes; High-Growth Towns = towns whose populations grew by 20%+ from 1850 to 1855, excluding growth due to boundary changes; Baptist Towns = towns in which one-third or more of the accommodations of the major denominations were Baptist in 1860; Methodist Towns = towns in which one-third or more of the accommodations of the major denominations in 1860 were Methodist; Unitarian Towns = towns in which one-third or more of the 1860 accommodations of the major denominations were Unitarian; Universalist Towns = towns in which one-third or more of the accommodations of the major denominations were Universalist. Major denominations included: Congregationalist, Methodist, Methodist Episcopal, Methodist Protestant, Baptist, Baptist Calvinist, Baptist Christian, Free-Will Baptist, Presbyterian, Episcopal, Roman Catholic, Unitarian, Universalist, Friends, Christian, Seventh-Day Adventists.

Sources: Massachusetts Secretary of State, Abstract of the Census of Massachusetts, 1855 (Boston, 1857) for cities of 10,000 in 1855, p. 217, for Declining and High-Growth Towns, pp. 204–215; United States Census, 1850, 1860, for town populations, 1850 and 1860; Massachusetts Secretary of State, Statistical Information Relating to Certain Branches of Industry . . . 1855 (Boston, 1856) for numbers employed in boot and shoe manufacture, fishing, and for town totals engaged in nonagricultural employment; United States Census, Social Statistics, Ms. National Archives, for denominational accommodation data. Election returns from Return of Votes for Presidential Electors, Return of Votes for Governor and Lieutenant Governor, Massachusetts Archives, Mss., Microfilm.

polled huge majorities in every type of town reported in Tables VII and VIII. Through a process of convergence, the largest cities and the most rural towns, towns growing rapidly and others which declined steeply, towns with only Congregationalist churches and those with none, Baptist and Unitarian, Methodist and Universalist towns — all joined the Republican throng. Older voters jettisoned past party attachments and new voters surged into the electoral arena causing turnouts to leap. The 80 percent of those eligible to vote who turned out in 1856 far outdistanced the previous record turnout in 1840.[42] Traces of past predilections, to be sure, lingered. Towns with substantial numbers of Roman Catholics, now numerous after a decade of mass immigration, were the least Republican. The fishing towns and those with only Congregationalist churches were the most Republican as earlier they had been the most Whig. Far more significant, however, were the changes. A generation earlier the Democrats had run comparatively well in the nonindustrial towns but by 1850 the rural towns became solidly Republican. The counterpoint between continuity and change is illustrated by the towns with only Congregationalist churches and those without any, the latter being "pure" dissenting towns with mostly Baptist, Methodist, and Universalist churches. These had once been the most heavily Democratic category, but in the 1850s they shifted into the Republican column though the party's majorities here lagged behind the staggering majorities piled up in the "pure" Congregationalist towns.

Signs of this voter revolution appeared in the 1848 presidential election when Free-Soilers — drawing on antislavery elements in both parties — polled nearly 30 percent of the state vote. The pattern of Free-Soil support was uneven. Free-Soilers ran best in the boot and shoe towns, ever a volatile group, the banner Anti-Mason group in 1834 and the strongest Know-Nothing towns in 1855. They also did relatively well in Quaker towns, in towns with only Congregationalist and Unitarian churches, and in "dissenting" towns. They ran behind their statewide poll in the big cities and fishing towns, which remained decisively Whig, and in the nonindustrial towns where the Democrats contained defections. (See Table IX.)

The Free-Soil performance was a harbinger of things to come, though Whig leadership underestimated the new party's staying

VIII. Banner Denominational Towns and the Party Vote, 1855–1860

	1855 Governor			1856 President			1858 Governor			1860 President			
	Whig %	Demo. %	Amer. %	Rep. %	Demo. %	Amer. %	Rep. %	Demo. %	Amer. %	Rep. %	Demo. %	Const. Union %	Brecken-ridge Demo. %
Statewide	66.9	33.1	66.5	73.6	26.4	11.5	65.7	34.3	28.7	72.2	27.8	13.2	3.5
Baptist Towns N = 7	45.7	54.3	69.2	61.0	39.0	2.8	64.3	35.7	21.6	67.5	32.2	4.7	.9
Methodist Towns N = 12	49.4	50.6	73.7	74.3	25.7	4.9	64.1	35.9	13.9	78.4	21.6	3.0	5.9
Unitarian Towns N = 12	73.0	27.0	59.1	76.8	23.2	11.1	62.6	37.4	44.0	75.2	24.2	12.0	4.3
Universalist Towns N = 2	44.3	55.7	59.3	66.8	33.2	11.6	51.0	49.0	11.6	77.2	22.8	4.7	5.3
Congregationalist Towns N = 12	74.9	25.1	64.5	86.2	13.8	4.7	80.4	19.6	11.8	91.6	8.4	2.4	3.2

Note: Whig, Republican, and Democratic percentages = % of two-party vote; American percentages = % of three-party vote; Constitutional Union and Breckenridge Democratic percentages = % four-party vote; Baptist, Methodist, Unitarian, and Universalist towns = towns in which 50% or more of the church accommodations were attributed to the respective denominations. Congregationalist Towns = towns with only Congregationalist churches. *United States Census*, 1860, pp. 408–409.

Sources: United States Census, 1860, *Social Statistics*, Ms., National Archives, for church accommodation data; election data from Return of Votes for Presidential Electors, Return of Votes for Governor and Lieutenant Governor, Massachusetts Archives, Mss., Microfilm.

IX. Massachusetts Party Vote by Types of Towns, 1848
(Whig and Democratic % = % two-party vote; Free-Soil % = % three-party vote)

	1848 President		
	W %	D %	Free-Soil %
Statewide	63.4	36.6	28.6
N = ( )	(30)		
Cities	67.8	32.2	25.4
Nonindustrial Towns	(57)		
	55.4	44.6	25.1
Boot and Shoe Towns	(18)		
	55.5	44.5	40.4
Fishing Towns	(12)		
	73.0	27.0	22.6
Towns with No Congregational Churches	(24)		
	55.6	44.4	35.0
Towns with Only Congregational Churches	(24)		
	64.0	36.0	32.0
Baptist Towns	(25)		
	58.3	41.7	27.4
Methodist Towns	(19)		
	64.0	36.0	30.5
Universalist Towns	(17)		
	57.4	47.6	31.0
Quaker Towns	(13)		
	69.7	39.3	37.6
Unitarian Towns	(27)		
	58.0	42.0	33.3
Boston	74.0	26.0	14.3

Notes: Cities = those with populations of 5,000+ in 1850; Nonindustrial Towns = towns with no industries employing 25%+ in 1847, excluding straw bonnets; Boot and Shoe Towns = towns in which 25%+ of the 1850 population was engaged in boot and shoe manufacture in 1847; Baptist Towns = towns in which 40%+ of religious accommodations in 1850 were Baptist; Methodist Towns = towns in which 40%+ of religious accommodations in 1850 were Methodist; Universalist Towns = towns in which 25%+ of religious accommodations in 1850 were Universalist; Quaker Towns = towns in which 10%+ of religious accommodations in 1850 were Quaker; Unitarian Towns = towns in which 40%+ of religious accommodations in 1850 were Unitarian.

Sources: *United States Census,* 1850, for cities of 5,000+; Massachusetts Secretary of State, *Statistics of . . . Industry in Massachusetts, . . . 1845* (Boston, 1846), for nonindustrial towns, persons employed in boot and shoe manufactures, and fishing; United States Census, 1850, *Social Statistics,* 1850, Ms., National Archives, for religious data; for election data, Return of Votes for Presidential Elector, Massachusetts Archives, Ms., Microfilm.

power and depth of commitment. Failing to pressure the Whigs to shift course on the slavery question, Free-Soilers forged an alliance with Democrats in 1851 and 1852, an alliance that was fragile and unstable, but by joining forces, the coalition elected a governor, gained control of the legislature in 1851 and 1852, and sent Charles Sumner to the United States Senate. For the Democrats, perennially a minority, here was a golden opportunity to gain power and to reform the commonwealth along Jacksonian lines — free banking, general incorporation, a secret ballot. For the Free-Soilers of Whig antecedents, the alliance was the only way to stay alive and to teach the Whigs that without Free-Soil votes, Bay State Whiggery was no longer the majority party.

The coalition crumbled in 1853 under the weight of pressure from the Democratic administration in Washington and internal friction. The Whigs recaptured the State House for two years but then a new political hurricane swept them permanently from the face of the Massachusetts political map. "There has been no revolution so complete since the organization of government," Charles F. Adams reported in his diary shortly after the Know-Nothing, or American party, landslide in 1854. "I no more suspected the impending result that I looked for an earthquake which would level the State House and reduce Faneuil Hall to a heap of ruins," confessed Charles Congdon, Whig editor of the *Boston Atlas*. Like the Free-Soilers, the Know-Nothings cut deeply into both major parties. They were exceptionally effective in mobilizing nonvoters with the class appeal latent in nativism.[43] There were but modest variations in Know-Nothing strength among different types of towns, foreshadowing the convergence of town voting which characterized the Republican vote. The American party did least well in the least industrialized towns and best in the boot and shoe centers. It ran more strongly in towns experiencing high rates of population growth than in declining towns. Most strikingly, it did about as well in "pure" Congregationalist towns as in "pure" dissenting towns, whereas a generation earlier these two categories had been the most heavily Whig and Democratic groups respectively. (See Table VII.)

Behind the convergence of different groups toward the Republican party, some by way of the Free-Soilers, many more via the American party, lay a popular rebellion, the sources of which were diverse and varied in timing, yet related by the common desire to throw off the state's traditional leadership. The Whig appeal as the party of material progress lost its magic as antislavery elements refused to still their agitation for the sake of southern votes for the tariff. Nor did the Whigs fare any better in promoting themselves as the party of moral progress. Appeasement of slavery abroad coupled with resistance to the rising tide of temperance sentiment at home stamped the Whigs as morally untrustworthy. By contrast the new Republican party which carried the state in the 1856 presidential election fashioned an ideology and program that attracted a broad spectrum of groups who had lost faith in the old parties. The Republicans combined an egalitarian appeal against aristocracy at home and in the South with an evangelical commitment against sin everywhere. They attracted major segments of the middle classes; skilled and unskilled native-born labor, whose consciousness and interests as wage earners placed new pressures on the political system; farmers and village folk in the towns left out of the state's industrial advance; Protestants alarmed by the massive influx of Irish Catholics; and finally, an increasingly aggressive pietism, spreading through the major denominations, and demanding that the state serve as an instrument of moral reform. In many voters these interests and impulses merged, reinforcing each other.

In the vanguard of those who helped to bury the Whigs stood the middle-class, independent, professional elements who had battled unsuccessfully against the Winthrops, Lawrences, and Websters to capture the Whig party for Free-Soilism. In the heat of that struggle, men who had been loyal Whigs in the past suddenly discovered that the party lay in the iron grip of a plutocracy. Attacks on the Lords of the Loom, entangled in an unholy alliance with the Lords of the Lash, became a stock-in-trade of Conscience Whigs and later of Free-Soilers. They pictured the Whig elite as a monied aristocracy unfit to govern a republic, traitors to the moral heritage of a Puritan commonwealth. "Everywhere out of New England we are heartily despised for this greediness of gain, this selfishness of the manufacturing interests now so identified with the Whig party," proclaimed Charles F. Adams.[44] At the 1848 Free-Soil convention Charles Sumner reminded the delegates that "the efforts to place the national government on the side of freedom have received little sympathy from corporations, or from persons largely interested in them."[45] The pernicious influence of great wealth, not the dangers of the mob, Sumner thought, menaced republican order. Did not Whigs such as Edmund Dwight pour thousands of dollars into elections to determine the results? "It is in this way, in part," Sumner claimed, "that the natural antislavery sentiment has been kept down; it is money, money, money, that keeps Palfrey from being elected."[46]

Sumner, Adams, and John G. Palfrey each took on one of the state's great Whig leaders — Robert Winthrop, Abbott Lawrence, and William Appleton — and sought to depict them as people who placed their personal and material interests above all others.[47] The Boston nabobs no longer represented the true sentiments of Bay State Whiggery. At times class resentment flowed freely in the rhetoric. Palfrey, a lifelong Whig elected to Congress as a Free-Soiler, became entangled in a nasty exchange with merchant-capitalist William Appleton. "Doubtless in Station and influence you have the advantage of me," Palfrey asserted, "but I as much as yourself am a free man of Massachusetts." He would not be intimidated by Appleton's "overbearing language" which only served to show how hard it was "to make a statesman out of a calico merchant."[48] Sumner agreed. "The money power has joined hands with the slavery power. Selfish, grasping, subtle, tyrannical. Like its ally, it will brook no opposition."[49]

The Whigs forthrightly rejected attacks on wealth. "Ours is no plutocracy," insisted the party's 1850 election address. The constitution of Massachusetts was "of the Grecian model," infused with "the spirit of law and progress of order and freedom." Under the beneficent guidance of the Whigs, wealth was so broadly diffused that "the poor do not reside in Massachusetts," while the public school system had "abolished classes and established universal equality."[50]

The attack on plutocracy found a receptive hearing in many of the state's small towns, towns that grew but slowly or even declined in population. Sweeping aside Whig opposition, the coalition of Free-Soilers and Democrats called a convention in 1853 which they controlled for the purpose of "modernizing" a fundamental law largely unaltered since the Revolution. The coalition rejected the notion that representation in the General Court should closely mirror population. Instead they proposed to restore annual representation to every town, which would have given the small towns a greater voice proportionately than the large ones.[51] Coalitionists argued that town representation, even though it departed from the principle of equal representation, would give the small towns due weight, whereas the large but equally apportioned districts the Whigs proposed would make representatives immune from direct accountability to voters, and strengthen caucus mongers and professional politicians.[52] The champions of the small towns thus rejected classic Whig arguments that city and country were "one people." "There is something in the power of Boston, something in the power of wealth concentrated there which creates sentiment somewhat different from that of the country," responded Francis Bird.[53] A third to half of the wealth of the state, coalition leader George Boutwell contended, was owned by a Boston clique that also controlled thirteen daily newspapers and, through a vast network of informal influence from Nantucket to the Berkshires, exercised immense power.[54] The cities, Richard H. Dana added, with their "immense floating population," were not communities but mere places dominated by "a great encampment of merchants, mechanics, and professional men" who were governed almost exclusively by "pecuniary purposes."[55]

The Whigs correctly recognized the motives behind town representation. "The scheme seems to have its basis in the jealousy of the influence of men of property," asserted Nathan Hale, "and in a design to concentrate political power in the hands of a minority of people, consisting chiefly of the farmers and artisans of the small towns."[56] The apportionment question remained unresolved until later in the decade for the Constitution of 1853 met defeat at the polls, but the convention afforded an opportunity for proto-Republicans to mobilize the hinterland against the Whig elite.

A parallel process was under way among the state's working people. Free-Soilers gave another twist to the antiplutocracy theme in 1848 when they explained why laboring men — among whom they included "the tillers of the soil, the mechanics, the manufacturers" — should not vote for Whig presidential candidate General Zachary Taylor, a Louisiana slave owner, who "when he wants an agriculturalist, buys him and when he wants a blacksmith, buys him." Surely a vote for Taylor could not "advance the cause of the laborer" or "increase the dignity of labor" because "the man who buys Peter and Jack and Nelson — black

men — to work and die for him, would just as readily buy
Johnson and Thompson and Smith and Jones — white men — if
he could do so." "What sort of a president is this for a free republic of laboring men?" asked William S. Robinson, Free-Soil editor
of the *Boston Daily Republican*.[57] Robinson, a former Whig editor in
Lowell, was driven out of the state's largest factory town for chal-
lenging the mill owners on the slavery question. In the early 1850s
the challenge broadened as a coalition of Free-Soilers and Democrats rallied segments of the city's working-class and middle-class
strata to defy the factory masters who had long dominated the
town. Their twin demand for a secret ballot to protect workers at
the polls and a ten-hour law to protect their health in the mills
swept the coalition to victory in 1851.[58]

By the 1850s workingmen were emerging as a distinct and important force in the Bay State. They were growing in numbers,
but more important, they were developing a consciousness. Almost a hundred strikes, big and small, occurred in Massachusetts
in the decades between 1830 and 1870, with a tempo of industrial
conflict gaining momentum by the 1850s. A corps of politicians
who became leaders of the Republican party emerged as champions of labor, men like Robinson, E. H. Rogers, James Stone,
Nathaniel Banks, Henry Wilson, and after 1860, Ben Butler. The
ten-hour movement did not succeed until the 1870s but the labor
Republicans were its leading advocates and other important party
figures such as Governors Washburn and Clafflin endorsed the
idea in the 1860s. Yet nothing so much symbolized the importance of working folks and the lower middle classes to the Republican alliance than the careers of Nathaniel Banks, the first Republican governor, and Henry Wilson, the first Republican
United States Senator, both founders of the new party.[59]

Banks, a Democrat, and Wilson, a Whig, each rose from humble
origins; one was the son of a Waltham mechanic and the other of a
poor, intemperate New Hampshire farmer. Both were au-
todidacts, self-improvers determined to get ahead. Each took the
pledge of total abstinence at an early age. In Waltham, Banks
repeatedly ran for public office without success. Despite attacks on
"the heartless corporations," and his appeal to workers as one of
their own, he was no match for the likes of Luke Wright, Whig
bank president. But by 1848 the tide had turned. Banks became a
central figure in the Free-Soil/Democratic coalition, ultimately

broke with the Democrats over Kansas-Nebraska, and led the antislavery elements in the House of Representatives as Speaker in 1855. "A general system of slave labor is incompatible with the labor of freemen," Banks preached.[60] When the Know-Nothing frenzy erupted, Banks joined the nativists.

Henry Wilson did the same.[61] Wilson, starting with little, prospered as a shoemaker in Natick, where he settled in the late 1830s. By 1840 he employed thirty-four hands. Unlike Banks, Wilson joined the Whig party, demonstrating valuable talents as a campaigner among ordinary folks. His reward was a seat in the legislature from 1841 until he cast his lot with the Free-Soilers later in the decade. Wilson became the foremost tactician and strategist of the emerging antislavery forces. A man of the people, he had the common touch missing in a Sumner, an Adams, or a Dana. Tirelessly, he roamed the commonwealth, sounding public opinion, encouraging supporters, attracting a circle of faithful lieutenants, men who must have been self-improvers much like himself. As a boot and shoe man, he had a special connection with the largest occupational group in the industrial labor force. The shoe manufacturers, in fact, came to play a special role in the Republican party: almost 10 percent of the Massachusetts legislature in 1860 were boot and shoe manufacturers, mostly Republicans, triple the percentage a decade earlier.[62] Like Banks, Wilson was an early Republican, and he too joined the Know-Nothings, hoping to direct the nativist current ultimately into antislavery channels. His reward came swiftly. The Know-Nothings sent him to the United States Senate in 1855, where he replaced the exhausted and disgraced Edward Everett, Harvard and Beacon Hill's "scholar in politics." As for Wilson, he did not "want the endorsement of the best society in Boston until I am dead — then all of us are sure of it — for it endorses everything that is dead."[63] Like Banks and other "labor" Republicans, Wilson believed that slavery was the enemy of free labor. President Grant, in trouble in 1872, chose Wilson as his running mate because he needed on the ticket a man who was a pious Congregationalist and an ardent prohibitionist, someone who "represented the great middling interest," a former shoemaker with "a stronger hold upon the public than almost any other public man."[64]

Unlike Banks and Wilson, who perceived the necessity of scrambling aboard the Know-Nothing bandwagon, the Whigs were surprised by the nativist eruption. Several weeks before the November 1854 elections, Edward Everett thought "the course and strength of the Know Nothings are alike wrapped in mystery." While some claimed "for them 50,000 votes," Everett doubted if "they cast a fifth of that number" for "no person of standing in the political world is known to have joined them." Everett's mistake was to think that the voters that year cared a fig for persons of standing. Election day rudely awakened him: The Know-Nothings captured the governorship and gained almost total control of the legislature. It surely was, Everett acknowledged, "the most astonishing result ever witnessed in our politics."[65]

The nativist triumph in Massachusetts was a temporary, popular political revolution with no parallel in the state's history. It was truly a mass movement, a democratic upheaval that swept through most groups and most parts of the state as voters ignored past loyalties and cast aside men of influence to elect people more like themselves, sensitive to their needs, persons in whom they could trust. Most of the nativist legislators were new men in politics; few had served previously in the General Court. They were much younger and less affluent than their predecessors. From the ranks of workingmen came 25 percent of the legislature, compared to 16 percent in 1848. Lawyers, by contrast, were scarcer, but boot and shoe manufacturers and clergymen were prominent. The leadership reflected the rank and file.[66] The temporary president of the first Know-Nothing legislature was a shoemaker, a Methodist, a prohibitionist, and a former Democrat; the permanent head was a Worcester machinist; and the Speaker of the House was a Baptist preacher who had never held public office. "I presume there is less mature education in the government than ever before at any time," Charles F. Adams dourly concluded.[67]

Mob rule, though peaceful and honoring all legal forms, had descended on the Bay State, some thought. In reality the great mass of workingmen and middle-class voters had rudely asserted themselves. They had abandoned the Whigs and Democrats because neither appeared willing or able to cope with the forces that people feared: the entrance of a large Irish Catholic population into a Yankee Protestant community; the chronic economic instability incident to industrialism; the frustrating and unfathomable disappointments of people taught to believe that hard toil paid off; the moral bankruptcy of Whigs, indifferent to the well-being of free labor yet insistent that the free white folks of Massachusetts return fugitive slaves to their southern masters. The collapse of the coalition in 1853 left voters without a feasible alternative. The Know-Nothings filled the vacuum.

In the eyes of many citizens an unholy alliance of the plutocracy and the foreigners threatened free labor, by which nativists meant, for course, Protestant labor. Both appeared to be allies of the slavocracy, devoted to the enforcement of the fugitive slave law, and enemies too of temperance and of constitutional reform that would protect the public schools from Catholic designs and preserve the power of the small towns against big-city wealth, corruption, ignorance, and superstition.[68]

From the perspective of party development, the Know-Nothings had mobilized a mass movement, something neither the Free-Soilers nor the coalitionists could manage. In the process, the Whigs collapsed and the Democrats were left severely weakened, while the Republicans bided their time and maneuvered to inherit a mass base which by 1856 found in antislavery and antisouthernism a more salient focus for its moral anxieties and social insecurities. "By your speeches and your votes you have spoken for Temperance, Liberty, and Protestantism . . ." proclaimed the Know-Nothing Speaker of the House at the end of the party's first tumultuous year in office.[69] As among the nativists, so among the Republicans a crusading, evangelical Protestantism figured significantly in the party formation.

The historical sociology of mid-nineteenth-century American Protestantism remains still poorly charted territory. The social forces that propelled pietism into an aggressive and ascending force in major denominations, that made the Methodists and Baptists the leading denominations, and that led churches to abandon their ambivalence and overcome internal divisions over slavery, temperance, and other questions of public morality await empirical investigation. It is clear, however, that the churches played an important role in the party revolution of mid-century.

"They are not anarchists nor revolutionists," insisted Congressman Nathaniel Banks, defending the three-thousand New England ministers who had petitioned Congress against the Kansas-Nebraska bill, triggering a rain of abuse from Democrats and Southerners.[70] A few years earlier prominent clergy had lent their moral authority to political compromise. Now in 1854, speaking with unprecedented unity and vigor, the clergy of New England, Henry Wilson rejoiced, had abandoned finally the "languid and equivocal utterances hitherto deemed all that prudence would allow."[71] Among them, if not in the forefront, were the Methodists, second largest denomination in the Bay State. In 1852 the denomination's organ, *Zion's Herald,* ended a ten-year silence on the slavery question.[72] The year before Methodists had publicly backed Charles Sumner's election to the Senate, opposed enforcement of the Fugitive Slave Law, and in 1856 were leading prayer meetings for Republican John C. Fremont. At the same time, Methodists became one of the most militant and persistent supporters of prohibition. In the twin struggles against slavery and intemperance, no Methodist stood more prominent than Gilbert Haven, who in the 1860s became editor of *Zion's Herald* and bishop in Boston.[73] In the 1850s Haven, the son of a Malden bookkeeper, served in various congregations around the state, struggling at times as at Westfield to convince his Democratic and Know-Nothing parishioners that slavery was the nation's besetting sin, racial brotherhood its compelling necessity. "The Gospel . . . is not confined to a repentance and faith that has no connection with social or civil duties," proclaimed Haven.[74] Other pietists among the Baptists, Congregationalists, and even Unitarians carried like messages to their flocks. In 1858 almost one hundred fifty towns in the state experienced religious revivals, dramatic evidence of the spread of evangelical Christianity in a state where even "the greatest leaders in New England Congregationalism swung their support to revivals."[75] The pietists preached individual improvement through self-denial and self-control, but they insisted, too, on social improvement through Christian legislation.

Methodist pietism's greatest popularity was probably among skilled workers and the lower middle classes, marginal people who nourished aspirations for success but who often encountered disappointment. Thus David Montgomery found a link between trade-union leadership in the mid-nineteenth century and Methodism, Republicanism, temperance, and the ideology of self-improvement.[76] In appealing to such elements, the evangelicals were unencumbered by socially prominent elite laymen, who in Massachusetts had gravitated largely to the Unitarian and Episcopalian churches. There, in those genteel islands of decorous faith, they became increasingly isolated from the great mass of Protestants in the state, in much the same way that Whig elites became politically isolated in the mid-1850s. In 1851 their candidate for governor, Boston's Robert C. Winthrop, went down to defeat, after refusing to endorse prohibition.[77] When the Whig remnants desperately threw their weight behind Know-Nothing Governor Henry Gardner's campaign to beat Republican Nathaniel Banks in 1857 and succeeded, they must have found comforting Gardner's fast-day proclamation which denounced clergy who meddled in politics and mixed secular with spiritual matters.[78]

Republican ascendancy gave Methodist leaders recognition and respectability they had not previously enjoyed. William Clafflin, a prominent Methodist layman, who like his father engaged in boot and shoe manufacture, became chairman of the Republican State Committee for seven years in the 1860s, served three terms on the national committee, and moved from lieutenant governor into the governorship. Before he left office, Clafflin signed a bill chartering Boston University, founded by his father, Lee Clafflin, together with other rich Methodist businessmen, who joined to erect a fitting monument to their own piety and benevolence as well as to their denomination's growing respectability and importance.[79]

IV

The end of Whig supremacy in Massachusetts and the emergence of the Republican alliance made government more sensitive to groups and interests which hitherto had felt slighted — evangelicals and middle-class humanistic reformers, businessmen on the make, neglected and backward regions, and to a lesser extent working people. The ascendancy of new men in the 1850s was heady stuff. On the evening of his inauguration as governor, coalition leader George Boutwell recalled strolling across Boston Common and telling Wilson and Banks: "It's mighty queer that the people of this Commonwealth have put their government into the hands of men who had no last and usual place of abode, destitute of even the means of well-to-do mechanics and tradespeople."[80] Not just antislavery but public finances, banking, railroads, and higher education all felt the impact of party realignment. Here we can only allude to such changes.

Harvard came under intense and bitter attack as a quasi-public institution that had become the privileged preserve of a "class of men in, and about the city of Boston who seem to think that they were born to guard, guide, govern, direct and control Harvard College." For the past half century, Henry Wilson told the 1853 constitutional convention, no "name that is not connected with the Unitarian sect in religion, and the Federal and Whig parties, in politics" had served on the Harvard Corporation.[81] Harvard instruction reflected the "bigoted and blind fanaticism" of those who controlled the college, men whose sympathies were "with the privileged few everywhere . . . the malignant enemies of liberal ideas and liberal men alike in the Old World and in the New."[82]

Appealing to both Orthodox Congregationalists and other evangelicals, Harvard's critics in 1851 eliminated the clerical section of the Board of Overseers as well as the State Senate and Council. Henceforth thirty members of the board, a majority, were to be chosen by ballot of the legislature. The coalition thereupon nominated ten persons from Free-Soil, Whig, and Democratic parties, but when the Whigs regained control of the state in 1853, the old policy of exclusivity returned. The 1853 constitutional convention adopted an amendment making clear that the legislature enjoyed "full power and authority to alter" the role of Harvard's governing board.[83] Though the constitutional revisions went down to defeat, pressures for pluralism in higher education persisted. Harvard had been admonished to educate the thousands, not the few, to become "head of our system of public instruction" and thereby come in close "contact with the beating pulse of the great heart of the Commonwealth, that the generous sympathies of the whole people may cluster around it."[84] No similar charges of elitism were leveled at the state's other denominational institutions. In 1858 a Republican legislature granted $50,000 to the Universalists' Tufts, $25,000 to the Trinitarian Congregationalists' Williams and Amherst and the same amount to the Methodists' Wesleyan Academy at Wilbraham. In 1865 Harvard was ready to sever all ties with the state; henceforth the alumni were to choose the Board of Overseers.[85]

Pluralism also influenced the state's policy toward banks.[86] In

1851 the Democrats with Free-Soil support pushed through general incorporation legislation for banks and other businesses. Few new banks were established under the new law, which placed them at a competitive disadvantage with existing banks, but some new banks petitioned the legislature to enlarge their capital. Leading Boston Whigs complained that small, interior banks and the boot and shoe interests received favored treatment. The creation in 1855 of a Bank of Mutual Redemption freed the interior banks from the restraining influence of the Suffolk System, dominated by eastern urban banking interests. The Suffolk System thereupon collapsed.[87]

Similarly, the northwestern portion of the state not served by the Western Railroad desperately sought a second through-rail network that would end its isolation and economic backwardness. When the Troy and Greenfield Railroad petitioned for state aid to assist in boring the Hoosac Tunnel, the Western Railroad, the state's most powerful corporation, vigorously opposed it as did the leading organ of Boston Whiggery, the *Boston Advertiser*. The battle raged for three years until 1854, when the last Whig legislature dared not deny the two million dollars sought to aid the Troy and Greenfield, which the coalition had championed.[88]

State spending, which had been growing slowly in the 1840s, suddenly doubled between 1850 and 1855. This development reflected new demands from citizens and communities to accommodate needs of an industrial society. The timing, degree, and precise categories of expenditures also reflected the political upheaval of the 1850s. The collapse of the Whigs weakened restraints on government spending, and the advent of new men in power, especially the Know-Nothings, unleased fresh claims on public largesse. The Hoosac Tunnel loan was only symptomatic of a larger trend.[89]

As the Republicans consolidated their control in the late 1850s, they narrowed divisions that had previously split the commonwealth. With surprising ease, a constitutional amendment adopted in 1857 replaced town representation with a district system, a measure of how well the Republicans had integrated the smaller towns into the governing majority, while at the same time Republican leadership cultivated former Whig rivals.[90]

When the Civil War ended, temperance and labor questions sorely strained the Republican alliance. By the late 1860s division between advocates of licensing and those of prohibition became vexing. Republicans tried to straddle the issue, but evangelicals, notably among the Methodists, bolted to a Prohibition party. The battle for control of the party seesawed between the two factions, one insisting on prohibition now and forever, the other for relaxing state control. Working people proved equally troubling. Neither the Know-Nothings nor the Republicans, despite their huge majorities, had enacted hours legislation or a secret ballot in the 1850s. In the 1860s skilled artisans launched a campaign for an eight-hour day while factory operatives sought a ten-hour bill, both expecting Republican support. Despite backing from prominent party leaders, workers and their unions met disappointment. Even the boot and shoe workers, the best-organized element in the labor force, failed to secure an act incorporating the Knights of St. Crispin. Frustrated workers, like prohibitionists, first fought for control of the party, and when defeated, formed a new party, the Labor Reform party, which had modest success between 1869 and 1871, and like the Prohibition party, cut into Republican strength.[91]

The free-labor ideology and the democratization of politics in the 1850s had raised expectations, especially among working folk and middle-class elements. When people encountered disappointment after 1860, they were a prey for demagogues, just as they had responded with keen enthusiasm earlier to Sumner when he preached against plutocracy, to Wilson and Banks when they proclaimed the dignity of free labor versus slave labor, and to Know-Nothings who promised to protect the native born from the strangers in the land. No one understood the new electoral realities better than Lowell's Ben Butler. Butler was a new political type, a master of mass politics, a demagogue, perhaps the first in a long line that stretches through America's industrial history from James Vardaman and Theodore Bilbo, to Joseph McCarthy and George Wallace.[92]

A poor youth of Baptist and Jeffersonian heritage, Butler learned early that prizes like admission to West Point were reserved for families of influence, but disappointment did not stop him. Ben graduated instead from Colby, a Baptist college, and returned to Lowell, where the militia and the bar became paths to success. He specialized in criminal law, taking cases other lawyers avoided, making vulgar appeals to juries on behalf of dubious clients, and prospering. By the 1850s he had accumulated $140,000, owned extensive real estate, and inhabited a mansion. In politics Butler began as a Democrat but got nowhere until the coalition successfully challenged the Whig textile magnates by advocating the secret ballot and ten-hour day. When the factory bosses threatened to discharge workers before the fall 1850 elections, Butler told a huge throng of workers that in defense of a free ballot he would take up the torch, if necessary, and reduce Lowell to what it had been a quarter century earlier — "a sheep pasture and a fishing place." The effect of his oratory "was marvellous," he later remembered, evoking yells of approval "like the agonized groans of wild animals when they feel the deadly knife at their throats."[93]

Butler's wartime service transformed a Breckenridge Democrat into a rabid Republican, a noted Southerner-baiter whose military exploits, especially in New Orleans, had made him the scourge of southern "traitors." He built a powerful personal faction within the Bay State Republican party, cemented with military contracts and the patronage with which President Grant rewarded him for support in Congress. The state's Republican leadership regarded him as a dangerous demagogue. In 1868 Richard H. Dana challenged Congressman Butler, but the chaste, patrician lawyer was no match for Butler in an Essex County district inhabited by thousands of shoemakers and other working people. "You must crush him now, or he will grind your faces in the dirt," Henry Adams warned.[94] Dana's failure proved fatal.

For the rest of his political career, Butler controlled a personal political "machine," first as a Republican, then as a Greenbacker, and again as a Democrat, always posing as the unbossed tribune of the people, exploiting class and ethnic resentments, the suffering and injustice to which "respectable" politicians seemed indifferent. Currency inflation, nationalizing the railroads, antimonopoly legislation, prohibition, women's suffrage, Chinese exclusion, Harvard baiting, an eight-hour law, reduced taxes and government spending — all these gave Butler an appeal which Wendell Phillips explained represented an "element of disturbance in the Republican party; and the moment he does not represent it, the great labor element that claps hands from Moscow to San Francisco will trample him under its feet."[95]

Butler finally won the governorship in 1880 as a Democrat.

Four years later he was on the hustings again, trying to block Democrat Grover Cleveland's bid for the presidency. Running as candidate of the Greenback and Anti-Monopoly parties, Butler was bankrolled by the Republicans, who hoped that he would cut into Democratic strength among workers in the eastern industrial states. Butler told workers they would starve if Cleveland won. Samuel Gompers, a leader of the new Federation of Organized Trades and Labor Unions, may have agreed. In any event, Gompers voted for him. "I am not a Butler man," he explained, "I am no man's man. Butler is my man."[96]

Butler, like Sumner, Banks, Wilson, and others, was a master of mass politics in mid-nineteenth-century America. He identified himself as a man of the people, courageously indifferent to the opinions of elites. A millionaire textile manufacturer who paid substandard wages in his own factory, he advised Massachusetts workers to trust him, not their bosses or community leaders, and not to rely on the accumulation of power in their own organizations such as trade unions. To prim President Rutherford B. Hayes, Ben Butler was "the most dangerous and wicked demagogue we have ever had."[97] Hayes, a skilled exploiter of anti-Catholic prejudice, failed to recognize that Butler, like himself and other Republicans, owed his ascendancy in part to the success with which he exploited the strains industrialization placed on American society.

The struggle against slavery in the South and plutocracy in the North destroyed a party system that in Massachusetts had appeared to rest on foundations of permanence. Neither Whigs nor Democrats with their variant formulas could contain the explosive tensions generated by economic development and demographic change. These pressures inspired popular crusades to purify the republic of sin — slavery, intemperance, plutocracy, the exploitation of labor — crusades which were channeled into the Republican party. The struggle gave a new birth of legitimacy to an experiment in popular government sorely strained by apprehension that, in the transition from the agrarian republic of the Founders to the nation soon to become the world's leading industrial power, democratic norms, egalitarian dreams, and Protestant morality lay in grave jeopardy. The class conflict accompanying industrialization elsewhere found expression in muted form in mid-nineteenth-century America, where the battle to purify and restore a republican order endangered by "the self-interest, private avidity, ambition, and avarice" the Founders had warned against fed a sectional holocaust which Lincoln and others understood to be purification by blood and fire.

Notes

1. Edith Ware, *Political Opinion in Massachusetts during Civil War and Reconstruction*, Studies in History, Economics, and Public Law of Columbia University, vol. LXXIV, no. 2 (New York, 1916), p. 5.
2. Henry Adams, "Review of Ticknor's 'Life, Letters, and Journals,'" *North American Review*, CXXIII (July 1876), 214–215.
3. Ware, *Political Opinion*, p. 36.
4. George S. Merriam, *Life and Times of Samuel Bowles*, 2 vols. (New York, 1885), I, 158.
5. George F. Hoar, *Autobiography of Seventy Years*, 2 vols. (New York, 1903), I, 158–159.
6. Edward L. Pierce, *Memoir and Letters of Charles Sumner*, 4 vols. (Boston, 1893), III, 9.
7. Ware, *Political Opinion*, p. 141.
8. For the political history of Massachusetts, 1830–1860, see Arthur B. Darling, *Political Change in Massachusetts* (reprinted, Cos Cob: J. E. Edwards, 1969); William G. Bean, "The Transformation of Parties in Massachusetts from 1848 to 1860" (doctoral dissertation, Harvard, 1922); Kinley Brauer, *Cotton versus Conscience* (Lexington: University Press of Kentucky, 1967); Thomas O'Connor, *Lords of the Loom: The Cotton Whigs and the Coming of the Civil War* (New York: Scribner's 1968); David Donald, *Charles Sumner and the Coming of the Civil War* (New York: Knopf, 1960).
9. Adams, "Review," pp. 214–215.
10. *Diary of Charles F. Adams*, edited by A. D. Donald, D. Donald, M. Friedlander, and L. H. Butterfield, 4 vols. (Cambridge, Mass.: Harvard University Press, 1964–1968), IV, 250.
11. *Official Report of the Debates . . . in the State Convention . . . 1853 . . . Massachusetts*, 3 vols. (Boston, 1853), I, 82; hereafter cited as *Mass. Const. Convention 1853.*
12. George Ticknor, *Life, Letters and Journals*, 2 vols. (Boston, 1909), II, 187–188.
13. See Peter Knights, *Plain People of Boston* (New York: Oxford University Press, 1971), pp. 78–102; Edward Pessen, *Riches, Class, and Power before the Civil War* (Lexington, Mass.: D. C. Heath, 1973), pp. 38–40.
14. William H. Channing, *Memoir of William Ellery Channing . . .* , 3 vols. (Boston, 1848), III, 227 ff.
15. For religious developments in Massachusetts, 1800–1833, see the monumental work of William G. McLoughlin, *New England Dissent, 1603–1937*, 2 vols. (Cambridge, Mass.: Harvard University Press, 1971), II, 1065–1282.
16. W. S. Hudson, *American Protestantism* (Chicago: University of Chicago Press, 1961), p. 96. See George S. Boutwell, *Reminiscences of Sixty Years in Public Affairs,* 2 vols. (New York, 1922), I, 11, for an account of his father's religious wanderings. Boutwell recalled that in the 1820s few towns were free of religious controversy. His father favored separation and a rational Christianity, yet in the 1820s joined the Methodists while also worshiping occasionally at the nearby Universalist church in Shirley.
17. The recent emphasis in American political history on the importance of religious affiliation as a determinant of voting behavior and party allegiance tends to neglect the nothingarians, in part because they were not organized or as visible as the affiliated. See, for example, Richard Jensen's findings that in eight Illinois townships in 1877–

1878 nothingarians outnumbered the pietists and liturgicals 1,563 to 1,284 and that in Hendricks County, Indiana, in 1874, there were 699 nothingarians or nonaffiliated and 918 affiliated. Richard Jensen in *Civil War History,* XVI (Dec. 1970), 325–343. Cf. Ronald Formisano, *The Birth of Mass Political Parties, Michigan, 1827–1861* (Princeton: Princeton University Press, 1971), pp. 340–342, which attempts to measure "religiosity" and relate it to party.

18. Daniel Webster, *Writings and Speeches of Daniel Webster,* edited by J. W. McIntyre, 18 vols. (Boston, 1906), XVII, 325.

19. For the finest modern study of the working class before the Civil War, see Paul Faler, "Workingmen, Mechanics and Social Change: Lynn, Massachusetts, 1800–1860" (doctoral dissertation, University of Wisconsin, 1971); see also Allen Dawley, *Class and Community: The Industrial Revolution in Lynn* (Cambridge, Mass.: Harvard University Press, 1976).

20. Darling, *Political Change,* p. 171; *Mass. Const. Convention 1853,* I, 591.

21. Elias Nason, *A Gazetteer of the State of Massachusetts* (n.p., 1874), p. 352.

22. Richard E. Sykes, "Massachusetts Unitarianism and Social Change: A Religious System in Transition, 1780–1800" (doctoral dissertation, University of Minnesota, 1966), p. 100.

23. Edward C. Kirkland, *Men, Cities and Transportation,* 2 vols. (Cambridge, Mass.: Harvard University Press, 1948), I, 285; see also Stephen M. Salsbury, *The State, the Investor, and the Railroad* (Cambridge, Mass.: Harvard University Press, 1967), chs. 1–4, 7.

24. Charles J. Bullock, *Financial History of Massachusetts* (New York, 1907), 35 ff.

25. Oscar Handlin and Mary F. Handlin, *Commonwealth* (New York: New York University Press, 1947), pp. 177–178.

26. Darling, *Political Change,* pp. 160–170; *Mass. Const. Convention 1853,* I, 821; *Boston Advertiser,* Aug. 3, 1850.

27. For workers see Faler, "Workingmen," *passim;* John R. Commons, Jr., et al., *History of Labor in the United States,* 2 vols. (New York, 1926), I, 292, 298, 338, 358–359, 380, 545–546; Vera Shlakman, *Economic History of a Factory Town: A Study of Chicopee, Mass.,* Smith College Studies in History vol. 20 (Northampton, 1834–1835), 98 ff.

28. See the fine account in Leonard Levy, *The Law of the Commonwealth and Chief Justice Shaw* (New York: Harper and Row, 1967), pp, 183–206.

29. Jonathan Messerli, *Horace Mann* (New York: Knopf, 1972), pp. 107, 221 ff.

30. McLoughlin, *New England Dissent,* II, 1189–1262.

31. Lyman Beecher, *Autobiography,* edited by B. M. Cross, 2 vols. (Cambridge, Mass.: Harvard University Press, 1961), I, 385, also 107–108.

32. Raymond Culver, *Horace Mann and Religion in the Massachusetts Public Schools* (New Haven: Yale University Press, 1929), pp. 55 ff, 100, 121, 136 ff, 145, 154, 157, 161, 184, 283. In the town of Groton, George Boutwell reported that in 1840 anticlericals led by a teacher and nonprofessionals ousted a school board controlled by ministers and doctors. See Boutwell, *Reminiscences,* I, 55.

33. *National Cyclopedia* (New York: J. T. White, 1892), 50 vols., I, 114–115; Boutwell, *Reminiscences,* I, 87. The *Springfield Republican,* the most important newspaper in Briggs's native western Massachusetts, 1830–1860, was run by the Unitarian Bowles family which employed on the paper's staff Dr. James G. Holland, who had extensive connections among the Congregationalist ministry, especially the Orthodox. See Merriam, *Samuel Bowles,* I, 62.

34. For Boston, see Pierce, *Charles Sumner,* III, 285, and Boutwell, *Reminiscences,* II, 71; for Springfield, see Michael Frisch, *Town into City: Springfield, Massachusetts, and the Meaning of Community, 1840–1880* (Cambridge, Mass.: Harvard University Press, 1972), pp. 40–41.

35. See James Schouler, "The Whig Party in Massachusetts," *Proceedings,* Massachusetts Historical Society, 2nd ser., L (Boston, 1917), 39–40; Schouler claimed that the Whigs were different from the Federalists in one important respect: "Men high born or low born were heartily welcomed in the Whig ranks. . . . The rich made friends with the poor, academic and men of culture . . . consorted with self-educated," but he acknowledged that mechanics and manual workers and immigrants were harder to win over.

Edward Everett, John G. Palfrey, and Horace Mann were each young men of modest circumstances whose talents were recognized and patronized and each advanced up the Whig ladder. The Whigs had similarly attempted to wean George Bancroft away from flirting with the Democrats by offering to make him secretary of state. See Russell B. Nye, *George Bancroft, Brahmin Rebel* (New York: Knopf, 1944), p. 92.

36. Sidney Nathans, *Daniel Webster and Jacksonian Democracy* (Baltimore: Johns Hopkins University Press, 1973), p. 7.

37. *Ibid.*, pp. 194, 220 n. 21.

38. Salsbury, *The State*, chs. 2, 4, 7.

39. See especially Brauer, *Cotton,* and Donald, *Charles Sumner.*

40. Webster, *Writings and Speeches,* XVI, 573.

41. For two recent analyses of Massachusetts voting see Kevin Sweeney, "Rum, Romanism, Representation, and Reform: Coalition Politics in Massachusetts, 1847–1853," *Civil War History,* XII (June 1976), 116–137; Dale Baum, "The Political Realignment of the 1850s: Know-Nothingism and the Republican Majority in Massachusetts," *Journal of American History,* LXIV (March, 1978), 959–986.

42. The turnout for 1856 is derived by extrapolation from the voter lists for 1850 and 1857 from Massachusetts Secretary of State, "Lists of the Cities and Towns . . . with the Total Number of Voters . . . 1850," *Senate Documents,* no. 30, pp. 1–5, and *Manual of the General Court, 1858* (Boston, 1858), pp. 115–123. Cf. J. R. Pole, *Political Representation in England and the Origins of the American Republic* (London: Macmillan, 1966), pp. 115–123; Pole found much lower "turnout" figures because he used the adult male population to compute turnout and that group included substantial numbers of noneligibles. The increased turnout may have reflected increased participation by young voters attracted to the Republican party. At least, Samuel Bowles of the *Springfield Republican* thought that "thousands of young men" had deserted the Whigs for the Republicans. See Merriam, *Samuel Bowles,* I, 127.

43. Virginia C. Purdy, "Portrait of a Know-Nothing Legislature: The Massachusetts General Court of 1855" (doctoral dissertation, George Washington University, 1970), 1, 79. See also Baum, "Political Realignment."

44. Brauer, *Cotton,* pp. 167–168; for R. H. Dana, another leader of the Conscience Whigs, see Jean Kenney, "An Analysis of Political Alignments in Massachusetts As Revealed in the Constitutional Convention of 1853" (master's thesis, Smith College, 1951), p. 34, and Samuel Shapiro, *Richard Henry Dana, Jr., 1815–1882* (East Lansing: Michigan State University Press, 1961).

45. Pierce, *Charles Sumner,* 187; see also III, pp. 1 ff, 37, 129, 179, and Donald, *Charles Sumner,* chs. 5–8.

46. Pierce, *Charles Sumner,* III, 212; cf. O'Connor, *Lords of the Loom,* pp. 88–89, on Whig fund-raising among corporations.

47. See *Boston Advertiser,* May 21, July 3, 1851; Brauer, *Cotton,* p. 168.

48. Frank O. Gatell, *John Gorham Palfrey and the New England Conscience* (Cambridge, Mass.: Harvard University Press, 1963), pp. 131–132. Palfrey had been a charity student at Exeter, a humiliation he never got over; see Gatell, p. 14.

49. Pierce, *Charles Sumner,* III, 187.

50. *Boston Advertiser,* Oct. 3, 1850.

51. For the constitutional convention see Kenney, "Analysis of Political Alignments"; A. B. Hart, ed., *Commonwealth History of Massachusetts,* 5 vols. (New York: States History Company, 1927–1930), IV, 18 ff. For the debates see the *Mass. Const. Convention, 1853,* I, 809–949; II, 38–58, 127–247, 314–468; III, 580–613.

52. *Mass. Const. Convention, 1853,* I, 829.

53. *Ibid.,* p. 938.

54. *Ibid.,* p. 895. The cities were also accused of draining the countryside of women: "The great object of our modern system seems to break down our farmers, so that their daughters may go to the cotton mills." See Shapiro, *Richard Henry Dana,* p. 72.

55. *Mass. Const. Convention, 1853,* I, 946–949.

56. *Ibid.,* P. 837.

57. W. S. Robinson, *"Warrington" Pen-Portraits . . .* (Boston, 1877), p. 186.

58. *Ibid.*, 48 ff; Benjamin F. Butler, *Butler's Books: Autobiography and Personal Reminiscences* (Boston, 1892), 93 ff; Michael Brunet, "The Secret Ballot Issue in Massachusetts Politics from 1851 to 1853," *New England Quarterly*, XXV (1952), 354–362.

59. For strikes see Massachusetts Bureau of Statistics and Labor, *Eleventh Annual Report, Strikes in Massachusetts*, Jan. 1880; for labor, see Faler, "Workingmen," *passim;* Shlakman, *Factory Town*, 98 ff; Commons, *History of Labor, I*, 337–338, 358–359, 545–546; E. E. Persons, "The Early History of Factory Legislation in Massachusetts," in S. M. Kingsbury, *Labor Laws and Their Enforcement* (New York, 1911), 25 ff; David Montgomery, *Beyond Equality* (New York: Knopf, 1967), pp. 117 ff, 200, 209, 245, 265–268, 277.

60. For Banks see Fred H. Harrington, *Fighting Politician: Major General Nathaniel P. Banks* (Philadelphia: University of Pennsylvania Press, 1948), p. 9.

61. For Wilson see Richard Abbott, *Cobbler in Congress: The Life of Henry Wilson, 1812–1875* (Lexington: University Press of Kentucky 1972).

62. For shoemakers see Boutwell, *Reminiscences*, I, 79; Horace B. Davis, "The Occupations of Massachusetts Legislators, 1790–1950," *New England Quarterly*, XXIV (1951), 94–95.

63. Abbot, *Cobbler in Congress*, p. 53.

64. *Ibid.*, p. 153; Hoar, *Autobiography*, I, 217; Purdy, "Know-Nothing Legislature," p. 91.

65. John R. Mulkern, "The Know-Nothing Party in Massachusetts" (doctoral dissertation, Boston University, 1963), pp. 102, 113; see also Pierce, *Charles Sumner*, III, 400–401.

66. Purdy, "Know-Nothing Legislature," 117 ff, 162 ff. On clergy see Butler, *Butler's Books*, p. 121, and Mulkern, "Know-Nothing Party, 122n. According to Harrington, *Fighting Politician*, pp. 23–24, Wilson and Banks liked to call Know-Nothingism a labor uprising. Banks explained the success of the nativists by arguing that employers had used the foreign vote against the native masses.

67. Mulkern, "Know-Nothing Party," p. 125.

68. William G. Bean, "Puritan versus Celt, 1850–1860," *New England Quarterly*, VII (1934), 71; Boutwell, *Reminiscences*, I, 220.

69. Mulkern, "Know-Nothing Party," p. 161.

70. Henry Wilson, *History of the Rise and Fall of the Slave Power in America*, 3 vols. (Boston, 1874), II, 399; Pierce, *Charles Sumner*, III, 394.

71. Wilson, II, 407; cf. to the clergy and the Fugitive Slave Law, pp. 309–310, 317 ff.

72. Timothy Smith, *Revivalism and Social Reform* (New York: Harper and Row, 1965), p. 205. See also George C. Baker, Jr., *An Introduction to the History of Early New England Methodism, 1789–1839* (Durham: Duke University, 1941), pp. 51 ff; Smith, *Revivalism*, pp. 181 ff.

73. William Gravely, *Gilbert Haven, Methodist Abolitionist* (Nashville: Abingdon, 1973), *passim;* Emory S. Bucke et al., eds., *History of American Methodism*, 3 vols. (Nashville: Abingdon, 1964), III, 326–327.

74. Smith, *Revivalism*, p. 36.

75. *Ibid.*, p. 75. See also Donald Mathews, *Slavery and Methodism* (Princeton: Princeton University Press, 1965), *passim*, and for New England Methodists' antislavery sentiments, pp. 120 ff, 131, 164, 171, 233.

76. Montgomery, *Beyond Equality*, pp. 198 ff, especially Edward Rogers, p. 200, W. H. Sylvis, p. 228; for Methodism in Lynn see Faler, "Workingmen," pp. 98 ff, 213.

77. For his refusal see *Boston Advertiser*, Nov. 19, 1851.

78. For Gardner see *National Cyclopedia*, I, 115; Mulkern, "Know-Nothing Party," pp. 52 ff, 275 ff. Gardner courted conservative Whigs by vetoing a personal-liberty law and refusing to permit removal of Charles G. Loring, a commissioner involved in a fugitive slave rendition. Sam Bowles in Merriam, *Samuel Bowles*, I, 174, reported that in the fall of 1856 "old fogey and conservative Whigs" were backing Gardner for reelection. For Unitarians and politics, see Sykes, "Massachusetts Unitarianism," *passim*, esp. pp. 114–149; Daniel W. Howe, *The Unitarian Conscience* (Cambridge, Mass.: Harvard University Press, 1970), *passim*, but esp. pp. 295–296; Octavius B. Frothingham, *Boston Unitarianism, 1820–1850* (New York: Putnam, 1890), *passim*, esp. pp. 2–3, 193–194, 196–197; John Ware, *Memoir of the Life of Henry Ware, Jr.*, 2 vols. (Boston, 1846), II, 147–151; *Boston Advertiser*, Apr. 24, 30, June 5, 7, 12, 1851.

79. *National Cyclopedia,* I, 117; E. Ray Speare, *Interesting Happenings in Boston University's History, 1839–1951* (Boston: Boston University Press, 1957), 5 ff. See Hoar, *Autobiography,* I, 193, on the Methodists in politics: "That denomination had always been strong and influential in the Worcester district and its members have always stood staunchly by the men of their own household when candidates for political office."
80. Boutwell, *Reminiscences,* II, 238; see also Robinson, *"Warrington,"* p. 122.
81. *Mass. Const. Convention, 1853,* III, 254–255.
82. *Ibid.,* pp. 256–262.
83. *Ibid.,* pp. 27–28.
84. *Ibid.,* p. 36.
85. William S. Tyler, *A History of Amherst College* (New York, 1895), pp. 142–143; Samuel E. Morison, *Three Centuries of Harvard* (Cambridge, Mass.: Harvard University Press, 1936), p. 309.
86. For debates in the constitutional convention see *Mass. Const. Convention, 1853,* II, 253–276; III, 50–73, 166–178, 318–361.
87. *Boston Advertiser,* Apr. 7, 15, 20, 22, 1850, Mar. 14, 1852.
88. Salsbury, *The State,* 280 ff; Kirkland, *Transportation,* I, 387 ff; *Boston Advertiser,* Apr. 3, 24, 26, 28, May 5, 14, 1851; *Mass. Const. Convention, 1853,* III, 20.
89. Bullock, *Financial History,* pp. 46 ff, 63; *Boston Advertiser,* Mar. 12, 14, Apr. 22, 1857.
90. Pierce, *Charles Sumner,* III, 519; IV, 97, 356–357; see also Sarah Forbes, ed., *Letters and Recollections of John M. Forbes,* 2 vols. (Boston: Houghton Mifflin, 1899), I, 183, 205; Robinson, "Warrington," p. 408; Abbott, *Cobbler in Congress,* p. 97; Ware, *Political Opinion,* pp. 122, 123, 125 n. 1, 137 n. 3, 175.
91. Ware, *Political Opinion,* p. 185 ff; Montgomery, *Beyond Equality,* pp. 230–267.
92. Butler, *Butler's Books;* Robert S. Holzman, *Stormy Ben Butler* (New York: Macmillan, 1954); Hans Trefousse, *Ben Butler: The South Called Him Beast* (New York: Octagon, 1974); Richard Harmond, "The 'Beast' in Boston: Benjamin F. Butler as Governor of Massachusetts," *Journal of American History,* LV (1968), 266–280.
93. Butler, *Books,* p. 93 ff.
94. Henry Adams, *Letters of Henry Adams,* edited by W. C. Ford (Boston: Houghton Mifflin, 1930), pp. 145–146.
95. Holzman, *Ben Butler,* p. 198.
96. *Ibid.,* p. 229.
97. *Ibid.,* p. 212.

Utopian Fiction and Its Discontents

Neil Harris

Neil Harris, professor of history at the University of Chicago, is the author of *The Artist in American Society: The Formative Years, 1790–1860* (1966), and *Humbug: The Art of P. T. Barnum* (1970). From 1975 to 1977 he was director of the National Humanities Institute at the University of Chicago.

OVER ONE HUNDRED utopian novels were published in America during the quarter century before World War I. In addition, there appeared a large number of science-fiction epics, as well as romances set in exotic places. All these genres shared a concern with other worlds, realms of life that contrasted with nineteenth-century experience. Whether they fit precisely within a utopian category or not, these experiments in time and place played with social conventions and frequently suspended the laws of history and nature.

Judged by contemporary reputation or literary survival, most of the books are minor documents. But their subterranean anxieties, largely ignored by later historians, are absorbingly up to date.

Many of these novelists were not professional authors. They had sound reasons for avoiding such a career. Their urge to describe other worlds was rarely based on any need for artistic fulfillment. More often they wrote from a passion to communicate some special idea. Their books, in fact, demonstrate the impact of modernization upon American life, presenting worlds ruled by strange machines, crowded with masses of people, and reverent toward scientific truth. The novels' solutions to political and economic problems built on the classic anxieties we associate with this period. But their fictional details answered more intimate and perhaps more fundamental personal fears. These crudely written books offer surprising insights into long-vanished sensibilities. Perhaps the best way to begin is to consider a few examples of this literature, and their rather unusual authors.

In 1895, in Cincinnati, a book was published which occasionally is described as a utopian novel, and is invariably a part of science-fiction bibliographies. It bore the unlikely title of *Etidorhpa; or, The End of Earth, the Strange History of a Mysterious Being and the Account of a Remarkable Journey.* The author was as distinctive as his title. John Uri Lloyd had been born in 1849 in upstate New York, the son of a surveyor and mathematician.[1] After an apprenticeship to several Cincinnati druggists, John Lloyd (along with a brother) came to own a drug firm. Lloyd also involved himself in research. During a long life he published eight scientific books, patented fifteen inventions, originated three hundred seventy-nine elixirs, and produced several thousand papers. Lloyd's collections of pharmaceutical formulas became standard texts in American colleges of pharmacy, and he assembled a distinguished library on botany and pharmacy, a library which published its own quarterly journal on the biological sciences. Heading various scientific and medical societies, he found the time to publish eight novels, all but one centered in northern Kentucky. By the time of his death in 1936 Lloyd had accumulated many honorary degrees and a comfortable fortune. In short, he was one of those extraordinary figures of nineteenth-century science: scholar, businessman, and bellettrist.

But this respectable scientist also published *Etidorhpa,* a novel that went through eighteen editions (of undetermined size), and was translated into seven languages. Some of the reviews, which the author reprinted in later editions, were enthusiastic. Benjamin O. Flower, social reformer, sometime mystic, and editor of the *Arena,* suggested that Lloyd had surpassed Alexander Dumas, Jules Verne, and Victor Hugo. Another critic termed *Etidorhpa* the "most unique, original, and suggestive new book" of the decade.[2] There was nothing else like it in print.

The novel describes a strange journey, begun when the member of a secret fraternity is kidnapped by his brothers for threatening to divulge the order's secrets. The sequence suggests the supposed abduction of William Morgan in the 1820s, an event touching off a decade of anti-Masonic agitation. Both abductors and victim are involved with alchemy and esoteric knowledge.

Sentenced to annihilation of identity, the potential apostate is suddenly transformed into an aged, unrecognizable man. Led by semihuman guides he then enters worlds where space, heat, time, and energy assume bizarre properties.

In its scope, the journey resembles other famous quests in Western literature. But unlike most of them, the aim of this allegory is principally to reveal the laws of nature. These laws are more complex, and permit more variety, than scientists ever dreamed. Strange forms of animal and vegetable life appear, including forests of gigantic mushrooms. Gravity loss, light without shadow, water without currents, mysterious energy sources, giant hands, temptations from friends, communion with angels — all are part of the book. Lloyd's fictive strategy is clever. He introduces a narrator who interviews the apostate, and challenges his experiences. He is met by experiments, descriptions, and diagrams that prove their possibility (however much they interrupt the narrative flow). Man, insists Lloyd, is limited and puny. No one could have forecast the wonderful inventions of the late nineteenth century. The marvels of *Etidorhpa* are real possibilities. Wonder is only an exemplification of ignorance.

But although its author was a scientist, and the book employs empirical demonstration, *Etidorhpa* is frequently antimaterialist. Experimental science is dangerous because it threatens the idea of immortality. Beware of the beginning of biological inquiry, is Lloyd's warning. Beware of your own brain. Reality is more than materialism; in *Etidorhpa* thought force is used to transmit ideas. The guide promises it will eventually replace the inadequacy of vocal language. But before this can happen, men will have to study strange spiritual phenomena and science abandon its materialist concentration. Spiritualistic investigations "unfortunately are considered by scientific men too often as reaching backward only," when in fact they lead directly to a wondrous future.[3] For many such pages the book proceeds, interweaving bizarre experiences with practical experiments and ending with a mystical vision: the abducted victim stands on the brink of another world, the distant country, prefiguring the progress of humanity when, like him, it will have comprehended the laws of creation and the meaning of life. He has reached the end of the earth.

This then was *Etidorhpa*. Questions must remain on every level of the book's meaning, but larger than the intricacies of its allegories is the basic fact of its appearance. What was a distinguished scientist doing with such a book? Why his suspicion of science? Why the turn to alchemy and mysticism?

If *Etidorhpa* stood alone, one might continue to examine Lloyd. But it shared a life with dozens of bizarre works depicting the existence of other worlds. As did *Etidorhpa*, they frequently combined careful descriptions of physical marvels with a passion for religious discussion, social improvement, and spiritualist investigation. One example is Amos K. Fiske's *Beyond the Bourn: Reports of a Traveller Returned from "The Undiscovered Country."*[4] In his own way, Fiske was as remarkable as Lloyd. He had been born in New Hampshire in 1842, and orphaned at an early age. Although forced as a child to work in a cotton mill, Fiske managed to attend Harvard College and graduate with honors in 1866. He married a sister of Francis J. Child, the Harvard philologist and ballad scholar, and became an editor for various newspapers including the *Boston Globe* and the *New York Times*. Fiske published only half a dozen books, but demonstrated a comprehensive mind. His works include studies of the Philippines and the West Indies; an analysis of banking; several volumes on Hebrew mythology and history; a proposed reorganization of labor and management; and, in 1891, his one utopia, *Beyond the Bourn*.

Fiske's novel is simpler than *Etidorhpa*, lacking its complex allegorical organization. But there is an added attraction. Alongside an account of a utopian planet, further evolved than earth, Fiske added a description of Heaven. His narrator, apparently killed in a train wreck, makes an ascent to Heaven, where he meets a number of old friends and is taken by angels to view a more advanced planet; after returning to Heaven he awakens to find that he has in fact survived the wreck.

In its basic argument, Fiske's novel is a self-conscious effort to combine traditional religion with Darwinian evolution. His utopian world is cooperative, brotherly, and technologically sophisticated. Air travel, submarines, selective breeding, and the security of immortality make life easy. But Fiske's description of Paradise forms his most interesting contribution. The orthodox meet with some surprises. The spirits of the dead, stripped of selfish animal appetites, can observe without reliance upon physical sensation. They require no material substance to perceive form and color. Contrary to popular belief, they do not stand around idly singing hymns but are in constant activity. With millions of globes to learn about, each with its own inhabitants, there are continuing marvels to discover. Heaven is far from dull.

Despite this enthusiastic description, however, Fiske warned against efforts to communicate directly with heavenly spirits. "The craving for such revelations," he argued, "becomes morbid and absorbing; it blinds the judgment . . . and leads to deception."[5] Nonetheless, spiritualists and mediums must have read *Beyond the Bourn* with satisfaction, for here, along with the social analysis of a utopian society, appeared a noncorporeal spiritual world, defying known natural laws, and demonstrating the existence of life after death.

Fiske and Lloyd were joined in their fictional enterprises by many others, of lesser fame and accomplishment. Cyrus Cole, for example, who published *The Auroraphone* in Boston, in 1890, published nothing else.[6] But this novel also is a heady mixture of utopianism, romance, religious debate, and soul transmutation. A group of Americans, traveling out west, stumble on communication with Saturn, through an instrument which combines features of the telephone and the telegraph. They find a planet torn by religious dissension. Saturnians had once worshiped the sun, whose power was revealed by the appearance of his son, Creeto. Creeto taught a religion of future rewards and punishments. In a thinly veiled satire on Christianity, Cole describes the arguments erupting about the religious doctrines. The followers of Creeto, Creetans, accept as a principle the permutation of personality. In a universe of homogeneous atoms, some of which form the soul, every individual during the course of time will inevitably acquire the personality of every other living organism, experiencing every pain and joy the universe embraces. Existence is unitary; if one individual or generation bears greater burdens than others, they will eventually reap their rewards.

While this doctrine unites Saturnians for a time, they face other problems. Marvelous machines enable them to master their environment. One, labeled the Electro-Camera-Lucida-Motophone, reproduces past events; the American visitors witness the destruction of Pompeii, the Battle of Gettysburg, and the Chicago Fire. Saturnians have also managed to create from matal, a strange element combining strength with lightness, duplicate human beings. The duplicates perform every function human beings do, except for reproduction; they are accountants, soldiers, and clerks. With the word *robot* still unborn, Cole happily had the Saturnians call their machines "dummies." But the dummies gain power, as Saturnian laziness leads to torpor. Learning to charge their own electrometers, the dummies revolt against their masters, killing thousands of citizens and capturing many cities. The Saturnians ruefully admit their mistake in moving forward so rapidly. "A certain amount of useful labor with the hands, daily performed," appears to be the price required by progress.[7]

The American visitors are impressed with Saturn's wonders, but even more excited by the Creetan theory of permutation. Without sacrificing belief in a benevolent deity, the creed explains all the evil in the universe. Knowing that one day even the fortunate and wealthy will experience the pains of the lower orders would surely produce greater social sympathy. This doctrine might permit brotherhood on earth. And Saturn's experiences, properly modified, would allow earthlings to avoid the dangers of machine insurrection.

Cole, Lloyd, and Fiske published their books within a period of five years. If talked about at all by literary historians, they are mentioned as part of the flowering of utopian fantasy which occurred in the two decades following publication of Edward Bellamy's *Looking Backward* in 1888. Their strange plots, metaphysical speculation, suspicion of science, and new mechanical marvels have usually been dismissed as irrelevant. Most commentators have concentrated upon the political and economic features of their utopian societies. The physical settings, the tastes of the interplanetary beings, and their religious convictions apparently required no explication.

Such selective analysis was partly accidental. Historians discovered our utopian literature in the 1930s and 1940s. This discovery became part of a larger effort to demonstrate a tradition of social and economic consciousness that American artists and writers could draw upon. Sensitive to charges of irrelevance and often committed to activist notions of the artist's political role, critics were delighted to demonstrate a pedigree for social involvement.

And the pedigree was comprehensive. More than one hundred ideal societies were depicted by novelists between the late 1880s and 1910; hundreds of other novels took as their themes labor strife and the class struggle. One early study of this literature,

Claude Flory's *Economic Criticism in American Fiction,* placed the utopias in the context of economic commentary. Flory insisted that the ablest American realists, from 1860 to 1900, were also the most vigorous economic critics. "The relationship," he explained, "is that both economic criticism — in the regular novel — and realism demand truth to life." Flory had located only sixty utopian novels; they did not fit his criteria for realism, to be sure. But he avoided the problem by declaring them a special genre, one which maintained an older, antebellum romanticism but was, "of course, almost exclusively economic" in its import.[8]

Other scholars — Alleyn B. Forbes, Lisle Rose, Walter Taylor, Robert Shurter — expanded the study of economic fiction; in 1947 Vernon Louis Parrington, Jr., published his study of utopian fiction, *American Dreams.* Several dissertations and more books supplemented these efforts and increased our knowledge of published utopias. But with some exceptions the thrust of this scholarship, and its invaluable bibliographies, has been largely to describe, annotate, and collate utopian fiction by economic and political themes.[9] The novels have been divided into collectivist, populist, nationalist, and single-tax categories, with descriptions of their solutions to agrarian discontent, monetary inequities, labor unions, and political representation. The physical details, the family structure, the social rituals, and the religious concerns have remained offstage, subordinated, and oddly separate. It is undeniable, of course, that most utopian novelists were vitally concerned with the pressing problems of industrialization — its economic hardships and inequalities. But they were dealing also with the cultural hardships of modernization; and on these their testimony is most eloquent.

All this, of course, in terms of larger effects and literary importance, was a peripheral literature; and one may gain more from scrutinizing what appear to be peripheral features than central objectives. Economic categorizing has isolated the utopian genre in America from other contemporaneous enterprises. A social link between the utopian peninsula and the literary mainland is achieved through the reputation of some of the novelists — William Dean Howells and Jack London, for example. But there are other ties with American intellectual history, and these ties are provided by the novels' physical settings, and more particularly, their fascination with technology.

The three novels by Lloyd, Fiske, and Cole share a delight in outlining various scientific marvels that men might yet experience. Utopian writers, more generally, depict various forms of radar and television, air travel, temperature control, new metals, exploitation of solar energy, and automated machinery. While utopians catalogue advances, however, they spend little time explaining their operation. The few who do are highly derivative, taking their information, without much change, from the pages of periodicals like *Popular Science*. Most critics, therefore, finding technological interests so clearly overshadowed by economic goals, have tended to ignore them, or classify the inventions as further evidence of the authors' visionary character.

But if these technologies are examined, not in terms of originality or thematic centrality, but to determine the problems they were meant to solve and their role in establishing credibility, other conclusions develop. Many utopias are a part of the literature of American science fiction, as much as they belong to the literature of economic criticism. Some students — Robert Philmus, Thomas Clareson, David Ketterer — have developed interesting definitions of science fiction which deserve further exploration.[10] But in this essay I am less concerned with definitions of form than with common details. Joint consideration permits the isolation of otherwise hidden themes; and these themes touch heavily on science and technology.

In the first place, technology was an enabling condition for the description of other worlds. In the early nineteenth century, American utopianism tended to be more practical than literary, household or village oriented, stressing primary relationships and work satisfactions. The famous experiments in group living scattered through New England and the Middle West sought to influence the rest of society by example. In Arthur Bestor's classic analysis, institutions seemed plastic; the country was young; and pure forms appeared attainable through isolation. Controlled experiments were social possibilities. The structure of national life, if illogical, was at least divisible; communication and involvement were voluntary acts.[11]

By the 1880s and 1890s it had become more evident that piecemeal reform was an unlikely introduction to utopian dreams. Urban and manufacturing technologies had created permanent interdependencies. The price of effective change was social comprehensiveness, on a national or worldwide scale. The continual attention utopian novelists gave to transport and communications reflected this commitment to interdependence. The very forms of their fictional societies would have been impossible without a new ecological consciousness, an awareness of the snowballing effects of physical innovation and the need for their careful control. Henry Olerich, who published *A Cityless and Countryless World* in 1891, confronted these relationships directly. Physical change, he wrote, necessarily created social change. New locomotives produced new roadbeds, more rapid commerce, a transformed trade. "A system in order to be natural and harmonious must be connected whole." "The very act" of discussing "a single topic unconnected with others is a sign of mental incompleteness," he concluded.[12]

The social order, then, had to be transformed totally or not at all. No part of the community could remain outside, as either exemplary or cautionary. Hostility to private interests and selfish individualism was nourished by experiences with the machine as system builder. Many of the novelists were moderately successful technicians and inventors: Chauncey Thomas, author of *The Crystal Button,* was a New England carriage manufacturer; Frederick U. Adams, who published *President John Smith* in 1899, designed machinery, including electric-light towers; John Bachelder, the author of *A.D. 2050: Electrical Development of Atlantis,* made important improvements on the sewing machine; Byron Brooks, still another utopian novelist, patented crucial improvements for the typewriter.[13] Some of these novelists, then, had been successful in adjusting to the occupational demands of the new industrial society; a few, like King Gillette, of safety-razor glory, even became wealthy. It was natural that they paraded gadgetry as proof of their own ingenuity, and to demonstrate an appreciation of social complexity.

Technology serviced another major utopian need: it rescued far-reaching schemes from improbability. Henry Olerich introduced in his novel a man who claimed to have been born on Mars. Americans might find this hard to believe, Olerich admitted generously; but after all, many incredible things had happened in the nineteenth century. "Telegraphy seemed impossible to Washington and his contemporaries," Olerich argued; "so did a 60 mile-an-hour train. We have divested them of all mystery."[14]

H. E. Swan, a Kansan, whose utopian novel *It Might Be* appeared in 1896, introduced a time machine which permitted visitors to witness the Crucifixion, and a wall paint which eliminated the need for artificial illumination by absorbing light during the day and emitting it at night. Some might scoff, but "had the picture of 1893 been drawn for our Puritan fathers, they would have called the artist crazy."[15] New machines were hostages, proofs that the limits of human intelligence could not be easily fixed.

A third value of technology to the utopians was its clear contrast with the wretched state of contemporary society. Machine efficiency might shame men into social improvement. "We have photographed starts too remote to be seen even with the most powerful telescopes," wrote Henry Olerich. "We have explored the bottom of the sea."[16] But women and children still spent long days in factories, farmers were abandoned to rural solitude, tramps terrorized the countryside. These disparities could not be tolerated. Machines raised expectations for physical comfort and social rationality. Their very presence invited dramatic institutional reform. Technology formed more than a footnote to utopian prescriptions; it lay at their heart.

But centrality was one thing, confidence another. Enthusiastic descriptions were coupled with doubts, strange speculations about Heaven, mysticism, and timidities. Indeed, despite their technical daring and apparent self-confidence, many of these utopian novels were the products of worried minds, and represented a flight from experience, adventure, and confrontation. The technological wonders were surrounded with restrictions and qualifications. Their purpose was to shield utopians from too much direct contact with either the organic world outside or their fellow human beings. The energies calling forth this literature of marvelous speculation were nourished by dreams of escape — escape from danger, from pressure, from threats both vague and specified. The keynote through all these novels was control, protection, security. Utopian societies were giant envelopes. Their combination of mystical religion and technological ingenuity is understandable when they are seen as anxious responses to a set of revolutionary changes undergone by this generation of Americans. These changes are associated with urbanization and industrialization, but they are the kinds of direct, physical experiences we often neglect in favor of larger abstractions. The changes that concerned them most, I believe, can be grouped within three large categories.

The first of these great revolutions was the harnessing of electricity. Up through the Civil War era the greatest symbol of scientific advance for the contemporary world was the steam engine, a gigantic emblem of natural power controlled by human ingenuity. But if steam power was ingenious, it was neither mysterious nor indecipherable. Its principles of operation were easily explainable; the energy that ran looms, boats, locomotives, and factories had obvious sources of fuel and comprehensible moving parts. Size and power stood in a direct relationship; great engines had the scale they seemed to deserve. Dirty, noisy, even threatening, the giant machines may have been, but they never disguised their nature or purpose.

Electrical energy, however, was less susceptible to ordinary logic; its systems were barely visible. The tiny wires and even the larger cables which transmitted the awesome power to move, to illuminate, to operate machinery seemed out of proportion to their task, minute conduits for a giant force. Experiments with electricity and writings about its properties had, of course, a long history by this time. In Europe, William Gilbert, Robert Boyle, and von Guericke had experimented in the seventeenth century, and their efforts were expanded by Benjamin Franklin and Alessandro Volta. But despite Volta's famous 1800 paper on electrical generation and the work of nineteenth-century scientists like Faraday, Davy, and Joseph Henry, it was not until the 1870s that a larger public familiarity with the uses of electricity developed.[17] The single exception was the electric telegraph.

Beginning in the 1870s, however, a series of major innovations exposed laymen to the still-novel force; illumination, communications, transport, and machinery were all transformed. Arc lights and then incandescent lighting, electric traction for railways and streetcars, the telephone, sewing machines (1889), automobiles (1892), vacuum cleaners (1899), all appeared in breathless succession. Electrical application appeared limitless, which is one reason why it figured so prominently in many utopian novels. Clean and portable, it seemed an ideal solution to problems of noise and pollution caused by steam.

But along with the sense of dominion which electricity stimulated there were forebodings and anxieties. The harnessing of natural forces, often far from the scene of application, seemed to some an arrogation of semidivine powers. The most dramatic symbol of this was the capture of that greatest token of the American sublime, Niagara Falls, to supply electricity for Buffalo in 1896. When this was accomplished, after years of effort and debate, the triumph of man over nature seemed assured.[18]

But so extraordinary a victory caused concern by its very scale. The new force was alternately dreaded and worshiped. Nowhere was this better evidenced than in the displays of late nineteenth century world fairs. By the 1890s enormous palaces at these expositions devoted themselves to electricity, while evening illuminations formed one of the chief glories of the fairs. Awe and fear mingled with one another. Many descriptions have been penned, but one of the most interesting was written by Joseph and Caroline Kirkland, at the Columbian Exposition of 1893. The Kirklands had come to the Electricity Palace from the Mining Building. In the latter, they wrote, "we could touch, measure, weigh, describe, depict what we were talking about"; but electricity was different.

[We] can not perceive the matter itself by any of our senses. It is without weight, length, breadth, or thickness. We can only see, hear, feel what it does, not grasp it or even conceive it in our minds. Certain treatments of matter produce certain forces, which are surely not matter; and those forces proceed to act in certain invariable ways with fearful speed and strength — that is all we know. The why and wherefore is as inexplicable to us as why or wherefore a liberated stone falls to the ground, or a planted seed germinates. . . . We speak without being spoken to, and bow without being introduced. We hover around the beautiful, terrible stranger, but we do not — willingly — shake hands. His glance is blinding, his voice is deafening, his touch is death. He is a law unto himself, and his enactments are immutable.[19]

The semireligious tone dominates; electricity is a god whose laws must be obeyed without question, but whose aid knows no limits. Omnipotent, omnipresent, perhaps electricity is the source for all life. The Kirklands, in fact, end their description of electricity by quoting Emerson's "Brahma" entire. The harnessing of electrical energy fit an old strain in the American consciousness which found all reality an expression of the Over-Soul; here was evidence for the mystical power animating the universe. Another visitor to the same fair described her entry into the Electricity Palace as a penetration of "the Great Enchanter, the King of Wonders of the 19th century," and lapsed into silent awe.[20]

But awe was matched by practical awareness of electricity's dangers, and the popular press played up these concerns. Fears about electrocution were legion. "It is an uncomfortable fact that chain lightning is being recklessly dispensed all over town," the *Philadelphia Inquirer* complained in the 1880s about the installation of electricity.[21] The *Boston Evening Transcript,* commenting on the electrocution of a horse by a live wire in New York, noted that authorities insisted that "there is no danger in the wires; but nobody believes them any longer."[22] The employment of electric lights was "fraught with great perils," insisted the *New York Tribune,* before going on to name electricity as the source for all kinds of mysterious accidents.[23] Business competitors exploited these fears as well. In 1879 Dan Rice, the clown and showman, warned against the electric light being featured by Cooper & Bailey's Great London Circus: "Persons predisposed to pulmonary complaints" should avoid the light since "it will shorten their days and in many cases it affects the tender brain of children."[24] The National Safety Congress was created from the concern of electrical engineers intent on reassuring the public. Thomas Edison did not help much when he stressed the perils of electrocution in his ill-fated campaign against alternating current. Neither did the development of the electric chair, adopted by New York in 1888 and first used two years later, partly on Edison's advice.[25]

The rhetoric of those favoring the electric chair as a death penalty revealed some of these early concerns. Writing in the *Forum,* Park Benjamin insisted that "no other mode of inflicting death could inspire stronger fear" in the lawless classes. "Even those accustomed to deal with electricity every day of their lives cannot divest themselves of an undefined impression of mystery which seems to surround the form of energy," he continued. "People still attribute to electricity almost every out-of-the-way natural phenomenon which they cannot understand. . . . No death is more dreaded than that which is mysterious."[26] Benjamin added that fears of electricity were hundreds of years old, but now much more evidence justified these fears and allowed defenders of law and society to exploit public alarm.

With these sinister implications in mind, one can understand why so many of the novelists enthroned electricity as a divinity, capable of remarkable achievements but requiring careful worship. Clean, powerful, and quiet electricity may have been, but it needed continual monitoring. In John Bachelder's *A.D. 2050* electricity, applied to every form of power, is a state secret, entrusted to a government commission of six men.[27] In Jack London's "Goliah," the world is reformed by an inventor who has developed a new form of energy, resembling electricity, which can destroy at will.[28] The inhabitants of William Taylor's *Intermere*, a utopian novel of 1901, know how to take the dangers out of electrical current, but refuse to pass the knowledge on to earthlings. "Neither your people nor any other people could be trusted with this secret in their present moral condition," warns a leader of Intermere. "A few learned men dependent upon the rulers in one nation, knowing it, could and would plot the destruction and exploitation of others. The sacrifice of human life . . . would be appalling."[29] Not only its own power, then, but the unprecedented power it brought those who controlled it made electricity fearsome.

The electrical revolution, however, released other meanings. It permitted existing fears to be translated into demands for a riskfree environment. Electricity itself could be perilous. But its extraordinary capacities apparently justified dreams of total comfort and unmeasured independence, independence of nature, of other animals, of any reminders of vulnerability. Electrical energy stimulated a recital of these anxieties, and the novelists paraded their concerns about indiscriminate contact, exposure to the elements, bodily invasion. They sought a level of safety that was breathtakingly total. Many utopias were set underground or placed within vast domes. Temperature control meant transcendence of natural caprice. "In truth," confessed a character in Albert Howard's *Milltillionaire*, "we have absolute control of the weather, and may evolve any special weather from the elements that are at any moment to embellish the occasion."[30] No fog, mist, steam, smoke, or noxious gasses survived this atmosphere; even the crops were grown by electricity, a calorifico-electeric ether which had replaced sunlight.

Electricity protected against more personal threats, which had grown under the pressure of urbanization. In *A.D. 2050* bedside keyboards were useful against burglars. "The building is guarded by an electric mechanism that notifies the occupants of the approach of anyone after the family retires. From the watch tower at Police Headquarters the whole or any part of the city can be instantly illuminated."[31]

No longer would man have to tolerate the presence of animals, or be distressed by claw and fang. The disappearance of horses, a prolific source of dirt and disease, was universally acclaimed. Utopian cities banished domestic animals. "Whatever the horse can do," promised one novelist, "the automobile can do a hundred times better."[32] Whole species were to be extirpated. "Humanity cannot but rejoice," cried a scientist in Chauncey Thomas's *Crystal Button,* "that the great carnivorous beasts of the feline, canine, and ursine families no longer exist." Their extinction resulted from "direct and systematic warfare in the interests of humanity." The hippopotamus, rhinoceros, crocodile, and tiger, Thomas continued happily, "have long ceased to devastate and make afraid." And repaying a biblical debt, he also announced the total destruction of the entire serpent family, "a long-wished for riddance that has but recently been effected."[33]

Thus most utopians had little reverence for wilderness or unspoiled nature. The wild was dangerous because it was unpredictable. Utopian pleasures were taken in parks, and nature organized by electricity. Solitary confrontations with natural challenges — of weather, terrain, or animal rivalry — were defined out of utopias, along with other risks.

The need for animals was reduced, moreover, because of changes in eating habits. A large number of these fictional communities were vegetarian, both for health and for moral reasons. Dietary reform had long been associated with more comprehensive social schemes in the United States; its appearance in this literature is not surprising.[34] But the frequency and emphasis are still impressive, and the justifications are revealing. In Edward Bellamy's sequel to *Looking Backward, Equality,* improved health results from a vegetarian diet. But the impulses to this reform were ethical. According to Bellamy the abandonment of flesh eating "was chiefly an effect of the great wave of human feeling, the passion of pity and compunction for all suffering — in a word, the impulse of tender-heartedness — which was really the great moral power behind the revolution. . . . The sentiment of brotherhood, the feeling of solidarity, asserted itself not merely toward men and women, but likewise toward the humbler companions of our life on earth and sharers of its fortunes, the animals."[35] Men had come to conceive of themselves as elder brothers in a great natural family; animal eating seemed a kind of cannibalism.

While some utopians tried to forget man's debt to nature, others wanted simply to improve the master design by destroying all aggressive impulses. On the Mars of James Cowan's *Daybreak* horses had not disappeared, but people were too tenderhearted to enjoy riding them; the horses might become fatigued. Even animals ceased to eat flesh. They were trained not to do so, or bred until the carnivorous instinct had disappeared.[36] On another Mars, this one the creation of Gustavus W. Pope, Martians became vegetarians in order to transcend their baser appetites. "Animal food," declared a Martian doctor, "has the inherent tendency to depress the development of the higher and nobler attributes of man, the moral sentiments and feelings, and it has the worse effect, also, of stimulating and fostering the instincts and passions of our lower nature." Earth people, he warned, despite any advances in civilization they might make, would always have discord so long as they devoured meat. Meat, according to Herman Brinsmade, contained "all of the poisonous, unexcreted waste matter" of dead animals, overstimulating the "eliminative organs" and producing an enormous number of fatal diseases. In Brinsmade's *Utopia Achieved,* a single-tax community, one of the heroes was Horace Fletcher, the food reformer who gave up a life of ease to teach the poor how to chew. Broth, graham puffs, zwieback, and malt honey were healthful as well as ethical imperatives.[37]

The substitution of electricity for animal power, and the complementary habit of vegetarianism were valued by the utopians as evidence of refined human feelings; stimulants which might lead to aggression or aggrandizement — alcohol, dirt, noise, animal food — were barred. Fears of aggressive energies, competitiveness, and self-enhancement dominate many of the novels. Activities which produced conflict or personal tension were discouraged. The reason for this obsession with order and regularity may lie in a second recent revolution which had affected the lives of millions of Americans, and that was the consciousness of crowding which invaded the late nineteenth century mind. Recent scholarship has paid greater attention to the ecological aspects of rapid urban growth, but in this period of increasing urbanization all its victims knew that higher population densities were influencing every aspect of urban life. Transport, recreation, housing, commerce, and family life all bore marks of the strain placed by numbers on facilities. This social pressure had many effects; one, no doubt, was to increase interest in avenues of escape, the wilderness appeal that historians have lately described.[38] Another effect was to intensify demands for privacy, and strengthen the argument that population density was in itself a cause of poverty, crime, and social alienation. The novelists, however, were committed to community and not to isolation; somehow they had to evoke physical settings suitable for large groups, without any sense of pressure or tension. Continual contiguity led to aggression, loss of control, and social decline. "Contact breeds contagion and decay," wrote Captain Nathan Davis in *Beulah.* Dense "populations which are in constant contact breed moral contagion and deadly corruption."[39] The solution was to plan an environment that used space efficiently, and avoided situations of crowding.

This, after all, was the first generation with so many indiscriminate crowd encounters; rural Americans, living on farms or in small towns, experienced large casual assemblages only occasionally, when they journeyed away from home or participated in political rallies and religious revivals. Even so, one finds among Poe, Hawthorne, and Melville an awareness of the nature of the pre–Civil War crowd. But the urbanites of the late nineteenth century, as the first generation of urban sociologists reiterated, were being bombarded with secondary contacts continuously, producing novel collective experiences. What arrangements could maintain order in so intense (and potentially anarchic) a social setting? This question was addressed by almost every utopian writer, whatever his economic orientation. The fictional strategy usually fell into three parts. First, avoidance of situations that involved social pressure, and a portrayal of the panic that would inevitably take place if control were to be lost. Second, construction of facilities which ordered public life and protected personal space simultaneously. And finally, encouragement of qualities of character and temper which preferred these controlled environments, and knew how to enjoy them.

On the first level, that of the object lesson, utopian novelists frequently referred to the horrors of social compression in contemporary America, contrasting them with the calm of utopian life. William Dean Howells's Altrurian traveler reacted with disgust to the noise and congestion of New York's elevated railroads. "Every seat in them is taken, and every foot of space in the aisle between the seats is held by people standing, and swaying miserably to and fro by the leather straps dangling from the roofs. Men and women are indecently crushed together, without regard for that personal dignity which we prize, but which the Americans seem to know nothing of and care nothing for. The multitude overflows from the car ... and the passengers are as tightly wedged on the platforms without as they are within. . . . Those who wish to mount fight their way into the car or onto the platform, where the guard slams an iron gate. . . ."[40] Howells blamed such horrors on plutocracy; with ten men doing the work of one, the movement of people to and from business was enormous. Referring implicitly to the work of George M. Beard, an early psychiatrist whose book *American Nervousness* made direct connections between urban life and mental disease, Howells connected the noise of trains to the growing prevalence of "neurotic disorders."[41]

Public ceremonies were like public transport — disorderly, crowded, and threatening. According to utopians, decorum was maintained only by force. "I was once summoned as a witness in one of our courts," recalled an American visitor to Altruria, "and I have never forgotten the horror of it; the hot, dirty room, with its foul air, the brutal spectators, the policeman stationed among them to keep them in order."[42] Cosimo Noto, a physician and novelist, symbolized disorder by concentrating on accidents in crowded streets and on railroad trains.[43] Henry Olerich blamed many social evils on the indiscriminate concentration of people in apartments. "The old, the middle-aged, and the young are all crowded in one little apartment. Their natural inclination . . . is very unlike. Yet they are compelled to be together. . . . How many matured children," he asked his readers, "when living in the same . . . apartment, make your home a dungeon — a battle-field on which the better sentiments of both parents and children are slain?"[44] For Bradford Peck, whose very title, *The World a Department Store*, summarized his commitment to order, a major drawback of nineteenth-century life was the shopping scene, "when crowds of women, becoming as they did frantic and almost wild, pushed and crowded one another to gain an opportunity of purchasing something, because some other woman wanted it."[45]

Several of the utopian and many of the science-fiction novels portrayed terrifying scenes of mass panic, when the normal controls failed. In Stewart Edward White's *The Sign at Six,* an old 'man holds New York in terror by cutting off electricity during the rush hour. "Where ordinarily is a crush," wrote White, "now was a panic — a panic the more terrible in that it was solid, sullen, inert, motionless. Women fainted and stood unconscious, erect. Men sank slowly from sight, agonized, their faces contorted, but unheard in the full roar of the crowd, and were seen no more. Around the edges people fought frantically to get out; and others, with the blind, unreasoning, home instinct, fought as hard to get in."[46] Several of the interplanetary stories feature cosmic catastrophe, meteor bombardments which reduce the delicate shell of civilization to rubble and send millions scrambling to escape destruction. In Louis P. Gratacap's novel of Mars, "strangely bewildered and uncontrolled" crowds fight to escape the meteor showers, the reverse of the buoyant throngs that the visitor had encountered just a short time before.[47] Panic scenes permitted writers to work out their fears, and sometimes to resolve them.

They did resolve them by devising miracles of ingenuity which carefully channeled the new crowds. Safety, dignity, and breathing space were stressed over and over again. Some novelists drew diagrams and maps of their ideal communities, scaled to the last foot of road width and building height. Mass transport, governed by elaborate mechanical safeguards, aided circulation. Garden cities and small towns replaced the dense concentration of urban life, while apartment hotels, with centralized cooking, eating, and washing facilities, were surrounded by parks and gardens. Neither concentration nor isolation was permissible, for each involved struggle and struggle meant anxiety. No device to ease worry was too small for discussion. In Albert Chavannes's Socioland, an ideal community set in Africa, streetcars were large, comfortable, and designed to reassure. At each end "is hung a large dial, and printed upon it are the names of the cross streets and important places passed on the trip. A needle on the dial, automatically moved by the running gear, travels in unison with the car, and always points to the exact spot reached, thus keeping the passengers informed of their present location. By this simple method much anxiety is avoided. . . ."[48] The great value of the telephone lay in its ability to bypass public encounters and crowd pressures. Broadcast sermons and music reached dispersed audiences. "Telephones have so far spoiled us," explained one utopian to a visitor, "that being in a crowd, which was the matter-of-course penalty you had to pay for seeing or hearing anything interesting, would seem too dear a price to pay for almost any enjoyment."[49] The population of Gustavus Pope's Mars was eight billion but there was no crowding; by a unique arrangement of great linear cities, some of them two thousand miles long, each family owned its own house, garden, and grounds.[50]

These technical contrivances, and the list could be extended indefinitely, all had a common objective: avoidance of confrontation and its resulting disorder. Utopians had an obsession with clarity. Everyone's place was demarcated. Some novelists prescribed uniforms (for men and women) as an effective means for social recognition.[51] Occasionally, in ominous prophecy, numbers were tattooed on the arm; elsewhere ceremonial parades demonstrated the coherence of the social order.[52]

But all these inventions, the novelists recognized, were doomed unless people adapted to crowd life by developing new, more regular habits. If social compression demanded mechanical resolution, it also required inner discipline and self-control. This was the purpose of education, explained one of Henry Olerich's Martians. We attach "a great deal of importance to order, promptness and regular habits," declared Mr. Midith. "We teach them to our children by practicing them ourselves. We are regular with our set meals, our work, our leisure, our exercises, our studies, our bathing, our dressing, our games, our rising, and our retiring. . . . We, no doubt, would be called cowards by you for not daring to infringe on our health by a night's carousal, the same as you would be called cowards by your savages for not daring to do what a cannibal delights in doing."[53] In Chauncey Thomas's city of Tone, citizens lived in giant apartment houses, resembling pyramids. While the earthly visitor is impressed by their cleanliness, he adds that if tenement dwellers at home were given such great buildings "they would soon reduce [them] to their own level of disorder, filth, and degradation. Of what account would be tiled floors, and porcelain walls . . . running water, ventilators, hot-air currents, and electric lights" to people who would not maintain them?[54] His utopian host, however, argued that the preliminaries of educating the workers in homemaking had been going on in Tone for centuries. Public instruction enabled workers' families to keep up their apartments.

The great state education systems promoted the transmission of these values, and public behavior, invariably restrained and peaceful, reflected their success. In Frank Rosewater's city of Red Cross, the earthly visitor winced a bit at the extremity of order. Underground subways led to electric-car stations; no one ever faced bad weather; parkways were lined with temples for social relaxation. "This parked environment seems too dainty for an out-world barbarian," joked the earthling. "It reminds me of the restraint I felt as a boy, every time I had to don my Sunday clothes." "I suppose you'd rather wade in mud and filth, with the dust flying into your face and soot and cinders falling all over you," his hostess remonstrated.[55] The exchange illuminates the psychological restraints produced by sanitary compulsions. It seemed like a flight backward to childhood, stern parents warning their children against dirty faces and torn clothing. But according to the novelists, it worked; the "feverish haste and flurry" of American crowds was gone; drunkenness and rowdyness had disappeared, at least in public.[56]

With their physical innovations and new social values, the utopians had apparently conquered all the anxieties which tortured civilized society. There was one area, however, which gave even the utopians difficulty, and it was connected with the third great consciousness revolution which took place in the late nineteenth century: acceptance of the germ theory of disease. Like electricity, here was another set of discoveries which promised security but also intensified older anxieties. From the 1870s onward popular understanding of the work of Pasteur, Lister, and Koch broadened in America. New conceptions of the etiology of disease gained influence. Interestingly (and sadly) enough, newspapers and popular science journals picked up the new theories faster than did physicians and medical schools.[57] But within a generation ancient traditions of miasmatic sources and spontaneous generation were discarded in favor of the dangerous microbes — insidious, omnipotent, invisible enemies of humanity, able to attack anyone and anywhere. Older contagion theory had posited a variety of atmospheric hypotheses; with a few exceptions scientists did not hold organic entities or animate contagion responsible for the spread of disease. But by the 1880s science had located and identified these tiny animal beings; nature herself, rather than poisonous gases or waste, produced pain and illness. Old fears now gained precision and legitimacy.

Along with the expectations of progress grew new torments. "We are surrounded by invisible legions of enemies," complained the *Arena,* enemies which inspire "a certain uncanny terror unknown by war."[58] Postage stamps, doorknobs, theater audiences, even money became suspect as spreaders of saliva, dust, and morbid germs.[59] The *New York Times* charged that in founding public libraries Andrew Carnegie was "establishing breeding grounds for every kind and degree of microbe known to science," and warned that those coming to libraries to "quench their thirst for knowledge" would incur "the same risk as those who should drink of polluted waters." Books in public use fairly "swarm with spores, germs, cells, and ferments," and among the colonies they foster "may be found the representatives of every variety of evil thing in which reside the power and potency of death." Could it be, asked the *Times* disingenuously, that the lengthening of human life achieved in the recent past was largely the result of increased use of newspapers — less apt to be breeding grounds for microbes — and decreasing use of books?[60] Sharing the general hysteria, the Missouri Valley Homeopathic Association adopted a resolution declaring kissing to be unsanitary.[61] The health commissioner of New York proposed that every piece of money in circulation be disinfected; English medical authorities warned against the use of doorknobs, and advised designing foot levers to prevent "fouling of the hand."[62] And *Harper's Weekly* declared it "the age of the microbe." "He disports himself with equal satisfaction in the air, the earth, and the waters. He invades our beverages and our foods. He finds our mouths desirable lurking places, our hair and fingernails habitual outposts; on occasion he swims in our blood. Everywhere he is seeking his own selfish ends. He is the agent of decay and the messenger of disease. . . . The whole world, though it long denied him recognition, now bows to him as the mightiest of conquerors."[63]

It was natural, then, that the novelists, with their already developed concerns about pressure, danger, and bodily integrity, should display the cruelest anxieties about germs. "Little is known of the micro-organic world," Jack London wrote in an essay, "The Human Drift," "but that little is appalling; and no census of it will ever be taken, for there is the true, literal, 'abysmal fecundity.' Multitudinous as man is, all his totality of individuals is as nothing in comparison with the inconceivable vastness of numbers of the micro-organisms. In your body, or in mine, right now, are swarming more individual entities than there are human beings in the world to-day."[64] To London these facts had extraordinary meaning. They seemed nature's reassertion of Malthusian laws. When man increased too rapidly and invaded the sources of his food and space, nature would reply with a wave of "death-dealing microbes" to decimate his ranks and so restore the balance. *The Scarlet Plague,* which Jack London published in 1912, described a world population of several hundred, the few survivors of seven billion after a mysterious plague had struck.[65] The electrical age was succeeded by cavemen.

Many utopians shared London's phobia, but devised plans to overcome it. Communities could organize to fight the menace of the microbe; public-health regulations and selective breeding would increase longevity and personal vigor. In Chauncey Thomas's Tone, citizens dealt "with disease as a deadly enemy that deserves no quarter." Marriage rules were strict. Invalids were treated within a domed hothouse, the Palace of the Sun, while monitoring stations searched for the presence of dangerous gases. The earthling applauded such innovations. "We used to be surrounded by invisible enemies that meant illness, if not death," he told his hosts, "and they found access not only to our factories and places of amusement, but also to our homes. Yet we had at our command no monitor to warn us of their presence. . . . The meters we most needed to cry 'Beware!' when the seeds of death hovered about us and our loved ones — those we lacked."[66] For the physician Cosimo Noto, disease was an obsession, justifying the most drastic methods of combat. Citizens of New Orleans, living under socialism and sanitation fifty years in the future, could not understand how nineteenth-century Americans could bear even to eat; there was "such a great number of microbes" in ordinary food that "everyone must have been constantly ill."[67] Science ran the spotless kitchens of utopian New Orleans. Dishes were sterilized after use, in specially designed machinery; the body was treated like "an electric battery," and rigorous legislation ensured that the air, water, and streets were spotless.

So strongly were utopians identified with sanitary regimentation that when a satire appeared, like W. N. Harben's *Land of the Changing Sun* (an attack upon socialism), it exaggerated for effect this worship of the body. Harben's dystopia exterminated all those found physically wanting. "Every heart-beat is heard by our medical men," reported the king, "and every vein is transparent."[68] Only the healthy lived in Alpha, under an electric sun, spied on continually by government agents.

Actually, Harben didn't have to travel far to exaggerate. In John Jacob Astor's *Journey in Other Worlds,* a utopian exploration which vaguely resembled *Etidorhpa,* earth people visited Saturn and Jupiter, and observe with the eyes of a spirit what life really was like on earth. One visitor, demonstrating Astor's own anxieties, "saw not only the air as it entered and left his friends' lungs, but also the substance of their brains, and the seeds of disease and death whose presence they themselves did not even suspect. . . . In some he saw the germs of consumption; in others, affections of the heart. In all he saw the incessant struggle between the healthy blood-cells and the malignant, omnipresent bacilli that the cells were trying to overcome."[69]

Of all these consciousness revolutions, microbe theory permitted the gravest of anxieties to surface, and this was the anxiety about death. In these worlds so controlled, so well planned, so secure, the ghostly stranger continued to appear. Death seemed anomalous to progressive thinkers in the late nineteenth century; it did not belong in a world so triumphantly organized. As Donald Meyer pointed out some years ago, for people "no longer disciplined to life and death by orthodox stoicism, no longer hedged narrowly by close economic and social circumstances," life was meant to join wish and reality. But no matter what marvels of machinery were achieved, or what ingenious institutions were developed, "the body remained vulnerable. Death could strike. . . . Disease, sickness, death, bearing no relation to right moral order, manifesting alien, material, outside forces, defeated wishes unfairly."[70]

As the ultimate source of disorder and confrontation, the reality of death, its customs and ceremonies, formed an obvious subject for the utopian novelists.[71] The generation reading their books was fascinated with grief and mourning. In both Britain and America spiritualist societies enjoyed a resurgence. Hundreds of mediums held séances to stimulate direct communication with spirits. They published books dictated by the distinguished dead, offering advice on everything from politics to religion. Novelists of the period — Howells, James, Harold Frederic, Richard Harding Davis — treated the phenomenon as a major social issue.[72] University commissions held hearings to determine fraudulence; distinguished scholars like William James in America and Henry Sidgwick in England, celebrities like Houdini and Sir Arthur Conan Doyle, paid their respects to this quest for certainty. The growth of mind-cure religions, like Christian Science and New Thought, reflected this desire for victory over the bonds of mortality. The same energies which had wrought revolutions in science and technology, which had tamed nature and identified man's microbe enemies, could now be turned to the conquest of the nonmaterial world.

Along with others of their day, then, the utopian novelists took on this last anxiety which the race could be spared: death, preceded by debilitating old age. Selective breeding and elaborate public-health programs, staples of the utopian genre, were tied to the prevention of physical decay. They studied "how best to nurture and care for those bodies," explained one of James Cowan's Martians, "and when that lesson was thoroughly learned, we found that sickness and pain were gone, and with them, also, all fear of death. For now we die when our days are fully ended. The span of our life has been doubled since we began to know and care for ourselves, and, at the close, death is anticipated and recognized as a friend."[73] Gustavus Pope's Martians were "free from those dreadful constitutional taints and inherited diseases, which have for ages past, and still afflict so many millions of our Terrestrial races. . . . Martians thoroughly understood the avoidable causes of disease and acted accordingly," their physicians exploring "the secret recesses of the human frame . . . with a skill unknown in our medical world," discovering and destroying the germs of disease.[74]

And when death eventually came, in utopia, it arrived gently, for mortals died in the full knowledge of their own immortality.

They would simply move on to inhabit a heaven as advanced as their model societies, destined either for peace everlasting or passage to a new life. For Louis P. Gratacap heaven could be found on Mars; for Dr. Mortimore it was inside the sun; for Arthur Willink it lay in the fourth dimension. But that heaven existed, and could be described, was devoutly believed by most of the utopian novelists.[75]

Thus the religiosity, the antimaterialism, and the technological absorption of Lloyd, Fiske, and Cole, the strange combinations of interests which mark utopian literature, seem more understandable. Machines and mysticism had a common objective: the allaying of human anxieties, and most of all, anxieties about aggression, accident, old age, and death. These were ancient fears, as old as the race. They were not eclipsed by the more immediate confrontations of labor and capital, or the specter of class warfare. Instead they were revitalized by a series of modern discoveries which, tantalizingly, promised greater security even while they threatened imminent destruction. And running alongside the physical dangers was the spiritual catastrophe: that no future life awaited the soul to compensate for the pain of the earthly life. Scientific progress had not only abetted physical danger; by stimulating (and supporting) secularized ideals, it was annihilating the last, best promise of religion: future life.

There were, in the 1890s, masterly, vigorous spirits in America who, like Theodore Roosevelt, opted for the Strenuous Life; who preached football and risk taking, and the expansion of experience as their response to an urbanizing world. The utopians, however, sought reconciliation and not challenge, and preferred comfort to confrontation. Despite its technology, advanced economics, and often rather aggressive secularism, this utopian vision was essentially religious, and aligned with a specifically American heritage. Like religious reformers of some three centuries earlier, faced with disorder the utopians sought to structure and even confine life, rather than expand it. The revolutions we have marked, until recently, as milestones of scientific progress, sobered them. Their optimism about the future rested on the achievement of an environmental stasis. Unlimited growth seemed as dangerous as decay.

That is why we can speak, with some justice, of the birth of the modernized sensibility in the utopian novel; for with all their strange trappings, their bizarre inventions, their scholasticism and occasional smugness, these utopians were awakening to the logic of the modern world. And many of them were afraid.

Notes

1. Information about Lloyd can be found in Allan Johnson and Dumas Malone, eds., *Dictionary of American Biography* (New York, 1928–), supplement II, pp. 389–390. Hereafter cited as *DAB*.
2. *Etidorhpa; or, The End of Earth, the Strange History of a Mysterious Being and the Account of a Remarkable Journey*, 6th ed. (Cincinnati, 1896), pp. 383–386. *Etidorhpa* is *Aphrodite* spelled backwards, but this fact does not help much in explicating the book's details.
3. Lloyd, *Etidorhpa*, p. 97. See also pp. 80–81.
4. Amos K. Fiske, *Beyond the Bourn: Reports of a Traveller Returned from "The Undiscovered Country"* (New York, 1891). A brief account of Fiske can be found in *DAB*, VI, 416–417.
5. Fiske, *Beyond the Bourn*, p. 169.
6. Cyrus Cole, *The Auroraphone: A Romance* (Boston, 1890).
7. *Ibid.*, p. 133.
8. Claude R. Flory, *Economic Criticism in American Fiction, 1792–1900* (Philadelphia: University of Pennsylvania, 1936), pp. 242–243.
9. One such exception is Kenneth M. Roemer, *The Obsolete Necessity: America in Utopian Writings, 1888–1900* (Kent, Ohio: Kent State University Press, 1976). Roemer's book is the most comprehensive published survey of American utopian fiction, and treats a broad range of social, intellectual, and economic issues. Unfortunately, it reached me just as I was finishing the final draft of this paper. It contains extensive bibliographies and plot summaries of the utopian novels. I was gratified to note Roemer's emphasis on the anxieties of the utopian novelists, and his attempt to qualify older, optimistic summaries of the novels.

    Among the earlier studies that I read are Alleyn B. Forbes, "The Literary Quest for Utopia, 1880–1900," *Social Forces*, VI (Dec. 1927), 179–189; Walter F. Taylor, *The Economic Novel in America* (Chapel Hill: University of North Carolina Press, 1942); and Vernon Louis Parrington, Jr., *American Dreams: A Study of American Utopias* (Providence: Brown University Press, 1947). A number of unpublished dissertations have aided my work immeasurably. They include Robert L. Shorter, "The Utopian Novel in America, 1865–1900" (Ph.D. dissertation, Western Reserve University, 1936); Margaret Wilson Thal-Larsen, "Political and Economic Ideas in American Utopian Fiction, 1868–1914" (Ph.D. dissertation, University of California at Berkeley, 1941); Ellene Ransom, "Utopus Discovers America, or Critical Realism in American Utopian Fiction, 1798–1900" (Ph.D. dissertation, Vanderbilt University, 1946); Charles J. Rooney, Jr., "Utopian Literature As a Reflection of Social Forces in America, 1865–1917" (Ph.D. dissertation, George Washington University, 1968); and Lisle A. Rose, "A Descriptive Catalogue of Economic and Politico-Economic Fiction in the United States, 1902–1909" (Ph.D. dissertation, University of Chicago, 1935).

    Two works that do indeed talk about various psychological aspects of American utopian fiction are Frederic Cople Jaher, *Doubters and Dissenters: Cataclysmic Thought in America, 1885–1918* (New York: Free Press, 1964), and the introduction in John L.

Thomas, ed., Edward Bellamy, *Looking Backward: 2000–1887* (Cambridge, Mass., Harvard University Press, 1967). See also the very interesting essay by Virgil L. Lokke, "The American Utopian Anti-Novel," in Ray B. Browne et al., eds., *Frontiers of American Culture* (Lafayette, Ind.: Purdue University Studies, 1968), pp. 123–153.

There is also, of course, a major literature of commentary and description on utopianism more generally, as well as studies of specific national utopian traditions. I have found particularly helpful W. H. G. Armytage, *Yesterday's Tomorrows: A Historical Survey of Future Societies* (Toronto: University of Toronto Press, 1968); J. O. B. Bailey, *Pilgrims Through Space and Time: Trends and Patterns in Scientific and Utopian Fiction* (New York: Argus, 1947); I. F. Clarke, *The Tale of the Future* (London: Library Association, 1961); Robert C. Elliott, *The Shape of Utopia: Studies in a Literary Genre* (Chicago: University of Chicago Press, 1970); many of the essays in Frank E. Manuel, ed., *Utopias and Utopian Thought* (Boston: Houghton Mifflin, 1965); and the extracts in Glenn Negley and J. Max Patrick, eds., *The Quest for Utopia: An Anthology of Imaginary Societies* (New York: Henry Schuman, 1952).

10. The single most valuable analysis of science fiction is Thomas Dean Clareson, "The Emergence of American Science Fiction: 1880–1915; A Study of the Impact of Science upon American Romanticism" (Ph.D. dissertation, University of Pennsylvania, 1956). Clareson has also worked with the journal *Extrapolations*, which has published in various issues checklists of American science fiction, and analyses of particular themes. A recent book, David Ketterer's *New Worlds for Old: The Apocalyptic Imagination, Science Fiction, and American Literature* (Garden City, N.Y.: Doubleday, 1974), offers a provocative definition of the genre. Other helpful books on science fiction include Kingsley Amis, *New Maps of Hell* (New York: Harcourt, Brace and World, 1960); Mark R. Hillegas, *The Future As Nightmare: H. G. Wells and the Anti-Utopians* (New York: Oxford University Press, 1967); Robert M. Philmus, *Into the Unknown: The Evolution of Science Fiction from Godwin to H. G. Wells* (Berkeley and Los Angeles: University of California Press, 1970); and H. Bruce Franklin, *Future Perfect: American Science Fiction of the Nineteenth Century* (New York: Oxford University Press, 1966). Many of these critics spend a good deal of time distinguishing among science fiction, science fantasy, utopian fiction, and other related categories. Because my interest, in this essay, lies in charting a range of concerns which afflicted late nineteenth century Americans, I have not pursued the matter of definition. Indeed, I have deliberately included in the utopian category much of this larger body of fiction. Most American utopian fiction, however, did employ the device that Philmus presents as basic to science fantasy, that is, "the rhetorical strategy of employing a more or less scientific rationale to get the reader to suspend disbelief in a fantastic state of affairs." Philmus, *Into the Unknown*, p. vii.

11. The Bestor comment I refer to was expressed most succinctly in Arthur E. Bestor, Jr., "Patent-Office Models of the Good Society: Some Relationships between Social Reform and Westward Expansion," *American Historical Review*, LVIII (Apr. 1953), 505–526. For some interesting comments on the relationship between the utopian novel and American technology, see John F. Kasson, *Civilizing the Machine: Technology and Republican Values in America, 1776–1900* (New York: Grossman, 1976), ch. 5.

12. Henry Olerich, *A Cityless and Countryless World: An Outline of Practical Cooperative Individualism* (Holstein, Iowa, 1893), pp. 8–9. See also Albert Merrill, *The Great Awakening: The Story of the Twenty-Second Century* (Boston, 1899), p. 168.

13. Charles J. Rooney, Jr., in "Utopian Literature As a Reflection of Social Forces in America," has presented the most careful statistical analysis of the utopian authors. Of the forty-one writers for whom Rooney could find biographical information, all were engaged in professional, business, or public careers; more than ten were in journalism, with the others in teaching, politics, business, medicine, and engineering. Most utopian novelists were middle class. See Rooney, "Utopian Literature," pp. 13–15.

14. Olerich, *Cityless and Countryless World*, pp. 20–21.

15. H. E. Swan, *It Might Be: A Story of the Future Progress of the Sciences, the Wonderful Advancement in the Methods of Government and the Happy State of the People* (Stafford, Kansas, 1896), p. 142. See also [M. Louise Moore], *Al-Modad, or Life Scenes beyond the*

Polar Circumflex: A Religio-Scientific Solution of the Problems of Present and Future Life, By an Untrammeled Free-Thinker (Cameron Parish, Louisiana, 1892), p. 79.

16. Olerich, *Cityless and Countryless World*, p. 3.

17. There is little that is very helpful on the social and intellectual effects of the spread of electrical usage, but among the informative books are Harold C. Passer, *The Electrical Manufacturers, 1875–1900* (Cambridge, Mass.: Harvard University Press, 1953); William T. O'Dea, *A Social History of Lighting* (London: Routledge & Kegan Paul, 1958); Harold I. Sharlin, *Making of the Electrical Age: From the Telegraph to Automation* (New York: Abelard-Schuman, 1963); and three essays, Bern Dibner's "The Beginning of Electricity," and Harold I. Sharlin's "Applications of Electricity" and "Electrical Generation and Transmission," all in Melvin Kranzberg and Carroll W. Pursell, Jr., eds., *Technology in Western Civilization*, 2 vols. (New York: Oxford University Press, 1967), vol. I.

18. For more details on the development of Niagara see Edward Dean Adams, *Niagara Power: History of the Niagara Falls Power Company, 1886–1918* (Niagara Falls, 1927), *passim.*

19. Joseph Kirkland and Caroline Kirkland, *The Story of Chicago* (Chicago, 1894), II, 115–116.

20. Josiah Allen's Wife [Marietta Holley], *Samantha at the World's Fair* (New York, London, Toronto, 1893), p. 558. The prophetic tone that electricity induced is revealed in other Holley comments made in the Electricity Building: "But who — who shall map out this vast realm that Benjamin F. Discovered? We stand jest by the sea-shore. We have jest landed from our boats. The onbroken forest lays before us. . . . A few trees have been felled by Morse, Edison, Field and others, so that we can git glimpses into the forest depths, but not enough to give us a glimpse of the mountains or the seas. The realm as a whole is onexplored; nobody knows or can dream of the grandeur and glory that awaits the advance guard. . . ." See also *ibid.,* pp. 545–565, 569; and Josiah Allen's Wife [Marietta Holley], *Samantha at the St. Louis Exposition* (New York, 1904), pp. 125–127. In St. Louis Samantha connected electricity with the coming of divine visitors, which someday men might be able to see and understand. See Lafcadio Hearn, "The Government Exhibit at New Orleans," *Harper's Weekly*, XXIX (Apr. 11, 1885), 240.

21. *Philadelphia Inquirer*, Jan. 4, 1890, p. 4. The article was a comment on the burning of an Edison building in New York City.

22. *Boston Evening Transcript*, Jan. 4, 1888, p. 4.

23. *New York Tribune*, Jan. 8, 1882, p. 6: "As the uses of electricity multiply, it is only fair that the belief in its dangers should multiply also; but, unlike most popular beliefs, modern experience has brought us practical verification of electrical perils."

24. Dexter W. Fellows and Andrew A. Freeman, *This Way to the Big Show: The Life of Dexter Fellows* (New York: Viking Press, 1936), pp. 172–173.

25. For a sample of Edison's rhetoric see Thomas A. Edison, "The Dangers of Electric Lighting," *North American Review*, CXLIX (Nov. 1889), 625–634. New York newspapers were filled with the controversy over the use of the first electric chair, and the limitations to be placed upon press attendance at the execution. For sample editorials, see *New York Tribune*, Jan. 22, 1889, p. 4; Mar. 16, 1889, p. 6; and June 20, 1889, p. 6. A novel has been written about the first execution by electric chair, which took place in 1890, in Auburn Prison, New York. See Christopher Davis, *A Peep into the Twentieth Century* (New York: Harper and Row, 1971). The mode of execution was embroiled in a controversy between Edison and his followers, who favored continuous (direct) current, and representatives of the Westinghouse alternating current.

26. Park Benjamin, "The Infliction of the Death Penalty," *Forum*, III (July 1887), 512.

27. A Former Resident of "The Hub" [John Bachelder], *A.D. 2050: Electrical Development at Atlantis* (San Francisco, 1890), p. 24.

28. Jack London, "Goliah," *Revolution and other Essays* (New York, 1912), pp. 71–116.

29. William Alexander Taylor, *Intermere* (Columbus, Ohio, 1901), p. 138.

30. M. Auburré Hovorrè [Albert W. Howard], *The Milltillionaire; or, Age of Bardization* (Boston, 1895), p. 17. In James Cowan, *Daybreak: A Romance of an Old World* (New York, 1896), it rained only at night, to increase the pleasures of the day. Many utopias

provided air-cooled buildings, covered or underground passageways, and huge hotels, all giving needed protection from rain or heat, if they were not controlled.

31. [Bachelder], *A.D. 2050*, p. 56. Rev. W. S. Harris, *Life in a Thousand Worlds* (Cleona, Pennsylvania, 1905), p. 234, describes life on Ploid, a world of highest invention, which has a telephone employing photographic wires: "Persons can be in bed at night, if they imagine they hear a robber in any room they can first turn on the photograph current and then the light flash. In this way one can look, without leaving his bed, into each room of the house." See also Swan, *It Might Be*, p. 55; and Gustavus W. Pope, *Journey to Mars. The Wonderful World: Its Beauty and Splendor; Its Mighty Races and Kingdoms; Its Final Doom* (New York, 1894), pp. 66–67.

32. Cosimo Noto, M.D., *The Ideal City* (New York, 1903), p. 79.

33. Chauncey Thomas, *The Crystal Button; or, The Adventures of Paul Prognosis in the Forty-ninth Century* (Boston and New York, 1891), pp. 100–101. In Merrill, *The Great Awakening*, the horse is practically extinct and found only in zoos, and in Paul Devinne, *The Day of Prosperity: A Vision of the Century to Come* (New York, 1902), a utopian host explains that electricity has made the horse superfluous. Moreover, since "robbery and stealing have gone out of fashion, we do not require watchdogs, and to keep dogs as a pastime . . . we should consider absurd," pp. 76–77. In Pruning Knife [Henry Francis Allen], *A Strange Voyage: A Revision of the Key of Industrial Co-Operative Government; An Interesting and Instructive Description of Life on the Planet Venus* (St. Louis, 1891), animals are also barred, to permit clean, odorless cities, pp. 62, 153. [Moore]'s *Al-Modad* outlaws horses, cows, hogs, dogs, and cats. There were a few small wild animals "but no offensive pests. Not a gnat, fly, ant nor anything in the slightest degree obnoxious," p. 96.

34. There is little in print that is either comprehensive or scholarly on the history of American dietary reform. Some information can be found in Janet Barkas, *The Vegetable Passion* (New York: Scribner, 1975), E. Douglas Branch, *The Sentimental Years, 1836–1860* (New York: Appleton-Century, 1934), ch. IX; and Gerald M. Carson, *Cornflake Crusade* (New York: Rinehart, 1957). Related material is well covered in James Harvey Young, *Toadstool Millionaires: Patent Medicines before Federal Regulation* (Princeton: Princeton University Press, 1961). But the best source on diet and social control is unpublished — Stephen W. Nissenbaum, "Careful Love: Sylvester Graham and the Emergence of Victorian Sexual Theory in America, 1830–1940" (Ph.D. dissertation, University of Wisconsin, 1969). William J. McGrath, *Dionysian Art and Populist Politics in Austria* (New Haven: Yale University Press, 1974), pp. 92–97, contains some interesting material on European vegetarianism.

35. Edward Bellamy, *Equality* (New York, 1897; reprinted, Upper Saddle River, New Jersey: Gregg Press, 1968), p. 286.

36. James Cowan, *Daybreak: A Romance of an Old World* (New York, 1896), p. 320.

37. Pope, *Journey to Mars*, pp. 234–235; Herman Hine Brinsmade, *Utopia Achieved: A Novel of the Future* (New York, 1912), p. 59. See also [Howard], *The Milltillionaire*; [Mary E. Bradley Lane], *Mizora: A Prophecy. A Mss. Found among the Private Papers of the Princess Vera Zarovitch, Written by Herself* (New York, 1889); The Lord Commissioner [John McCoy], *A Prophetic Romance, Mars to Earth* (Boston, 1896); Prof. W[illis] Mitchell, *The Inhabitants of Mars: Their Manners and Advancement in Civilization and Their Opinion of Us* (Malden, Mass., 1895); [Moore], *Al-Modad*; and Noto, *Ideal City*, are also among the novels in which a vegetable diet assumes great importance. Many of the other utopian novels mention, simply as a matter of course, the vegetarian diets of their residents. So common a convention did dietary fads become among utopians that in his antisocial, dystopian novel *The Scarlet Empire* (New York, [1906]) David M. Parry played with various reforms, including laws compelling equal use of the muscles on both sides of the mouth for chewing — a reflection of Fletcherism — as well as laws controlling the trimming of fingernails and regulating the length of a step.

38. For explorations of this theme, with differing emphases, see John Higham, "The Reorientation of American Culture in the 1890s," in John Weiss, ed., *The Origins of Modern Consciousness* (Detroit: Wayne State University Press, 1965), pp. 25–48; Roderick Nash, *Wilderness and the American Mind* (New Haven: Yale University Press,

1967); and Peter Schmitt, *Back to Nature: The Arcadian Myth in Urban America* (New York: Oxford University Press, 1969).

39. Capt. Nathan Davis, *Beulah; or, A Parable of Social Regeneration* (Kansas City, Missouri, 1904), p. 209.

40. W. D. Howells, *Letters of an Altrurian Traveller,* in Clara and Rudolph Kirk, eds., *The Altrurian Romances* (Bloomington, Ind.: Indiana University Press, 1968), p. 253.

41. W. D. Howells, *Through the Eye of the Needle,* in *ibid.,* p. 281.

42. *Ibid.,* p. 372.

43. Noto, *Ideal City,* p. 180.

44. Olerich, *Cityless and Countryless World,* p. 65.

45. Bradford Peck, *The World a Department Store: A Story of Life under a Cooperative System* (Lewiston, Maine, 1900), p. 78.

46. Stewart Edward White, *The Sign at Six* (Indianapolis, 1912), p. 27.

47. L. P. Gratacap, *The Certainty of a Future Life in Mars, Being the Posthumous Papers of Bradford Torrey Dodd* (New York, Paris, Chicago, Washington, 1903), pp. 203–204.

48. Albert Chavannes, *In Brighter Climes; or, Life in Socioland: A Realistic Novel* (Knoxville, Tennessee, 1895), p. 44.

49. Bellamy, *Equality,* p. 255. "It is a curious paradox," stated Mr. Barton, a spokesman for Bellamy's utopia, "that while the telephone and electroscope, by abolishing distance as a hindrance to sight and hearing, have brought mankind into a closeness of sympathetic and intellectual rapport never before imagined, they have at the same time enabled individuals, although keeping in closest touch with everything going on in the world, to enjoy, if they choose, a physical privacy, such as one had to be a hermit to command in your day."

50. Pope, *Journey to Mars,* p. 193 and *passim.* Another ribbon scheme was provided by Edgar Chambless in *Roadtown* (New York, 1910), a plan "to lay the modern skyscraper on its side and run the elevators and the pipes and the wires horizontally instead of vertically," p. 19. Continuous lines of houses, containing transportation systems as well as utilities, would stretch through the countryside, with farms on either side. In describing his future cities, Chambless intoned a catalogue of the evils distressing utopian novelists. There will be, he promised, "no streets, no street cars and no 'subway air'; no kitchens, no coal bins, no back yards or back alleys full of crime and tin cans; no brooms, no feather dusters, no wash day; no clothes line, no beating the carpet or shaking the rug out the window . . . no dish washing, no cooks, no maids, no janitors . . . no dust, no noise . . . no moving vans, no coal wagons, no garbage carts . . . no horses except for pleasure drives . . . no fire engines, no cabs nor taxicabs, no mixing of pedestrians and vehicles . . . no grade crossings and no 'death avenue'; there will be no bargain rushes, no small shops, no middleman's profits, no bill boards . . . no waste of money for little bottles and cans and bags, no adulterated food . . . no snow to shovel . . . no street cleaners, no water wagons, no swill-tubs, no rain barrels, no manure carts . . . no beds to make . . . no fire escapes, no waiting in rain or snow to catch a car . . . no news boys, no messenger boys, no mail carriers, no traffic policemen, no teamsters . . . no street car conductors, no expressmen, no delivery boys, no peddlers, no pushcart men, no waiters to tip, no insurance agents . . . ," pp. 165–168. The emphasis throughout was on tidiness, economy of motion, lack of irritation, convenience, safety, and an end to the many varieties of brokers and middlemen that had come between the consumer and the products he used.

51. Uniforms can be found in, among other novels, Richard Hatfield's *Geyserland: 9262 B.C.: Empiricism in Social Reform, Being Data and Observations Recorded by the Late Mark Stubble, M.D., Ph.D.* (Washington, 1908); [Howard], *The Milltillionaire;* Peck, *The World a Department Store;* and Bellamy, *Looking Backward.*

52. Numbered tatoos were employed in William Wonder [Thomas Kirwan], *Reciprocity (Social and Economic) in the Thirtieth Century: The Coming Co-Operative Age* (New York, 1909), pp. 145–146. In Devinne, *Day of Prosperity,* everyone carries a permanent passport, which records his travels, birthplace, parents' background, schooling, marriages, etc., accompanying "its possessor from the cradle to the grave," p. 138. For an excellent description of a utopian parade, see John Ira Brant, *The New Regime, A.D. 2202* (New York, London, 1909), p. 22.

53. Olerich, *Cityless and Countryless World,* pp. 351–352.

54. Thomas, *Crystal Button,* p. 85.

55. Frank Rosewater, *The Making of a Millennium: The Story of a Millennial Realm, and Its Law* (Chicago, 1908), p. 50.

56. See, for example, Peck, *The World a Department Store,* p. 61; Rosewater, *Making of a Millennium,* pp. 78–79; and Henry Wallace Dowding, *The Man from Mars; or, Service for Service's Sake* (New York, 1910), p. 173.

57. For background on American reception of germ theory see Phyllis Allen Richmond, "American Attitudes toward the Germ Theory of Disease (1860–1880)," *Journal of the History of Medicine and Allied Sciences,* IX (Oct. 1954), 428–454.

58. Frank B. Vrooman, "Public Health and National Defence," *Arena,* XIII (Aug. 1895), 425.

59. Among other examples, the *Literary Digest,* XI (June 29, 1895), 258; *Literary Digest,* XI (Oct. 5, 1895), 674; *New York Times,* Feb. 4, 1904, p. 8; *Boston Evening Transcript,* Jan. 4, 1888, p. 6; *New York Tribune,* Dec. 11, 1881, p. 6; *Independent,* LIX (Dec. 1, 1905), 1492; *New York Times,* Aug. 5, 1900, p. 6; *Chicago Record-Herald,* Feb. 22, 1904, p. 6; and *Chicago Record-Herald,* Apr. 11, 1904, p. 6.

60. "Microbes in Books," *New York Times,* Feb. 8, 1904, p. 8.

61. "On Kissing," *New York Times,* Nov. 9, 1902, p. 6.

62. See the various extracts and the introduction to section 11 in Ray Brosseau and Ralph K. Andrist, *Looking Forward: Life in the Twentieth Century as Predicted in the Pages of American Magazines from 1895 to 1905* (New York: American Heritage Press, 1970), particularly "The Danger of Door-knobs," and "The Home of the Microbes," both on p. 282.

63. "The Mercenary Microbe," *Harper's Weekly,* XXXVIII (Dec. 30, 1893), 1243.

64. Jack London, "The Human Drift," in *The Human Drift* (New York, 1917), p. 21. "The Human Drift" was originally published in 1911.

65. Jack London, *The Scarlet Plague* (New York, 1912). See also Jack London, *Short Stories* (1914; reprinted, New York: Hill and Wang, 1960).

66. Thomas, *Crystal Button,* pp. 229–230.

67. Noto, *Ideal City,* p. 196.

68. W. N. Harben, *The Land of the Changing Sun* (New York, 1894), p. 66. For more on eugenic reforms see Fayette Stratton Giles, *Shadows Before; or, A Century Onward* (New York, 1894), p. 206; H. George Schuette, *Athonia; or, The Original Four Hundred* (Manitowoc, Wisconsin, 1910), pp. 184–185; and Dr. W. O. Henry, *Equitania; or, The Land of Equity* (Omaha, n.d.), *passim.*

69. John Jacob Astor, *A Journey in Other Worlds: A Romance of the Future* (New York, 1894), p. 438.

70. Donald Meyer, *The Positive Thinkers: A Study of the American Quest for Health, Wealth and Personal Power from Mary Baker Eddy to Norman Vincent Peale* (Garden City, N.Y.: Doubleday, 1965), p. 48.

71. Many of the utopian novels incorporated rules concerning cremation as a healthier way of disposing of the dead than traditional burial methods. See, for example, Olerich, *Cityless and Countryless World;* and [Bachelder], *A.D. 2050,* p. 30.

72. For literary involvement with spiritualism see Howard H. Kerr, *Mediums and Spirit-Rappers, and Roaring Radicals: Spiritualism in American Literature, 1850–1900* (Urbana: University of Illinois Press, 1972). For American spiritualism, and up-to-date bibliographic references, see R. Laurence Moore, "The Spiritualist Medium: A Study of Female Professionalism in Victorian America," *American Quarterly,* XXVII (May 1975), 220–221.

73. Cowan, *Daybreak,* p. 65.

74. Pope, *Journey to Mars,* pp. 312, 314. See also Taylor, *Intermere,* pp. 116–118; Cole, *The Auroraphone, passim;* Alfred Denton Cridge, *Utopia; or, The History of an Extinct Planet* (Oakland, California, 1884), *passim;* Francis Worcester Doughty, *Mirrikh; or, A Woman from Mars: A Tale of Occult Adventure* (New York, 1892), *passim;* and Fiske, *Beyond the Bourn, passim.*

75. Gratacap, *Certainty of a Future Life in Mars;* D. Mortimore, M.D., *The Spirit of God as Fire; The Globe within the Sun Our Heaven* (New York, 1870); Arthur Willink, *The World of the*

Unseen: An Essay on the Relation of Higher Space to Things Eternal (New York, London, 1893). There existed, in the late nineteenth century, a literature of heavenly description, both inside the utopian genre and outside it. It could be argued, of course, that detailed heavenly description forms a utopian literature by itself. One such work is Edward Stanton, *Dreams of the Dead* (Boston, 1892). For more on heavenly description see Elmer F. Suderman, "Elizabeth Stuart Phelps and the Gates Ajar Novels," *Journal of Popular Culture,* III (Summer 1969), 91–100; and Ann Douglas, "Heaven Our Home: Consolation Literature in the Northern United States, 1830–1880," *American Quarterly,* XXVI (Dec. 1974), 496–515.

Psyching Out the City

William R. Taylor

"All is changed, changed utterly,
A terrible beauty is born."
— W. B. Yeats, "Easter 1916"

William R. Taylor, author of *Cavalier and Yankee: The Old South and American National Character* (1961) and professor of history at the State University of New York, Stony Brook, is currently at work on *The Rise and Fall of Modern Times: New York and the Urbanization of Aesthetic Perception, 1890–1932.*

THE MODERN SKYSCRAPER city ringed by successive industrial and residential districts appeared with startling suddenness at the end of the nineteenth century. Before that time cities had expanded without assuming any particular or characteristic shape. The process through which these sprawling, low-rise cities of the nineteenth century gave way to modern cities consumed the first three decades of the new century. It was a process, moreover, fully as disruptive in its consequences as the more frequently discussed transition from country to city that was taking place at much the same time. The disruption was of every kind: economic, social, and aesthetic. The very conception of the city was radically transformed as a wide range of new activities and values accrued in popular thinking to the idea of city life. The economic and social costs of such a process have been extensively discussed by historians and others. Less attention, indeed very little at all, has been given to examining how such a radical process of change was perceived by those who experienced it, or how they learned to live with it and to enhance its disruptive character with a new aesthetic that found positive qualities in its forms and modalities.

Chicago was the first American city to develop a typical "downtown" of tall buildings clustered about activities that ranged from commercial to service: office buildings, banks, wholesale and retail stores, hotels, theaters, and restaurants, all fed by railroads and other arteries of public transportation.[1] For a long time it was the most modern of such cities, widely acclaimed as the home of the skyscraper. But the same developments that created Chicago soon transformed other American cities. New York, in particular, early became known for its modernity, and it soon surpassed Chicago as the embodiment of a new style of urban life. Its importance as a port of entry, its constricted location that made at once for high population density and vertical construction, and its vigorous ethnic, theatrical, and literary life helped it establish a reputation for modern urbanity.

The stamp of modernity was early placed upon New York, in part by a succession of photographers and other graphic artists who were sensitized to the visual character that the city was assuming and who saw in these new shapes and forms a vision of the future. For the French avant-garde painter Picabia, for example, New York had become by 1914 "the Cubist City."[2] For a whole generation of photographers, its buildings, its streets, and its people became close to an obsession. New York was as important to photography, moreover, as photography was to New York. The creative potential of photography, an art already half a century old by the turn of the century, was strikingly unfolded in the work of those who first tried to grasp the meaning of these changes.

One common problem faced by all significant urban photographers in this period was that of how to visually relate the people of the city to their surroundings. There was, first of all, an aesthetic problem to be confronted. The modern city violated virtually every artistic convention developed over the centuries for linking man to his environment, even those that were suited to the visual character of older European cities such as Venice, Paris, and London. During the nineteenth century landscape painting, at the hands of Constable, Turner, Millet, and the Impressionists, developed into a major artistic genre, and photographers were quick to adapt many of its conventions. Photographs of people in a setting of fields, hills, woods, rivers, lakes, or shore were commonplace by the end of the century. In particular, photographers, like painters, were excited by the magic of light reflected from water. In the face of such conventions the visual properties of modern cities like New York must have seemed a kind of anti-pastoral obverse of the beautiful. It was one thing to portray people scattered across fields, at work and at play; it was quite another to depict them against a background of concrete, glass, and asphalt. There was something, too, about man in relation to machine that seemed initially incongruous, even grotesque. Tall buildings, furthermore, blocked the horizon, created dark sunless canyons, overshadowed waterways, and dwarfed those bits of vegetation their construction had not eradicated. Clouds of smoke replaced trees against the sky, a network of rails, the familiar stream or waterway. It proved difficult to portray people in such settings without dwarfing or dehumanizing them.

In view of such problems, it is scarcely surprising that few photographers before 1915 sought to capture broad panoramic sweeps of the modern city. Those perspectives on the city that have become the familiar conventions of today's photography and cinema, the skyline view and the bird's-eye view, had to await a more minute exploration of the city's new visual character and represent a later visual accommodation to it. Indeed, it is very likely that during these transitional years before the modern city became a recognized visual entity it was difficult for anyone, photographer or not, to conceive of these sprawling, amorphous communities as a whole. Such an impossibility, moreover, places the present discussion in a context of the history of perception and helps give it a significance beyond the history of art and architecture.

If the photograph can be shown to record in some fashion how the modern city was perceived and how such perceptions changed over time, then historians have at their disposal a valuable and largely unexploited source. There are two aspects of photography that tend to support such a claim. First, the photographer is both a man of his time, sharing its interests and anxieties, and, at the same time, a kind of antenna for the public, probing, clarifying, and channeling the visual signals of a new environment. The photographer's relation to a public is a complicated one, like that of any graphic artist, since he must both anticipate public taste and, if he is to be understood and appreciated, finally satisfy it. Any art form, to stay alive, must speak meaningfully to some public, however small. During the opening decades of the century, the public for photography enlarged immeasurably. Public interest and taste, moreover, dogged that of photographers. As with the Empire State Building, where the photographer Lewis Hine perched his camera one day, the public swarmed the next.

The second aspect of photography sets it apart from the other graphic arts. The photograph not only reflects the perceptions of the photographer, it often records and documents some of the perceptions of his subjects, when the subjects are people. Being photographed, in this period, was an event, something that happened to you and your surroundings, something novel and memorable. The photograph itself thus became a bit of "reality" snatched from a moment of someone's existence. Sometimes, for example, the very artlessness of the way people group themselves before the camera tells us something about how they conceive of themselves and how they wish to be seen. Indeed, as we look at these photographs today, part of their interest and humanity lies in the different meanings that were ascribed to the experience of having one's picture taken.

What began to appear in the nineties was, then, a new kind of urban photograph that, even in the beginning, was easily set off from most earlier photographic work about the city. Among the first such photographs were quite a number by Alfred Stieglitz that were taken in the years immediately after his return from Europe in 1890. These photographs speak directly to the time and place, to New York in transition to modern city. They provide evidence about the beginning phase of the process through which photographers were to size up modern urban life.

The occasion for Stieglitz's photographic scrutiny of the modern city is a little unclear. By 1890 he had completed some study in Germany, had exhibited photographs abroad and mastered existing photographic technology. He was soon to abandon any pretense of following a vocation other than photography. Bolstered by independent means, which freed him from some of the economic pressures that preoccupied other contemporary photographers, he launched himself into the New York photographic and artistic world in a series of bold and imaginative steps that led to the founding of his influential quarterly, *Camera Work*, in 1903, and to the opening a few years later of the Photo-Secession Gallery at 291 Fifth Avenue, the first in a succession of moves that kept him a focus of modernism in the arts for almost half a century.[3] Unlike Jacob Riis, he was not a reformer bent on changing men's minds. He did not, like Lewis Hine or Jacob Riis, take up the camera in the course of other work. Taking pictures, at least for a time, was his work.

In his approach to the city, he was neither carping nor idealizing. He struck, over all, some sort of balance between communicating a sense of loss and a sense of aesthetic excitement, except for the fact that he seemed possessed by the city to a singular degree — annoyed by it, antagonized, exhausted to the point where he had to get away, yet continually fascinated and drawn back, at least in these years, for still another look. Indeed, he himself traced the inauguration of his photographic career to an experience of the city that seems curiously like a religious conversion. When he returned to America in 1890 Stieglitz had found the city, by contrast with European cities, dirty, empty of excitement, and without culture or artistic interests of any traceable kind. For a time he went through a period of what sounds like deep depression, which included, for example, weeping at night. In reminiscing to his biographer he associated his early work and the end of his feelings of depression with a succession of aesthetic experiences in and of the city. One of these was his discovery of theater in the winter of 1893, when he almost accidentally witnessed the Italian actress Eleanora Duse in a notable production of *Camille* and, at about the same time, the comic team of Weber and Fields in a performance that came as almost a revelation to him. He closely associated these two experiences with his first photographs in his new probingly realistic manner. "This is the beginning of a new era," he later recalled exclaiming to a fellow photographer as he finished the first of these new prints. "Call it a new vision if you wish."[4]

The photograph that evoked these remarks was made during a Washington's Birthday blizzard in 1893 and is entitled "Winter, Fifth Avenue." The exposure was made as Stieglitz, equipped with a recently purchased hand camera, stood at the corner of Fifth Avenue and Thirty-fourth Street facing south (Plate 1). It portrayed coaches lumbering north along a deeply snow-rutted avenue against background and foreground of laterally driving snow. The buildings lining the street are reduced to shadowy abstractions and the human figures to tiny silhouettes. It was considered a work of great technical brilliance, one that pushed photographic technology beyond its recognized limits. At the time

1. Alfred Stieglitz, *Winter, Fifth Avenue*

it was taken, for example, Stieglitz reported that the light was so dim that he himself had doubts about what he would capture on his plates. Those who first saw the plates were doubtful about whether recognizable forms would emerge in prints made from them.[5] Yet the result, in accord with Stieglitz's hunch, was a photograph of some considerable interest. In it a carriage in the near foreground (which Stieglitz actually described as a "stagecoach") appears to be arriving out of some mythical past into the midst of a busy, modern city, with the almost magical blizzard providing the illusion necessary for such a transforming vision. The photograph is also well composed and interestingly ambiguous. The long straight line of ruts running laterally across the picture parallels the lines of driving snow and therefore seems to suggest either a country road penetrating the city or an added bit of geometric design to score off against the vertical lines of the modern buildings. It is easy to see why such a photograph would have seemed to Stieglitz "a new vision" and to promise a new kind of potentiality for photography. It was all done, moreover, without the artificial procedures that often characterized pictorial photography of the day. No pigmented paper had been used in printing from the plate to simulate brush strokes, nor had the negative been scratched or scored to the same effect, both techniques that even the best of his contemporaries commonly used. Nor had it been necessary to "import" a Whistlerian fog by artificially softening the focus. Instead, the photograph was as sharp and the focal distance as great as lens and available light would permit. The picture was thus the direct result of the unfiltered play of New York winter light upon a slow photographic plate, a triumph of what would become known as "straight" photography, in order to distinguish it from its more heavily cosmetic stylistic rival.

Not long afterward Stieglitz made another photograph of a somewhat similar kind, a picture of a horsecar and team standing at the terminal, the horses steaming as the driver, back to camera, attends to them (Plate 2). Once again, the steaming horses have an almost primeval quality, as though they had just sprung fresh from creation. In the background is the old Post Office with its Doric columns and rectilinear windows capped with snow. This photograph, too, has a visual immediacy and the arresting quality of expressing temporal displacement and skewed chronology. For

2. Alfred Stieglitz, *The Terminal*

Stieglitz the making of these two photographs was powerfully associated with his theatrical initiation of a few days before: "The steaming horses being watered on a cold winter day, the snow covered streets and the Stagecoach in 'Winter — Fifth Avenue,' my sense of loneliness in my own country, all seemed closely related to my experience when seeing Duse."[6] Just as clearly, from Stieglitz's obtaining of these visual effects, a new kind of street theater had been born.

During the next fifteen years or so Stieglitz continued to develop and broaden his conception of urban photography. Between "The Asphalt-Paver" of 1892, the earliest picture that roughly fits this form — and a photograph of considerable interest — and his "Excavating, New York," a picture that still retains in 1911 some of the qualities of his early work, Stieglitz made at least a score of other photographs of great variety and range. "The Asphalt-Paver" is a good example of how this process began. In this particular photograph the center of attention and subject is a paving machine located in the foreground of the picture and virtually enveloped in smoke from a nearby asphalt-melting fire. A single human figure whose outline is scarcely discernible against the machine is bent over it. The smoke rises in a great cloud to partly obscure the bare branches of a row of trees behind and, farther off, the geometric line of a viaduct. This viaduct crosses the picture at a slight angle. There is no horizon, no clear division of earth and sky. The whole photograph, in fact, is a study of shades of gray. The darkest forms are those of the viaduct and the vertical stack of the paving machine, which cross at right angles in the center of the picture. Even lighter than the sky is the cloud of man-made smoke. The meaning of such photographs, at least out of context, is somewhat enigmatic. The objects portrayed, for example, the paving machinery and the viaduct behind, seem very much from the present, in contrast to "Winter, Fifth Avenue." Their lines are contrasted with the lacework of bare branches, the soft outline of the smoke, and with what little one can detect of the single, hunched human figure. Stieglitz seems characteristically to have employed smoke to soften and qualify the starkly linear quality of his urban scenes. Sometimes, in his cityscapes, mushrooms of smoke billowing from stacks almost seem to take the place of trees in the conventional landscape, as in his picture of rail yards, "The Hand of Man" (Plate 3). Even more telling, in this

3. Alfred Stieglitz, *The Hand of Man*

case, is the bleak, wintry tonal range. There is no beauty here, at least not in any easily recognizable form, though the picture has the quality of offering a perception of where things are, as measured against the more or less constant values of earth and sky. All in all, one would have to say, the photograph presents a not very optimistic reading on the building of roads. Some kind of hostile invasion of the natural world is clearly under way in such a portrayal of man-in-the-machine as an enemy encampment.

The direction in which Stieglitz was moving in his portrayal of New York becomes clearer if one contrasts two photographs, one of a Paris street scene made in 1894 during a wedding trip to France and the other a New York street scene made eight years later. The Paris photograph, "Wet Day on the Boulevard," is of a tree-lined street. Despite the rain and grayness of tone, this is an aesthetically agreeable picture, in perspective and subject very much in the manner of contemporary Pissaros. The wet, puddled street reflects what light there is, and there is an interesting bustle of people freely moving about in carriages or under umbrellas: all in all, a scene out of the European urban past. Paris and other European cities were always to strike Stieglitz in this way, as they did most contemporary photographers. Another photograph of Paris made by Stieglitz seventeen years later, for example, is roughly similar in character. There is no analogous portrayal of a New York street scene by Stieglitz, nor, so far as I can determine, by any other "art" photographer of the time. New York streets were usually photographed by Stieglitz, as by others, at night or when mostly deserted, the parks virtually empty. More and more, the vertical lines of buildings rising on either side of the street, or the geometric patterns of buildings and streets viewed from above, tended to dominate or dwarf any human figures in sight. A good example of this is "Spring Showers, New York," made in 1902. In the foreground of this photograph is a sapling surrounded by a fence, a small remnant of nature caught in a cage. Near the small tree is a street cleaner in a white coat, back to camera and broom in hand, working alone. Way off in the distance and barely discernible are some carriages and what appear to be the forms of pedestrians, but the scene is overshadowed by the obscure forms of tall buildings rising on either side of the street. As though to emphasize the strikingly vertical character of the picture, the print itself is tall and thin, as contrasted with the horizontal and rectilinear squatness of the two Paris prints.

The significance of such a shift in emphasis does, I think, pose something of a problem, though certain things can be said that do clarify the situation somewhat. For one thing, such a shift was not unique to Stieglitz. A growing and analogous photographic interest in abstraction began to mark the work of a number of photographers at just about this time. Such a change can be soon seen in the work of Edward Steichen, Paul Strand, and Alvin Coburn, to name but three, as well as in that of Lewis Hine. While the precise terms in which they worked differed interestingly from artist to artist, a comparable development took place in each of them. The answer, therefore, does not seem to lie in biography. A careful examination of Stieglitz might tell us something about the idiosyncratic style in which he worked, might help explain his total commitment to his art and, indeed, much else, but it could scarcely supply an answer to the central riddle: why does this particular kind of geometric and abstract vision of the city appear in just these years? This was not, as we know, a phenomenon of photographers alone, since such painters as John Marin and Joseph Stella seem to have perceived something comparable only just a little later. Nor was it the product of any particular avant-garde influence. While many of those involved were associated with the Photo-Secession movement and with Stieglitz's "291" gallery, Hine and Stella worked alone and apart from the others. Stieglitz's *Camera Work,* while an invaluable source during the whole of its existence from 1903 until its discontinuation in 1917, is scarcely dominated by this kind of photography, since most Photo-Secession work does not conform to this pattern. The examples cited here have had to be culled from masses of photographs of a widely differing character. *Camera Work,* furthermore, contains little editorial comment on the city as a subject of photography, and apart from a few references in letters, there is little recognition in Stieglitz's writings that such a development was taking place. Since Stieglitz himself was editor and retained a controlling voice throughout this period concerning what was printed, one would have expected him, had he been fully conscious of the importance of this shift in his own perception, to have given some indication of it at least in the selection and grouping of his own photographs included in the volumes for

1905, 1911, and 1913. The only hint of this kind came in 1910 when he grouped together a number of cityscapes made during the previous year. Nor does the appearance of modernism in European painting and sculpture seem to hold the answer. The notorious Armory Show in 1913 and the arrival in the Stieglitz circle of European modernists such as Picabia and Duchamp came too late to provide a satisfactory explanation. Stieglitz's own style of abstract representation was well developed by 1910, the year before the first Futurist Manifesto and the year of his first, faltering exposure, during a trip to France, to the art of Picasso and Matisse.[7] Instead, the change in Stieglitz, as in the others, seems to be the product of the ecological promptings of New York itself, an almost communal experience of the city on the part of those who lived there and whose perception was in some way specially attuned to what they saw.

One of the most interesting careers in American photography began some nine years earlier in 1901 when Frank Manny, superintendent of New York's Ethical Culture School, placed a camera in the hands of a young botany teacher from Wisconsin named Lewis Hine — in order for him to improve his teaching.[8]

Hine's career as a photographer was closer to that of Jacob Riis than to those of more consciously artistic photographers like Stieglitz and those associated with the so-called Photo-Secession movement, which he originated and led. During the next thirty years or so Hine, with seeming artlessness, photographed America's new laboring classes from the time of their arrival at Ellis Island. He found them, child and adult, in their homes, on the streets, sometimes at rest or at play but most often at work.

While his photography was not confined to New York, the city was the focus of his most interesting studies — and all but a few of his pictures concerned subjects that were in some sense urban. Indeed, his photography was informed almost from the start by an interest in urban sociology acquired first at the University of Chicago and then at Columbia, where he completed a Pd.M. in 1905. Out of this latter association, in fact, came his lifelong involvement in Progressive social reform and in the beginnings of investigative journalism. He served first as staff photographer for Paul Kellog's *Survey*, an influential national magazine focusing on all aspects of social service and reform. Subsequently, he was photographer for the National Child Labor Committee, for the

Russell Sage Foundation, which then had a pronounced sociological orientation, and finally for such prominent "muckraking" national magazines as *McClure's* and *Everybody's*.

The most striking feature of Hine's photographs lies in the way they question the relation of his human figures to their setting. It is the faces we remember in these pictures: the face of a child standing beside a power loom, the white faces of boy miners, the concentrated look on the face of a construction worker dangling from a beam of the Empire State Building, the slightly puzzled look on the face of a boiler worker lying in the end of a boiler. For Stieglitz the setting always seems to dominate, and his human figures, when they appear at all, seem part of the setting. Indeed, the feeling we often get from Stieglitz's pictures of the city as a soulless place partly derives from the way human figures are submerged in his urban photography. The titles he sometimes gave to his photographs support such a reading: "The Asphalt-Paver," "The City of Ambition," and, for a railroad yard, the ironic title "The Hand of Man." With Hine, human figure and setting are kept in balance and one's attention is absorbed in examining the character of the juxtaposition. His documentary style is inclined less to judge than to question the seeming disparity of, for example, child and machine. The precise way in which this relationship between subject and setting is presented varies from picture to picture, but from the outset Hine was unusually successful in capturing the formal character of his settings and in isolating the details that give them visual meaning. In particular, he dwelt upon the pervasively abstract and geometric character of both city and machine. His "Madonna of Ellis Island" (Plate 4), for example, is an extraordinary early photograph taken of an immigrant woman with her two children, which is part of a sequence of such portrayals made about 1905. This is a very modern "madonna," compassionate and ironic, as the title would suggest. She is seated on a bench against the background of one of the high windows of the immigration hall. The window, with its parabolic curve and its somewhat blurred geometric tracery, faintly suggests a church window. The group of figures is arranged so as to parallel the lines of the window, one child seated on each side of the mother. The woman, to judge from other photographs of the same time and location, is probably Jewish; if so, still a further ironic turn on the title. But here, as in almost all Hine's work, it is through the

4. Lewis Hine, *The Madonna of Ellis Island*

portrayal of the faces that he achieves his most powerful effect. In this case, the faces are illuminated by bright sunlight shining through the hall, and all three are smiling, somewhat enigmatically, again with the slight suggestion that there is more to it all than simple joy and relief after a safe arrival. The mother, in fact, appears quite unconsciously to have assumed a Mona Lisa smile. Is this, one is made to wonder, simply a happy family group? Perhaps. For example, the family is grouped together in a way that suggests closeness and, through the clustering of hands, tenderness, too. Yet there are puzzling features in the way these three faces are caught by the camera. In traditional madonnas the mother's face is generally bowed over or attentive to that of the infant. This mother's is not. She looks at neither child. Instead her eyes are slightly averted, her smile faint and enigmatic, with perhaps a touch of complacency. There is a suggestion that her thoughts may concern something a long way removed from the present moment. Neither child, moreover, is looking at her, nor are they looking at one another. The older has what appears to be a "faraway" look, across her mother's lap and over her baby sister. Even the infant, whose eyes reflect the bright light originating behind the camera, is made to give the impression that she, too, is wrapped in some private reflections.

These faces drawn from the crowds of immigrants moving through Ellis Island are, in other words, highly individualized and, in this case as in others, photographed in such a way as to suggest that, conceivably, figures so portrayed have separate destinies in the New World. This ability to individualize his subjects, even in pictures of large groups like his "Breaker Boys" (Plate 10), is achieved by such devices as highlighting the eyes or patterns of wrinkles around the eyes. This preoccupation is characteristic of Hine's photographic work until the twenties and undoubtedly explains some of the force his work carried as evidence with legislators and reformers bent on social justice. It is this very ambiguity in the expression of his subjects that gives his work such power and "directness." His photograph "Forty-Year-Old Woman," made at Hull House in 1905, portrays a lidded, wrinkled face that is virtually sphinxlike in the ambiguity of its expression (Plate 5). The title, too, is characteristically ironic, since to the "comfortable classes" this woman must have appeared closer to sixty than to forty. What kind of experience, the viewer

5. Lewis Hine, *Forty-Year-Old Woman*

must have wondered, has etched those premature wrinkles and lowered those lids? Such faces radiate the historical mystery of the abrasive transition from peasant to urban slum dweller.

Hine, in selecting his subjects, seems to have had an extraordinary sensitivity to the effect of his camera upon those he photographed. His subjects in their responses span the whole range from extreme self-consciousness before the camera to utter indifference. Hine seems to have sensed, too, that these responses to the camera's presence were an important part of what he could reveal as a photographer. In puzzling through his gallery of urban figures and trying to define what we see, it is important to remember that the camera itself was an unseen participant. Uncertainty before the camera and how to respond to it figure as significantly in his work as uncertainty about the machine and the new shapes and forms of an urban setting. Much of the value of his photographs as historical documents derives from these flickerings of uncertainty and what we can infer from them about what people perceived was happening to them. Some adult subjects appear to have ignored the camera or pretended to, like those performing in *cinema verité,* partly to avoid a feeling of self-consciousness and partly because they *were* busy and only tolerated interruption. And then, too, remaining at work must have been important as well because for many of these subjects their working selves must have been their most comfortable identities. Staring at the camera lens or looking vaguely off into the distance would have struck them as awkward and artificial. Children, who are more "open" anyway and who identify less with their work, appear to have expressed this experience much more directly and overtly — and with the widest range of gestures and stances.

Photographers seldom photographed themselves in this period, at least with full paraphernalia, and there are accordingly few pictures of what people confronted when their photographs were taken. One interesting exception is a 1910 portrait by Hine of a family in a New York tenement (Plate 6). Part of what makes this such a striking photograph is the presence of a wall mirror in the upper right-hand corner of the picture, which seems to be reflecting a black-hooded camera with clouds of smoke rising in the background. The rest of the photograph shows what Hine found in the way both of setting and of human response. For example, here the camera seems to have had a still further effect

6. Lewis Hine, *Family in New York Tenement*

of causing crowding and congestion in the room. The family group seems almost herded into a corner. Other effects are evident. A small child seated on the lower right seems in the midst of a cry or gasp, it is hard to know which. The baby in the mother's arms is slightly blurred, probably from having started at the flash or having stirred during the exposure. Another child standing by the window is starey-eyed. The other children give evidence of varying degrees of interest and surprise. Only the mother can maintain something approaching normal composure in the face of it all.

In other ways, too, the photograph portrays what is essentially an adult's world. A fancy nineteenth-century clock, conceivably a family heirloom, stands on the mantelpiece on top of a lace cloth, well away from the reach of children. Beside it are a small porcelain figurine, a vase, a bottle of medicine. What appears to be a cut-glass pitcher and one or two other items along with a coal-oil lamp stand on the dresser behind the group. On top of the lamp is a man's hat, or so it appears, perched almost jauntily. On the walls are several "pictures" — it is hard to tell whether they are prints, photographs, or aquatints, and whom or what some of them represent. One such picture is cut off by the camera, another obscured by what seems to be an item of clothing hanging on the wall. A frame containing what looks like several photographs is partly obscured by the hat. Only the milk, Karo syrup and baby bottle on the table by the mirror and the small child's stool give evidence of the seven children in residence.

It takes some careful looking to find what may be the most important object in the room, a sewing machine off in the left-hand corner piled high with clothing. Is it the family's clothing that is being made or is it "putting-out" work? Only one leg, the wheel, and what looks like a spool beneath are caught by the flash. Thus, we see this family and we see, furthermore, what they see, in this case even the camera in their midst. We perceive the texture, the perspectives, the feeling of congestion — or is it closeness? — to which these individuals must have been alive. Yet much that we think we see or sense is very much conjecture, and our overall impressions fully confirm the importance of ambiguity in photographic representation. What we see is very much a visual event constructed or, better, puzzled out, by the viewer. The clock, for example, says one-thirty. Is no one in school or is it summer or Saturday? If this is a "family" photograph why is there no man present? No particular hardship is depicted in this case (although the number of other rooms is also unknown), and one is left to wonder what the photograph "means," or was intended to mean. Most forcibly, perhaps, one is left with the impression that this small domestic "invasion" has trapped its subjects in a singular moment of history, frozen a frame from lives in which viewers may see undefined destinies. In particular, it has caught something about the physical scale of life, the human density and the old-world aesthetic values of those portrayed, and something too, perhaps, about the spatial limitations of those undertaking a novel social existence in one of the most densely populated urban areas of the world. The belongings of several generations of family life, such as the picture of some ancestor on the wall, are crammed, like the people themselves, into a corner of a single room, as if to dramatize the discomfort of a transition from a more spacious to a severely constricted social scene. Indeed, the very absence of melodramatic evidence of poverty and the presence of some bourgeois comfort make this aspect of the picture even more dramatic.

This kind of meaning tends, I believe, to supersede obvious and intended meanings of the time, even in those photographs of a more overtly documentary kind, as in those of children whom Hine caught in factories, mills, mines, or on city streets. One sees them today looking into his camera, some of them insolently, some almost introspectively, close enough some of them to be able to see their own faces reflected in the lens. Still, it would be difficult to determine what being photographed meant to his subjects. It must have meant many different things. To the black man dying of tuberculosis whom Hine photographed in 1908 in a Washington slum it appears to have been yet another indignity to be suffered stoically by someone too sick and too weak to do more than cast his outer garments over the head of his bed and let rubbish collect at his feet (Plate 7). To the "newsies" taken at close range in 1910 the occasion seems to have called for a macho show of adulthood with much mugging and puffing of smoke (Plate 8). To the Negro orphan, aged about two, the experience was both frightening and significant, to judge from her erect pose, her wide eyes, and the tight grip of her hands on the arms of her baby rocker (Plate 9). To his "Breaker Boys" from the mines or to his

7. Lewis Hine, *Slum Negro Dying of Tuberculosis*

8. Lewis Hine, *Newsies at Skeeter Branch*

9. Lewis Hine, *Little Negro Orphan, Washington, D.C.*

10. Lewis Hine, *Breaker Boys*

mill workers, picture taking seems to have brought a few moments of respite from hard, draining work (Plate 10). Few give the impression of according the experience the significance that viewers must have given it, nor do Hine's subjects appear to have expected anything like redress from the appearance of an alien photographer in their midst. The camera must have seemed to them still another machine, leveled at them to uncertain effect. Yet, ironically to Florence Kelly, Jane Addams, and other social reformers, the camera had become the one incorruptible measure of social condition — another kind of mechanistic instrument of scientific measure. None of the ambiguity of Hine's work, for example, was apparent to Florence Kelly, who saw the photograph as providing a kind of metric scale of reality. "The camera," she wrote, "is convincing. Where records fail and where parents forswear themselves, the measuring rod and the camera carry conviction."[9]

For Hine himself, the machine he carried about was necessitated by a breakdown or failure of language to portray social circumstance. The ability of language to get at the character of human pathos, he felt, had been steadily eroded by three-quarters of a century of sentimentalizing and sermonizing. Such a development had left the actualities of human existence glossed over with a soft and impenetrable shell. For him it was narrative art that had suffered most as a gauge of reality. "If I could tell a story in words," he wrote to Paul Kellogg in 1922, "I wouldn't need to lug a camera" — an odd formulation which suggests that Hine may have underestimated the unique force of his own work.[10] One of the great virtues of his photographs lay precisely in their not telling *a* story in the traditional mode but, instead, in their inviting plural, even conflicting, interpretations.

Photographers like Hine were never wholly innocent about the importance of illusion in photographic work, although they rarely discussed this aspect of their art. At the same time, even the best and most artistically self-conscious photographers of the time, like other artists, seem never to have been fully conscious of the range of meaning that could be assigned to their work. Their obsession was the operational aspect of camera work. They almost prided themselves on their accidental artifice, the way they acted from hunches, the happy effects obtained from minor mishaps such as double exposure or kicking the leg of the tripod while the shutter was open. Once they had broken their dependence upon painterly modes and perspectives, they quickly began to explore the potentialities of their machinery in an openly experimental fashion. They seemed, in fact, to have been fully as preoccupied with learning from their machinery as with "instructing" or guiding it. This search gave a somewhat restless character to the best photography of the period. No photographic mode or style, except perhaps the studio portrait, settled down or remained in any sense constant. To be a photographer of standing between 1890 and 1930 — to set an arbitrary outer limit — meant to experiment and hence to change, to feel one's way in a medium that played tricks with light, flattened distances, blanched out color, and distorted human features at close range. For them it was a complicated business of learning to see the world afresh through a narrow squint of a single glass eye, like a Cyclops.

Hine is in this sense quite representative. He had changed his own style of social documentary photography out of all recognition by the end of his life. From the outset his pictures had betrayed an interest in abstract design, as a photograph like "Madonna of Ellis Island" suggests. He had always shown an interest in the machinery surrounding his human figures, especially in the pictures of children at work in the prewar years. Increasingly over the years, however, his machines were moved from margin or background to visual center and soon began to assume an importance as great as or greater than that of his human figures. His "Steamfitter" of 1921 could almost be a still from Chaplin's *Modern Times* fifteen years later (Plate 11). Finally, his figures were almost literally swallowed up by machines, as in "Man at Dynamo" of 1921 (Plate 12), dwarfed by them into Lilliputian figures dancing about on abstract forms, or hidden within them. There is some evidence of this interest in machinery in a photograph taken as early as 1910 that portrays a group of children in the process of clambering up the corner of a railroad boxcar, a photograph somewhat uncharacteristic of Hine in this period since the camera has caught the spectacle from the rear and no child's face can be seen. A later, more striking example is "Boilermaker" (1929), which shows a worker flat on his stomach and perched in the end of a huge cylindrical boiler, boiler cap in hand, poised for a moment and looking at the camera with interest (Plate 13). Other geometric shapes fill the picture: the regular lines of wartlike welts recede down the boiler and there is an

11. Lewis Hine, *Steamfitter*

12. Lewis Hine, *Man at Dynamo*

abstract arrangement of what appear to be crates or boxes at the upper left. If photographs such as this make a statement, it is not precise. Yet any viewer is left to ponder the oddity of such a normal-looking man, his hair carefully combed, lying with apparent comfort in such a space-age habitat. The ironic play, if one was even intended, seems to be directed neither at the man nor at the machinery. The man's steady eye, indeed, seems to send some kind of question back to the viewer for reconsideration: what do *you* think of what you see? It is, in fact, a long way from the crowded tenement of 1908, both formally and in substance.

This preoccupation with abstraction in genre photography is apparent even in Hine's early work. One of his newsboys, Danny Mercurio, is shown against a foreground of starkly geometric blocks of cement sidewalk that recede like merging parallel lines into the background. The background is further dominated by a fretwork of rectilinear window casements in a distant building. Another newsboy, photographed at about the same time, is shown standing against a perfectly plain brick wall. In what seems at first the straightest of documentary photographs, Hine in 1910 photographed a Bowery derelict, hands in pockets, who appears virtually cornered by camera and flash. In this case the soft lines of the huddled, dazed figure are set off against the ornate geometric masonry of the dark wall behind him and against the equally fancy tile work underfoot (Plate 14). In another, similar contrast, a woman beggar partly obscures an advertisement for safety razors and stands surrounded by abstract Art Deco ironwork railings. And so forth. It is hard to find photographs at any period of his work that do not embody this preoccupying intermixture of humanity and geometric form.

Hine was, of course, not alone among photographers, to say nothing of artists more generally, in taking such an interest in abstract machine forms. Paul Strand at the time had shifted his interest to machines, to photographs of motion-picture cameras he was then using, for example, their mechanism open to view, as in his "Double Akely" of 1922 or his earlier "Automobile Wheel" (1917). And this was the moment at which American "Precisionists" such as Charles Sheeler appeared on the art scene with representational abstractions of a geometric character. This almost simultaneous discovery of the "beauty" of abstract form by photographers, sculptors, painters, and architects warrants more

13. Lewis Hine, *Boilermaker*

14. Lewis Hine, *The Bowery, New York City*

careful examination. The gradual emergence of this mechanistic vision among photographers seems to be a preoccupation of an autobiographical sort, a kind of running portrait of the artist as or in machine, through which for a few years these photographers allow their "machinist" selves to play a more and more prominent part in what they see.

This sudden appearance of a mechanical Narcissus is evident even in the prewar years. With the twenties came an even more apparent and widespread recognition by all kinds of artists that they were in part welders, chemists, machinists, aviators, motorists, students of optics — a whole range of technological specializations. They possessed, in other words, a fractured consciousness of being part artist and part scientist-engineer that was embedded in perspective as well as in form and subject. These were years, of course, in which art generally carried on a love affair with science and technology, and the effects of this romance had a dramatic impact on the shape and imaginative image of cities as well as upon the way men saw themselves. The motorcar exerted horizontal pressures on the vertical, aggregate character of cities in much the same way that the welder's torch modified the human figure in the work of such sculptors as Giacometti. The flat perspectives of the camera appear to have played some role in inspiring the flat, almost photographic human faces that appear in the paintings of such Viennese Expressionists as Gustav Klimt and Egon Schiele, just as the aerial photograph flattened the profile of cities and further heightened their perceived geometric character. The human face, like the modern city, was caught by the camera at crazy angles and flattened by the lens. It was never to look the same again. A revolutionary new chemistry of paints did the rest, making brilliant, posterlike colors almost irresistible.

What was true of the graphic arts was even more pronouncedly true of architecture. For all his Whitmanesque rhetoric, Frank Lloyd Wright had the soul of an engineer and only his brilliantly intuitive sense of the potential of reinforced concrete made his abstract and geometric cantilevering possible. Finally, what began in studio and laboratory reached the public through an equally revolutionary change in printing, graphics, and photoreproduction that brought the modern art of book design and illustration into existence and created a whole new industry of advertising.

Among the best photographers, the new modern consciousness

arrived very early, partly because photographers were almost by necessity machinists and emulsion chemists, whose darkroom laboratories interpreted what their cameras saw. In 1934 Paul Strand, who had studied with Hine, lamented the slowness with which photographers relinquished the idea that a camera was a brush or a pencil and recognized it for "what it is, a machine."[11] Even Stieglitz, perhaps the least modish and most restless artist among the Photo-Secessionists, caught the fever and seemed for a time imaginatively caught up by the new interest in the machinery of the sky, in airplanes and dirigibles. This symbiosis of camera, city, machine, and abstract form was never more interestingly expressed than in the striking portfolio of photographs which Hine took in 1931 and 1932 to document the erection of the world's highest skyscraper, the Empire State Building. As in "Empire State Building" (1931), his human figures crawl about doing their work on an immense framework of steel against a background of other urban geometry that is rendered even more abstract by a gauze of smoky haze (Plate 15).

Indeed, the groping of photographers in pictures such as these now seems uncertainly and cautiously heuristic rather than ironic. Their aim appears to have been one of attempting to recover or re-create human scale, one of finding some way of reimposing it in a new and disruptive visual setting, for very much the same reasons one suspects landscape painters like Millet and Constable place human figures engaged in everyday activities in the foreground of even their most far-ranging landscape perspectives. For the photographers the effect seems to have been one of weighing and testing the human impact of these new urban perceptions. Photographers, like others living through this period of transition, were educating their eyes, attuning their perceptions in a way that often made their conscious artistic objectives and expressed verbal attitudes seem irrelevant or in conflict with these now apparent but less conscious gropings. The overall effect, however, was to further enhance the aesthetic excitement of the modern city and thus to join hands with others whose work tended toward the same end.

The full significance of the work by photographers during these crucial decades cannot be fully appreciated unless their explorations in urban spatiality and perspective are seen in the context of still larger and parallel efforts to enhance the aesthetic

15. Lewis Hine, *Empire State Building*

character of urban life. Photography, as we have seen, arrived in the twentieth century with an accredited capacity to document the everyday life of city people. It soon demonstrated an equally dramatic capacity to portray the modern city from striking new perspectives which became part of an emerging urban sense of identity. This sense of identity was composed in part of those coded perceptions, now largely taken for granted, which at the time registered the dramatic accommodation that city dwellers were forced to make with a new technological and aesthetic environment that had drastically altered the shape and scale of communal life.

It is this emerging sense of urban identity, if one may so describe it, that seems such a historic development. It was the product of a process in which art came to the aid of sensibility, a process that began with the adumbration of visual images to represent how it felt to live in such utterly new surroundings, surroundings which the city dweller found a kind of house of mirrors, in which perceptions and self-perceptions were crazily confounded, in which one could both see and see oneself from strange new angles. But it soon became clear that more than visualization was involved in these new perceptions. The objects portrayed in the new photography — like the skyline view of the city — soon began to take on aesthetic values of their own. What began as orientation to a new setting ended as romance, although the line between documentary representation and flattering portrayal remained thin and elusive. In a matter of decades the city underwent a process of aesthetic transformation — from aesthetic *terra incognita* to the "stylish" city of urban mythology — the New York of Crowninshield's *Vanity Fair* and Busby Berkeley musicals.

In retrospect it seems evident that such a process of visualizing — or, if you will, spatializing — experience was central to the two decades after 1910 both in America and in Europe. Not only was it preeminently an age of architecture — keyed to such names as Frank Lloyd Wright, Le Corbusier, and those of the Bauhaus group in Germany — but it was an age of the architectonic, too. The aesthetic interest in geometric abstraction already noted in photography and the close association of this interest with urban life was suddenly evident everywhere by the twenties. New York continued to remain focal to these developments, as the inspiration and subject of portrayal and as a source of artistry. The dazzling futuristic drawings of cities by the architectural renderer Hugh Ferris, the stark vertical stage sets by Gordon Craig, and the bold and colorful geometrics that permeated the design work of the Bauhaus, the Vorticists, and Art Deco found their counterparts in painting and in sculpture, in the New York–inspired work of the French painter Picabia, in the New York Precisionist work of Sheeler and Demuth, and in the representational urban abstractions of New York by Joseph Stella. Much of this fretted against the static limits of existing art forms. In particular, painters and designers, like photographers, were preoccupied, almost obsessed, with the problem of representing movement — through multiple perspective, through the shattering of geometric image, through almost any means that gave expression to the kinetic reality of urban life, the sense of haste, pressure, and near-frenzy that came to be associated with New York, as in cinema comedy. This new preoccupation was accompanied by a developing aesthetic of kinetics and of the film, which began to get an airing in Stieglitz's *Camera Work* and other intellectual journals.

This heightened preoccupation with the visual, spatial, and kinetic, while it held implications for every art form, seemed most immediately threatening to literary art since, more than any other, it seemed bounded by linear temporal limits. Despite the fact that this was a great age of literary experiment and of creativity it is possible to detect a strong undertow from these new forces undercutting the sufficiency of verbal discourse. This development was most apparent in the dance and cinema, where the silent poetry of movement tended altogether to supplant verbal expression, but it seemed an undeniable feature of the sudden upsurge in dramatic art of all kinds and of the series of historic collaborations that took place between dramatist and musician from Richard Strauss and Hugo von Hofmannsthal to Bertolt Brecht and Kurt Weill. A feeling that words were insufficient, timebound, somehow lacking in imaginative reality, while it drew some literary artists to bolder and bolder experimentation, also dictated changes in the traditional setting in which readers encountered literary art: the magazine. A new kind of collaboration developed, not only between writer and illustrator, but between editor and layout man, which gave increasing prominence to the visual experience of the magazine reader. Graphics, as they came to be called, were sheared from their dependence upon literary expression and began to assume a certain autonomy. In advertising, for example, verbal expression as set off from photography and graphics more and more assumed the subordinate role of the subtitle in the silent film.

We have grown so accustomed to finding good fiction and "liberal" reporting surrounded by slick, sophisticated advertising — the short story or Talk of the Town and the ad for French perfume — that we forget how novel it must once have seemed. Nor can we reckon how much these glossy pages, either now or then, figure in one's perception of the accompanying fiction. It seems clear enough, however, that this juxtaposition of style and stylishness is historically significant, and it seems likely that the fiction that appeared in this new pictorial setting must have seemed at once, by a process of infectious proximity, better "furnished" socially and more visually class conscious.

One process, therefore, that can be traced through this whole period from the nineties to the end of the twenties is one through which groups within the urban middle classes gradually assume visual possession of the whole city, as we have seen with these photographers. It is a process of aesthetic appropriation through which an older and narrower parochial consciousness gives way to a more expansive and inclusive point of view about the city. The older point of view lives on, of course, in ethnic neighborhoods in which possessive pride in one's neighborhood gives way much more slowly to possessive pride in the city. For a time the problems inherent in such an enlarged point of view about the city — the political implications, for example, in aesthetically underwriting modern skyscraper architecture — remained submerged in the joyousness of aesthetic discovery of the modern city.

The history of our own time is in part the story of how this bright, possessive vision of the modern city is gradually challenged and gives way to the at once more somber and introverted attitudes about the city and the culture of cities which we now hold. By the end of the twenties this process of replacement was well under way. After the thirties the metropolis, however much it might be "used" as a setting, would never again hold the bright place in American imagination that it had obtained during the previous thirty years. These were years of orientation, accommodation, and aesthetic compromise, as we have seen, but they were also years of intense, exploratory, aesthetic excitement where even the "compromised" artistic product seemed enhanced by the very innocence of the period in which it had been produced. Like the English landscape after Turner and Constable and the still life after Cezanne, the artistic journey of the city thereafter plunged inward, even downward into those "interborough fissures of the mind" first evoked in Hart Crane's vivid portrayal of the new York subway in *The Bridge* of 1929. These and later evocations of the city of New York were to form part of a new repertoire of urban expressionism that has since dominated American literary and artistic culture. An already somewhat threadbare consensus about how the city was to be perceived — and how its forms, shapes, and tempo were to be valued — shattered into private symbolisms of the kind already discernible earlier in the evocations of the city in Eliot and Pound. Later versions of this use of the city for private symbolism were to be found in the phantasmagoric Manhattan of Ralph Ellison's *Invisible Man,* and more recently in the nightmarish mockery of New York as a center of fashion and sophistication in Sylvia Plath's *Bell Jar,* or in the ghoulish evocation of the city and city life in the photography of Diane Arbus.

The city led still another kind of subterranean existence as part of the consciousness of still other writers and artists who carried the city with them wherever they went, internalized, half dissociated from place, a metaphor for the artificially complex, the supererogatory, the pressured and frantic pace of modern life they were yearning to shake off, as in Chaplin's great film of the thirties, *Modern Times.* This is the city that will not release its hold on the fugitive in Hemingway's "Killers" or on Robert Penn Warren's Nick Burden as he drives through the western desert, as on a host of fictional heroes hiding out in far-flung places, any more than earlier it had fully relinquished its grasp on Fitzgerald's narrator Nick Carraway after he had left New York and returned to the Middle West.

In either case, the tones were soon to be autumnal. It seemed evident that a certain conception of the city, of New York, the idea of the city as the very embodiment of modern times and the idea of modern man as capable of mastering, even anticipating the demands of such an environment, had passed into history. No art form ever promised such mastery more unreservedly than architecture or portrayed it more appealingly than in the tap-dancing sequences of Busby Berkeley's film choreography, as his hero floated almost effortlessly through city streets. But by the time Berkeley designed the dances for his films, musical comedy was itself becoming nostalgic for the twenties and the mastery evoked in the dances was already a fading memory of a hope.

Notes

1. Sam Bass Warner, Jr., *The Urban Wilderness: A History of the American City* (New York: Harper and Row, 1972), pp. 85–100.
2. "Votre New York est la cité cubiste, la cité futuriste. Il exprime la pensée moderne dans son architecture, sa vie, son esprit." Francis Picabia, quoted from a newspaper interview in 1913. Exhibition Catalogue, Galeries Nationales du Grand Palais, 23 Janvier–29 Mars 1973, p. 66.
3. Biographical information is chiefly derived from Dorothy Norman, *Alfred Stieglitz: An American Seer* (New York: Random House, 1973), and William Innes Homer, *Alfred Stieglitz and the American Avant-Garde* (Boston: New York Graphic Society, 1977).
4. Norman, *Alfred Stieglitz*, p. 36.
5. *Ibid.*
6. *Ibid.*, p. 37.
7. *Ibid.*, pp. 104–106.
8. Judith Mara Gutman, *Lewis W. Hine, 1874–1940: Two Perspectives* (New York: Grossman, 1974), p. 16. Other biographical information about Hine is drawn from this source.
9. *Ibid.*, p. 17.
10. *Ibid.*
11. Paul Strand, "Alfred Stieglitz and a Machine," in Waldo Frank et al., eds., *America and Alfred Stieglitz: A Collective Portrait* (Garden City, N.Y.: Doubleday, 1934), p. 285.

The Melting Pot

Arthur Mann

Arthur Mann, Preston and Sterling Morton Professor of American History at the University of Chicago, is the author of *Yankee Reformers in the Urban Age* (1954), and of a two-volume biography of Fiorello La Guardia. His contribution to this book is part of a larger study on American nationality.

THE MELTING-POT concept dissolved in the discontents of the late 1960s. Not only did it antagonize white ethnics, blacks, Chicanos, Indians, and Puerto Ricans; radicals attacked it as another example of repressive America. Meanwhile, interest in ethnicity revived in the media, academia, the foundations, and government. By the time the President signed the Ethnic Heritage Studies Programs Act of 1972, hardly anyone had a good word to say for the melting pot.

The few who did took the position that all the social movements of the day were destroying American unity. Eric Hoffer, the San Francisco longshoreman-writer, was the most widely read spokesman for that point of view. He advised minorities to join the mainstream, condemned radical intellectuals for wanting to remake the world in their own image, and lauded the United States as the only successful mass society in history. Defiantly, Hoffer attributed the achievement to traditional values: the work ethic, technological innovation, self-reliance, civility, cleanliness, order, self-discipline, love of country, and "the process of amalgamation in the melting pot."[1]

Both sides to the controversy gave the impression that an old American symbol was at issue. Actually, during the greater part of the national past, the melting pot was known in only its literal sense; namely, as a vessel in which inanimate substances — not human beings — were fused or melted. It was so defined in Noah Webster's dictionaries, which since 1806 had been compiling American additions to the English language. And that rendering remained the common usage into the next century.

None of the standard works on the history of the American language include the term at all. It found no place in Sir William Craigie's *Dictionary of American English* (four volumes, 1936–1944) or in Mitford Mathews's *Dictionary of Americanism* (two volumes, 1951). H. L. Mencken, though sensitive to the influence of immigration, mentioned it in neither the original (1936) edition nor two supplements to his celebrated *American Language*.

Yet the *idea* of the melting pot, as against the *phrase,* was as old as the Republic. From Crèvecoeur in the 1780s through succeeding generations into the next century, writers urged the need to "amalgamate," "fuse," "blend," "smelt," and even "melt" America's different ethnic groups into a "composite" people. Other writers took the opposite tack and joined Walt Whitman in hailing America as "this nation of many nations." Both groups of intellectuals and the models they projected deserve attention. But the phrase itself, "the melting pot," became a national symbol only in this century.

I. A Great Play, Mr. Zangwill

Not until 1934, with the publication of the second edition of *Webster's New International Dictionary of the English Language,* did lexicographers say of the melting pot: "The United States as a place of amalgamation of races and mores. . . ." The entry attributed that meaning to "a phrase coined by Israel Zangwill as the title of a play (1908) treating of immigration problems." But the next edition of *Webster's New International,* copyrighted in 1961, dropped the attribution; and at present no one knows for sure who originated the phrase. If not Zangwill, the fact remains that his four-act drama on intermarriage, which caught the public fancy in the years before World War I, made "the melting pot" a common expression of American speech.

The Melting-Pot takes place in immigrant New York City. David Quixano, a Russian-born Jew, and Vera Revendal, a Russian-born Christian, fall in love. Despite the opposition of their relatives, they decide to marry, until they learn that Vera's father, a colonel in the tsar's army, had been personally responsible for the slaughter of David's family in the Kishinev pogrom of 1903. The marriage is put off; but by the play's end not even so horrible an obstacle as the "shadow of Kishinev" can hold back the irresistible course of love in the "American crucible."

Zangwill pulled out the stops in developing his theme. The attractive young couple are reconciled in the roof garden of a settlement house where the idealistic Vera is a resident and David's brilliant new symphony on the American dream has just been successfully performed. It is the final scene. The set contains a view of lower Manhattan and the Statue of Liberty against the backdrop of a stirring sunset. David and Vera, standing hand in hand, speak:

VERA

Look! How beautiful the sunset is after the storm!
[DAVID *turns. The sunset, which has begun to grow beautiful jut after* VERA's *entrance, has now reached its most magnificent moment; below there are narrow lines of saffron and pale gold, but above the whole sky is one glory of burning flame.*]

DAVID
[*Prophetically exalted by the spectacle.*]

It is the fires of God round His Crucible.

[*He drops her hand and points downward.*]

There she lies, the great Melting-Pot — listen! Can't you hear the roaring and the bubbling? There gapes her mouth

[*He points east.*]

— the harbour where a thousand mammoth feeders come from the ends of the world to pour in their human freight. Ah, what a stirring and a seething! Celt and Latin, Slav and Teuton, Greek and Syrian, — black and yellow —

VERA
[*Softly, nestling to him.*]

Jew and Gentile —

DAVID

Yes, East and West, and North and South, the palm and the pine, the pole and the equator, the crescent and the cross — how the great Alchemist melts and fuses them with his purging flame! Here shall they all unite to build the Republic of Man and the Kingdom of God. Ah, Vera, what is the glory of Rome and Jerusalem where all nations and races come to worship and look back, compared with the glory of America, where all races and nations come to labour and look forward!

[*He raises his hands in benediction over the shining city.*]

Peace, peace, to all ye unborn millions, fated to fill this giant continent — the God of our *children* give you Peace.

[*An instant's solemn pause. The sunset is swiftly fading, and the vast panorama is suffused with a more restful twilight, to which the many-gleaming lights of the town add the tender poetry of the night. Far back, like a lonely, guiding star, twinkles over the darkening water the torch of the Statue of Liberty. From below comes up the softened sound of voices and instruments joining in "My Country, 'tis of Thee." The curtain falls slowly.*][2]

Zangwill dramatized a process that had gone on and would go on. Intermarriage was in the American tradition. But the author of *The Melting-Pot* was saying a good deal more than that. He was saying that the authentic, the best, the real American ought to be an American of mixed ancestry. Zangwill made intermarriage a cause. Its success depended, obviously, on the disappearance of ethnic groups and their institutions.

Zangwill received help toward that end from no less a person than the President of the United States. When *The Melting-Pot* opened on October 5, 1908, in the Columbia Theater, Washington, D.C., the audience included Theodore Roosevelt and members of his official family. At the end of the performance, when the author was called up to the stage, the President shouted from his box: "That's a great play, Mr. Zangwill." To the author's wife, who had joined him in the presidential box, Roosevelt said, "*This* is the stuff."[3] A week later, while Zangwill was preparing his work for publication, he wrote to Roosevelt for permission to dedicate *The Melting-Pot* to him. Roosevelt consented, writing back: "I do not know when I have seen a play that stirred me as much."[4]

Launched with the most favorable publicity, *The Melting-Pot* went on to become a huge popular success. After showing in the nation's capital, it ran for six months in Chicago, and then for 136 performances in New York City. Thereafter, for close to a decade, it played in dozens of cities across America. In 1914 it was produced in London, again before full houses and admiring audiences. Lord Bryce joined Theodore Roosevelt in praising *The Melting-Pot*, as had Jane Addams, Hamlin Garland, Booth Tarkington, Augustus Thomas, Brand Whitlock, Burns Mantle, Constance Skinner, and many other prominent figures in politics and the arts.

Small wonder that in 1926 the New York *Herald Tribune* said of Zangwill: "Seldom has an author so molded thought by the instrumentality of a single phrase." If not the originator of the phrase, Zangwill was its most important popularizer. His play affected the thinking of a larger number of people than those who saw it performed on the professional stage. Widely reviewed in newspapers and magazines on both sides of the Atlantic, and published in 1909, it became a text in schools and colleges, and amateur theatrical groups often produced it. "Oh," wrote a Connecticut teacher, "oh, it is splendid to see the little Citizens — Latins, Celts, Jews and Gentiles, all repeat it understandingly." To keep up with the continuing demand, Zangwill's publisher (Macmillan) reprinted the book at least once a year until the United States entered World War I in 1917.[5]

And yet, when Zangwill composed his ode to America as "God's Crucible," he was a Zionist of thirteen years' standing. Critics pointed out the contradiction between his being, simultaneously, a Jewish nationalist and a militant assimilationist. Nor was that the sole paradox in a man who said of himself that he embodied "violent contraries." Zangwill took pride in his controversial twistings and turnings. As a character in another of his plays said for the author: "Ah, sir, the human heart contains four chambers, so surely there is room for contradictions."[6]

Zangwill felt pulled in different directions because he touched base in different cultures but did not fully belong to any of them. Stated sociologically, *The Melting-Pot*'s author was a classically marginal type. The validity of his prophecy of a mixed American "race" must of course stand or fall according to the evidence. But his personal chemistry also demands examination, for it affected his ability to add an influential phrase to the language of American nationality.

II. *The Writer As Lay Priest*

When Israel Zangwill died in 1926 at sixty-two in his native England, obituary writers on both sides of the Atlantic mourned the passing of "the Disraeli of modern letters." He was the first English Jew after Lord Beaconsfield to make his mark in literature and by far the best-known Jewish writer of his generation in the English-speaking world. Turning out a book a year for more than thirty years, Zangwill was primarily a playwright and novelist, but he also wrote poetry, short stories, history, travel accounts, literary criticism, and political journalism. His admirers thought him the equal of Arnold Bennett, John Galsworthy, G. K. Chesterton, H. G. Wells, Bernard Shaw, and other Victorian-Edwardian notables. To Theodore Roosevelt's way of thinking, Zangwill was a much better playwright than Shaw.

Roosevelt had a taste for moralizers, and Zangwill approached his craft as a holy calling. "The true man of letters," he wrote in 1896, "was and must always be a lay priest, even though he seems not to be religious in the popular sense. . . ."[7] Many another intellectual of that time also viewed the writer as society's conscience; Victorians looked upon literature as very serious business. To men of Zangwill's background, though, it took on a particular urgency.

Born in the London ghetto of poor Russian immigrants in 1864, Zangwill belonged to a generation of men and women compelled to create a new identity for themselves.[8] Parliament, by a historic act in 1858, had granted complete civil rights to Jews. They welcomed the emancipatory act, but the invitation to enter English society as equals placed them under severe strain. They could no longer go on thinking, as they had done for centuries, that they and their hosts were peoples apart. Legal emancipation forced England's Jews to come to terms with their Englishness.

Elsewhere in the Old World and for the same reasons, Jews also had to reconsider who they were. First in France, then in other countries, legislation raised Jews to full citizenship. Except for the Roman destruction of the second Temple, wrote Zangwill, no era in the history of the Diaspora was more radically upsetting than that of emancipation. At issue was whether Jews could be true to themselves while they tried to be like others.

The resolution of that question, as Zangwill knew from personal experience, sometimes drove a wedge between fathers and sons. He grew to manhood in the Whitechapel district of London's East End, an immigrant community much like New York City's Lower East Side. In both there was a generational conflict over the degree to which Jews should accommodate to the host society. Zangwill's father, Moses, a devoutly Orthodox, Yiddish-speaking peddler, saw no reason to make any adaptations at all, and chose to spend the last years of his life in Palestine. It is said that he disapproved of his Anglicized son.

For his own part, the son yearned to be both English and Jewish. Zangwill attended Jews' Free School in Whitechapel, Lord Rothschild's institution for the children of poor immigrants, and then taught there while commuting to the University of London, from which he earned a degree in 1884, with honors in English, French, and moral and mental science. At the university he formed, for the first time, associations and friendships with non-Jews. The circle widened as Zangwill, in the 1890s, achieved a reputation as "one of the foremost writers" of his native land. Eventually, he not only moved out of the ghetto, but also outgrew many of its taboos and commandments.

In 1903, just before his fortieth birthday, Zangwill married an English Christian, Edith Ayrton, herself a writer and the daughter of a liberal professor. Shortly thereafter, in a newspaper interview, Zangwill said: "With Israelitish stiffneckedness we have spurned intermarriage, the only natural process by which two alien races can be welded into one. To speak most dispassionately, we have in the long run got only what we deserved." The newspaper reporter described him, sympathetically, as "the very archetype of his race — shrewd, witty, wise, and patient; spare of form and bent of shoulder, and with a face that suggests nothing so much as one of those sculptured gargoyles in a mediaeval cathedral."[9]

But the outsider who wanted to become part of English life no more accepted the Christianity of the host people than he did the Orthodox Judaism of his father. Zangwill's religion was humanism. One of his plays proposed the creation of a new church, with Mazzini and Emerson and Swinburne as saints to transcend the creedal and ancestral differences that had long divided mankind. Mrs. Zangwill shared her husband's faith. Their first son was neither baptized nor circumcised. Initiated into no tribe or sect, the infant belonged to humanity.[10]

Actually, Zangwill had given up Judaism years before marrying. With Heine he liked to say that it "was not a religion, but a misfortune." That rejection of his heritage notwithstanding, Zangwill remained intensely absorbed in things Jewish. "I can never forget," he said at the height of his literary fame, "that I am one of the Children of the Ghetto."

Whenever Zangwill spoke of the ghetto, he had in mind time as well as place. "The ghetto looks back to Sinai," he declared, "and forward to the milennium." According to his reading of history, Jewish life fell into two major eras, the biblical and the ghetto. The latter was breaking up, Zangwill wrote again and again, and Jewish lay priests like himself must prepare the way for the future.

The way was confusing, for the ghettos of the Old World, defenseless against the forces of modernity, had turned into a battleground for contending messiahs. Zangwill warned Jews against following the lead of Moses Mendelssohn, whose children had converted to Christianity; of Ferdinand Lassalle, the father of German socialism; of Heinrich Heine, who had made a religion out of art; of Disraeli, the high prophet of Tory patriotism. Their dispensations rested on the assumption that someone was superior to someone else — the Christian to the Jew, the worker to the capitalist, the aesthete to the philistine, and the aristocrat to the people.[11]

Such distinctions ran counter to Zangwill's universalism. In addition to a creedless church to which everyone could belong, he and his wife found substitutes for their respective ancestral faiths in the peace and feminist movements. Neither cause pitted one group or class against another; and transnational in scope, both promised to extend the family of mankind.

But however inclusive his sympathies — and Zangwill's interests were very large — Jews were his primary concern. The major part of his literary work was about them. For that output he had a larger American than British audience; indeed, the book that first brought him widespread acclaim — a novel about English Jewish life called *Children of the Ghetto* (1892) — was commissioned by the Jewish Publication Society of America to dispel unflattering

Jewish stereotypes. Zangwill, then twenty-eight, had re-created the world in which he had grown up. He followed his initial triumph with *The King of the Schnorrers, Ghetto Tragedies, Dreamers of the Ghetto,* and *Ghetto Comedies.* In 1899 *Children of the Ghetto* was produced as a play in New York, and in that year Zangwill visited the United States for the first time.

Dependent on Jews for his literary materials, Zangwill's principal political cause was also Jewish. In 1895, as a result of the Dreyfus affair, he joined Theodore Herzl and others in founding the Zionist movement. But he came to believe that neither the Arabs nor the Turkish government, to which Palestine belonged, would ever give up the ancient homeland to the Jews. In 1905, together with like-minded secessionists from the Seventh Zionist Congress, Zangwill set up the Jewish Territorial Organization to establish a Jewish state *wherever* possible. For a while he thought British East Africa a likely place. When condemned for betraying the original movement, Zangwill replied that he was no less a Zionist because he regarded Palestine as irretrievable. "Our Messiah is Zionism," he assured an audience in Manchester, England; "we shall know again what it is to love mountains and rivers that are our own. . . ."[12]

Three years later, while he was still promoting that cause, *The Melting-Pot* opened in Washington, D.C.

And so we come back to the puzzle with which we started — namely, Zangwill's recommendations, at one and the same time, that the Jews form their own national state and that they disappear through intermarriage. Zangwill explained that the first proposal was for persons who did not care to remain in their homelands or who could not, as in pogrom-ridden Russia, whereas the second applied to men and women who wanted to stay where they were. By that formula Zangwill solved to his satisfaction the Jewish problem, which he had defined as the inability or unwillingness to stop being Jewish in the post-ghetto era.

III. The Ethnic Apparition

From Zangwill's point of view, *The Melting-Pot* could not have come out at a better time. The American people were then engaged in a debate over the immigration problem. In 1911, while

Zangwill's play was being shown across America, the Government Printing Office published a forty-one-volume report by the Dillingham Commission on immigration. Its major point was that the new immigrants, from southern and eastern Europe, threatened both American society and the American stock. The implications of that conclusion culminated in the next decade in restrictive legislation.[13]

But until then, the immigration policy of the United States was an open question. It consisted of two parts. First, were the new immigrants to blame for the social disorders of the American city — for slums, congestion, poverty, broken families, juvenile delinquency, crime, prostitution, drunkenness, mental illness, illiteracy? Second, were the new immigrants so different from the old in cultural background and physical appearance as to make their absorption impossible?

Restrictionists answered yes to both questions and urged Congress to close the doors to immigration. Antirestrictionists argued that the old and the new immigrants shared a common humanity; that the most recent newcomers were not the causes but the victims of urban decay; and that the host people could best solve the problems of the city through housing reform, better schools, higher wages, fewer hours of work, trade unionization, industrial insurance, and other progressive measures. Between the restrictionists and the antirestrictionists lay a large body of opinion, probably representative of most Americans, who had yet to make up their minds about what to do but were apprehensive about the possible effects of the new immigration on America's future.

The best index to their mentality was *The American Scene,* an account by Henry James of his visit to the United States in 1904–1905. An expatriate since the 1860s, James had settled in the Old World because the New had been "too vague, and, above all, too uniform" to provide him with the "diversity of type" he needed as "a story-seeker and picture-maker." The ethnic variety he found in America almost a half century later should therefore have appealed to the artist in James. Instead, its immensity overwhelmed him.

The American Scene abounded in such expressions as "remorseless Italian," "depths of the Orient," "Slav' origin," "rays of the Croatian," "Moldavian eye," "Galician cheek," "hard glitter of Israel," "unprecedented accents." Not only at "terrible little Ellis

Island," but everywhere he traveled outside the South, James was haunted by "the 'ethnic' apparition." Worse still, in the presence of "the ubiquitous alien," he felt "a chill in his heart" and "a sense of dispossession." He had grown up in New York City and had lived in Boston; the one was now under "the Hebrew conquest" and the other under "an Irish yoke." Astonished to find an Armenian immigrant in the New Hampshire woods, and feeling alien to Italo-American workers in the New Jersey countryside, James complained that elsewhere in the world a man could take a "rural walk in his England or his Italy, his Germany or his France" — but not "in the land of universal brotherhood. . . ." The sense of dispossession was so great that James yearned for "the luxury of some such close and sweet and whole national consciousness as that of the Switzer and the Scot."[14]

In comparison to the views of H. G. Wells, another British visitor to the United States at the beginning of the century, James's reactions to the American population mix were very mild indeed. An Anglo-Saxon supremacist, Wells urged restriction on his American friends and was astonished that so few of them shared his view that the new immigrants were polluting the American bloodstream.[15] James, having neither Wells's racist certitudes nor his socialist fondness for solving problems through radical legislation, went back to England without telling the United States what to do. But in his apprehensions over the ethnic apparition, the self-called "expatriated observer" and "brooding critic" expressed the feelings of millions of old-stock Americans.

As a result of the new immigration, James asked, what was to become of the Americans "ethnically . . . physiognomically, linguistically, *personally* . . . ?"[16]

Zangwill, in contrast to James and Wells, assured Americans that the alien influx from southern and eastern Europe was not a threat or even a cause for worry. Progressive reformers like Theodore Roosevelt were capable of coping, rationally and humanely, with the economic and social dislocations of the modern city. Meanwhile, the melting pot would thaw disturbing ethnic differences and forge a common American race. Some twenty years later the *Literary Digest* said of Zangwill: "He made a phrase that long postponed restricted immigration in America."[17]

Neither Zangwill nor any other person affected legislation to that extent. His play served a political purpose in an age that liked writers to translate urgent public issues into human terms. Zangwill's personal anxiety over the Jewish problem meshed with the American public's concern over the immigration problem. He succeeded in dramatizing that problem, as Hamlin Garland did the farm problem, Upton Sinclair the labor problem, Frank Norris the trust problem, and Winston Churchill (the American) the problem of political corruption.

Their solution was something else. Many a reader, though moved by Upton Sinclair's novel about the disintegration of a working-class family in Chicago's stockyards, rejected the Socialist author's call for a classless America. Just so with *The Melting-Pot*: one could be sympathetic to Zangwill's young immigrant couple in New York City without endorsing his crusade for intermarriage.[18]

IV. Protean Appeal

The oratorical and oracular finale of *The Melting-Pot* was typical of the play as a whole, and Zangwill was criticized for composing a tract for the times rather than an enduring work of art. His harshest critics were Britons who cared for none of his plays. "Nonsense, nonsense, nonsense" — that is how G. K. Chesterton dismissed *The Melting-Pot*. John Palmer, who, years before, had promised never to attend another of Zangwill's plays, remarked that *The Melting-Pot* achieved "the limit of vulgarity and silliness." A. B. Walkley, the *London Times*'s prestigious drama critic, also expressed contempt. "Romantic claptrap," he wrote, "this rhapsodising over music and crucibles and statues of Liberty."

The thin-skinned Zangwill retorted that it was wrong to think that the only worthwhile art was "art for art's sake." On occasion he himself had written works in that spirit, he noted, but *The Melting-Pot* was no less artistic because it dealt with a great social problem. Zangwill scorned the likes of Walkley, "the library-fed man of letters," for not understanding what liberty meant to someone who had been hunted down in a Russian cellar by a murderous mob. One of the functions of art, the lay priest maintained, was to make vivid the highest aspirations of mankind.[19]

Most reviewers agreed with Zangwill rather than with Chesterton and Walkley. Burns Mantle was so moved by *The Melting-Pot*'s idealism that he called it "something of a master work. . . ." Percy

Hammond liked it because it "is all so sincere, so certainly from the heart, that it thrills with conviction." Still another Chicagoan praised it for being "a mighty prophecy, an eloquent plea. . . ." The *English Review* testified that it "laps the pulse strings of our humanity, refreshing as the 'gentle dew from heaven.' " The *Athenaeum* thought Zangwill right for "using the stage as the preacher does the pulpit. . . ."[20]

The sharpest rebuttal to Walkley came from Augustus Thomas, one of America's better-known playwrights, who wrote that "Mr. Zangwill's 'rhapsodizing' over music and crucibles and statues of Liberty is a very effective use of a most potent symbolism. . . . I have never seen men and women more sincerely stirred than the audience that was present when I saw 'The Melting Pot.' . . . The impulses awakened by the Zangwill play were those of wide human sympathy, charity and compassion; and for my own part I would rather retire from the theater, and retire from all direct or indirect association with journalism, than write down the employment of these factors by Mr. Zangwill as mere claptrap."[21]

But in the battle among the critics, which continued as long as *The Melting-Pot* continued to be performed and read, the issue turned less on Zangwill's technique than on his message. "Not since Walt Whitman wrote *Leaves of Grass* have we had so inspiring a picture of America," exclaimed Holbrook Jackson in 1914. Another admirer alluded to an even more popular American classic when he said that Zangwill's work was "calculated to do for the Jewish race what Uncle Tom's Cabin did for the coloured man." Jane Addams reached back in her comparison to the authors of the Declaration of Independence and of the Constitution, declaring that *The Melting-Pot* performs "a great service to America by reminding us of the high hopes of the founders of the Republic."[22]

This extravagant praise — placing the British playwright in the American pantheon alongside such democratic saints as Whitman, Harriet Beecher Stowe, and Jefferson — raises the question of what, precisely, Zangwill's message was. Jefferson believed in amalgamation (for whites only), but Stowe did not, and Whitman praised ethnic variety. Clearly, not everyone who liked *The Melting-Pot* believed in a mixed American race. Zangwill's play contained additional themes that pleased reviewers and accounted for its enthusiastic reception among the public.

For example, in an article called "Plays That Make People Think," the *American Magazine,* edited by Lincoln Steffens, thanked Zangwill for calling attention to a social problem that really mattered to Americans. "What are we going to do with our immigrants?" that publication asked in a review of *The Melting-Pot.* It offered no answer other than the observation that "no thoughtful person will deny that the social future of this country depends largely upon the answer to that question." Among many persons, Zangwill's play succeeded because it was a "problem play."[23]

It was appealing, too, for celebrating America's superiority over Europe. Like previous foreign admirers since the eighteenth-century Enlightenment, Zangwill identified the New World with democracy and the Old with aristocracy. Vera's brutal father and empty-headed mother, the Baron and Baroness Revendal, stood for a social order where the upper classes devour the lower. In contrast, David spoke for a humane society. He decorated his room with the American flag, hummed the national anthem on the street, and dedicated his symphony to the American promise of a fresh start for everyone.

Not even Thomas Jefferson had drawn a more striking polarity between America and Europe, and Zangwill's portrait of the United States embarrassed American reviewers at the same time that it pleased them. Here is how the *Independent* put it: "*The Melting-Pot,* written by an English Hebrew, is altogether American, more American than Americans, for even on the Fourth of July we hardly dare be so unqualifiedly optimistic over the future of the country, so wildly enthusiastic about the success of our great experiment of amalgamation, as Mr. Zangwill is. But it will do us good in this case to see ourselves as others see us, to learn how the fair Goddess of Liberty looks to those who have fled to her protection from Russian pogroms."[24]

Therein lay another reason for *The Melting-Pot*'s success. Civilized opinion had for years deplored Russia's murderous policies against the Jews, and audiences were therefore prepared to sympathize with Zangwill's young refugee. Indeed, the playwright's loathing for the Kishinev massacre, expressed through David Quixano and his bride-to-be, was indistinguishable from the Roosevelt administration's earlier and official protest against the barbaric event.

Zangwill also touched a responsive chord in American audiences by attacking their homegrown plutocracy. Quincy Daven-port, Jr., a cynical millionaire who apes the European aristocracy and tries to force Vera to marry him, is a stock villain. He and his kind were popular targets during the Progressive era. Theodore Roosevelt captured the public imagination as a trust-busting President, and a generation of muckraking journalists equated big money with dirty money. So did *The Melting-Pot.* When Davenport offered to produce David's symphony, David refused, and in-dicted the rich for "undoing the work of Washington and Lincoln, vulgarizing your high heritage, and turning the last and noblest hope of humanity into a caricature."[25]

The most obvious key to Zangwill's protean appeal was that Jane Addams and Theodore Roosevelt could both endorse his work. Roosevelt opposed "hyphenated Americanism," declaring that immigrants and their descendants must slough off their heritage and be loyal only to the United States. He was an amal-gamationist. But Miss Addams, who devoted her life to immi-grants at Chicago's Hull House, was a pluralist. She believed that not only the newcomers but America as well would profit by the preservation of ancestral cultures. She liked Zangwill's work be-cause its author shared her faith in democracy.[26]

Some reviewers denounced Zangwill for asserting that the real American did not as yet exist and would have to wait until the Davids and Veras of the United States mated. "This extraordinary idea of the function of America emanates, of course, from an author who is himself foreign in nationality and alien in race," objected Clayton Hamilton in the *Forum.* "It might be instructive to Mr. Zangwill to look up the ancestry of certain representative Americans of the past. . . ." To Hamilton and men of his point of view, "the present pouring in of alien millions is fraught with menace to our future." That hostility would lead, by the 1920s, to the triumph of restrictive legislation.[27]

But the strongest criticism of Zangwill's views on intermarriage came from the American Jewish press and pulpit. He was ridiculed for holding, simultaneously, such diverse views as Zionism, Jewish territorialism, and assimilation. More important, he was condemned for proposing the extinction of American Jews in the melting pot. "Not for this did prophets sing and martyrs die," the *American Hebrew* protested in an editorial devoted to Zangwill's play. "Not for this have the million refugees from Russia sought America. . . ." Zangwill's talent as a writer made his message all the more dangerous. *"The Melting Pot* is certainly lighted by the intellectual fires of a God-given genius," a Jewish reviewer observed; but "that is all the worse for you and me, brother, who are to be cast into and dissolved in the crucible."[28]

As with Walkley and others who dismissed his play as bogus art, Zangwill answered back to critics who deplored it as objectionable sociology. In an afterword to the revised (1914) edition of *The Melting-Pot,* he defended himself against the charge of inconsistency. Those Jews who wanted to live in Palestine or work for still another homeland should do so, Zangwill said; but Jews who intended to live in America should accept the absorption that David Quixano advocates. Zangwill saw no reason why he had to offer "a panacea for the Jewish problem, universally applicable."[29]

But the essential quarrel between the British playwright and his critics was not his ability to juggle the claims of Zionism and assimilation — it was the survival of Jews as Jews in America.

Zangwill complained that he had been misunderstood on the subject of intermarriage. In 1914 he wrote: "The action of the crucible is . . . not exclusively physical — a consideration primarily important as regards the Jew. The Jew may be Americanized and the American Judaised without any gamic interaction." Two years later, when World War I raised hyphenated Americanism to a new level as a political issue, Zangwill observed that the resurgence of ancestral loyalties "has only made the majority of Americans more conscious than ever of their Americanism, more determined than ever to be a non-European and politically homogeneous people. I say politically homogeneous" — he emphasized the point — "because the actual physical fusion is a long process and is not even necessary, any more than it is necessary in Britain for Welshmen to marry Highland women. . . ."[30]

These reservations nowhere appear in the texts of either the original or the revised editions of *The Melting-Pot.* The play's central theme is Vera's and David's union. Her parents oppose it because David is a Jew, and his uncle is against it because Vera is a Christian. And not only in the final scene, but throughout the play, David talks incessantly about the American crucible. To it he dedicates his life and the symphony that will make him a famous composer.

"No, uncle," the young musical genius exclaims, "the real

American has not yet arrived. He is only in the Crucible, I tell you — he will be the fusion of all races, the coming superman. Ah, what a glorious Finale for my symphony — if I can only write it."[31]

That vision was unambiguous, as was Zangwill's prediction in the afterword that Americans "will ultimately harden into a homogeneity of race, if not even of belief." He granted that continuing immigration and the persistence of both the synagogue and anti-Semitism would slow down the process of homogenization for Jews, but their melting-pot fate was inevitable. "Once America slams her doors [to immigration]," Zangwill concluded in the afterword, "the crucible will roar like a closed furnace."[32]

And yet we cannot discount his disclaimer that there need be no "gamic interaction" for Jews. Zangwill was confused. In his violent contraries he veered from wanting to be a Jew to not wanting to be a Jew. The prophet of universalism never reconciled his philosophy with his background. He belonged to a generation of English Jews that struggled, painfully, to devise alternatives to the tight little communities that Jews had been obliged to build and nourish in the ghetto era. Men of that sort were unsure of their identity. One of Zangwill's alternatives was national regeneration through a Jewish state, and the other was disappearance into the melting pot.

In the end he despaired of both.

V. Disillusionment and Renunciation

Zangwill was born into a Victorian world that had faith in unlimited progress, and he died in a decade of embittered intellectuals. The turning point was World War I. Zangwill was a Tolstoyan pacifist but he supported England against Germany — despite the hateful alliance with Tsarist Russia — in the hope that a better world would emerge from the peace. The shape of post–World War I society shattered that hope, and ultimately, his faith in mankind.

In a speech in New York City's Carnegie Hall in 1923, Zangwill pronounced political Zionism "dead." The "small people" who had succeeded Theodore Herzl as leaders of the movement, Zangwill said, would never be able to dislodge the Arabs from

Palestine. By that time, too, the founder of the Jewish Territorialist movement had also given up the dream of creating a Jewish state somewhere else in the world. For his criticism of Zionist leaders, and also for his urging "a Jewish vote in the United States," Zangwill was denounced by Samuel Untermyer, Louis Marshall, and other Jewish leaders in America.

He was no less disenchanted with the United States. "If America had not gone into the war," he wrote in the 1920s, "a draw would have resulted and militarism would have been killed instead of reviving it in other countries." For the League of Nations he had contempt. It was a "League of Damnations" that had been "palmed off on" Woodrow Wilson in exchange for an unjust treaty. Zangwill also deplored America's stand on war reparations as "isolationist."

More dismaying still was the rise of the Ku Klux Klan. In a polemic against Dr. Hiram Evans, the Klan's Imperial Wizard, Zangwill scornfully remarked that under Evans's "Nordic dispensation" Christ himself would be turned back at Ellis Island. But Zangwill knew that it was not just the hooded knights, but the American people speaking through a large majority in their Congress, who approved the passage of immigration-restriction laws on the theory of Anglo-Saxon superiority. Disillusioned with the United States for forsaking its founding ideals, the author of *The Melting-Pot* called for a revival of the Judaism he had rejected as a youth. Moses Zangwill's son had come full cycle.[33]

His death a few years later was a public event. New York City's most prestigious newspaper ran his obituary on the first page, and Carnegie Hall was hired for a mass memorial meeting. But in death, as well as in life, Israel Zangwill was a controversial figure. Which of his many books, it was asked, were likely to last? Few obituary writers selected Zangwill's most famous play. As the *New York Times* put it in an editorial: "The country and the Immigration law are far away from that pious belief, expressed in the play about which such a hullabaloo was made here some twenty years ago, that the melting pot is 'God's crucible.' . . ."[34]

Pious belief — the epitaph was cruel but the choice of language was not altogether inappropriate for a writer who had thought of himself as a lay priest. The work that in 1908 Theodore Roosevelt called a great work had its moment and then fell to the level of a period piece. Nobody recognized better than the Victorian dreamer of the ghetto himself that he was dated. Israel Zangwill died after a nervous breakdown, irritated, as he said, with "the whole human race."[35]

VI. The Melting Pot Before and Since Zangwill

In the debate over the immigration bill of 1924, many a congressman said he was voting for restriction because the melting pot had failed to weld America's ethnic groups into a homogeneous people. Despite that repudiation, Zangwill's metaphor survived, and in the 1950s Funk and Wagnalls still defined it as a "nickname for the United States of America." Dictionary makers aside, to whom in particular did it appeal? And why?

Before turning to that question, we must first establish the fact that American writers anticipated Zangwill's amalgamationist vision. Four stand out, not only because of their stature, but also because of the frequency with which historians quoted them: J. Hector St. John de Crèvecoeur, Ralph Waldo Emerson, Frederick Jackson Turner, and Theodore Roosevelt. Together, they span the years of the national experience down to the appearance of Zangwill's play. Further, each used words similar to those in *The Melting-Pot*, and Emerson came close to coining the figure of speech later attributed to Zangwill.

"I could point out to you a family," wrote Crèvecoeur during the Revolutionary era, "whose grandfather was an Englishman, whose wife was Dutch, whose son married a French woman, and whose present four sons now have four wives of different nations." Crèvecoeur, himself born in France, married a native American of English stock. His conclusion about the new nation-state? "Here individuals of all nations are melted into a new race of men. . . ."[36]

Emerson, appalled by the anti–Irish Catholic feelings of his fellow New Englanders, entered the following protest in his journal: "I hate the narrowness of the Native American Party. It is the dog in the manger. It is precisely opposite to all the dictates of love and magnanimity, and therefore, of course, opposite to true wisdom." Then, in a soaring passage that surpassed Crèvecoeur's apostrophe to intermarriage, the Transcendentalist declared:

Man is the most composite of all creatures. . . . As in the old burning of the Temple at Corinth, by the melting and intermixture of silver and gold and other metals a new compound more precious than any, called the Corinthian brass, was formed; so in this continent, — asylum of all nations — the energy of Irish, Germans, Swedes, Poles, and Cossacks, and all the European tribes — of the Africans, and of the Polynesians — will construct a new race, a new religion, a new state, a new literature, which will be as vigorous as the new Europe which came out of the smelting-pot of the Dark Ages, or that which earlier emerged from . . . barbarism. *La Nature aime les croisements.* [37]

For some thirty-five years until his retirement in 1924, Professor Frederick Jackson Turner taught that "the evolution of a composite nationality" was basic to understanding American history. First at the University of Wisconsin and then at Harvard, he emphasized the role of the frontier in that development. The most famous of his essays (1893), whose major ideas he repeated in the next three decades, maintained: "In the crucible of the frontier, the immigrants were Americanized, liberated, and fused into a mixed race, English in neither nationality nor characteristics." [38]

Theodore Roosevelt, in a history of the West that Turner reviewed, had made a similar point in 1889:

it is well always to remember that at the day when we began our career as a nation we already differed from our kinsmen of Britain in blood as well as in name. . . . The modern Englishman is descended from a Low-Dutch stock, which, when it went to Britain, received into itself an enormous infusion of Celtic, a much smaller infusion of Norse and Danish, and also a certain infusion of Norman-French blood. When this new English stock came to America it mingled with and absorbed into itself immigrants from many European lands, and the process has gone on ever since.

Proud of his own mixed ancestry, Roosevelt later said: "We Americans are the children of the crucible." He was delighted to have the author of *The Melting-Pot* dedicate his book to him. [39]

Clearly, Zangwill was correct in thinking that there had been support for the melting-pot concept well before he put it into dramatic form. But we must distinguish between the normative and descriptive parts of that concept. Like Emerson before him, Zangwill celebrated a process that he thought Americans ought to encourage. Roosevelt and Turner and Crèvecoeur, in contrast, not only praised the amalgamation but believed it to be a widespread reality.

Did the evidence support them?

The absence of eighteenth-century statistics makes it impossible to determine just how much intermarriage took place in Crèvecoeur's America. Yet, on the basis of what his contemporaries wrote about New England, New York, Pennsylvania, South Carolina, and the Southern backcountry, it seems to have been more customary than not for persons of different ethnic groups to marry their respective sort. Actually, in scattered passages of his own writing, Crèvecoeur made that observation of English, Scottish, Dutch, Swedish, and French communities with which he was familiar. The most careful history of the subject thus far concluded: "In the late eighteenth century the idea that the 'American' was a 'new man' by reason of physical amalgamation was the exceptional opinion of a romantic French immigrant."[40]

Ralph Waldo Emerson did not confuse his personal preference with the conditions he saw around him. Until the large migration from Ireland after 1845, Bostonians formed the most homogeneously English-derived population of any large American city. A generation later, according to statistics compiled at the time, the Catholic newcomers had a lower rate of intermarriage than even the city's few blacks. The Irish and the host people clashed for social and intellectual as well as religious reasons; and the resulting divide reinforced in both groups "the natural tendency to mate with their own kind."[41]

That practice lasted well beyond the initial Yankee-Irish confrontation. The first Catholic President of the United States, whose paternal great-grandfather made the immigrant crossing in 1850, was a fourth-generation Bostonian of unmixed Irish descent. In contrast to Theodore Roosevelt's devotion to the crucible, John Fitzgerald Kennedy summed up his understanding of America in a book by the title of *A Nation of Immigrants*.

Turner and Roosevelt asserted that new western areas had been much more hospitable to the fusing process than old eastern cities. But neither man offered supporting evidence, and a quarter century after Turner's death in 1932, the interpretation failed "objective tests" of a computer-based history of a frontier community in Trempealeau, Wisconsin. Its population consisted of native Americans from eastern states and of immigrants and their descendants from Germany, Norway, Poland, Bohemia, Scotland, Switzerland, Ireland, and England. Except for the last named, who *seem* immediately to have merged with the native Americans, the others settled among their own kind and established their separate churches, festivals, clubs, games, stores, and the like. The press took such diversity for granted in reporting the county's news.

At the end of the thirty-year period examined (1850–1880), Trempealeau's ethnic groups had yet to form a common religious, social, and cultural life. This was contrary to the Turner-Roosevelt thesis, as was the rate of intermarriage. In 1880 an overwhelming majority were still choosing mates from their group. By that criterion, "the melting pot in Trempealeau worked slowly in the early years. . . ."[42]

Actually, Trempealeau County was very much like Turner's own Portage, Wisconsin, where he was born in 1861 and grew up. The population, divided equally between the native- and foreign-born, was a mosaic rather than an amalgamation of different ethnic groups. Turner himself, in a reminiscent mood shortly before he retired from Harvard, described the Portage of his youth as

a mixture of raftsmen from the "pineries," — (the "pinery road" ran by my door), of Irish (in the "bloody first" ward), Pomeranian immigrants (we stoned each other), in old country garbs, driving their cows to their own "Common," of Scotch with "Caledonia" near by; of Welsh (with "Cambria" adjacent); with Germans some of them university-trained (the Bierhall of Carl Haertel was the town club house); of Yankees from Vermont and Maine and Conn. Chiefly, of New York–Yankees, of Southerners (a few relatively); a few negroes; many Norwegians and Swiss, some Englishmen, and one or two Italians. As a local editor and leader of his party, my father reported the community life . . . harmonized the rival tongues and interests of the various towns of the county, and helped to shepherd a very composite flock. My school fellows were from all these varied classes and nationalities, and we all "got on together" in this forming . . . society . . .

It remains to be said that the frontier historian married a Midwesterner of his own New England origins.[43]

But Turner's Portage and the then contemporary Trempealeau — as well as the Boston of John Kennedy's forebears — belonged to the era of unrestricted immigration. And here we must return to Israel Zangwill, whose death coincided with the end of that era. To what extent did the amalgamationist ideal persist in the next half century? To what degree was it realized? Both questions require qualified answers. Not only have Americans held ambivalent attitudes toward mixed marriage; the data for such unions in the last fifty years are so fragmentary and elusive that we do not have a full picture of what went on.

This much can be said, however, with reasonable certainty. First, the ideal lived on, as evidenced by the popularity of *Abie's Irish Rose* (the play broke all pre-1930s box-office records) and of subsequent movies, novels, and television shows treating the same theme. Second, sociological studies reveal that the descendants of immigrants intermarried much more frequently than did the foreign-born. Third, the most common form of such unions took place within the ancestral religion, so much so that in the 1940s scholars referred to the emergence of a "triple melting-pot," one each for Protestants, Catholics, and Jews. Fourth, since World War II it has been by no means unusual for persons to marry outside the faith. This last applies even to Jews, who, at the beginning of the twentieth century, had the lowest rate of intermarriage of immigrant groups from Europe.

It is therefore incorrect to state flatly, as some writers have, that the melting pot never happened. Millions of Americans of mixed ancestry know otherwise. Intermarriage did occur, and is still occurring, and anyone who doubts it has only to look around. Indeed, the phenomenon's sharp increase among Jews since the early 1960s has caused some Jewish leaders to fear for the group's survival.[44]

But if applicable to many individuals, the melting pot is an inappropriate label for American society. It denies the legitimacy, and value, of ethnic groups. It underestimates the strength of family, religious, ethnic, and racial constraints against intermarriage. It deprecates the right to marry inside as well as outside the group. Were mixed ancestry the sole measure, a Theodore Roosevelt, but not a John Kennedy, would be an admissible American type.

Not even in its own terms does the amalgamationist credo stand up. Zangwill assumed that a single stock would issue from mixed marriage beds, but experience proved otherwise. The unions between Irish Catholics and German Catholics, or between Swedish Lutherans and Yankee Congregationalists, or between Russian and German Jews — plus all other combinations — have added further variations to the American population mix.

But the melting-pot metaphor had always meant more than intermarriage, and after Zangwill's death it increasingly signified homogenization through institutions. The school was held to be the most important. Typically, in a 1927 presidential address to the National Education Association, the Illinois superintendent of public instruction said: "The great American school system is the very pit of this melting pot. Here the ancient foreign prejudices are melted out of the youth and the best that was brought and the best that is here are fused together." Forty years later a widely adopted American history textbook claimed that, as a result of educational and other institutions, by "the middle of the twentieth century the melting process was astonishingly complete."[45]

At the same time, though, Americans also invoked the melting pot as a symbol of diversity. That had not been Zangwill's major emphasis; he was less interested in what went into the crucible than in what came out of it. Still, he did stress its varied ingredients, and it was not uncommon after 1950 for historians to refer to the melting pot solely in that way. Similarly, in the post–World War II struggle to remove Anglo-Saxon biases from the immigration laws, reformers equated the melting pot with America's original policy of welcome to strangers from everywhere.[46]

The laws were no sooner repealed in the mid-1960s than self-called "unmeltable ethnics" denounced the melting-pot concept as "genocidal." Aside from mistaking Zangwill's phrase for an Anglo-Saxon invention, the opponents won their point, as evidenced by the passage of the Ethnic Heritage Studies Programs Act of 1972. Officially, the United States is not, nor ought it to be, a melting pot. And there, at present, the matter rests.

Notes

1. Eric Hoffer, *First Things, Last Things* (New York: Harper, 1971), p. 102. See also Eric Hoffer, *The Temper of Our Time* (New York: Harper, 1967).
2. Israel Zangwill, *The Melting-Pot: Drama in Four Acts* (New York: Macmillan, 1909), pp. 198–200.
3. Mrs. Zangwill of course liked Roosevelt's praise, but she thought very poorly of his taste in general. His reaction to *The Melting-Pot* "is encouraging from a box office standpoint," she wrote to a friend, "because I always feel that Roosevelt is a glorified man in the street, a . . . commonplace person raised to the *nth* power and what would appeal to him would also be likely to appeal to the masses. Among other things Roosevelt said to me," she went on to say, " 'I'm not a Bernard Shaw man or an Ibsen man, Mrs. Zangwill. No, *this* is the stuff.' Poor Israel. I had to repeat it to him to keep him humble. Not that the Shaw contrast matters but I thought everyone recognized Ibsen as a great genius." Edith Zangwill to Mrs. Yorke, Oct. 7, 1908, Annie Russell Papers, New York Public Library.
4. Roosevelt to Zangwill, October 15, 1908. Theodore Roosevelt, *Letters of Theodore Roosevelt,* edited by Elting E. Morison, 8 vols. (Cambridge, Mass.: Harvard University Press, 1951–1954), VI, 1289.
5. There is an enormous amount of material about Zangwill's play, consisting of reviews, advertisements, and playbills, in the Robinson Locke Collection of Dramatic Scrapbooks and the Walker Whiteside Collection, Theater Collection, New York Public Library, Astor, Lenox and Tilden Foundations. Also see Walter Rigdon, ed., *The Biographical Encyclopaedia and Who's Who of the American Theatre* (New York: Heineman, 1966), p. 31. For sales figures of *The Melting-Pot,* see enclosure in Zangwill to Brett, June 16, 1921, Macmillan Company Records, New York Public Library. The quotation from the Connecticut teacher is in Israel Zangwill, *The War for the World* (New York, 1916), p. 37.
6. Israel Zangwill, *The War God* (New York, 1912), p. 47.
7. Quoted in Maurice Wohlgelernter, *Israel Zangwill: A Study* (New York: Columbia University Press, 1964), p. 195.
8. For biographical details, I have relied on Wohlgelernter's *Zangwill* and Joseph Leftwich's *Israel Zangwill* (New York: Yoseloff, 1957), both full of useful information and insight.
9. *New York Herald,* Nov. 6, 1904.
10. Israel Zangwill, *The Next Religion* (New York, 1912); Wohlgelernter, *Zangwill,* p. 25.
11. Israel Zangwill, *Dreamers of the Ghetto* (New York and London, 1898), pp. 289–429. The preceding quotations are to be found in Wohlgelernter, *Zangwill,* p. v; Barnet Litvinoff, "Zangwill's Ghetto Is No More," *Commentary,* X (Oct. 1950), 363.
12. Israel Zangwill, "The East Africa Offer," in Maurice Simon, ed., *Speeches, Articles, and Letters of Israel Zangwill* (London: Soncino, 1937), pp. 226–227. For Zangwill's activities in the Zionist movement, see Wohlgelernter, *Zangwill,* pp. 38–40.
13. For a superb analysis of the Dillingham Commission, see Oscar Handlin, "Concerning

the Background of the National-Origin Quota System," in President's Commission on Immigration and Naturalization, *Hearings* (Washington, D.C.: Government Printing Office, 1952), pp. 1839–1863.

14. Henry James, *The American Scene,* edited by Leon Edel (London, 1907; reprinted, Bloomington, Ind.: Indiana University Press, 1968), pp. 84–87, 118–120, 125, 132, 139, 195, 199, 206, 245, 265, 454–455.
15. H. G. Wells, *The Future in America: A Search after Realities* (New York, 1906), pp. 71–77, 119–120, 133–151, and *passim.*
16. James, *American Scene,* p. 64.
17. "Zangwill," *Literary Digest,* XC (Aug. 21, 1926), 33.
18. Cf. Philip Gleason, "The Melting Pot: Symbol of Fusion or Confusion?" *American Quarterly,* XVI (Spring 1964), 20–46.
19. For the quarrel between Zangwill and his English critics, see John Palmer, "The Melting-Pot," *Saturday Review* CXVII (May 16, 1914), 628; Zangwill, *War for the World,* p. 33; Israel Zangwill, Afterword to *The Melting-Pot* (New York, 1914), pp. 198–199.
20. The quotations, in the order of their appearance, are in Burns Mantle, *Chicago Tribune,* Oct. 20, 1908; "Mr. Zangwill's New Dramatic Gospel," *Current Literature,* XLV (Dec. 1908), 671, 673; *English Review* XVII (Apr. 1914), 132; *Athenaeum,* no. 4501 (Jan. 31, 1914), p. 171.
21. *New York Daily Tribune,* Dec. 8, 1909.
22. Holbrook Jackson, "Israel Zangwill," *Living Age* CCLXXXII (Sept. 26, 1914), 795; Zangwill, Afterword, p. 208; *Athenaeum,* no. 4501, p. 171.
23. *American Magazine,* LXIX (Jan. 1910), 411.
24. *Independent,* LXVII (Oct. 21, 1909), 931–932.
25. Zangwill, *The Melting-Pot,* p. 91.
26. Roosevelt wrote a good deal about the subject of immigration over a long period of time, without changing his mind about the dangers of "hyphenated Americanism." See, for example, *The Works of Theodore Roosevelt,* edited by Hermann Hagedorn, 20 vols. (New York, 1926), XIII, 13–26; XIV, 192–207; XVIII, 278–294, 371–376, 388–405. On Jane Addams's attitudes toward pluralist Chicago, see Steven J. Diner's insightful essay, "Chicago Social Workers and Blacks in the Progressive Era," *Social Service Review,* XLIV (Dec. 1970), 393–410. For the relationship between Addams's domestic pluralism and her internationalism, see John C. Farrell, *Beloved Lady: A History of Jane Addams' Ideas on Reform and Peace* (Baltimore: Johns Hopkins Press, 1967).
27. Clayton Hamilton, "The Melting-Pot," *Forum* XLII (Nov. 1909), 434–435.
28. Quoted in "Mr. Zangwill's New Dramatic Gospel," *Current Literature,* XLV, 672. Even Reform rabbis, who, since the Pittsburgh Platform of the mid-1880s, had taken the position that Jews were not a people but a religious denomination, officially disapproved (in 1908 and 1909) of intermarriage as "contrary . . . to the Jewish religion. . . ." See David Philipson, "The Central Conference of American Rabbis, 1889–1939," in *American Jewish Year Book 5701* (Philadelphia: Jewish Publication Society, 1940), pp. 205–206. For the dismissal of Reform rabbis who, among other things, preached intermarriage, see Arthur Mann, ed., *Growth and Achievement: Temple Israel 1854–1954* (Cambridge, Mass., 1954), pp. 45–83.
29. Zangwill, Afterword, p. 208.
30. *Ibid.,* p. 207; Zangwill, *War for the World,* p. 39.
31. Zangwill, *The Melting-Pot,* pp. 37–38.
32. Zangwill, Afterword, pp. 210, 213.
33. "Zangwill," *Literary Digest,* XC, 33. *New York Times,* Aug. 2, 1926; Edward Price Bell, "Creed of the Klansmen, Interviews with H. W. Evans, Israel Zangwill . . . ," *Chicago Daily News Reprints* (1924), p. 11; Zangwill, "A Few Reflections: Is America Forsaking the Ideals of Her Founders?" in Simon, *Speeches,* pp. 106–112.
34. *New York Times,* Aug. 3, 1926.
35. Quoted in "Zangwill," *Literary Digest,* XC, 33.
36. J. Hector St. John de Crèvecoeur, *Letters from an American Farmer* (London, 1782; reprinted, New York, 1904), pp. 54–55.

37. Ralph Waldo Emerson, *Journals of Ralph Waldo Emerson*, edited by Edward Waldo Emerson and Waldo Emerson Forbes, 10 vols. (Boston, 1909–1914), VII, 115–116.

38. Frederick Jackson Turner, *The Frontier in American History* (New York, 1920), pp. 22–23.

39. Theodore Roosevelt, *The Winning of the West*, 4 vols. (New York, 1889–1896), I, 20; Theodore Roosevelt, *The Foes of Our Own Household* (New York, 1917), p. 58.

40. Winthrop D. Jordan, *White over Black: American Attitudes toward the Negro, 1550–1812* (Chapel Hill: University of North Carolina Press, 1968), p. 337. Cf. Carl Bridenbaugh, *Myths and Realities: Societies of the Colonial South* (Baton Rouge: Louisiana State University Press, 1952), p. 134: "We surely err," Professor Bridenbaugh writes, ". . . if we apply the concept of the *melting pot* to the Back Settlements, which, to choose a Biblical metaphor all its inhabitants would have readily understood, much more accurately resembled the Tower of Babel. Fate designated the Back Settlements as the scene of cultural conflict for many decades." For Crèvecoeur's own writings on unmelted ethnic communities, see his *Letters from an American Farmer*, p. 51, and his *Journey into Northern Pennsylvania and the State of New York*, translated by Clarissa S. Bostelmann (Paris, 1801; reprinted, Ann Arbor: University of Michigan Press, 1964), pp. 31–41, 90–100, 253, 323–324, 344–359, 427–442, 458–460, 502, 527, 563. This latter view, namely, on the persistence of ethnicity, is corroborated by William Winterbotham, *An Historical, Geographical, Commercial and Philosophical View of the United States, and the European Settlements in America and the West Indies*, 4 vols. (London, 1795), II, 437–440; Timothy Dwight, *Travels in New England and New York*, edited by Barbara Miller Solomon, 4 vols. (Cambridge, Mass.: Belknap Press of Harvard University Press, 1969), I, xxxiv–xxxix, 365; III, 322, 329; IV, 327; and David Ramsay, *The History of South-Carolina from Its First Settlement in 1670, to the Year 1808*, 2 vols. (Charleston, 1809), I, 1–25. For an earlier view of multi-ethnic New York than Crèvecoeur's but much the same as Dwight's later view, see Peter Kalm, *Travels into North America* (London, 1771–1772); I have used the most recent American edition, *Peter Kalm's Travels in North America*, edited by Adolph B. Benson, 2 vols. (New York: Wilson-Erickson, 1937), I, 115–143.

41. Oscar Handlin, *Boston's Immigrants, 1790–1865: A Study in Acculturation* (Cambridge, Mass.: Harvard University Press, 1941), pp. 182–183.

42. Merle Curti, *The Making of an American Community: A Case Study of Democracy in a Frontier County* (Stanford: Stanford University Press, 1959), pp. 99–105, 444.

43. For Turner's ancestry, see Ray Allen Billington, *Frederick Jackson Turner: Historian, Scholar, Teacher* (New York: Oxford University Press, 1973), pp. 3–5. The quotation about Portage, Wisconsin, can be found in Edward N. Saveth, *American Historians and European Immigrants, 1875–1925* (New York: Columbia University Press, 1948), p. 123.

44. There is now a considerable but nevertheless inconclusive and sometimes contradictory literature about the rates, variables, and patterns of intermarriage in the United States for this century. See, for example, the best and most recent compendium of its sort, Milton L. Barron, ed., *The Blending American: Patterns of Intermarriage* (Chicago: Quadrangle, 1972). Compare it to the pioneering work of Julius Drachsler, *Intermarriage in New York City: A Statistical Study of the Amalgamation of European Peoples* (New York, 1921). Advocates of the "triple melting-pot" theory include: Ruby Jo Reeves Kennedy, "Single or Triple Melting-Pot? Intermarriage Trends in New Haven, 1870–1940," *American Journal of Sociology*, XLIX (Jan. 1944), 331–339; Kennedy, "Single or Triple Melting-Pot? Intermarriage Trends in New Haven, 1870–1950," *ibid.*, LVIII (July 1952), 56–59; Milton L. Barron, *People Who Intermarry: Intermarriage in a New England Industrial Community* (Syracuse: Syracuse University Press, 1946), pp. 342–344 and *passim;* Will Herberg, *Catholic, Protestant, Jew: An Essay in American Religious Sociology* (New York: Doubleday, 1955), pp. 18–58. Comparative rates of religious intermarriage for the 1950s can be gleaned from U.S. Bureau of the Census, "Religion Reported by the Civilian Population of the United States: March, 1957," *Current Population Reports*, series P-20, no. 79, Feb. 2, 1958, p. 8. For the rising rates of intermarriage between Jews and non-Jews, and the concern of Jewish leaders over that phenomenon, see Erich Rosenthal, "Studies of Jewish Intermarriage in the United

States," *American Jewish Year Book 1963* (Philadelphia: Jewish Publication Society, 1963), pp. 3–53; Rosenthal, "Jewish Intermarriage in Indiana," *American Jewish Year Book 1967* (Philadelphia: Jewish Publication Society, 1967), pp. 243–264; Werner J. Cahnman, ed., *Intermarriage and Jewish Life: A Symposium* (New York: Herzl Press, 1963); Albert I. Gordon, *Intermarriage: Interfaith, Interracial, Interethnic* (Boston: Beacon Press, 1964); Louis A. Berman, *Jews and Intermarriage: A Study in Personality and Culture* (New York: Yoseloff, 1968); Fred Massarik and Alvin Chenkin, "United States National Jewish Population Study," *American Jewish Year Book 1973* (Philadelphia: Jewish Publication Society, 1973), pp. 292–306.

45. Francis G. Blair, "American Melting Pot," *Proceedings of the National Education Association of the United States,* LXV (1927), 34; Arthur S. Link, *The Growth of American Democracy* (Boston: Ginn, 1968), p. 414.

46. For the melting pot as a symbol of diversity and welcome, see Oscar Handlin, *The American People in the Twentieth Century* (Cambridge, Mass.: Harvard University Press, 1954), p. 161; Arthur Mann, *La Guardia: A Fighter against His Times, 1882–1933* (Philadelphia: Lippincott, 1959); John R. Alden, *Rise of the American Republic* (New York: Harper, 1963), pp. 507–508; Neil Larry Shumsky, "Zangwill's *The Melting Pot:* Ethnic Tensions on Stage," *American Quarterly* XXVII (Mar. 1975), 29–41; "Code for the Melting Pot," *Time,* LIX (June·2, 1952), 16; "No More Melting Pot," *New Republic,* CXXVII (July 7, 1952), 8; Meg Greenfield, "Melting Pot of Francis E. Walter," *Reporter,* XXV (Oct. 26, 1961), 24–28; "New Mix for America's Melting Pot," *U.S. News and World Report,* LIX (Oct. 11, 1965), 55–57.

Marcus Lee Hansen: America's First Transethnic Historian

Moses Rischin

Moses Rischin is professor of history at San Francisco State University and currently president of the Immigration History Society. He is the author of *The Promised City: New York's Jews, 1870–1914* (1962), and editor of *The American Gospel of Success* (1968) and *Immigration and the American Tradition* (1976).

IN A WORLD IN FLUX, the historian must strike a balance between change and tradition. The historian of American immigration and culture particularly sits poised on the knife's edge, seeking universal categories of analysis and understanding while immersing himself in a loving study of distinct peoples, places, and ways of life in disarray. He is the boomer engineer committed to democracy and equality, progress and growth, mobility and technology, science and medicine, individualism and freedom. But he is also the artist, priest, and guardian of culture, the admirer of fragile arts and crafts and tastes perfected over generations, of customs, traditions and folkways that afford people quiet content, of obsolescent manners, civilities, persons, and things that please. He is both a modern American and many others, perennially at odds with his varied personae. He is of necessity divided between his commitment to the promise of the great society and a concern for the identities of all its components. An understanding of the emergence during World War I of America's first transethnic historian should contribute to our comprehension of Marcus Hansen as a precursor to Oscar Handlin, both as a historian and as an American shaped by historical circumstances that have made for the internationalization of American history.

Few historians have become so powerfully identified with a

grand theme and the lonely pioneering of that theme as has Marcus Lee Hansen (1892–1938).[1] He was the first and only American historian between the two world wars to conceptualize, legitimate, and give stature and universality to the ethnic dimension in American life, at least in its European aspects. The works of Hansen's distinguished contemporaries Theodore Blegen, George Stephenson, and Carl Wittke are undeniably impressive but lack the broad sweep and overarching vision that made immigration as a process the common experience of all Americans from the earliest comers to the latest arrivals. Hansen, on the other hand, found in the inspiring myth of immigration both a common denominator and a strategy to unite an ethnically fragmented and divided nation in need of an epic that would celebrate the pan-European, if not quite the pan-ethnic, origins of the American people. Hansen's premature death, the posthumous publication of his major works, and his association with a rural midwestern Turnerian tradition in eclipse have tended to shroud in elegy the full significance and originality of the nation's first transethnic historian.

Hansen's ambition to integrate the diverse stories of Whitman's nation of nations into a saga of North Atlantic civilization without betraying the integrity of any of its parts fell tragically short of its aim. But the ardor and integrity of his quest and the conditions surrounding his emergence as the pioneer historian of immigration have much to tell us about our own compelling need to take the measure of our ever-changing, multi-ethnic nation and world, where common modes of discourse are essential.

Hansen's scholarly reputation has been based essentially on two books, *The Atlantic Migration,* more accurately the North Atlantic migration, and *The Mingling of the Canadian and American Peoples.* Remarkable in their sweep, both portray primarily the emigration process with but incidental attention to the complexities of settlement and acculturation. Aptly called the internationalizer of the Turnerian tradition, Hansen was a proud disciple of America's most influential historian. Like his mentor he was a student of history's silent social forces. From the outset of his career Hansen was committed to the study of the significance of immigration to the United States, as related to the "universal phenomenon" in the total context of Europe's development. "This is the story to be told forgetting European political boundaries and dealing with man in his economic and geographic relations," asserted Hansen in 1924, in the year of decisive immigration-restriction legislation, in the introduction to his doctoral dissertation, "Emigration from Continental Europe, 1815–1860, with Special Reference to the United States."[2] The perhaps unintended epigrammatic turn of title may have troubled Turnerians. But Hansen's commitment to the study of immigration in "relation to the universal phenomenon" at least left no doubt as to Hansen's American destination.

There was also the other Hansen, the brooding cultural historian whose voice was slower to find its pitch. This Hansen was as fully concerned with immigrants as bearers of European culture as with the process of emigration itself, with the ongoing texture of American life as much as with its social dynamics, with the contemporary scene as much as with the records of the past. Continually Hansen counterpointed his study of the immigration process with imaginative probings into the relations between immigrant and American cultures. His pathbreaking article of 1927, "The History of American Immigration As a Field for Research," reflected the breadth if not quite the depth of his cultural perceptions, and contains many suggestions that are still fresh and worth pursuing a half century later. In 1929 in the newly launched *New England Quarterly*, he adventurously glided across three centuries as he sketched the cultural implications of "The Second Colonization of New England," confidently projecting for that historic region a second flowering inspired by the later immigrants after the period of gestation had run its course.[3] In 1934, an invitation to deliver a series of lectures at the University of London spurred Hansen to put his larger views of American culture into organized form. The results, entitled "The Influence of Nineteenth Century Immigration upon American History," published in part in *The Immigrant in American History*, boldly explored a series of themes that touched both directly and indirectly on the cultural impact of immigrants upon America. In a particularly daring lecture in what might be called comparative regional history, Hansen attempted to demonstrate how New England, the South, and the Scandinavian Midwest became linked in an alliance that culminated in Prohibition. "Immigration and Puritanism" brilliantly displayed a range that he was only beginning to find, that his successors have failed to pursue, and that might have developed into an original full-scale interpretation of nineteenth-century American culture.[4]

A historian of varied interests and abilities, Hansen was an advocate and evangelist, as well as a brilliant research scholar of immigration history. At his death he was just emerging as a national spokesman and interpreter of the larger meaning and implications of immigration for American culture and life. "I do have in me a streak for what is called 'popular' writing,"[5] confessed Hansen to Turner early in his career. Like Turner, he was committed to the study of American history to better know himself so that he might tell others who they were and might become.

His last two public addresses were superbly interpretative. In these lectures, given in the final year of his life, far more than in his scholarly works, were revealed the drives that animated the essential Hansen. The first of these was Hansen's classic statement "The Problem of the Third Generation Immigrant," read at the annual meeting of the Augustana Historical Society on May 15, 1937. Stressing the phenomenon of third-generation interest in the immigrant past, he pointed to the opportunities for third-generation historical activity and the critical obligation to pursue them.[6] His unfinished and little-known second address followed just ten days later in Indianapolis. There at a session of the National Conference of Social Work jointly sponsored by ten national organizations devoted to immigrant welfare, Hansen spoke to the grand theme "Who Shall Inherit America?" In what in effect was his farewell address, he confessed that his interest in the immigrants of the nineteenth century was not primarily in their search for work and land, the dominant theme of his great book *The Atlantic Migration,* but "in their unconscious character as the carriers of culture from an old world to a new."[7] For the first time he lectured before an audience of social activists eager for a prophetic look ahead rather than a documented glance backward. Obviously moved by the occasion, the University of Illinois historian cast scholarly restraint aside. In no uncertain terms, he proceeded to indict the social policy of the United States for failing to seize the unique cultural opportunity extended to the new American nation by the varied immigrant cultures brought to it in the course of the great migration.

The United States, almost alone among new nations, has had offered to it the manysided culture of a continent but in its social policy it has scorned to take any but that represented by a small part of the old world from which its people come. Is it any wonder that for over a century observers have deplored the uniformity of the American cultural scene and have commented on the pioneer drabness that characterizes towns and cities, men and women? It is easy to explain it . . . by saying that Americans have been so busy taming a wild continent that there has been no energy or ingenuity left for other pursuits. The truth is, they made a blunder when consciously or unconsciously they decreed that one literature, one attitude toward the arts, one set of standards should be the basis of culture.[8]

More precisely, based on "scanty historical study," Hansen conceded, he outlined a pattern of "ruthless" Americanization that had foreclosed the possibilities for a uniquely variegated national culture. This pattern (he argued tendentiously), much influenced by contemporary Civil War "revisionism," had been set in motion by the Civil War, "which destroyed the Old South" and "in a less obvious way the varied immigrant America of the North" that had crystallized at the mid-century. The Civil War, "the dominant factor in determining what the prevailing concept of 'Americanization' should be," left no place for the perpetuation of a plurality of cultures that might have helped define Americanization in more generous terms. That "interlude in the normal development of the continent," as Hansen, echoing Turner, described the Civil War elsewhere, was a disaster for all future prospects for genuine cultural diversity. The subsequent tides of immigration, noted Hansen, renewed and fortified the immigrant subcultures. At times there appeared some hope "that succeeding generations of Americans would inherit some of the less material and inspiring features of the civilization that they represented. . . ." But a series of catastrophes beginning with the depression of the 1890s and the emergence of a second generation eager "to forget everyone and everything that antedated the moment when the foreign born father first stepped upon American soil" confirmed the American tradition of cultural conformity. World War I ratified that impulse with a vengeance for the second generation of later immigrants and dealt a mortal blow to a prestigious German-American culture that succumbed to the ravages of superpatriotism and intolerance. "Little could be expected to survive the hundred per-centism of that period and apparently little did," the historian dolefully concluded.[9]

Yet, ultimately, Marcus Hansen seemed to hope, the saga of immigration would become in and of itself a force for culture and its renewal in ways not quite foreseeable. "If told as trans-pired . . . the epic of migration can add an ideal to take the place of one of the many that recent decades have shattered," he pledged in closing his Augustana address. But at Indianapolis, he cast out a challenge to the nation as well. "Within the next genera-tion, the United States will decide what it wants to accept and what it wants to reject. That is the next problem of immigration that the nation must solve." Three years later, his three major works rolled off the Harvard and Yale university presses almost simulta-neously. Monuments to Hansen's all too brief career, they ap-peared, ironically, just as again a world war rang down the pos-sibilities for a reaffirmation and renewal of the nation's multicul-tural heritage. By then even Hansen's innocuous suggestion in his 1927 article that Carl Schurz's career as a German-American was more important than his role as an American statesman proved unseemly and was deleted when the article was reprinted in *The Immigrant in American History*.[10] For the third time, what might be called Hansen's Second Law, the principle of war and catastrophe, had come to nullify Hansen's First Law, the principle of third-generation interest in the immigrant past.

What combination of forces had nurtured Marcus Lee Hansen? In the years between the two world wars, Hansen, it would ap-pear, had occupied a unique vantage point from which to view the immigration story and the total American cultural scene. In a nation of highly visible ethnics, his ethnic identity proved an un-usually fecund source for creative scholarship. A self-conscious Scandinavian-American, he shared actively in the coming of age of American Scandinavia. It was he who informed fellow Scan-dinavian-Americans in his Augustana address, without detailing all the reasons, that after three generations of American living it was inevitable that they should have virtually co-opted the first generation of immigration historians. Protestant, Nordic, and midwestern, they inhabited and gave a tone to the outer prairies which evoked a lyric vision of a lost nineteenth-century agrarian America. Indeed, to self-conscious New Englanders, Scandina-

vian-Americans appeared far more akin to their own heroic
Puritan ancestors than did they, their bloodline descendants. To
the enthusiastic young Brahmin historian Samuel Eliot Morison,
Ole Rolvaag's Beret was indisputably a latter-day Anne
Bradstreet. Coming from nations that had been neutral if not
impartial during World War I, Scandinavian-Americans remained relatively unscarred by the war and its aftermath. By
contrast, other major ethnic groups continued to live in the long
shadow of war guilt, revolution, and imputed racial and cultural
inferiority; soon they would even become connected in the popular mind with totalitarian, dictatorial, and other un-American
governments that had come to rule their countries of origin.
Furthermore, Scandinavian-Americans, long identified with cog-
nate political and cultural traditions, were coming to be associated
with a new Scandinavia of northern Europe, immune from the
turmoil of the Continent and apparently able to balance change
and tradition with rare good sense.

For half a century, Norway, Sweden, and Denmark had been
divorced from power politics. In the aftermath of World War I,
no group of countries championed the League of Nations more
ardently. None was more consistently identified with a keen sense
of human solidarity and with the quest for a moral equivalent of
war. No one better exemplified cosmopolitan humanitarianism
than Fridtjof Nansen, intrepid Arctic explorer, deviser of the international Nansen passport, first high commissioner of refugees
for the League of Nations, and the recipient in 1922 of the Nobel
Prize for peace. Perhaps it was more than coincidence that 1927,
the year of the publication of Hansen's seminal article "The History of American Immigration As a Field for Research," saw Ole
Rolvaag's immigrant epic of the prairies, "the climax of a literary
tradition that began in the 1870's," Dorothy B. Skårdall reminds
us, attain bestsellerdom and saw a nonstop flight from New York
to Paris turn twenty-five-year-old Charles Lindbergh into an instant American symbol and popular idol, the pioneer of a new
epic in transatlantic migration, the prairie Viking become lone
eagle.[11]

For Americans of Scandinavian origin, past, present, and future appeared to have fallen into place. For them, Americanness
and Scandinavianness had attained an enviable harmony that
reflected a moral equilibrium and international poise denied most

of their hyphenated and unhyphenated contemporaries. The University of Minnesota, at the heart of American Scandinavia, seemed to be the only major institution of higher learning in the country able to provide a setting for immigration scholars that blended unobtrusively into the surrounding region and that summoned up a sense of community rather than of conflict, of shared frontiers rather than divided worlds. There, Scandinavian-American historians Theodore Blegen, George Stephenson, and others could draw on a hospitable milieu where their research and teaching enhanced rather than compromised their American identity. Indeed in 1926, Stephenson became the first historian to undertake a general survey of American immigration. Following an opening chapter analyzing the causes of emigration from the United Kingdom, Stephenson chose to portray the Scandinavians in the following chapter and then proceeded to depict the other ethnic strains. "It is the opinion of a competent Swedish observer that the establishment of Swedish-America is the greatest and most significant accomplishment of the Swedish people," Stephenson exulted.[12]

No son of Scandinavia was better outfitted for a rediscovery of America and a reinterpretation of its history from the perspective of immigration than was Marcus Lee Hansen. The rising status of Scandinavian-Americans and their heightened American self-consciousness combined to crystallize the impulse to find profound fulfillment in the telling of the saga of the American Canaan. But unlike Minnesota's immigrant historians and others who became primarily ethnic and grass-roots historians, Marcus Hansen aimed from the first to encompass the total immigration epic. "It differs from other studies," he noted in the opening lines of his doctoral dissertation, "in being a flank instead of a direct attack upon the problem; instead of studying emigration, as such, it investigates the economic, social and political environment in which the movement operated that its fullest significance may be appraised. . . ." Hansen showed little patience for scholars differently inclined. "The student of American history is not interested primarily in nationalities," he admonished fellow Scandinavians who limited their researches to single countries. Hansen, unlike most of them, was not closely associated with the major immigrating Scandinavian nationalities, the Lutheran churches, or a state where Scandinavian-Americans could aspire to hegemony.

Scandinavian-American colleagues did not recall hearing him speak the Scandinavian tongues, and even suspected that others had aided him in researching Scandinavian sources.[13] Deliberately, Hansen did not publish a single article in his lifetime that focused on Scandinavian America. He was one of them but not quite one of them.

From his parents, particularly his father, the historian acquired a combination of traits that must have profoundly conditioned his image of himself, his psychology, and his goals. When the senior Markus Hansen migrated to the United States from Langeland in 1871 at age twenty, America was the promised land. Scandinavian immigrants especially were welcomed by prairie-state boards of immigration, which proclaimed in most of the languages of northern Europe the agrarian and domestic virtues of their commonwealths. The highly individualistic elder Hansen was determined to start afresh and to become a new-world Christian. But unlike so many of his Danish fellow-countrymen in rebellion against the staid church establishment of their homeland, he did not turn to the new Zion of the West, the Church of Jesus Christ of Latter-Day Saints. Instead of becoming a Mormon, the elder Hansen became a Baptist, trained for the ministry, and devoted his life to founding Baptist churches for Danish and Norwegian immigrants throughout the prairie West. On two occasions, as family lore had it, the pioneer minister's career was nearly terminated. Just before Mark's birth, a Dakota blizzard almost wiped out the Hansen family. Somewhat earlier, apparently, in Centerville, Iowa, a young Norwegian newcomer caught pneumonia from the rigors of a wintry baptism. After her death, the elder Hansen was hanged in effigy, barely escaping with his life. Young Mark, the sixth of seven children and his father's namesake, was conditioned early to view the whole Midwest as the hub of his universe. In 1929 in a letter to Turner, Hansen paid homage to his America with the characteristic ardor of a second-generation American. The pre–Civil War society of the Northwest was "the foundation of our present day American Civilization," he rejoiced, "because it certainly moved West, it is moving East, and from the little I know about the contemporary South, I believe it is not a stranger there."[14]

The education of young Hansen proceeded by stages that exposed him to the full range of Western civilization. As the historian would later insist, based on his own rich experience, the Midwest was as close to European culture as was the East. Home, school, and college, the University of Iowa and Harvard — each in turn were to contribute to his growth. In the multicultural Hansen household, Danish and Norwegian (his mother was a native of Christiana, subsequently Oslo) shared equal time with English. The Danes, even more readily than other Scandinavians, were noted for rapidly assimilating the language of their adopted land; Danish Baptists especially were passionately committed to bilingualism, if not quite to the trilingualism that was the special Hansen heritage. In the course of attending a series of high schools in Michigan, Illinois, and Minnesota, family, church, and folk culture were augmented with four years of Latin and introductory German along with the usual subjects. Following a brief spell as a schoolteacher, Hansen matriculated in 1912 with his sister, Ruth, and his brother, Clarence, at Central College in Pella, Iowa, a state to which the Hansens had just moved. At this small Baptist college, especially indebted to the early support of H. B. Scholte, the forceful Dutch dissenter and University of Leyden graduate, young Hansen added to his solid school Latin, acquired a grounding in Greek as well, and rounded out his studies in classic and modern Western culture.[15]

With the outbreak of World War I, Hansen's education entered a new phase. Even as he resolved to write the epic of immigration now that it had come to a close, he determined also to become an American-American. At the University of Iowa, he learned to read French and tutored in that language just as he had assisted earlier in Latin at Central College. But his major interest lay in American history, particularly western history. In his two years at Iowa he took no fewer than five courses, equivalent to eighteen units, related to the westward movement: the territorial growth of the United States, the history of the old Northwest, the history of the Louisiana Purchase, the evolution of the western states, and a special one-year seminar on the West, taken with Louis Pelzer, a Turnerian who had not studied with Turner. Upon graduation in 1916, young Hansen was given a special award by the Sons of the American Revolution, Des Moines chapter, for standing first in American history. A graduate year at Iowa completed Hansen's vicarious apprenticeship to Turner, crowned by *Old Fort Snelling:*

1819–1858, his M.A. thesis, a full-length book published the following year by the State Historical Society of Iowa.[16]

To Hansen, *Old Fort Snelling* was more than a work of local history. The oldest fort in the old Northwest, it had become the symbol of his America. At the junction of the Minnesota and Mississippi rivers, Fort Snelling, exulted Hansen, had always flown the Stars and Stripes, had never been taken by a foreign power, had not fired its cannon upon foes, or been besieged by Indians. "Its history was not made by the rifles and sabers of the soldiers," he insisted, and therefore was unique in the history of the nation. "The axe and the plow of the pioneer who worked in safety beneath its potential protection have left their history upon the landscape of the great Northwest." Ironically, Hansen's tribute to the peace symbol of his West appeared in summary in July 1917, in the first issue of *Iowa and War*.[17]

In September 1917, encouraged by Pelzer and the Iowa History Department, Hansen went east to Harvard on a fellowship to study with Frederick Jackson Turner. Nineteen seventeen was a momentous time in the country's history as it was in the lives of both Hansen and Turner. In January, Wilson had called for the establishment of a League of Nations, peace without victory. In February, both houses of Congress passed the literacy-test bill over the President's veto bringing unrestricted immigration to a close. And in April, Congress declared war on Germany, ending a century of American isolation. For Hansen there was a personal turning point as well. In March 1917, the elder Markus Hansen died in Iowa City after forty years of ministering to Danish and Norwegian immigrants. With him departed his son's most intimate tie with the Old World and the era of the great migration, with the New World and the settlement of his West.[18]

The elder Hansen, had he lived on, would not have recognized his promised land. Almost overnight, America had become un-America. Europe's civil war of empires had detonated America's psychic war of ethnics, nakedly dividing the nation along European lines as had no war in its history. All foreign-sounding Americans fell under suspicion. All foreign speakers appeared sinister. All foreign languages seemed subversive. Culture, customs, and the dinner table had become politicized. In May 1918, in Hansen's beloved Iowa, Governor William Harding proclaimed that freedom of speech "guaranteed by federal and state Constitutions" did not guarantee "the right to use a language other than the language of this country." Although the proclamation was modified to permit Danish sermons, Governor Harding's Independence Day message on the subject of language and loyalty singled out the Danes and the widespread use of Danish in schools and churches for special censure. "When they get through, they are full grown, 100 per cent Dane," he was reported to have said. "Now, think of a man who was brought from the filth of Denmark and placed on a farm for which he has paid perhaps $3 an acre. Ye gods and fishes, what Iowa has done for him he never can repay." Danish-American voters registered near total shock. In three heavily Danish-American precincts, the Harding vote went from 252 in 1916 to 25 in 1918, from 55 percent of the ballots to less than 7 percent. There was no doubting that an epoch in American life had come to a close. Assigned to artillery officers' training at Camp Taylor, Kentucky, Hansen, in a letter to his family written one month before the war ended, playfully mocked the predicament of a patriotic man of peace.

I am afraid that being an historian is not conducive to fitting in easily with army traditions. I don't like to look on myself merely as a part of a machine and I guess I don't fit in well — there's something peculiar with my appearance or attitude or something — I don't know what, that, in times of peace is an advantage. Sometime I shall preach a sermon on the parable of the Publican and the Sinner but instead of taking the words of the Sinner for my text I shall take those of the Publican: "I thank God that I am not like other men" and preach a sermon on individuality. . . .[19]

Upon his discharge from the army, Hansen was commissioned by the Iowa State Historical Society to prepare two monographs on welfare campaigns and welfare work for the "Iowa Chronicles of the World War." The occasion gave him the opportunity to bare his dim view of war. "Welfare work," he wrote, "bears a direct relation to the movement for world peace. . . . If war must come it must come alone, stripped of those evil companions — moral and intellectual waste, physical degeneration, and spiritual death." Three years later, in the final passages of his doctoral dissertation, Hansen again felt driven to editorialize darkly on another facet of his lost America. "Visas and three per cents are confusing; compared with a dozen years ago America is indeed almost a forbidden land."[20]

The experiences that stirred young Hansen during the war and its aftermath were matched by the crisis in the life of the nation's leading historian. For the first time since 1893, the historian of the frontier was forced to shift his gaze radically from west to east. Driven to transfer his historical sights from the American heartland to the Europe that long had been his anti-America, Frederick Jackson Turner was stirred to apply the lessons of American history to the Old World with a passion that up to then had eluded him.[21]

More than a quarter of a century earlier at the University of Wisconsin, two young professors, both recent Johns Hopkins Ph.D.'s in American history, had cosponsored a master's dissertation on the sources of German immigration to Wisconsin. Expanded into a doctoral dissertation, it was to be the only study in immigration history supervised by Turner at his alma mater.[22] Subsequently Turner and Charles Haskins, colleagues at Wisconsin and later at Harvard, and lifelong friends, went their opposite scholarly ways, Turner to the study of the West on the wings of his frontier thesis, Haskins to the study of medieval Europe. World War I brought them together again in renewed collaboration. The revived association of the Americanists' Americanist and the medievalists' medievalist signaled the emergence of a revitalized Turner.

In the intervening decades when almost half the whole white population of the country consisted of immigrants and their children, a higher proportion than at any time in the nation's history, Turner and his disciples had been busily occupied carving out their own super-American identities, aiming to unite all Americans, but particularly western Americans, by defining for them a unique frontier heritage that distinguished America from Europe, "the valley of democracy" from the eastern seaboard, early American pioneers from later European immigrants. "The advance of the frontier has meant a steady movement away from the influence of Europe. . . . To study this advance . . . is to study the really American part of our history," rang out Turner's famous declaration of historical independence. But ironically, though it had the highest percentage of immigrant voters of any state, the frontier alchemy was not at all apparent in Wisconsin. There in the 1890s particularly, religious, educational, and linguistic issues proved acutely divisive. In a state with the greatest proportion of German immigrants and their descendants in the nation, Professor Turner, no longer "Fritz" (the family nickname for young Turner), could take even less comfort in Americans still untransformed by a frontier rebirth than could young William Dean Howells in an earlier Ohio. Until the outbreak of World War I, his oft-cited pronouncement of 1891 proclaiming the unity of Atlantic civilization remained rhetorical. "Our destiny is interwoven with theirs; how shall we understand American history without understanding European history? We do not understand ourselves." The dialectic, momentum, and contagion of Turner's frontier thesis left little room for immigration, despite its nominal place in his historical design. Moreover, Turner seemed unreceptive and ill at ease with those rustic scholars most highly motivated and best equipped for research into the immigrant peopling of the United States. Most notable was the case of the prideful Norwegian-born Laurence Larson, who reached the United States at age one — "brought to U.S., 1870," he noted with apologetic bravado in *Who's Who in America*. A president-elect of the American Historical Association and Hansen's department chairman, Larson nursed a lifelong suspicion that his unredeemable foreign birth caused Turner to lose interest in him as a student, leading Larson to turn from American to medieval history under the tutelage of Charles Haskins.[23]

Turner's sole excursion into immigration history — a popular series in the *Chicago Herald* in 1901 — mirrored Turner's insufficiencies. Although significantly more insightful than the writings of his contemporaries, these articles revealed how inhibiting was his Jacksonian code of values. When confronted with distinctions of language, religion, culture, and race, he found it difficult to respond appropriately. Neither Carl Wittke, a member of Turner's seminar at Harvard in 1913, nor Theodore Blegen, who worked at Minnesota with Solon Buck, a Turner product, received any encouragement from their mentors. Impelled solely by their own personal needs, Blegen and Wittke pursued their researches in immigration history independently. The only doctoral dissertation in the field sponsored by Turner at Harvard,

George Stephenson's study of public land policy, was at best only incidentally immigration history.[24]

In the fall of 1917, however, Turner and Hansen crossed paths at a critical time for them both. Together the two Wilsonians were entering a new phase of their education. Turner's course on the West fell into eclipse, his seminar had to be cancelled, and the longtime professor of American history volunteered to teach the European history survey to the Student Army Training Corps. Subsequently, Turner joined other history faculty in offering a new course that aimed to explain to returning students America's role in the reconstruction of the world. By then World War I had totally converted Turner from a Jacksonian isolationist into a Wilsonian internationalist. Eager to instruct the Old World of its common destiny with the New by reminding it of its long-term debt to the American democratic example, he dimly discerned a pattern that would place the immigration story within an international framework of frontier and section where native and immigrant, America and Europe, would find their common democratic cause. To his old friend Charles Haskins, now chief of the Division of Western Europe of the American Commission to Negotiate the Peace, Turner entrusted a personal memorandum in 1918, destined for Woodrow Wilson, projecting a United States of Europe based on the Pax Americana. "We have given evidence that immigrants from all nations of the world can live together peacefully under a single government that does justice," he wrote. Five years later, in Boston, Turner waxed apocalyptic in a Washington's Birthday address: "We have built up the American peace for a whole continent. . . . Unless Europe learns of some such way, her civilization is doomed to fall in a great catastrophe. . . . Will the United States escape?"[25]

Even more decisively than his mentor, Hansen, after 1917, veered sharply away from American history. Except for his seminar and thesis work in immigration history (based almost entirely on European sources) with Turner, he did not register for a single course in American history in his graduate years at Harvard. Instead, he took a series of courses in English history with Charles McIlwain, Roger B. Merriman, and Wilbur Cortez Abbott, a course in bibliography with Haskins, and a two-semester sequence offered by the economics department in nineteenth-century economic history that focused first on Europe and then on the United States. To top it off, he completed his graduate program with three courses in international law taken in three successive years.[26] Clearly Hansen was preparing for his lifework as had no Turner student before him. The binding together of the history of Europe and America into one seamless web via the North Atlantic migration had become his life mission.

Doubtless Turner discerned in Hansen — born in rural Wisconsin like himself — unusual talents of mind, of person, and of culture that synchronized with his own and yet transcended Turner's limitations. The "good historical farmer" impressed Turner with his ability, his thoroughness, his clearheadedness, and above all, his "sound judgment." Although Turner characteristically inquired of students, "Of what stock are you?" it is unlikely that he gave much thought to the fact that Hansen identified himself as Danish and Baptist and listed "Scandinavian" rather than Danish, Norwegian, or Swedish as a language that he both spoke and read. It is equally doubtful that Turner was quite aware that the Danes were the least nationalistic, the least numerous, and the most mobile, continental, and assimilating of the Scandinavian immigrants. Unlike a great research foundation that cast a wide net in search of a scholar coming from "a nonimperialistic country with no background of domination of one race over another" to direct a comprehensive study of the Negro in America, Turner came upon Hansen by chance. But Marcus Hansen, like Gunnar Myrdal, would prove a rare find. The American dilemma for Turner's generation was the immigrant, central to the American consciousness but as yet unintegrated into an egalitarian vision of a nation of ethnics. At a time when the European and the immigrant presence was deafening, Hansen, like Myrdal at a later time, would "approach the situation with an entirely fresh mind."[27]

Hansen's overarching internationalist view of immigration drew inspiration from three distinct sources. A Danish-American, Hansen was stirred by the example of the renowned Danish literary critic and historian Georg Brandes, "who devoted himself to the investigation not of Danish writers but the writers of the western nations" and so "made more understandable the cultural development of each separate nation." Certain and pervasive was the influence of Charles Haskins. In 1922, in his presidential address to the American Historical Association, Haskins insisted that it was "the historian's business to tie Europe and America together in the popular mind" because they were "in the same boat." Haskins's dismay at the proliferation of separate professorships and even departments of European and American history spurred Hansen in his continual efforts to transcend the parochialisms of the academy. At a session of the American Historical Association devoted to a reassessment of Turner's frontier thesis two years after his death, Hansen advanced the suggestion that for one year all American historians study European history and all European historians do the reverse. Students would then be provided with history courses sharing common themes that were continuous, balanced, and faithful to the larger human experience. Above all, Turner's heightened sense of the critical importance of relating the Old World to the New via the story of the immigrant experience and the influence on Europe of the American democratic presence helped give thrust to the young historian's researches. In 1932, the year of Turner's death, the publication of Carl Becker's *Heavenly City of the Eighteenth Century Philosophers,* dedicated jointly to Charles H. Haskins and Frederick J. Turner, his teachers and friends, best testified to their roles in the making of Marcus Hansen as well.[28]

Turner spared no efforts to promote his protégé. Thanks primarily to Turner's support, Hansen became the first historian to be awarded two successive fellowships by the newly founded Social Science Research Council. The two years that he spent in Europe permitted him to complete the major research for *The Atlantic Migration.* Writing to his family from Berlin in the spring of 1926, the good internationalist resignedly bemoaned the obstacles to international amity and Atlantic cooperation.

. . . it does make me disgusted when I consider how we Americans have meetings and conferences, and worry gray over the settlement of world questions, and then to notice how light-heartedly and feverishly the Europeans plunge into one action after another unconcerned as to where it will lead them. They need a little American cold practicality to help them — Europe is the most fertile and diversified region on the globe. No famines to contend with as in the east, no fevers as in the tropics, no great physical barriers as in America. They have been the "spoiled children" of the universe and all their troubles they have brought on themselves — but they don't see it. If we only could be separated from them, but we can't! I expect to have many things to worry about in my life du [sic] to them. In the meantime I'll make the most of their libraries.

But to Turner, after commenting on "daily rumors of contemplated Anarchist and Bolshevist coups," Hansen, looking back to the nineteenth century, wrote more optimistically:

The more I study the origins of the emigration movement in the middle of the last century, the more I realize what a tremendous reputation American democracy had in Europe at that time and the interest with which all its developments were followed by the common man. I am almost beginning to think that Nineteenth Century European Democracy owes less to the "leaven" of the French Revolution than it does to the practical experience of the United States during the first half of the century — an example that came before them every day in the newspapers. I have a suspicion that you suggested this idea on one occasion in seminar. I am finding many evidences of its truth. So once having been a model to save Europe politically we must now be an example to save them industrially. You see I haven't lost any of my hundred percentism by living abroad.[29]

Turner's active promotion of Hansen's career reflected both his esteem for Hansen and his overpowering urge to take a hand in contributing a cosmopolitan and internationalist dimension to American history that earlier had defied his own grasp. In addition to Hansen, the two other historians to receive the first Social Science Research Council Fellowships in 1925 also reflected the internationalist thrust: Edgar W. Knight was to study the folk high schools in Scandinavia, in effect, Denmark; and Thomas P. Martin, a Turner student, interested in the international aspects of the antislavery movement, was to study the influence of trade on Anglo-American relations, 1815–1875. Indeed, a year earlier, Turner had arranged for his last doctoral student, Merle Curti, to research "The Young America of 1852" in France and Germany. However, Turner's eagerness to persuade leading departments of history to endow a chair in immigration history proved of no avail. Nor did Turner succeed in his overzealous efforts to convince his friend Max Farrand, the director of the new Huntington Library, dedicated to Anglo-American studies, of the wisdom of appointing Hansen a research associate on the grounds that "one cannot understand Anglo-American civilization apart from the influence of the immigrant stocks." Yet Hansen, totally committed to the study of immigration history, never relented in his determination to find his proper place. Despite his diverse talents and interests, he remained unmoved by opportunities in other fields. He turned down a professorship in current international politics and the problems of international organization. He probably would have rejected appointments in religious and cultural history as well, had they been tendered. ". . . I hope to work as persistently to secure the means by which the phenomenon of immigration may be explored to its depths as I have worked in prospecting over the field and charting the most promising veins," avowed Hansen in 1927 in a letter to his friend Arthur M. Schlesinger, Sr.[30]

Finally, Hansen was able to choose between Iowa and Illinois. At Iowa he would have been assigned to teach only two courses. They were American social history and aspects of European social history, custom-tailored to his transatlantic and internationalist perspective and complementary to each other. Even Carl Becker, who wrote mainly American history while teaching modern European history almost exclusively, had never been given such an opportunity. The Iowa library, however, was in no position to support Hansen's acquisition needs in immigration history. By contrast, Illinois offered magnificent library resources that included a formidable collection of immigrant newspapers rescued from oblivion in 1917 (now on deposit at the Midwestern Library Center). Despite the heavier teaching load at Illinois, he therefore accepted Laurence Larson's invitation to join the Illinois history department. There, alongside a Turnerian course on social and economic forces in nineteenth-century America, Hansen introduced a one-year sequence in American immigration history that proved a genuine innovation. While the lack of graduate students with a language competence proved disappointing, as he wrote Turner, undergraduates with language skills in Swedish, German, Polish, Italian, and Czech prepared family histories that were the real stuff of the immigration story.[31]

The University of Illinois presented another attraction, a home away from home. In 1911 a faculty–graduate student Scandinavian Society, Heimskringla, had been founded by lonely Scandinavian-Americans as a cultural haven in a university town where

339

not a trace of Scandinavian institutional life was to be found. Upon coming to Illinois in 1907, Laurence Larson, a charter member of Heimskringla and the product of ethnically rich and diversified Iowa and Wisconsin, had reacted to the drab uniformity of Urbana with a sense of cultural shock. "It seemed that every influence, personal and institutional, that had held me in the old grooves had been removed," recalled Larson. A generation later Hansen would not quite know that experience. At Heimskringla's monthly meetings Hansen's homebred Scandinavian culture was broadened and deepened by exposure to the new Scandinavian culture and the old, from the sculpture of Carl Milles and the Norwegian Landsmaal movement and evenings with Ole Rolvaag, Carl J. Hambro, and Halvdan Koht to readings in Old Norse. Heimskringla's most active member and its stalwart historian from the time of his arrival, Hansen regularly presented papers at its meetings based on his own researches that reflected his evenhanded devotion to the cultures of all the Scandinavian peoples. These were, in the order that they were presented: "The Relative Proportions of the European Stocks Represented in the American Population of 1790, with Special Reference to the Swedish Element," drawn from a larger study of the minor stocks in the American population in 1790 that he had prepared for the American Council of Learned Societies; an insightful sketch of "The First Eighteen Years of Heimskringla As Revealed by the First Volume of Records"; "The Career of Fridtjof Nansen" in collaboration with Clarence Berdahl; "The Proposed Scandinavian American Exhibit at the Chicago Exposition of 1933"; "The Future of Norwegian Culture in the United States"; "My Tour of Scandinavia in the Summer of 1935" (illustrated); and "The Danish American Archives at Aalborg." In 1937, the year Laurence Larson was president-elect of the American Historical Association, Hansen served as toastmaster at Heimskringla's twenty-fifth anniversary banquet.[32]

The mid-1930s were years of growing maturity for Hansen as he struggled to define the conflicting impulses and emotions that coursed through his mind in his attempt to give shape to his researches. In 1934, after accepting an invitation to lecture at the University of London, he wrote Laurence Larson just before sailing from New York, "It will give me a unique pleasure to get up and tell them that the United States is the child, not of England, but of Europe, and to trace the foundation and development of Continental institutions alongside the transplanted English." But when he reached London after a six-month stay on the Continent, he rejoiced. It proved "almost like coming home" to "kindred ground" as it had been for George Ticknor over a century earlier, who upon landing in Falmouth "could have fallen down and embraced it like Julius Caesar."[33]

Hansen's sabbatical leave in 1934 was devoted primarily to the study of the Scandinavian immigration for the years 1870–1890, the years central to his own family story, and to the second volume of his projected immigration epic. Of the six months he spent in Scandinavia, he devoted three to Denmark, where his encounter with the real and imagined worlds of familiar faces, ancestral graces, and group memories attained the personal cogency and poignance of a family reunion. "The people are a cross-section of those with whom we have lived in Minnesota and elsewhere (or vice-versa); and this is one place where you are understood at once when you give your name as 'Hansen,' " he wrote his family from Copenhagen. Hansen saturated himself in small Denmark. He traveled no less than twenty-one hundred miles and made a special pilgrimage to his father's native village on the island of Langeland. "The place is dominated by two hills on one of which is the old mill and on the other the church," he wrote. "The church was open so I went in and sat down. The interior is a little gem — altar, baptismal font and pulpit — associated with the family since medieval times." He was excited and thrilled by dimly glimpsed cultural nuances. "I am convinced that there is a peculiar type of Danish humor which can be found on every page of the newspapers and which crops up constantly in conversation." But in his mother's Oslo, as in Denmark, he was perplexed by unanticipated language barriers that he had not encountered in his researches. "I ought to be able to speak with the natives but just as the Danish in Copenhagen was a foreign language compared with the Danish we learned, so the Norwegian is, to me, practically unintelligible." If the depression seemed remote in Scandinavia, where there was still a "good word" for "Democracy," Hansen's chance meeting in Copenhagen with speechless refugees from Nazi Germany cast a deep shadow. "I've never seen living beings with such frightened and hunted looks in their eyes," he wrote Arthur M. Schlesinger, Sr. "I begin to understand the French Revolution a little more."[34]

Hansen had never resolved the dilemma of ethnicity. In his final public addresses, he lamented the cultural cost of Americanization when he wrote of the immigrant:

He was not a musician nor an artist but he did have an appreciation of music and art that the Yankee lacked and no matter how small the village about which his social life had revolved some means of satisfaction existed. Public opinion assured that it should. But how different was America — certainly, the America with which he associated! Square boxes for homes and long boxes for churches; no painting but the crude sign that swung over the tavern door; no songs but unintelligible camp meeting hymns; no music but the fiddler's string squeaking "Turkey in the Straw." What was worse than the absence of the arts was the contempt in which the native American held all accomplishments of this nature. Strong and healthy men should not be concerned with such trivialities so long as there were trees to be cut, stones to be rolled or even horses to be traded. In his effort to recreate part of what had been lost the immigrant settler could expect no cooperation or encouragement from his Yankee neighbor.

Yet Hansen's ambivalence is no better demonstrated than in his view of the American Civil War. On the one hand, he argued, it was a prime determinant of the nation's misguided Americanization policy that legislated cultural uniformity. On the other, he was convinced that the remarkable Americanizing influence of the Civil War, joining immigrants and natives in a common objective and blurring ethnic differences, had prevented the crystallization of the minority problems that had helped to destroy Europe.[35]

In his last public address, "Who Shall Inherit America?," Hansen anticipated the consequences of the disappearance of immigration. He might even have foreseen that what might be called Hansen's disappearance-of-immigration thesis could be employed to justify new educational legislation to alleviate the sense of cultural deprivation, if not depression, that followed upon the erosion of ethnic cultures and institutions. Clearly, Hansen's analysis provided a no less valid historical rationale for legislation that "would restore by law an equality that formerly had been guaranteed by the conditions of American life" than had Turner's disappearance-of-free-land thesis for vindicating the programs of the New Deal. Hansen may have doubted the merits of the New Deal but not the historical claims for its vindication. Like Oscar Handlin, he doubtless would also have been skeptical of the wisdom of the Ethnic Heritage Studies Act funded by Congress in 1974. But like Handlin he too would have reasserted the genuineness of the problem and called in fresh accents for the application of greater historical understanding and social imagination to the problems of ethnicity, community, and culture. The withering away of elemental continuities and the freeing of the individual has of course been the dialectic central to the writings of Oscar Handlin, where it has been given universal dimensions.[36]

Marcus Lee Hansen's career spanned an era that anticipated our own and with whose most advanced strivings he was wholly identified. It opened with the passing of the old American ethnic frontier and the launching of a new Europe where new republics, small nations, and minority peoples seemed slated to find their places alongside the great powers. Enhanced mutuality between New World and Old seemed an inevitable goal that would enrich both. It closed with global catastrophe.

To Hansen the myth of the archetypal immigrant grafted onto the myth of the frontier was essential for the creation of his own saga, in which the universal phenomenon of immigration was bound into the special histories of all the ethnics. "Hands across the seas" sentiments and ties that would foster world peace, understanding, and the recognition and regeneration of the nation's genuine multicultural tradition seemed the natural consequence of the great American experiment in the twentieth century.[37] The extension of Hansen's grand vision to encompass Americans of non-European as well as of European origin has been the central ongoing task of his successors. The first historian to contemplate the cultural experience of the United States in totally democratic and pluralistic terms, Hansen truly was America's first transethnic historian.[38]

Notes

1. See Oscar Handlin, Introduction to Torchbook edition, *The Atlantic Migration, 1607–1860* (New York: Harper, 1961), pp. x–xvii; Allan H. Spear, "Marcus Lee Hansen and the Historiography of Immigration," *Wisconsin Magazine of History*, XLIV (1961), 258–268.
2. John Higham, *History* (Englewood Cliffs, N.J.: Prentice-Hall, 1965), p. 192; Moses Rischin, "Beyond the Great Divide: Immigration and the Last Frontier," *Journal of American History*, LV (1968), 51–52; M. L. Hansen, "Emigration from Continental Europe, 1815–1860, with Special Reference to the United States" (Ph.D. dissertation, Harvard University, 1924), pp. 10, 309. See also Frank Thistlethwaite, "Migration from Europe Overseas in the Nineteenth and Twentieth Centuries," *XIᵉ Congrès International des Sciences Historiques, Rapports V: Histoire Contemporaine* (Uppsala: Almquist and Wiksell, 1960), 32–33; Harald Runblom and Hans Norman, eds., *From Sweden to America: A History of the Migration* (Minneapolis: University of Minnesota Press, 1976), pp. 11–18; and Charlotte Erickson, *Emigration from Europe, 1815–1914: Select Documents* (London: Adam and Charles Black, 1976) for the long-term Hansen influence.
3. M. L. Hansen, *The Immigrant in American History* (Cambridge, Mass.: Harvard University Press, 1940), pp. 191–217, 154–174.
4. M. L. Hansen, *A Course of Eight Public Lectures on the Influence of Nineteenth Century Immigration upon American History — Syllabus and Bibliography* (University of London, 1934–1935; in University of Illinois Archives); Hansen, *The Immigrant*, pp. 97–128.
5. M. L. Hansen to F. J. Turner, July 11, 1926, Turner MSS, Huntington Library, San Marino, California.
6. M. L. Hansen, *The Problem of the Third Generation Immigrant* (Rock Island, Ill.: Augustana Historical Society Publications, 1938).
7. M. L. Hansen, "Who Shall Inherit America?" *Interpreter Releases*, XIV (July 6, 1937), 233; cf. Hansen, *The Immigrant*, p. 157.
8. Hansen, "Who Shall," pp. 229–230.
9. Hansen, *A Course*, p. 3; Hansen, *The Immigrant*, p. 183; Hansen, "Who Shall," pp. 228–229; Hansen, *The Atlantic Migration* (Cambridge, Mass.: Harvard University Press, 1940), p. 306; Hansen, *The Problem*, pp. 11–12; cf. Frederick C. Luebke, *Bonds of Loyalty: German-Americans and World War One* (Dekalb: Northern Illinois University Press, 1974), pp. 329–330.
10. Hansen, *The Problem*, p. 20; Hansen, "Who Shall," p. 233; Hansen, *The Immigrant*, p. 211; cf. *American Historical Review*, XXXII (1927), 513.
11. K. C. Babcock, *The Scandinavian Element in the United States* (Urbana: University of Illinois Press, 1914), pp. 9–11; Henry Steele Commager, ed., *Immigration and American History Essays in Honor of Theodore C. Blegen* (Minneapolis: University of Minnesota Press, 1961), pp. 6–7; Merle Curti, "Sweden in the American Social Mind of the 1930's," in *The Immigration of Ideas*, edited by J. Iverne Dowie and J. Thomas Tredway (Rock Island, Ill.: Augustana Historical Society, 1968), pp. 159 ff.; Neil T. Eckstein, "The Marginal Man As Novelist: The Norwegian-American Writers H. H. Boyesen

and O. E. Rolvaag As Critics of American Institutions" (Ph.D. dissertation, University of Pennsylvania, 1965), p. 71; S. Shepard Jones, *The Scandinavian State and the League of Nations* (Princeton: Princeton University Press, 1939), p. xiii; Paul Tabori, *The Anatomy of Exile* (London: Harrap, 1972), pp. 279–281; Dorothy Burton Skårdall, *The Divided Heart: Scandinavian Immigrant Experience through Literary Sources* (Lincoln, Neb.: University of Nebraska Press, 1974), pp. 27–28; John William Ward, "The Meaning of Lindbergh's Flight," *American Quarterly* (Spring 1958), 3 ff.

12. Commager, *Immigration, passim;* George M. Stephenson, *A History of American Immigration* (Boston: Ginn, 1926), p. 29.

13. *American Historical Review,* XXXVII (1932), 372; C. F. Hansen, "Marcus Lee Hansen: Historian of Immigration," *Common Ground,* II (1942), 1; Clarence Clausen to author, Jan. 27, 1975; Clarence A. Berdahl to author, Jan. 1, 1975.

14. C. F. Hansen, "Hansen," pp. 1–2; *Seventy-Five Years of Danish Baptist Missionary Work in America* (Philadelphia: American Baptist Publication Society, 1931), *passim;* Nels Sorensen Lawdahl, *De Danske Baptisters Historie i Amerika* (Morgan Park, Ill.: Forfalterns forlag, 1909), *passim;* W. Glyn Jones, *Denmark* (New York: Praeger, 1970), pp. 70–71; William Mulder, *Homeward to Zion: The Mormon Migration from Scandinavia* (Minneapolis: University of Minnesota Press, 1957), pp. 35, 38–39; Thomas P. Christensen, "The History of the Danes in Iowa" (Ph.D. dissertation, University of Iowa, 1924), p. 111; M. L. Hansen, "Official Encouragement of Immigration in Iowa," *Iowa Journal of History and Politics,* XIX (1921), 159 ff.; Diary notations by Einar Haugen, Nov. 27, 1929 (courtesy of Einar Haugen); M. L. Hansen to F. J. Turner, Nov. 27, 1929, Turner MSS, Huntington Library; cf. M. L. Hansen, "Phantoms on the Old Road," *Palimpsest,* II (Feb. 1921), 38 ff.

15. Kristian Hvidt, *Flugten til Amerika eller Drivkraefter i masseudvandrigen fra Danmark 1868–1914* (Aarhus: Universitetsvorlaget, 1971), p. 504; the State University of Iowa, Transcript of M. L. Hansen; Jacob Van der Zee, *The Hollanders of Iowa* (Iowa City: State Historical Society of Iowa, 1912), pp. 276–279.

16. Iowa Transcript; *Daily Illini,* Nov. 15, 1928 (University of Illinois Archives), p. 1; M. L. Hansen, *Old Fort Snelling: 1819–1858* (Iowa City: State Historical Society of Iowa, 1918).

17. Hansen, *Old Fort Snelling,* p. 201; M. L. Hansen, "Old Fort Snelling," *Iowa and War,* I (1917).

18. F. J. Turner to Louis Pelzer, Feb. 10, 1917, Turner MSS, Huntington Library; *Danish Baptist Missionary Work,* p. 287.

19. "Iowa War Proclamations," *Iowa and War,* edited by B. F. Shambaugh (Iowa City: State Historical Society of Iowa, 1919), p. 44; Christensen, "History of the Danes," pp. 140–145; Peter C. Petersen, "Language and Loyalty: Governor Harding and Iowa's Danish-Americans During World War I," *Annals of Iowa,* XLII (1974), 411–412, 415; M. L. Hansen to sister, Oct. 1918 (courtesy of Lydia Hansen). Cf. Luebke, *Bonds of Loyalty,* p. 252; Moses Rischin, ed., *Immigration and the American Tradition* (Indianapolis: Bobbs-Merrill, 1976), pp. xxxv–xxxvi, 171 ff.

20. M. L. Hansen, *Welfare Campaigns in Iowa* (Iowa City: State Historical Society of Iowa, 1920); M. L. Hansen, *Welfare Work in Iowa* (Iowa City: State Historical Society of Iowa, 1921), p. 263; Hansen, "Emigration," p. 309.

21. Ray Billington, *Frederick Jackson Turner* (New York: Oxford University Press, 1973), pp. 353 ff.

22. Kate A. Everest, "How Wisconsin Came By Its Large German Element," *Wisconsin State Historical Society Publications,* XII (1892), 299; Edward N. Saveth, *American Historians and European Immigrants, 1875–1925* (New York: Columbia University Press, 1948), pp. 124–125.

23. Howard R. Lamar, "Frederick Jackson Turner," in *Pastmasters: Some Essays on American Historians,* edited by Marcus Cunliffe and Robin Winks (New York: Harper and Row, 1969), p. 89; David P. Thelen, *Robert M. LaFollette and the Insurgent Spirit* (Boston: Little, Brown, 1976), p. 14; Roger E. Wyman, "Wisconsin Ethnic Groups and the Election of 1890," *Wisconsin Magazine of History,* LI (Summer 1968), 269 ff.; F. J. Turner, *The United States, 1830–1850* (New York: Henry Holt, 1935), p. 288; Laurence

M. Larson, *Log Book of a Young Immigrant* (Northfield, Minn.: Norwegian American Historical Association, 1944), pp. 258 ff.; Larson, "Log Book of a Young Immigrant" (original manuscript), pp. xxix–4 (University of Illinois Archives); cf. *Who's Who in America, 1932–1933* (Chicago: A. N. Marquis, 1932), p. 1375.

24. Saveth, *American Historians*, pp. 127–135; Billington, *Turner*, pp. 171–172, 486–487; Carl Wittke to author, May 1967; Theodore Blegen to author, June 1, 1967.

25. Billington, *Turner*, p. 355; Henry Nash Smith, *Virgin Land* (Cambridge, Mass.: Harvard University Press, 1950), p. 302; F. J. Turner, "American Sectionalism and World Organization," edited by W. D. Diamond, *American Historical Review*, XLVII (1942), 549; Wilbur R. Jacobs, ed., *Frederick Jackson Turner's Legacy: Unpublished Writings in American History* (San Marino: Huntington, 1965), p. 148.

26. Marion C. Belliveau, registrar, Harvard University, to Moses Rischin, Sept. 29, 1972; Academic and Professional Record of M. L. Hansen, Harvard Appointments Office.

27. F. J. Turner to M. L. Hansen, June 20, 1926, Turner MSS, Huntington Library; Hansen's Academic and Professional Record; Babcock, *Scandinavian Element*, pp. 62–65; Kristian Hvidt, *Flight to America: The Social Background of 300,000 Danish Emigrants* (New York: Academic Press, 1975), pp. 166–171; Gunnar Myrdal, *An American Dilemma* (New York: Harper, 1944), pp. vi–vii.

28. Dixon R. Fox, ed., *Sources of Culture in the Middle West* (New York: D. Appleton-Century, 1934), pp. 109–110; Charles Haskins, "European History and American Scholarship," *American Historical Review*, XXVIII (1923), 226–227; Gerald Thorsen to author, Jan. 23, 1975.

29. F. J. Turner to J. F. Jameson, Nov. 14, 1922, Jameson MSS, Box 85, Library of Congress; M. L. Hansen to F. J. Turner, May 24, 1926, Turner MSS, Huntington Library; M. L. Hansen to folks, Mar. 9, 1926 (courtesy of Lydia Hansen); M. L. Hansen to F. J. Turner, May 24, 1926, Turner MSS, Huntington Library; cf. Wilbur R. Jacobs, ed., *The Historical World of Frederick Jackson Turner, with Selections from His Correspondence* (New Haven: Yale University Press, 1968), pp. 159–161.

30. Ray Billington, *The Genesis of the Frontier Thesis: A Study in Historical Creativity* (San Marino: Huntington Library, 1971), p. 254; F. J. Turner to M. L. Hansen, Nov. 12, Dec. 21, 30, 1926, Aug. 21, 1927, Turner MSS, Huntington Library; cf. Jacobs, *Historical World*, pp. 118–119; M. L. Hansen to Arthur M. Schlesinger, Sr., Jan. 16, 1927, Schlesinger MSS, Columbia University.

31. M. L. Hansen to Laurence Larson, Apr. 3, 29, 1928 (University of Illinois Archives); M. L. Hansen to F. J. Turner, Nov. 27, 1929, Turner MSS, Huntington Library; Michael Kammen, ed., *What Is the Good of History? Selected Letters of Carl L. Becker, 1900–1945* (Ithaca: Cornell University Press, 1973), p. xviii.

32. Lucien W. White to author, June 28, Oct. 26, 1971, Nov. 1974; Larson, *Log Book*, p. 301; *Heimskringla Commemorative Booklet, 1911–12 . . . 1936–37* (Urbana, Ill.: Heimskringla, 1937), pp. 14–17; American Council of Learned Societies, *Report of the Committee on Linguistic and National Stocks in the Population of the United States* (Washington: Government Printing Office, 1932), pp. 391–396; diary notations by Einar Haugen, Nov. 17, 27, Dec. 19, 1929 (courtesy of Einar Haugen).

33. M. L. Hansen to Laurence Larson, July 3, 1934, Jan. 24, 1935 (University of Illinois Archives); David Tyack, *George Ticknor and the Boston Brahmins* (Cambridge: Harvard University Press, 1967), p. 79.

34. M. L. Hansen to Dean M. T. McClure, Sept. 25, 1935 (University of Illinois Archives); C. F. Hansen, "Hansen," p. 6; M. L. Hansen to folks, Aug. 15, 1934 (courtesy of Lydia Hansen); M. L. Hansen to Ruth Hansen, Nov. 2, 1934 (courtesy of Lydia Hansen); M. L. Hansen to Arthur M. Schlesinger, Sr., Dec. 6, 1934, Schlesinger MSS, Columbia University.

35. Hansen, "Who Shall," p. 227; Esther McKenzie to Arthur M. Schlesinger, Sr., June 13, 1939, Schlesinger MSS, Columbia University; Hansen, *The Immigrant*, pp. 140 ff.; Hansen, *The Atlantic Migration*, p. 306.

36. Hansen, *The Immigrant*, p. 59; cf. Oscar Handlin, *The Uprooted*, 2nd ed. (Boston: Little Brown, 1973), pp. 274 ff.; Rischin, *Immigration*, pp. xlviii–xlix, 363–371; Maldwyn A. Jones, "Oscar Handlin" in Cunliffe and Winks, *Pastmasters*, pp. 273 ff.

37. Oscar and Mary Handlin, "The New History and the Ethnic Factor in American Life," *Perspectives in American History* IV (1970), 9 ff.; Nathan I. Huggins, "National Character and Community," *Center Magazine,* VII (July-Aug. 1974), 66.

38. This paper was first outlined in the spring of 1969 at a seminar of the Migration Research Group, University of Uppsala, Sweden, where the author served as a Fulbright-Hays fellow. In a very different form, it was given in the spring of 1973 as the O. Fritiof Ander lecture at California Lutheran College. A radically revised and expanded version of this paper was prepared in May 1974 for the conference on ethnicity at Santa Barbara jointly sponsored by the Center for the Study of Democratic Institutions and the Immigration History Society. In its present form, it has undergone additional revision and amplification.

   Based primarily on original sources, fugitive printed materials, and personal recollections and references, this study owes much to the cooperation of the Harvard, Illinois, and Iowa University archives, the Huntington Library, and the generous assistance of the following persons: Selig Adler, Sue Åkerman, Marion C. Belliveau, Clarence Berdahl, Ray Billington, the late Theodore Blegen, Thomas N. Brown, Niles Carpenter, Clarence Clausen, the late John Cogley, Esther McKenzie Coppock, Merle Curti, Manning Dauer, John P. Diggins, Harriet Dorman, Lowell K. Dyson, Lawrence Gelfand, Joseph Giovinco, George Green, Einar Haugen, John Higham, Kristian Hvidt, Sr. M. Gilbert Kelley, Almont Lindsey, the late Frederick Merk, William J. Petersen, Carlton C. Qualey, Arthur M. Schlesinger, Jr., the late Elizabeth B. Schlesinger, Richard Schwerin, Franklin D. Scott, the late John L. Shover, Leonard Smith, Rudolph J. Vecoli, Lucien W. White, and the late Carl Wittke. Above all, I am grateful to the late O. Fritiof Ander and to the late Lydia E. Hansen for their selfless aid and stimulation.

347

Selected Bibliography of the Published Works of Oscar Handlin

Robert Mirak

Robert Mirak, who completed his dissertation on the Armenians in America in 1965 under Professor Handlin's direction, is an adjunct professor of history at Boston University and is involved in his family's enterprises. Specializing in immigration history, he has recently contributed the Armenian entry to the *Harvard Encyclopedia of American Ethnic Groups,* and acted as project director of the H.E.W. Armenian Ethnic Heritage Project.

THE FOLLOWING BIBLIOGRAPHY of Professor Handlin's published writings includes books, articles, and major reviews, in that order, by year through 1977. His many prefaces and forewords to other works have generally not been included, nor is indication given of his editorship of publications or periodicals, such as the twenty-five-volume Library of American Biography (Boston: Little, Brown and Company, 1954–), and the publications of the Center for the Study of the History of Liberty in America (Cambridge, Mass.: Harvard University Press, 1961–1977). Citations of reviews by Professor Handlin are in abbreviated bibliographical form; reprints and translations have generally been omitted.

1937

"The Eastern Frontier of New York." *New York History,* XVIII (Jan. 1937), 50–75.

1939

Review:
Upton, William Treat, *Anthony Philip Heinrich: A Nineteenth-Century Composer in America* (New York, 1939), in *New England Quarterly,* XII (Dec. 1939), 773–775.

1940

Reviews:
Dulles, Foster Rhea, *America Learns to Play: A History of Popular Recreation, 1607–1940* (New York, 1940), in *New England Quarterly,* XIII (Sept. 1940), 567–569.

Kelly, Sister Mary Gilbert, *German Immigrant Colonization Projects in the United States, 1815–1860* (New York, 1939), in *American Historical Review,* XLV (July 1940), 973–974.

1941

Boston's Immigrants, 1790–1865: A Study in Acculturation. Harvard Historical Studies, Vol. L. Cambridge, Mass: The Belknap Press of Harvard University Press, 1941; xvii + 287 pp. Awarded the John H. Dunning Prize of the American Historical Association, 1942. Revised and enlarged edition, *Boston's Immigrants* [1790–1880]: *A Study in Acculturation* (Cambridge: The Belknap Press of Harvard University Press, 1959; xvii + 382 pp.).

1942

"Land Cases in Colonial New York, 1765–1767: The King *v.* William Prendergast." *New York University Law Quarterly Review,* XIX (Jan. 1942), 165–194. With Irving Mark.
"A Russian Anarchist Visits Boston." *New England Quarterly,* XV (Mar. 1942), 104–109.
Reviews:
Dean, Leon W., *The Admission of Vermont into the Union* (Montpelier, 1941), and Frederick F. Van de Water, *The Reluctant Republic: Vermont, 1724–1791* (New York, 1941), in *New York History,* XXIII (Jan. 1942), 86–87.
McConnell, John W., *The Evolution of Social Classes* (Washington, D.C., 1942), in *New England Quarterly,* XV (Dec. 1942), 754.
Van de Water, Frederick F., *The Reluctant Republic: Vermont, 1724–1791* (New York, 1941), and Leon W. Dean, *The Admission of Vermont into the Union* (Montpelier, 1941), in *New York History,* XXIII (Jan. 1942), 86–87.
Warner, W. Lloyd, and Paul S. Lunt, *The Social Life of a Modern Community,* Yankee City Series, Vol. I (New Haven, 1941), and *The Status System of a Modern Community,* Yankee City Series, Vol. II (New Haven, 1942), in *New England Quarterly,* XV (Sept. 1942), 554–557.
Williams, T. Harry, *Lincoln and the Radicals* (Madison, 1941), in *New England Quarterly,* XV (June 1942), 381–383.

1943

"History" (an annual review of publications). *American Year Book, 1942* (New York: Thomas Nelson and Sons, 1943), 843–848.
"Laissez-Faire Thought in Massachusetts, 1790–1880." *Journal of Economic History,* III, Supplement (Dec. 1943), 55–65. From a paper presented at the third annual meeting of the Economic History Association, Princeton, N.J., Sept. 3–4, 1943.
Reviews:
Adams, James Truslow, ed., *Atlas of American History* (New York, 1943), in *New England Quarterly,* XVI (Dec. 1943), 681–683.
Greene, Lorenzo, *The Negro in Colonial New England* (New York, 1942), in *New England Quarterly,* XVI (June 1943), 346–347.

1944

"History" (an annual review of publications). *American Year Book, 1943* (New York: Thomas Nelson and Sons, 1944), 842–848.
"Immigrant in American Politics." David F. Bowers, ed., *Foreign Influences in American Life* (Princeton: Princeton University Press, 1944), 84–98.
"Radicals and Conservatives in Massachusetts after Independence." *New England Quarterly,* XVII (Sept. 1944), 343–355. With Mary F. Handlin.

SELECTED BIBLIOGRAPHY

Reviews:

Adams, James Truslow, *The American: The Making of a New Man* (New York, 1943), in *New England Quarterly*, XVII (June 1944), 319–321.

Beard, Charles A., and Mary R. Beard, *Basic History of the United States* (New York, 1944), in *Partisan Review*, XI (Fall 1944), 466–468.

Binkley, Wilfred E., *American Political Parties: Their Natural History* (New York, 1943), in *New England Quarterly*, XVII (Mar. 1944), 117–119.

Lord, Clifford L., and Elizabeth H. Lord, *Historical Atlas of the United States* (New York, 1944), in *New England Quarterly*, XVII (Sept. 1944), 461–462.

Lord, Robert H., John E. Sexton, and Edward T. Harrington, *History of the Archdiocese of Boston . . .* , 3 vols. (New York, 1944), in *New England Quarterly*, XVII (Dec. 1944), 606–609.

Snow, Edgar Rowe, *Great Storms and Famous Shipwrecks of the New England Coast* (Boston, 1943), in *Mississippi Valley Historical Review*, XXXI (Sept. 1944), 310.

1945

"History" (an annual review of publications). *American Year Book, 1944* (New York: Thomas Nelson and Sons, 1945), 872–878.

"Origins of the American Business Corporation." *Journal of Economic History*, V (May 1945), 1–23. With Mary F. Handlin.

Reviews:

Perry, Ralph Barton, *Puritanism and Democracy* (New York, 1945), in *Partisan Review*, XII (Spring 1945), 268–269.

Warner, W. Lloyd, and Leo Srole, *The Social Systems of American Ethnic Groups*, Yankee City Series, Vol. III (New Haven, 1945), in *New England Quarterly*, XVIII (Dec. 1945), 523–524.

Willison, George F., *Saints and Strangers: Being the Lives of the Pilgrim Fathers . . .* (New York, 1945), in *Mississippi Valley Historical Review*, XXXII (Dec. 1945), 441–442.

1946

"American Immigration Policy." *Harvard Alumni Bulletin*, XLIX (Oct. 26, 1946), 121–124.

"History" (an annual review of publications). *American Year Book, 1945* (New York: Thomas Nelson and Sons, 1946), 923–926.

Reviews:

Curti, Merle, et al., *Theory and Practice in Historical Study* (New York, 1946), in *New England Quarterly*, XIX (Dec. 1946), 538–540.

Dorfman, Joseph, *The Economic Mind in American Civilization: 1606–1865*, 2 vols. (New York, 1946), in *New England Quarterly*, XIX (June 1946), 251–253.

Grinstein, Hyman B., *The Rise of the Jewish Community of New York, 1654–1860* (Philadelphia, 1945), in *William and Mary Quarterly*, III (July 1946), 444–445.

Smith, Chard Powers, *The Housatonic: Puritan River* (New York, 1946), in *Mississippi Valley Historical Review*, XXXIII (Dec. 1946), 481–482.

1947

Commonwealth: A Study of the Role of Government in American Economy: Massachusetts, 1774–1861. New York: New York University Press, 1947; xiii + 364 pp. With Mary F. Handlin. Studies in economic history, prepared under the direction of the committee on research in economic history, Social Science Research Council. Revised edition, *Commonwealth: A Study of the Role of Government in American Economy: Massachusetts, 1774–1861* (Cambridge, Mass.: Harvard University Press, 1969; xvii + 314 pp.).

"Democracy Needs the Open Door." *Commentary*, III (Jan. 1947), 1–6.

"In the Dark Backward." *Partisan Review,* XIV (July 1947), 371 ff.
"Revolutionary Economic Policy in Massachusetts." *William and Mary Quarterly,* IV (Jan. 1947), 3–26. With Mary F. Handlin.
Review:
Firey, Walter, *Land Use in Central Boston* (Cambridge, Mass., 1947), in *New England Quarterly,* XX (Dec. 1947), 551–553.

1948

"Danger in Discord: Origins of Anti-Semitism in the United States." *Freedom Pamphlet* (New York: Anti-Defamation League of B'nai B'rith, 1948). With Mary F. Handlin.
"Our Unknown American Jewish Ancestors." *Commentary,* V (Feb. 1948), 104–110.
"Prejudice and Capitalist Exploitation." *Commentary,* VI (July 1948), 79–85.
Reviews:
American Jewish Committee, *American Jewish Year Book,* XLIX (1948), in *Commentary,* V (Mar. 1948), 288–289.
Fairchild, Henry Pratt, *Race and Nationality As Factors in American Life* (New York, 1947), in *Commentary,* V (May 1948), 476–477.
MacDonald, Dwight, *Henry Wallace: The Man and the Myth* (New York, 1948), in *Partisan Review,* XV (Apr. 1948), 499–500, 502–503.
Smith, Abbot Emerson, *Colonists in Bondage* (Chapel Hill, 1947), in *William and Mary Quarterly,* V (Jan. 1948), 109–110.

1949

This Was America: True Accounts of People and Places, Manners and Customs, As Recorded by European Travelers to the Western Shore in the Eighteenth, Nineteenth, and Twentieth Centuries. Cambridge, Mass.: Harvard University Press, 1949; xi + 602 pp. Twentieth Anniversary Edition (Cambridge, Mass.: Harvard University Press, 1969; xi + 602 pp.).
"American Culture — The Socialist View." *Atlantic Monthly,* Feb. 1949, pp. 59–62.
"A Century of Jewish Immigration to the United States." *American Jewish Year Book,* L (1948–1949), 1–84. With Mary F. Handlin.
"Group Life within the American Pattern." *Commentary,* VIII (Nov. 1949), 411–417.
"New Paths in American Jewish History." *Commentary,* VII (Apr. 1949), 388–394.
Reviews:
Barron, Milton L., *People Who Intermarry: Intermarriage in a New England Industrial Community* (Syracuse, 1946), in *New England Quarterly,* XXII (Mar. 1949), 121–123.
Community Service Society of New York, *The Family in a Democratic Society: Anniversary Papers of the Community Service Society of New York* (New York, 1949) and New York School of Social Work, and Community Service Society of New York, *Social Work As Human Relations: Anniversary Papers of the New York School of Social Work and the Community Service Society of New York* (New York, 1949), in *New York Times Book Review,* Aug. 21, 1949, p. 25.
Friedman, Lee M., *Pilgrims in a New Land* (Philadelphia, 1948), in *Mississippi Valley Historical Review,* XXXVI (Dec. 1949), 533–534.
New York School of Social Work, and Community Service Society of New York, *Social Work As Human Relations: Anniversary Papers of the New York School of Social Work and the Community Service Society of New York* (New York, 1949), and Community Service Society of New York, *The Family in a Democratic Society: Anniversary Papers of the Community Service Society of New York* (New York, 1949), in *New York Times Book Review,* Aug. 21, 1949, p. 25.
Payne, Robert, *Report on America* (New York, 1949), in *Saturday Review of Literature,* Mar. 5, 1949, p. 17.

1950

"America Recognizes Diverse Loyalties." *Commentary,* IX (Mar. 1950), 220–226.
"The American Scene." A. E. Zucker, ed., *The Forty-Eighters* (New York: Columbia University Press, 1950), 26–42.

"New England at Mid-Century." *Social Studies Topics,* Oct. 1950.

"A Note on Recent Texts in American History." *Journal of General Education,* IV (Apr. 1950), 300–302.

"Origins of the Southern Labor System." *William and Mary Quarterly,* VII (Apr. 1950), 199–222. With Mary F. Handlin.

"The Withering of New England: The Prophets of Gloom." *Atlantic Monthly,* Apr. 1950, pp. 49–51. From a paper read at the annual meeting of the American Historical Association, Dec. 1949.

Reviews:

Becker, Carl, *Progress and Power* (New York, 1949), in *Partisan Review,* XVII (Feb. 1950), 202.

Bernard, William S., ed., *American Immigration Policy: A Reappraisal* (New York, 1950), in *New York Times Book Review,* Feb. 19, 1950, p. 26.

Bettelheim, Bruno, and Morris Janowitz, *Dynamics of Prejudice* (New York, 1950), in *New York Times Book Review,* Feb. 12, 1950, p. 29.

Blegen, Theodore C., and Philip D. Jordan, eds., *With Various Voices: Recordings of North Star Life* (St. Paul, 1949), in *Mississippi Valley Historical Review,* XXXVII (June 1950), 137–138.

Brownell, Baker, *The Human Community: Its Philosophy and Practice for a Time of Crises* (New York, 1950), in *New York Times Book Review,* Nov. 26, 1950, p. 46.

Cadman, John W., Jr., *The Corporation in New Jersey: Business and Politics, 1791–1875* (Cambridge, 1949), in *American Historical Review,* LVI (Oct. 1950), 129–130.

Commager, Henry Steele, *The Blue and the Gray,* in *Nation,* Dec. 23, 1950, pp. 680–681.

Doll, Eugene Edgar, *American History As Interpreted by German Historians from 1770 to 1815* (Philadelphia, 1949), in *William and Mary Quarterly,* VII (Apr. 1950), 323–324.

Golden, Harry L., and Martin Ryewell, *Jews in American History* (Charlotte, N.C., 1950), in *American Jewish Historical Quarterly,* XL (Dec. 1950), 191–192.

Historical Statistics of the United States, 1789–1945: A Supplement to the Statistical Abstract of the United States (Washington, 1949), in *Mississippi Valley Historical Review,* XXXVI (Mar. 1950), 697–698.

Nevins, Allan, *Ordeal of the Union,* 2 vols.: *The Emergence of Lincoln* (New York, 1950), in *Nation,* Dec. 2, 1950, pp. 512–513.

Redding, J. Saunders, *They Came in Chains: Americans from Africa* (Philadelphia, 1950), in *New York Times Book Review,* July 30, 1950, p. 7.

Rochester, Anna, *American Capitalism, 1607–1800* (New York, 1949), in *William and Mary Quarterly,* VII (July 1950), 516–517.

1951

The Uprooted: The Epic Story of the Great Migrations That Made the American People. Boston: Little, Brown and Company, 1951; 310 pp. Awarded the Pulitzer Prize in History, 1952. Translated into Russian, Italian, and Czech. Second edition, enlarged (Boston: Little, Brown and Company, 1973; x + 333 pp.).

"American Views of the Jew at the Opening of the Twentieth Century." American Jewish Historical Society, *Publications,* XL (June 1951), 323–344. Another version, "How U.S. Anti-Semitism Really Began," *Commentary,* XI (June 1951), 541–548.

["Today's Jewish Student"]. *Commentary,* XII (Dec. 1951), 531–532.

"Yearning for Security." *Atlantic Monthly,* Jan. 1951, pp. 25–27.

Reviews:

Arendt, Hannah, *The Origins of Totalitarianism* (New York, 1951), in *Partisan Review,* XVI (Nov.–Dec., 1951), 721.

Catton, Bruce, *Mr. Lincoln's Army* (New York, 1951), in *Nation,* Mar. 17, 1951, p. 255.

Holbrook, Stewart H., *The Yankee Exodus* (New York, 1950), in *William and Mary Quarterly,* VIII (Jan. 1951), 140–141.

Johnson, Gerald W., *This American People* (New York, 1951), in *Nation,* Nov. 10, 1951, p. 408.

Kazin, Alfred, *A Walker in the City* (New York, 1951), in *Saturday Review of Literature,* Nov. 17, 1951, p. 14.

LaFarge, John, *No Postponement: U.S. Moral Leadership and the Problem of Racial Minorities* (New York, 1950), in *New York Times Book Review,* Jan. 21, 1951, p. 22.

Mims, Edward, Jr., *American History and Immigration* (Bronxville, N.Y., 1950), in *Mississippi Valley Historical Review,* XXXVII (Mar. 1951), 738–739.

1952

"Freedom or Authority in Group Life." *Commentary,* XIV (Dec. 1952), 547–554.

"The Immigrant Contribution." R. W. Leopold and A. W. Link, eds., *Problems in American History* (Englewood Cliffs, N.J.: Prentice-Hall, 1952), 643–690.

"The Immigration Fight Has Only Begun." *Commentary,* XIV (July 1952), 1–7.

"International Migration and the Acquisition of New Skills," Bert F. Hoselitz, ed., *The Progress of Underdeveloped Areas* (Chicago: University of Chicago Press, 1952), 54–59. Norman Wait Harris Memorial Foundation Lecture, 1951.

"Marcus Lee Hansen." *Commentary,* XIV (Nov. 1952), 492–493.

"Memorandum Concerning the Background of the National Origin Quota System." President's Commission on Immigration and Naturalization, *Hearings* (Washington, D.C.: U.S. Government Printing Office, 1952), pp. 1838–1863.

"Party Maneuvers and Civil Rights Realities." *Commentary,* XIV (Sept. 1952), 197–205.

Reviews:

Aaron, Daniel, ed., *America in Crisis* (New York, 1952), in *New York Times Book Review,* Nov. 9, 1952, p. 56.

Anderson, Thornton, *Brooks Adams: Constructive Conservative* (Ithaca, 1951), in *Mississippi Valley Historical Review,* XXXIX (June 1952), 144–145.

Davis, Moshe, *Yahadut Amerika Be-Hitpathutah* [The Shaping of American Judaism] (New York, 1950), in *Historia Judaica,* XIV (Fall 1952), pp. 165–166.

Kilpatrick, Carroll, ed., *Roosevelt and Daniels: A Friendship in Politics* (Chapel Hill, 1952), in *Nation,* Aug. 9, 1952, p. 115.

Riesman, David, and Nathan Glazer, *Faces in the Crowd* (New Haven, 1952), in *New York Times Book Review,* May 25, 1952, p. 6.

Saroyan, William, *The Bicycle Rider in Beverly Hills* (New York, 1952), in *Saturday Review of Literature,* Oct. 11, 1952, p. 27.

Siegfried, André, *Nations Have Souls* (New York, 1952), in *New York Times Book Review,* Jan. 27, 1952, p. 18.

Willison, George F., *Behold Virginia: The Fifth Crown* (New York, 1951), in *Nation,* Mar. 1, 1952, p. 208.

1953

Israel and the Mission of America. Brookline, Mass.: Hebrew Teachers College Press, 1953; 9 pp. Hebrew Teachers College Commencement Address, June 14, 1953.

"The Diffusion of Ideologies: The American Immigrant and Ideologies." *Confluence,* II (Sept. 1953), 95–104.

"Payroll Prosperity." *Atlantic Monthly,* Feb. 1953, pp. 29–33.

"Second Chance for the South." *Atlantic Monthly,* Dec. 1953, pp. 54–57.

"We Need More Immigrants." *Atlantic Monthly,* May 1953, pp. 27–31.

Reviews:

Garvan, Anthony N. B., *Architecture and Town Planning in Colonial Connecticut* (New Haven, 1951), in *Journal of Economic History,* XIII (Winter 1953), 121–122.

Harris, Sara, *Father Divine: Holy Husband* (Garden City, N.Y., 1953), in *New York Times Book Review,* Oct. 25, 1953, p. 14.

Kent, Donald Peterson, *The Refugee Intellectual: Americanization of the Immigrants of 1933–1941* (New York, 1953), in *New York Times Book Review,* Apr. 26, 1953, p. 14.

Kipnis, Ira, *The American Socialist Movement, 1897–1912* (New York, 1952), in *New England Quarterly*, XXVI (Mar. 1953), 109–110.

Marcus, Jacob R., *Early American Jewry*, 2 vols. (Philadelphia, 1951–1953), in *Commentary*, XIV (Aug. 1953), 184–185.

Tryon, Warren S., ed., *A Mirror for Americans: Life and Manners in the United States, 1790– 1870 . . .* , 3 vols. (Chicago, 1952), in *William and Mary Quarterly*, X (Apr. 1953), 323–324.

1954

Adventure in Freedom: Three Hundred Years of Jewish Life in America. New York: McGraw-Hill, 1954; xiii + 282 pp. Reprinted (Port Washington, N.Y.: Kennikat Press, 1971; xiii + 282 pp).

The American People in the Twentieth Century. Cambridge, Mass.: Harvard University Press, 1954; x + 244 pp.

Harvard Guide to American History. Cambridge, Mass.: The Belknap Press of Harvard University Press, 1954; xxiv + 689 pp. With A. M. Schlesinger, S. E. Morison, F. Merk, A. M. Schlesinger, Jr., and P. H. Buck.

"Les Américains devant leur Passé." *Diogène*, V (Apr. 1954), 27–40.

"American Jewish Pattern after 300 Years." *Commentary*, XVIII (Oct. 1954), 296–307.

"History in Men's Lives." *Virginia Quarterly Review*, XXX (Autumn 1954), 534–554.

"Independence at Yorktown." *Atlantic Monthly*, Dec. 1954, pp. 27–32.

Reviews:

Bruce, J. Campbell, *The Golden Door: The Irony of Our Immigration Policy* (New York, 1954), in *Commentary*, XVII (May 1954), 509–510.

Bruce, J. Campbell, *The Golden Door: The Irony of Our Immigration Policy* (New York, 1954), and Milton R. Konvitz, *Civil Rights in Immigration* (Ithaca, 1953), in *Yale Review*, XLIII (Summer 1954), 639–640.

Konvitz, Milton R., *Civil Rights in Immigration* (Ithaca, 1953), and J. Campbell Bruce, *The Golden Door: The Irony of Our Immigration Policy* (New York, 1954), in *Yale Review*, XLIII (Summer 1954), 639–640.

Young, Kimball, *Isn't One Wife Enough?: The Story of Mormon Polygamy* (New York, 1954), in *New York Times Book Review*, Apr. 11, 1954, p. 6.

1955

Chance or Destiny: Turning Points in American History. Boston: Little, Brown and Company, 1955; 220 pp.

Général rapporteur, *The Positive Contributions by Immigrants: A Symposium Prepared for UNESCO by the International Sociological Association and the International Economic Association.* Paris: UNESCO, 1955; 202 pp.

"The Acquisition of Political and Social Rights by the Jews in the United States." *American Jewish Year Book*, LVI (1955), 43–98. With Mary F. Handlin.

"Does the People's Rule Doom Democracy?" *Commentary*, XX (July 1955), 1–8.

"Explosion on the *Princeton*." *Atlantic Monthly*, Feb. 1955, pp. 63–68. Reprinted in *Chance or Destiny . . .* (Boston: Little, Brown, and Company, 1955).

"A Liner, A U-Boat, and History." *American Heritage*, VI June 1955, 40 ff.

"The Louisiana Purchase." *Atlantic Monthly*, Jan. 1955, pp. 44–49. Reprinted in *Chance or Destiny . . .* (Boston: Little, Brown and Company, 1955).

"Mr. Seward's Bargain." *Atlantic Monthly*, Apr. 1955, pp. 63–68. Reprinted in *Chance or Destiny . . .* (Boston: Little, Brown and Company, 1955).

"The United States." O. Handlin, général rapporteur, *The Positive Contributions by Immigrants . . .* (Paris: UNESCO, 1955), pp. 17–48. With Mary F. Handlin.

"What Europeans Think of America." *Boston Globe*, Jan. 3–9, 1955.

"Why Lee Attacked." *Atlantic Monthly*, Mar. 1955, pp. 61–66. Reprinted in *Chance or Destiny . . .* (Boston: Little, Brown and Company, 1955).

Reviews:

Blegen, Theodore C., ed., *Land of Their Choice: The Immigrants Write Home* (Minneapolis, 1955), in *New York Times Book Review*, Dec. 25, 1955, p. 3.

Borrie, W. D., *Italians and Germans in Australia* (Melbourne, 1954), in *Population Studies*, IX (Nov. 1955), 189–190.

Gordis, Robert, *Judaism for the Modern Age* (New York, 1955), in *New York Times Book Review*, Nov. 6, 1955, p. 57.

Hayek, F. A., ed., *Capitalism and the Historians* (Chicago, 1954), and Allan Nevins, *Study in Power: John D. Rockefeller, Industrialist and Philanthropist*, 2 vols. (New York, 1953), in *New England Quarterly*, XXVIII (Mar. 1955), 99–107.

Nevins, Allan, *Study in Power: John D. Rockefeller, Industrialist and Philanthropist*, 2 vols. (New York, 1953), and F. A. Hayek, ed., *Capitalism and the Historians* (Chicago, 1954), in *New England Quarterly*, XXVIII (Mar. 1955), 99–107.

1956

"Barefoot Patriots." *Colliers*, CXXXVIII (Dec. 21, 1956), 84–89.

"Changing Nature of the Republican Party." *Current History*, XXXI (Aug. 1956), 65–69.

"Crisis in Teaching." *Atlantic Monthly*, Sept. 1956, 33–37.

"Do the Voters Want Moderation?" *Commentary*, XXII (Sept. 1956), 193–198.

"Ethnic Factors in Social Mobility." *Explorations in Entrepreneurial History*, IX (Oct. 1956), 1–7. With Mary F. Handlin.

"Immigrants Who Go Back." *Atlantic Monthly*, July, 1956, pp. 70–74.

"Introduction." I. J. Benjamin, *Three Years in America, 1859–1862*, translated by C. Reznikoff, 2 vols. (Philadelphia: Jewish Publication Society of Philadelphia, 1956), I, 1–36.

"A Museum for Liberty." *This Week*, Jan. 29, 1956.

"Where Equality Leads." *Atlantic Monthly*, Nov. 1956, pp. 50–54.

Reviews:

Furnas, J. C., *Goodbye to Uncle Tom* (New York, 1956), in *New York Times Book Review*, June 24, 1956, p. 6.

Siegfried, André, *America at Mid-Century* (New York, 1955), in *Commentary*, XXI (Mar. 1956), 290–291.

Wittke, Carl, *The Irish in America* (Baton Rouge, 1956), in *American Historical Review*, LXII (Oct. 1956), 158–159.

1957

Race and Nationality in American Life. Boston: Little, Brown and Company, 1957; 300 pp.

Readings in American History. New York: Knopf, 1957; xxvi + 715 pp.

"American Jewish Committee." *Commentary*, XXIII (Jan. 1957), 1–10.

"American Views of the Past." Massachusetts Historical Society, *Proceedings*, LXX (Boston: Massachusetts Historical Society, 1957), 227–236. Prepared for the 1952 conference of the American Council of Learned Societies.

"The Atlantic Report: Israel." *Atlantic Monthly*, Nov. 1957, pp. 22 ff.

"Civil Rights after Little Rock." *Commentary*, XXIV (Nov.1957), 392–396.

"Desegregation in Perspective." *Current History*, XXXII (May 1957), 257–260.

"Introduction." Charles Reznikoff, ed., *Louis Marshall: Champion of Liberty* (Philadelphia: Jewish Publication Society, 1957), pp. ix–xliii.

"Textbooks That Don't Teach." *Atlantic Monthly*, Dec. 1957, pp. 110–114.

"Tomorrow's City." *Boston Sunday Globe*, Apr. 7, 1957.

"What U.S. Jewry Will Be Like in 2000." *National Jewish Monthly*, May 1957, pp. 5 ff.

"Worlds Apart: Classes and Masses in the Communist State." *Atlantic Monthly*, May 1957, pp. 53–56.

Reviews:

Burlingame, Roger, *The American Conscience* (New York, 1957), in *New York Times Book Review*, Mar. 17, 1957, p. 6.

SELECTED BIBLIOGRAPHY

Divine, Robert A., *American Immigration Policy, 1924–1952* (New Haven, 1957), in *Mississippi Valley Historical Review*, XLIV (Dec. 1957), 573–574.

Paleologué, Maurice, *An Intimate Journal of the Dreyfus Case* (New York, 1957), in *Commentary*, XXIV (July 1957), 88–89.

Wright, Richard, *White Man, Listen!* (Garden City, N.Y., 1957), in *New York Times Book Review*, Oct. 20, 1957, p. 3.

1958

Al Smith and His America. Boston: Little, Brown and Company, 1958; x + 207 pp.

Suggestions for Colleges in the Commemoration of the Theodore Roosevelt Centennial. New York: Theodore Roosevelt Association, 1958; 14 pp.

"College and Community in 1900." Harvard Library *Bulletin*, XII (Spring 1958), 149–160.

"John Torrey Morse." *Dictionary of American Biography*, XXII (New York: Charles Scribner's Sons, 1958), 475–476.

"Rejoinder to Critics of John Dewey." *New York Times Magazine*, June 15, 1958, pp. 13–14, 19–20.

"Time to Change Our Government?" *Boston Sunday Globe*, Sept. 14, 1958.

"Zionist Ideology and World Jewry." *Commentary*, XXV (Feb. 1958), 105–109.

Reviews:

Dubnow, Simon, *Nationalism and History* (Philadelphia, 1958), in *Commentary*, XXVI (Aug. 1958), 175–176.

Kallen, Horace M., *Utopians at Bay* (New York, 1958), in *Saturday Review of Literature*, Aug. 2, 1958, p. 28.

Redding, J. Saunders, *The Lonesome Road: Story of the Negro's Part in America* (Garden City, N.Y., 1958), in *New York Times Book Review*, Apr. 20, 1958, p. 30.

Schuyler, Robert Livingston, ed., *Dictionary of American Biography, Supplement 2*, Vol. XXII, in *New York Times Book Review*, July 20, 1958, p. 7.

Wibberley, Leonard, *Coming of the Green* (New York, 1958), in *Saturday Review of Literature*, Apr. 5, 1958, p. 36.

1959

Ed., *Immigration As a Factor in American History.* Englewood Cliffs, N.J.: Prentice-Hall, 1959; 206 pp. Earlier version, "The Immigrant Contribution," R. W. Leopold and A. W. Link, eds., *Problems in American History* (Englewood Cliffs, N.J.: Prentice-Hall, 1952), pp. 643–690.

John Dewey's Challenge to Education: Historical Perspectives on the Cultural Context. John Dewey Society Lectureship Series, Vol. 2. New York: Harper, 1959; 59 pp.

The Newcomers: Negroes and Puerto Ricans in a Changing Metropolis. Cambridge, Mass.: Harvard University Press, 1959; xiii + 171 pp.

"Alfred E. Smith." *Colliers Encyclopedia* (New York: Crowell-Collier, 1959 and following editions).

"The Significance of the Seventeenth Century." J. M. Smith, ed., *Seventeenth Century America* (Chapel Hill: University of North Carolina Press, 1959), 3–12.

1960

American Jews: Their Story. New York: Anti-Defamation League of B'nai B'rith, 1960; 48 pp.

Ed. and trans., *Journey to Pennsylvania*, by Gottlieb Mittelberger. Cambridge, Mass.: The Belknap Press of Harvard University Press, 1960; xix + 102 pp. A John Harvard Library volume. With John Clive.

"Comments on Mass and Popular Culture." *Daedalus*, Spring 1960, pp. 325–332.

"Ethics and Eichmann." *Commentary*, XXX (Aug. 1960), 161–162.

"Immigration." *Colliers Encyclopedia* (New York: Crowell-Collier, 1960 and following editions).
Reviews:
Coyle, David Cushman, *The Ordeal of the Presidency* (Washington, 1960), in *New Republic,* CXLII (Mar. 28, 1960), p. 20.
Lipset, Seymour Martin, and Reinhard Bendix, *Social Mobility in Industrial Society* (Berkeley, 1959), in *American Historical Review,* LXV (Jan. 1960), 339–340.
Potter, George R., *To the Golden Door: Story of the Irish in Ireland and America* (Boston, 1960), in *New York Times Book Review,* Apr. 3, 1960, p. 6.

1961

Ed., *American Principles and Issues: The National Purpose.* New York: Holt, Rinehart and Winston, 1961; xvi + 576 pp.
The Dimensions of Liberty. Cambridge, Mass.: Harvard University Press, 1961; 204 pp. With Mary F. Handlin.
"Alfred Emanuel Smith." *Encyclopaedia Britannica,* 14th ed. (Chicago: Encyclopaedia Britannica, Inc., 1961–1973). With Henry F. Pringle.
"Ben Gurion against the Diaspora." *Commentary,* XXXI (Mar. 1961), 193–196.
"The Civil War As Symbol and As Actuality. *Massachusetts Review,* V (Fall 1961), 133–143.
"The Failure of Communism and What It Portends." *Atlantic Monthly,* Dec. 1961, pp. 40–45.
"Federal Aid to Parochial Schools: A Debate." *Commentary,* XXXII (July 1961), 6–11.
"Historical Perspectives on the American Ethnic Group." *Daedalus,* Spring 1961, pp. 220–232.
"Immigration in American Life: A Reappraisal." H. S. Commager, ed., *Immigration and American History* (Minneapolis: University of Minnesota Press, 1961), pp. 8–29.
"Introduction to the Torchbook Edition." Marcus Lee Hansen, *The Atlantic Migration, 1607–1860* (New York: Harper and Row, 1961), x–xvii.
"Judaism in the United States." James Ward Smith and Albert L. Jamison, eds., *The Shaping of American Religion,* Vol. I of *Religion in American Life* (Princeton: Princeton University Press, 1961), pp. 122–161.
"Live Students and Dead Education." *Atlantic Monthly,* Sept. 1961, pp. 29–34.
"The Social System." *Daedalus,* Winter 1961, pp. 11–30.
"Voluntary Basis of Private Education." *Catholic World,* CXCIII (July 1961), 217–221.
Reviews:
Benson, Lee, *Turner and Beard: American Historical Writing Reconsidered* (Glencoe, Ill., 1960), in *American Historical Review,* LXVII (Oct. 1961), 147–148.
Elkins, Stanley M., *Slavery: A Problem in American Institutional and Intellectual Life* (Chicago, 1959), in *New England Quarterly,* XXXIV (June 1961), 253–255.
Kramer, Judith R., and Seymour Leventman, *Children of the Gilded Ghetto* (New Haven, 1961), in *New York Times Book Review,* Oct. 1, 1961, p. 16.
Pelling, Henry, *American Labor* (Chicago, 1960), in *Mississippi Valley Historical Review,* XLVII (Mar. 1961), 714–715.

1962

"Are the Colleges Killing Education?" *Atlantic Monthly,* May 1962, pp. 41–45.
"The Church and the Modern City." *Atlantic Monthly,* Aug. 1962, pp. 101–105.
"Jewish Resistance to the Nazis." *Commentary,* XXXIV (Nov. 1962), 398–405.
"Out of Many, One." *Rotarian,* Mar. 1962, pp. 20 ff.
"Qualities of Victory: Perseverance." *Nation's Business,* L (Mar. 1962), 68–71, 74–75.
Reviews:
Fosdick, Raymond B., et al., *Adventure in Giving: The Story of the General Education Board* (New York, 1962), in *New York Times Book Review,* Nov. 25, 1962, p. 24.
Halperin, Samuel, *The Political World of American Zionism* (Detroit, 1961), in *American His-*

torical Review, LXVII (July 1962), 1133.

Williams, William Appleman, *The Contours of American History* (Cleveland, 1961), in *Mississippi Valley Historical Review,* XLVIII (Mar. 1962), 743–745.

1963

The Americans: A New History of the People of the United States. Boston: Little, Brown and Company, 1963; 434 pp.

Ed., *The Historian and the City.* Cambridge, Mass.: M.I.T. Press and Harvard University Press, 1963; xii + 299 pp. Publication of the Joint Center for Urban Studies of the Massachusetts Institute of Technology and Harvard University. With John Burchard.

Three Lectures: The Heritage of Mind in a Civilization of Machines. Waterville, Me.: n.p., 1963; 60 pp. With Frank Stanton and Gerard Piel.

"Are There Really Ghettoes in America?" *U.S. News and World Report,* LV (July 22, 1963), 70–72. Interview.

"The Eisenhower Administration: A Self-Portrait." *Atlantic Monthly,* Nov. 1963, pp. 67–72.

"The Gullibility of the Neutrals." *Atlantic Monthly,* Mar. 1963, pp. 41–47.

"James Burgh and American Revolutionary Theory." Massachusetts Historical Society, *Proceedings,* LXXIII (Boston: Massachusetts Historical Society, 1963), 38–57. With Mary F. Handlin.

"The Modern City As a Field of Historical Study." O. Handlin and J. Burchard, eds., *The Historian and the City* (Cambridge, Mass.: M.I.T. Press and Harvard University Press, 1963), pp. 1–26.

"Racial Danger." *Boston Sunday Globe,* June 2, 1963.

Reviews:

Arendt, Hannah, *Eichmann in Jerusalem* (New York, 1963), in *New Leader,* Aug. 5, 1963, pp. 19–21.

Darin-Drabkin, H., *The Other Society* (New York, 1963), in *American Scholar,* Summer 1963, pp. 484, 486.

Glazer, Nathan, and Daniel Patrick Moynihan, *Beyond the Melting Pot* (Cambridge, 1963), in *New York Times Book Review,* Sept. 22, 1963, p. 3.

Higham, John, ed., *The Reconstruction of American History* (New York, 1962), in *Daedalus,* Winter 1963, pp. 172–174.

Myrdal, Gunnar, *An American Dilemma* (New York, 1944), in *New York Times Book Review,* Apr. 21, 1963, p. 1. Review-discussion.

1964

A Continuing Task: The American Jewish Joint Distribution Committee, 1914–1964. New York: Random House, 1964; v + 118 pp.

Fire-bell in the Night: The Crisis in Civil Rights. Boston: Little, Brown and Company, 1964; 110 pp.

Ed., "Chief Daniel Nimhan *v.* Roger Morris, Beverly Robinson, and Philip Philipse — An Indian Land Case in Colonial New York, 1765–1767." *Ethnohistory,* XI (Summer 1964), 193–246. With Irving Mark.

"The City Grows." in Stefan Lorant, ed., *Pittsburgh: The Story of an American City* (Garden City, N.Y.: Doubleday, 1964), pp. 81–128.

"Convention Address." *Bulletin of the Florida State Teachers Association,* XXXIX (June 1964), 28–33.

"L'intégration des Noirs." *Notes et Documents* (Paris), no. 95 (1964), pp. 1–6.

"Is Integration the Answer?" *Atlantic Monthly,* Mar. 1964, pp. 49–54.

"Jews in the Culture of Middle Europe." Leo Baeck Memorial Lecture, 7 (New York: Leo Baeck Institute, 1964). Lecture commemorating the last representative figure of German Jewry in Germany during the Nazi period.

"Libraries and Learning." *Atlantic Monthly,* Apr. 1964, pp. 96 ff.

"Man and Magic: Encounters with the Machine." *American Scholar,* Summer 1964, pp. 408–419.

"Out of Many: A Study Guide to Cultural Pluralism in the United States." (New York: Anti-Defamation League of B'nai B'rith, 1964).

Review:

Lipset, Seymour Martin, *The First New Nation: The United States in Historical and Comparative Perspective* (New York, 1963), in *American Historical Review,* LXX (Oct. 1964), 180–182.

1965

"American Jewry's Dilemmas: Assimilation and Acculturation." *Jewish Advocate* (Boston), Oct. 14, 1965.

"Making the Most of Leisure." *Parents' Magazine,* June 1965, pp. 60 ff.

"Poverty from the Civil War to World War II." U.S. Department of Labor, *Monthly Labor Review,* July 1965, pp. 836–837. Adapted from West Virginia University Conference on Poverty, Morgantown, W.Va., 1965.

"Reader's Choice." *Atlantic Monthly,* Oct. 1965, pp. 166 ff.

"Reconsidering the Populists." *Agricultural History,* XXXIX (Apr. 1965), 68–74.

"Science and Technology in Popular Culture." *Daedalus,* Winter 1965, pp. 156–170.

"Why Marching Is Wrong." *Boston Sunday Globe,* Dec. 5, 1965.

Reviews:

Broom, Leonard, and Norval D. Glenn, *Transformation of the Negro American* (New York, 1965), John Ehle, *The Free Men* (New York, 1965), Walter Lord, *The Past That Would Not Die* (New York, 1965), and Robert Penn Warren, *Who Speaks for the Negro?* (New York, 1965), in *New York Times Book Review,* July 4, 1965, p. 3.

Ehle, John, *The Free Men* (New York, 1965), Leonard Broom and Norval D. Glenn, *Transformation of the Negro American* (New York, 1965), Walter Lord, *The Past That Would Not Die* (New York, 1965), and Robert Penn Warren, *Who Speaks for the Negro?* (New York, 1965), in *New York Times Book Review,* July 4, 1965, p. 3.

Lord, Walter, *The Past That Would Not Die* (New York, 1965), Leonard Broom and Norval D. Glenn, *Transformation of the Negro American* (New York, 1965), John Ehle, *The Free Men* (New York, 1965), and Robert Penn Warren *Who Speaks for the Negro?* (New York, 1965), in *New York Times Book Review,* July 4, 1965, p. 3.

Warren, Robert Penn, *Who Speaks for the Negro?* (New York, 1965), Leonard Broom and Norval D. Glenn, *Transformation of the Negro American* (New York, 1965), John Ehle, *The Free Men* (New York, 1965), and Walter Lord, *The Past That Would Not Die* (New York, 1965), in *New York Times Book Review,* July 4, 1965, p. 3.

1966

Ed., *Children of the Uprooted.* New York: G. Braziller, 1966; xxii + 551 pp.

Ed., *The Popular Sources of Political Authority: Documents in the Massachusetts Constitution of 1780.* Cambridge, Mass.: The Belknap Press of Harvard University Press, 1966; xi + 962 pp. With Mary F. Handlin.

"Academic Freedom in International Educational Exchange." *International Educational and Cultural Exchange,* II (Fall 1966), 9–16.

"Americanizing Our Immigration Laws." *Holiday Magazine,* Jan. 1966, pp. 8 ff.

"At Last: A Fair Deal for Immigrants." *Reader's Digest,* May 1966, pp. 29 ff. Condensation of *Holiday Magazine* article, Jan 1966.

"The Goals of Integration." *Daedalus,* Winter 1966, pp. 268–286.

"Lyndon B. Johnson Address on Voting Rights, 1965." Daniel J. Boorstin, ed., *An American Primer,* 2 vols. (Chicago: University of Chicago Press, 1966), II, 918–929.

"Reader's Choice." *Atlantic Monthly,* July 1966, pp. 136–138; Aug. 1966, pp. 116–118; Oct. 1966, pp. 141–143; Nov. 1966, pp. 158 ff; and Dec. 1966, pp. 138 ff.

SELECTED BIBLIOGRAPHY

1967

The History of the United States. 2 vols. New York: Holt, Rinehart and Winston, 1967; Vol I.,
  xvi + 640 pp.; Vol II., xiv + 688 pp.
"Reader's Choice." *Atlantic Monthly,* Jan., 1967, pp. 117–120.
"The Role of the Academic Community." Allan A. Michie, ed., *Diversity and Interdependence
  through International Education* (New York: Education and World Affairs, 1967), 47–53.

1968

America: A History. New York: Holt, Rinehart and Winston, 1968; xxi + 1069 pp.
Ed., *Dissent, Democracy, and Foreign Policy: A Symposium.* New York: Foreign Policy Associa-
  tion, 1968; 47 pp.
"Dissent, Democracy, and Foreign Policy." O. Handlin, ed., *Dissent, Democracy and Foreign
  Policy: A Symposium* (New York: Foreign Policy Association, 1968), 3–29.
"E Pluribus Unum! Or?" Clarence Senior and William S. Bernard, eds., *Toward Cultural
  Democracy* (New York: Selected Academic Readings, 1968), 131–140.
"Prefatory Comments." *International Migrations Review,* Spring 1968, pp. 5–6.
"Recommended Summer Reading." *American Scholar,* Summer 1968, pp. 530–532.
" 'This Promiscuous Breed': Sources of Diversity in the American Character." J. Benjamin
  Townsend, ed., *This New Man: A Discourse in Portraits* (Washington, D.C.: Smithsonian
  Institution Press, 1968), pp. 6–21.
"Worlds of Arthur Koestler." *Atlantic Monthly,* Dec. 1968, pp. 92–96.
Review:
Hofstader, Richard, *The Progressive Historians* (New York, 1968), in *New York Times Book
  Review,* Nov. 17, 1968, p. 28.

1969

"Monuments to the Past." *American Jewish Historical Quarterly,* LIX (Sept. 1969), 16–22.

1970

The American College and American Culture: Socialization As a Function of Higher Education.
  New York: McGraw-Hill, 1970; 104 pp. Written for the Carnegie Commission on
  Higher Education. With Mary F. Handlin.
The American University As an Instrument of Republican Culture. Leicester, England: Leicester
  University Press, 1970; 20 pp. Sir George Watson Lecture delivered in the University of
  Leicester, Mar. 6, 1970.
"The New History and the Ethnic Factor in American Life." Bernard Bailyn and Donald
  Fleming, eds., *Perspectives in American History,* IV (1970), 5–24. With Mary F. Handlin.
"The Vulnerability of the American University." *Encounter,* XXXV (July 1970), 22–30.
  Concluding comment in *ibid.,* XXXVI (Jan. 1971), 89–90.
Reviews:
Comette, Elizabeth, trans. and ed., *Seeing America and Its Great Men . . .* (Charlottesville, Va.,
  1969), in *Journal of American History,* LVI (Mar. 1970), 898–899.
Josephson, Matthew, and Hannah Josephson, *Al Smith: Hero of the Cities . . .* (Boston, 1969),
  in *Journal of American History,* LVII (June 1970), 193–194.

1971

Facing Life: Youth and the Family in American History. Boston: Little, Brown and Company,
  1971; ix + 326 pp. With Mary F. Handlin.

SELECTED BIBLIOGRAPHY

Statue of Liberty. Vol. III of Wonders of Man. New York: Newsweek, 1971; 172 pp. With the editors of the *Newsweek* Book Division.
"History: A Discipline in Crisis?" *American Scholar,* Summer 1971, pp. 447–465. Adaptation of address to American Historical Association, Dec. 1970.

1972

A Pictorial History of Immigration. New York: Crown Publishers, 1972; 344 pp.
["Revisionist Historians"]. *Freedom at Issue,* Sept.–Oct. 1972, p. 2.
Charles Weiner, ed., *Exploring the History of Nuclear Physics* (New York: American Institute of Physics, 1972). Proceedings of the American Institute of Physics–American Academy of Arts and Sciences Conferences on the History of Nuclear Physics, 1967 and 1969. Participant.

1973

"Watergate: Reflections from Afar." *Freedom at Issue,* Sept.–Oct. 1973, pp. 11–13.

1974

One World: The Origins of an American Concept. Oxford: Clarendon Press, 1974; 21 pp. Inaugural lecture delivered before the University of Oxford on Feb. 23, 1973.
"The Anti-Americanism of the Intellectuals." *Campus Colloquy,* I (1974), 39 ff.
"Education and the American Society." *American Education* (U.S. Department of Health, Education, and Welfare), X (June 1974), 6–8.
"Historical Factors in the Decline of the University." S. Hook, P. Kurtz, and M. Todorovich, eds., *The Idea of a Modern University* (New York: Prometheus Books, 1974), 81–85.

1975

The Wealth of the American People: A History of American Affluence. New York: McGraw-Hill, 1975; vii + 266 pp. With Mary F. Handlin.
"The Capacity of Quantitative History." Bernard Bailyn and Donald Fleming, eds., *Perspectives in American History,* IX (1975), 7–26.

1976

"Edward Chase Kirkland." *Proceedings of the American Antiquarian Society,* LXXXV (1976), 360–363.
"Twenty Year Retrospect of American Jewish Historiography." *American Jewish Historical Quarterly,* LXV (June 1976), 295–309.
Reviews:
Feldberg, Michael, *Philadelphia Riots of 1844: A Study of Ethnic Conflict* (Westport, Conn., 1975) in *Labor History,* XVII (Spring 1976), 291–292.
Morgan, Edmund S., *American Slavery, American Freedom: The Ordeal of Colonial Virginia* (New York, 1975), in *American Historical Review,* LXXXI (Oct. 1976), 957–958.
Woodruff, William, *America's Impact on the World: A Study of the Role of the United States in the World Economy, 1750–1970* (New York, 1975), in *Business History Review,* L (Spring 1976), 127–218.

SELECTED BIBLIOGRAPHY

1977

"Living in a Valley." *American Scholar,* XLVI (Summer 1977), 301–312.
Review:
Collier, Peter, and David Horowitz, *The Rockefellers: An American Dynasty* (New York, 1976), in *Bankers' Magazine,* CLX (Winter 1977), 104.

Students of Oscar Handlin
Recipients of
Doctor of Philosophy Degrees
Harvard University 1951–1978

HISTORY

1951 George Wallace Chessman
1952 Rowland Tappan Berthoff
Arthur Mann
William B. Whiteside
1953 Bernard Bailyn
1954 Arthur Stanley Bolster, Jr.
1955 Mary Cobb Nelson
1956 Thomas Nicholas Brown
Morton Keller
1957 Donald Barnard Cole
Martin Bauml Duberman
J. Joseph Hutchmacher
Benjamin Woods Labaree
Moses Rischin
1958 David Brody
Edwin Fenton
William J. Grattan
Sydney V. James
1959 Milton Berman
Robert Earl Roeder
Richard Beatty Sherman
Sam Bass Warner, Jr.
1961 Paul Goodman
Stephen M. Salsbury
Warren S. Tryon

1962 Gunther Barth
Harold Gorvine
Nathan Irvin Huggins
1963 Roger Lane
1964 David Heathcote Crook
Robert Michael Fogelson
David Jay Rothman
1965 Neil Harris
Robert Mirak
1967 Daniel Horowitz
Jon Alvah Peterson
1970 Marvin Frederick Lazerson
1971 Alan Charles Dawley
1972 Barry Michael Dym
1973 Redmond James Barnett
Henry Binford
Anthony J. Kuzniewski, Jr.
1974 Barry Lawrence Salkin
1975 Margaret E. Conners
1976 Donald Davis
Stephen M. Diamond
Calvin B. Holder
Jonathan Prude
1977 Robert A. Silverman
1978 Ernest Kurtz

HISTORY OF AMERICAN CIVILIZATION

1953 William G. McLoughlin
Barbara Miller Solomon
1954 James Roger Leiby
Kenneth S. Lynn II
1955 Francis L. Broderick
Robert D. Cross
David Levin
William Mulder
1956 Barbara Cross
William Robert Taylor
1958 Anne Firor Scott

1960 Paul Raymond Baker
1961 Frederick Cople Jaher
1962 Stephan A. Thernstrom
1963 Dorothy Burton Skårdal
1968 William Esmond Rowley
1969 Helen Lefkowitz Horowitz
Richard Sennett
1972 Richard Howard Ekman
Barry Gewen
1974 Keith Edward Eiler
Robert Jerrett III